Jacques Bainville and the
Renaissance of Royalist History
in Twentieth-Century France

Jacques Bainville and the Renaissance of Royalist History in Twentieth-Century France

WILLIAM R. KEYLOR

Louisiana State University Press
Baton Rouge and London

ques Bainville, 1879–1936
er-Viollet

Design: Albert Crochet
Typeface: VIP Palatino
Typesetter: G & S Typesetters, Inc.
Printing and binding: Thomson-Shore, Inc.

LIBRARY OF CONGRESS CATALOGING IN PUBLICATION DATA

Keylor, William R   1944–
    Jacques Bainville and the Renaissance of Royalist history in twentieth-century
France.

    Bibliography: p.
    Includes index.
    1. Bainville, Jacques, 1879–1936.   2. France—Historiography.   3. Royalists—
France.   4. France—Politics and government—20th century.   I. Title.
DC36.98.B314K48   944.081   79–10604
ISBN 0–8071–0465–5

For Rheta

Contents

Acknowledgments

I would like to express my gratitude to the following individuals who read the entire manuscript of this book at various stages of its progress and supplied useful suggestions for its improvement: Jacques Barzun, Rudolph Binion, Stewart Campbell, Arthur Danto, Bert M.-P. Leefmans, Robert O. Paxton, Fritz K. Ringer, Nancy Lyman Roelker, Martin Siegel, Robert Soucy, Fritz Stern, and Hilah Thomas.

I am indebted to the following organizations and institutions for having provided me with financial assistance to defray many of the costs related to this study: the Fulbright-Hays Commission, the Woodrow Wilson Foundation, the American Council of Learned Societies, and the Graduate School of Boston University.

I have also received valuable assistance from the staffs of the following libraries: Les Archives Nationales, La Bibliothèque Nationale, Les Archives de la Préfecture de Police (Département de la Seine), La Bibliothèque Jacques Doucet, La Bibliothèque de l'Arsenal, the Library of the British Museum, Hoover Library of Stanford University, Butler Library of Columbia University, Widener Library of Harvard University, the New York Public Library, and the Boston Public Library.

I am also grateful to the following individuals who granted me personal interviews and, in some cases, permitted me access to private correspondence in their possession: Hervé Bainville, the late Madame Jacques Bainville, Madame de Coudekerque-Lambrecht, François Leger, Pierre Gaxotte, Pierre Juhel, Charles Popin, the late Marcel Wiriath, and René Wittmann. The Librairie Arthème Fayard kindly allowed me to examine its records of the number of editions and printed copies of Jacques Bainville's major works.

Above all, I wish to thank my wife, Rheta Grenoble Keylor, for her continual encouragement and frequent suggestions for improving both the form and the content of this study, and my mother, Thelma Keylor, for timely assistance over the years.

Prologue

The role of the intellectuals is something that particularly needs to be studied in France, as a basis for getting beyond the confusing and interminable conflicts of which its history seems to be composed. For not only have the intellectuals played a leading part in these conflicts, but they have also interpreted and labeled them in such a way as to influence all subsequent thought about them. It was they who formulated the issues which they claimed divided the country and defined the principles which were at stake.

Theodore Zeldin

One of the most remarkable developments in modern French cultural history was the appearance during the first four decades of the twentieth century of a small group of historians who succeeded in popularizing an avowedly monarchist interpretation of their nation's past. This phenomenon is particularly remarkable in that it coincided with the establishment of a relatively secure consensus in support of the democratic political system of the Third Republic after three decades of crisis and instability. It was this puzzling paradox—the popularity of a royalist version of French history in a society which had supposedly accepted the political evolution from autocracy to republicanism—that originally inspired my interest in the subject of this book.

There have been several studies of modern French royalism. Most of them have concentrated either on the activities of the royalist political organization, the Action Française, or on the intellectual contributions of its undisputed master, Charles Maurras.[1] Both topics deserve the careful scrutiny from scholars that they

---

1. Many of the best such studies have been written by non-Frenchmen. See, for example, Eugen Weber, *Action Française* (Stanford, Calif.: Stanford University Press, 1962); Edward R. Tannenbaum, *The Action Française* (New York: Wiley, 1962); Ernst Nolte, *Three Faces of Fascism*, trans. Leila Vennewitz (New York: Holt, Rinehart, and Winston, 1966), pt. 2; Samuel Osgood, *French Royalism under the Third and*

have received. But it also seems worthwhile to examine the ways in which the *historians* belonging to the Action Française influenced the historical thought of modern Frenchmen. For the political ideology of the Action Française was to a great extent shaped by its idiosyncratic interpretation of French history. Moreover, its program for political counterrevolution was presented to the French public as a series of lessons for the present drawn from the past. Indeed, historical argumentation constituted perhaps the most important weapon in the intellectual arsenal of the royalist movement.[2]

Several prominent members of the Action Française considered themselves historians of a sort—Maurras, Léon Daudet, and Pierre Lasserre, to mention only the most memorable. But these men were first and foremost journalists and *littérateurs* who dabbled in historical writing. History remained for them subsidiary to political and literary criticism. The bona fide historians in France during this period who wrote from a narrowly royalist perspective—men such as Pierre Gaxotte, Louis Bertrand, Franz Funck-Brentano, and Pierre de La Gorce—were not members of the inner circle of the Action Française leadership. The first three were sympathizers and supporters of the political organization controlled by Maurras and his select group of associates. The latter was a liberal monarchist with no formal ties to the Maurrassian clique.[3]

Only one man can be legitimately regarded as both a leader of the modern French royalist movement *and* a full-fledged historian. That man was Jacques Bainville. Sharing with Maurras and Daudet

---

Fourth Republics (The Hague: Nijoff, 1960); William C. Buthman, *The Rise of Integral Nationalism in France* (New York: Columbia University Press, 1939); and Michael Curtis, *Three Against the Republic: Sorel, Barrès, and Maurras* (Princeton: Princeton University Press, 1959).

2. For a discussion of the role of historical writing in the intellectual and political campaigns of the French royalist movement, see Stephen Wilson, "A View of the Past: Action Française Historiography and its Socio-Political Function," *Historical Journal*, 19, I (1976), 135–61.

3. A number of individuals who merit mention in this regard are difficult to categorize. Louis Dimier was both an influential member of the Action Française *and* a respected art historian, but he defected in the mid-twenties and became an outspoken critic of the royalist movement. Charles Benoist was a former diplomat

a preeminent position in the royalist directorate, Bainville exercised a considerable influence on the political and intellectual elite of France in the heyday of the Action Française. He was in fact the most important royalist historian in twentieth-century France.

The task of explaining the popularity of Bainville's works required that I attempt to isolate those characteristics of his writing that seemed to account for its public appeal and to determine the extent of his influence. I rapidly learned that to measure intellectual influence or appeal is a difficult assignment. One can cite the circulation figures of newspapers and periodicals to which a particular writer contributed regular articles, as other scholars have already done for many of the journals that are relevant to this study.[4] But such figures reflect only the dissemination of a writer's ideas, not their popularity. For his contribution was only a portion of the intellectual fare served in the journal that was purchased. The figures for the number of printed copies of an author's books are somewhat more illuminating in this regard. (See Appendix.)

But such figures neither reveal the nature of an author's appeal nor help to isolate from the corpus of his thought the particular ideas that captured the attention or approval of his readers. Here we are forced, as a last resort, to rely on the commentary of contemporary critics. The masters of literary criticism in the Parisian press prided themselves on their ability to discern and identify the preferences of the reading public. Actually they were no mere recorders of literary taste; they were also its shapers and arbiters. On both accounts their testimony deserves careful attention.

The biographical details of Bainville's career have been a secondary consideration in this study, which has focussed on his historical thought and—so far as this was possible to assess—its influ-

turned historian who had joined the Action Française because of his hatred of democracy rather than because of any sentiments in favor of a royalist restoration, which he regarded as impossible. Other noted historians whose paths crossed that of the royalist movement in various ways include Philippe Ariès, André Bellesort, Eugène Cavaignac, Gustave Fagniez, Raoul Girardet, Daniel Halévy, and the Marquis de Roux.

4. See Weber, *Action Française*, 183, 368, and Charles Micaud, *The French Right and Nazi Germany, 1933–1939* (New York: Octagon Books, 1964), 239–40.

ence on his contemporaries. This is so for two principal reasons. First, his life was essentially uneventful, particularly in comparison with the exploits of his two more flamboyant colleagues, Maurras and Daudet, whose daily encounters with friend and foe formed the material from which adventure novels are written. Unlike most of the leading members of the Action Française, Bainville never participated in a violent political demonstration, nor endured an assault on his person. He was neither arrested, convicted, imprisoned, nor forced into exile. A conventional *père de famille*, he was neither a bon vivant like Daudet nor a misanthropic, deaf bachelor like Maurras. He spent virtually his entire adult life in the same neighborhood of Paris, methodically composing his newspaper articles by day and his historical works at night. What was significant about the man was his thought, which both reflected and influenced the society in which he lived so inconspicuously.

But even if the details of his life could supply a deeper understanding of political and intellectual trends in his society, the dearth of biographical information precludes such a reconstruction. He died at the comparatively young age of fifty-seven and therefore left no memoirs. He seldom wrote letters, since his circle of friends was largely confined to Parisians—the royalist writers with whom he shared an office during the day and the literary and political personalities with whom he frequently socialized in the evening. His published works are scarcely useful as sources of information about his private life, except insofar as they reveal him to have been a man whose most intimate feelings seldom surfaced to divert the reader's attention from the author's reflections on the state of society, culture, and the world. He may only occasionally be traced in the reports of the police informers planted by the Préfecture and the Sûrêté in the *Action française* editorial offices, which recorded virtually every memorable utterance and activity of the other leading members of the movement. Perhaps the reticence for which Bainville was renowned extended even to the presumed privacy of his office, or perhaps what he said and did was of no interest to spies in search of conspiracies to report. Either way, the consequence to the historian is the same: he must look else-where for biographical information.

Such biographical details as do appear in this study have been pieced together from disparate sources: letters supplied by Bain-ville's son, Hervé, as well as others published by friends after his death; a diary he kept during the year 1914 (which affords a rare glimpse into his personal sentiments, since it was not intended for publication); those infrequent references to his own life that appear in his published works; and the written testimony of his friends and colleagues. Among the most valuable sources were the many personal interviews which have helped to fill in the gaps in the meager written record of his life. For though he left few revealing papers, Bainville left a number of friends and relatives (including a wife and son) who gave generously of their time to speak to me about the man.

One cannot begin a study of Bainville's historical writings with-out calling attention to one overriding characteristic of his work that distinguishes it from that of most French historians of his gen-eration. This is his essentially philosophical approach to the past. By the turn of the century, professional historians in France had appropriated the terminology and what was thought to be the methods of the natural sciences; their goal was to transform history from a philosophical enterprise that produced unsubstantiated, speculative, and often polemical generalizations into a rigorous so-cial science based on the analysis of concrete historical facts. In the face of this trend Bainville blithely approached his subject matter as a logician rather than as a scholar. Beginning with a limited number of postulates that he never felt impelled to question, he proceeded to select and employ historical facts that confirmed these postulates. He passed over facts that could upset his foregone conclusions.

It is no exaggeration to say that Bainville's works were largely variations on a few simple themes. Taken as a whole, they reveal very little development in his understanding of history. He es-chewed the practice customary among historians of revising, refin-ing, and updating one's judgments as new data are discovered and new techniques of analysis are developed. His arguments were presented as historically accurate because they were logically unassailable. As we shall see, while this deductive approach to historical understanding displeased most scholars, it found a sympathetic audience among nonspecialists intent on discovering meaning in history.

The underlying assumption of Bainville's world view was his unwavering belief in the superiority of the cultural values of Western civilization and his conviction that the disappearance of that heritage would plunge humanity into a new age of barbarism. He began his career at a time when Europe dominated the world economically, militarily, and culturally. But he lived to witness the appearance of new historical forces that eventually terminated the era of European supremacy. Particularly after the First World War, which had depleted so much of the old world's material and spiritual resources, he devoted the major part of his intellectual talents to a reaffirmation of the cultural values of the West, of Europe's claim to the dual title of policeman and preceptor of the world.

Yet Bainville recognized that the concept of a common European civilization was a mythical representation of what was in reality an unruly continent of sovereign nations competing with one another for preeminence. He was incapable of envisioning the emergence of a federative principle under which the European nations could join forces and cooperate for the purpose of preserving their common heritage and maintaining Western dominance in the world. He accepted without qualification the primacy of the nation-state because of his conviction that all efforts to unify European civilization were destined to fail. The only practical alternative to such utopian schemes for a united Europe was the mechanism that had operated, albeit imperfectly, since the origin of the modern state system itself in the seventeenth century: the principle of the balance of power. Only by banding together in shifting coalitions to deter any one nation from disrupting the European order could the European powers preserve the harmony that was the *sine qua non* of their predominance in the world.

Bainville's belief in the superiority of European civilization in general was in no way incompatible with his espousal of a rather narrow brand of French nationalism. He shared with many of his compatriots a view of France as the modern bearer of the illustrious cultural tradition that had been forged in ancient Greece, disseminated throughout the civilized world by the Romans, and rediscovered by the Italian humanists during the Renaissance. This view enabled Bainville to regard his own nation's interests as synonymous with those of the universal culture that constituted the legacy of Western civilization. As the repository of Western values in the modern world, France was uniquely suited to preside over the political affairs of Europe, to preserve the balance of military forces among the contending states (with a slight edge in her favor), and to impose her own superior culture upon the rest of the continent for its own good.

But Bainville realized that diplomatic mastery, military hegemony, and cultural domination require a foundation of economic prosperity and social stability in the nation that would exert them. And these conditions in turn depend on a viable political system, which Bainville believed, following Maurras, to be the engine of national strength. An enlightened state alone was capable of protecting the industrious, conscientious citizenry of France from the three principal threats to its well being: the meddling of rapacious, bumbling bureaucrats from above, the periodic insurrections of the envious multitude from below, and military invasion by enemies from without. In the absence of such a state, the great civilization of which France was the custodian would go the way of ancient Greece and Rome. To avoid such a calamity remained Bainville's principal preoccupation throughout his life.

It comes as no surprise that such contemporary concerns dominated the thinking of Bainville the political journalist. But what set him apart from most other commentators on current affairs was his practice of resorting to history as a source of instructive precedents for contemporary events. Indeed, the key link between his two callings as historian and journalist was his conception of the past as a vast storehouse of potentially useful guidelines for the present. This belief derived from his classical view of human nature as an immutable collection of instincts which, in conjunction with certain environmental constants, perpetually shaped human behavior in a uniform manner throughout the ages. Such a rigidly deterministic conception of history appeared to leave little room for the exercise of human freedom to promote progress, since it tended to portray man as a passive creature at the mercy of overpowering instincts and environmental pressures. Yet the bleak pessimism for which Bainville became famous was leavened with a generous dose of hope. Mankind could not intervene to reverse the course of history at will, for the psychological and geographical determinants that condition human behavior were ineradicable. But this did not mean that man was compelled to submit meekly to his fate. For while history was not infinitely malleable, neither was it entirely predetermined. At certain critical turning points in history, at what Bainville called the "decisive moments,"[5] man was afforded the rare opportunity to shape his destiny. Herein lay the source of Bainville's obsession with understanding the past and extracting its lessons for the future. Only by profiting from the previous experience of men who were faced with similar challenges could modern man exploit the few occasions that might occur during his lifetime to redirect the course of history.

These were the philosophical postulates about man, nature, and history on which Bainville based the specific political principles that formed the crux of his royalist ideology. The assumption that the rigid mechanism of historical evolution yielded only infrequent opportunities for the intervention of human will to affect its course served as a logical justification for political autocracy. It implied the necessity for an omnipotent, omniscient leader capable of calmly accessing the historical precedents of contemporary events, vigilantly awaiting the decisive moment, and then swiftly intervening to divert the course of historical development in a desirable direction. Such a function could never be entrusted to the collective will of ill prepared, impulsive voters, who were naturally preoccupied with the parochial concerns of their personal existence. Nor could

5. See Jacques Bainville, _Les Moments décisifs de l'histoire de France_, ed. Pierre Gaxotte (Paris: Cayla, 1949).

it be assigned to a group of squabbling politicians swayed by the mercurial whims of their constituents and the corrupting influence of their own personal ambitions. Only an absolute, hereditary monarch could pretend to the aura of legitimacy, the sense of continuity, the flexibility, patience and independence that would enable him to act decisively at the opportune moment to protect the interests of his realm. In light of Bainville's uncritical acceptance of French national interest as the primary standard of judgment in all matters political, the restoration of the French monarchy represented the logical extension of this philosophical system.

It was with these general observations in mind that Bainville addressed the overriding problem that haunted him to the day of his death: the progressive decline of France's position in the world according to all the criteria of national vitality that he had postulated. His investigation of this development produced the somber realization that his country had degenerated within less than a century from the most powerful, prosperous, and populous nation in Europe into a pale shadow of her former self. The symptoms of national decadence appeared at every turn, exposing this once great nation as militarily vulnerable, diplomatically impotent, and plagued by the internal disabilities of political polarization, social dissension, economic sluggishness, and demographic stagnation. Even France's formerly undisputed cultural leadership had dissipated in the course of the nineteenth century. The entire edifice upon which France had rested her historic claim to the title of the universal civilization of Europe had been gradually corroded by the doctrines of cultural nationalism in Germany, Italy, and other fledgling nations whose ruling elites had once accepted French ways as the supreme standard.

This sorry situation presented a marked contrast to the glorious days of the *ancien régime*, when Richelieu and Louis XIV supervised the affairs of the continent and French manners set the standard of conduct for the courts of Saint Petersburg, Vienna, and Potsdam. Even more mortifying was the contemporary contrast between this ignominious national degeneration and the simultaneous emergence of France's historic enemy as the dominant power in Europe. Indeed, this juxtaposition of Gallic decadence and Teutonic vitality produced what Claude Digeon has called a "national inferiority complex" in France.[6] Many of Bainville's contemporaries who began their careers at the turn of the century adopted a pessimistic view of their nation's future and desperately sought an explanation for the apparent supersession of France and French civilization in the modern world.

Such an explanation Bainville was eager to provide by invoking the past. The comparison between the France of 1900 and the France of 1660, as well as between the France and the Germany of 1900, supplied a political lesson: Germany's national strength derived from her monarchical institutions, while France's inferiority was attributable to her abandonment of a strong, solid monarchy for an impotent, unstable democracy. This argument represented a rejoinder to the republican historians at the state-controlled university, many of whom had portrayed France's present political system as the culmination of an age of national progress and prosperity that had begun in 1789.[7] Bainville strove to demonstrate that the Revolution had produced a series of national disasters that dissipated the accumulated resources that had made the France of the Bourbons the leading power in the Western world. In this way he successfully exploited the widespread nostalgia in early twentieth-century France for the national grandeur and security of the pre-revolutionary past, as well as the increasingly pervasive apprehension of what the future held in store.

This campaign of historical revisionism reflected once again Bainville's classical view of man and history. In order to explain away the historical developments of the nineteenth century that had deprived his nation of its former military supremacy and saddled it with malfunctioning political institutions, he cast doubt upon the ultimate significance of historical evolution itself. He attempted to rescue France from the ravages of modernity by postu-

6. Claude Digeon, *La Crise allemande de la pensée française, 1870–1914* (Paris: Presses Universitaires de France, 1959), 372.

7. See my *Academy and Community: The Foundation of the French Historical Profession* (Cambridge, Mass.: Harvard University Press, 1975), Pt. 1, Chaps. 3 and 4; Wilson, "A View of the Past," 136–39.

lating certain eternal principles of stability that resist the transforming influence of time. From the perspective of the classical (rather than the evolutionary) view of history, the apparent decline of the Greco-Roman-French tradition in the nineteenth century was to be regarded not, as in the writings of many German historians, as the culmination of an ineluctable trend of historical evolution, but rather as merely a temporary digression. Just as the Renaissance humanists had rediscovered the sources of Western culture's eternal grandeur after centuries of neglect, Bainville hoped to witness a rebirth of classical civilization in the twentieth century and the reestablishment of France's position as the modern representative of that heritage. His classical conception of history as the unfolding of a predetermined blueprint rather than as an evolutionary process and of human nature as a timeless, immutable entity permitted Bainville to imagine the possibility of retrieving the lost past. The republican regime in France was merely a temporary deviation from the proper principles of statecraft that had guided the French monarchy as it unified the nation and shaped it into the dominant power in Europe. Those very principles could be reinstated to conduct France along the path to national recovery in the modern world. Hence, what might have at first seemed a pessimistic vision of irretrievable loss proved to be a prescription for full retrieval.

This blatant appeal to those Frenchmen who longed for a return to the good old days was not the only basis of Bainville's popularity. There was also the crucial matter of his style. To appreciate the significance of this phenomenon, one must recall the sweeping metamorphosis of French historical writing that occurred during the last quarter of the nineteenth century. The men who transformed the study of history into an academic discipline in France were motivated by a strong antipathy for what they regarded as the glib, simplistic writing of the early nineteenth-century historians. The founders of the academic historical profession in France sought to discredit the impressionistic, picturesque prose that abounded during the romantic period, when history was widely regarded as a source of diversion rather than as a serious scholarly undertaking. Once history attained the status of an academic discipline practiced by professionals, historical writing was judged by the quality of its scholarship rather than by the form in which it was presented. Style was relegated to an inferior position in the hierarchy of values that governed the historian's guild.[8]

Like most of the other members of the royalist historical school, Bainville had received no formal academic training in history. He was what professional historians would (and did) consider a dilettante. His extensive experience as a short story writer, essayist, and critic infused his historical writing with a literary quality that secured it a prominent place in the realm of belles lettres and distinguished it from the erudite scholarship conducted at the centers of higher learning. The sparkling quality of his writing contributed to the commercial success of his works by flattering the literary taste of the general reader, who had neither the expertise nor the inclination to read an opaque monograph on some recondite topic by a professional historian. The scrupulous attention that Bainville devoted to the form of the historical narrative did not satisfy scholars who justifiably criticized his casual attitude toward sources and citations. But it endeared him to a large section of the reading public. The clarity of his prose—his ability to express his ideas in a form comprehensible to average Frenchmen beyond the small circle of scholarly specialists—assured him access to an audience that few French historians before or since have ever reached.

These features of his writing appealed in particular to two groups in French society with reasons of their own to disdain academic historical writing: the free-lance literary intelligentsia and the bourgeoisie. The lettered set that contributed regularly to the dozens of Parisian periodicals and newspapers that flourished under the Third Republic favorably received Bainville's major works for two reasons. The first was political. The literary fraternity had been, with some notable exceptions, ideologically conservative if not explicitly antirepublican since the advent of the Third

8. See Gabriel Monod, in *Revue historique*, I (January–June 1876), 32; Charles-Victor Langlois, *Questions d'histoire et d'enseignement* (Paris: Hachette, 1902), 164, 226; Keylor, *Academy and Community*, 52, 84–85.

Republic and particularly since the Dreyfus Affair. The academic intelligentsia, on the other hand (again with notable exceptions), had rallied to the cause of Dreyfus and the Republic.[9] Secondly, these *gens de lettres* reacted vociferously to the efforts of professional historians to reduce the role of literary studies in the curriculum of the French educational system as well as to the attempt by the proponents of "scientific literary history" in the university to usurp the function previously performed by nonacademic critics writing for the newspapers and reviews. This dispute even assumed the character of a test of patriotism, with members of the literary world accusing the "pedants" from the university of poisoning France's classical literary culture with historical doctrines and methods imported from the seminars across the Rhine.[10] Bainville effectively played upon these resentments and insecurities in his programmatic manifestoes and his historical writings, thereby gaining a large and distinguished following among the custodians of France's literary tradition.

The second group in French society that appears to have responded with enthusiasm to Bainville's popular brand of historical writing was the bourgeoisie. The campaign of intellectual persuasion that he undertook was directed at this social group above all.[11] He was convinced that the unlettered proletariat lacked the sophistication to profit from the lessons of the past and that the academic elite was firmly attached by the force of tradition or self-interest to the republican regime in power. But the middle-class elite could be depended on eventually to defend its own interests (and thereby the interests of the nation) by rallying to the cause of social order and national security. It therefore seemed potentially susceptible to the appeal of monarchism as the surest means of achieving those

9. The Sorbonne historian Alfred Rambaud was perhaps the most notorious professorial defector from the united front established by the French academic elite in defense of Dreyfus. Archives Nationales, Sûreté (hereinafter cited as AN), F⁷ 12721, 1898–1900, "Ligue de la Patrie Française."

10. See Phyllis H. Stock, "New Quarrel of Ancients and Moderns: The French University and its Opponents, 1899–1914" (Ph.D. dissertation, Yale University, 1965).

11. Stephen Wilson notes that the audience of the Action Française as a whole was "predominantly bourgeois." Wilson, "A View of the Past," 148.

two objectives. All that remained was the need to cure the French bourgeoisie of its traditional vulnerability to the sentimental appeals of the revolutionary mystique and to convert it to the cause of royalist counterrevolution. This ambitious objective Bainville never achieved. But he did succeed in rendering the political ideology of the Action Française palatable to a large part of the respectable *bien pensant* population of France.

Two developments within French society after the Franco-Prussian War contributed to the removal of the most formidable barriers between the French public and the type of works produced by Bainville. These barriers were illiteracy and the prohibitive price of books. The establishment of a nationwide, state-controlled, compulsory system of primary and secondary education between 1880 and 1902 eventually produced a comparatively large clientele of literate citizens whose patronage enabled free-lance historians such as Bainville to earn a living outside the university system. Once the obstacle of illiteracy was removed, it was only a matter of time before the French publishing industry took steps to lower costs in order to tap the potential market for popular historical literature. Inexpensive editions of historical works began to appear, and some of them became instantaneous best sellers in the tradition of the most popular novels. That works of history could achieve such a commercial success doubtless reflected the nostalgia that afflicted many Frenchmen of Bainville's generation, to whom the present seemed barely tolerable and the future, ominous. But it was also traceable to the enterprising spirit of such magnates of the French publishing trade as Bainville's friend Arthème Fayard, whose Grandes Etudes Historiques series became a forum for several commercially successful works of popular history during the interwar period.[12] Not the least of these were Bainville's *Histoire de France* and his *Napoléon*, two of the most widely read history books in twentieth-century France.

But unlike other historical popularizers in France, who unabash-

12. Other popular collections that featured the works of Action Française historians were Hachette's *Récits d'autrefois, Hier et Aujourd'hui* and Grasset's *Les Leçons du Passé*.

edly catered to the public taste for color and romance in historical literature, Bainville refused to view history solely as an art and the historian as an entertainer. Persuasion rather than amusement was his objective. And to persuade, at least in the modern world, implied the obligation to present one's historical arguments in the guise of a scientific demonstration. The prestige of science was such that no historian who wrote to instruct rather than merely to entertain could afford to acquire a reputation of hostility to the scientific study of the past. Such a writer was in danger of exposing himself to the devastating accusation of romanticism from the academic promoters of *la science historique*. Since the term "science" admitted of many meanings, Bainville was able to adapt it to the requirements of his own ideology. His mentor Maurras had set out to liberate royalist political theory from the romantic, irrationalist political tradition of Chateaubriand and the "sentimental" royalists of the Bourbon Restoration by identifying it with the positivist philosophy of that "scientific" royalist Auguste Comte. Bainville in turn sought to establish royalist history on a "scientific" footing by linking it to the tradition of historical positivism represented by three of the most eminent French historians of the second half of the nineteenth century: Hippolyte Taine, Albert Sorel, and Fustel de Coulanges. By redefining scientific history in this way, he was able to combat his professional adversaries in the republican university with their own weapons.

This doctrine of historical positivism derived from the conviction that human behavior is governed by a determinant system of historical laws that bind men's actions to certain predictable consequences. A modified version of the Enlightenment tradition of natural law, this deterministic world view formed the basis of Comtean sociology and, later, of Maurrassian political theory. In Bainville's works it served as an instrument for exposing the historical causes of the decline of French civilization during the nineteenth century. Moreover, his apparent ability to identify the causal links between past and present gave him a serene confidence in his predictions. The historian thus became more than a mere recorder of past events; he was a counselor of the present and a prophet of the future as well. It was this steadfast claim to oracular powers that gave a sense of urgency to most of Bainville's writings. He envisioned a future fraught with peril if France continued to embrace the false principles that governed her political life, and he was determined to warn his country of those dangers in order to provide it with the opportunity to escape their consequences.

The most effective selling point in the royalist interpretation of history was Bainville's proven ability (or good fortune, as his more skeptical critics would claim) to predict future developments with an enviable degree of accuracy. While most professional historians in France appeared to be preoccupied with probing the musty corners of the distant past, Bainville was gaining a nationwide audience for his ominous prophecies of doom and his prescriptions for national salvation. The repeated confirmation of his prognostications, particularly of future conflicts between France and Germany, earned him a reputation as both a political clairvoyant and a "scientific" historian. For what did "science" mean to the layman if not a branch of knowledge in which the observation of individual facts yields generalizations that enable the observer to predict the future? It was this simplistic definition that apparently satisfied many French readers of Bainville's time, who displayed little interest in the scholarly achievements of history but who eagerly devoured the polished historical essays of this skillful dilettante. In a language that all literate Frenchmen could comprehend and appreciate, Bainville told them where they had been, where they were, and where they were likely to be in the years to come.

Abbreviations

AF   *Action française*

AN   Archives Nationales

APP   Archives de la Préfecture de Police, Département de la Seine

RAF   *Revue de l'Action française*

RU   *Revue universelle*

PART ONE

The Road to Royalism

CHAPTER ONE

The Emergence of a Royalist
1879–1900

I owe you everything except life itself.
> Jacques Bainville to Charles Maurras

At the very beginning of the twentieth century, amid the political turmoil precipitated by the Dreyfus Affair, a young French writer of twenty-one who had recently returned from a scholarly sojourn in Germany published a biography of Ludwig II of Bavaria. The book was hardly a ground-breaking contribution to historical scholarship. Since his mysterious death in 1886, the demented monarch had inspired a plethora of biographical studies that attempted to disentangle his bizarre career and personal life. What distinguished this work was the curious political affiliation of the author, Jacques Bainville. During the year of its publication Bainville had joined a new political movement dedicated to the restoration of the monarchy in a France which, since 1871, had adopted and preserved one of the few republican political systems in nineteenth-century Europe. Charles Maurras, the master of the new royalist group, had acquired control of a fortnightly journal, the *Revue de l'Action française*, and, later, a publishing house, the Nouvelle Librairie Nationale.[1] He had recruited a talented team of young writers which began to turn out an uninterrupted stream of royalist propaganda designed to undermine the legitimacy of the Third Republic.[2]

---

1. The Nouvelle Librairie Nationale was never actually owned by members of the Action Française, nor did it possess a monopoly on all of the movement's writers. But it did function, in the words of Ernst Nolte, as a "central publishing house" of the Action Française. See Nolte, *Three Faces of Fascism*, 93–94.
2. The authors of the two standard histories of the Action Française in English differ in their evaluation of its leading members. Edward Tannenbaum's "café intellectuals" (*Action Française*, 45–63) are treated in Eugen Weber's study as "influen-

Bainville soon began to submit articles to the biweekly journal on a regular basis and his *Louis II de Bavière* became, at least in the eyes of his colleagues in the movement, a major literary contribution to the renaissance of French royalism. Though the book undeniably belonged to the genre of historical biography, its author possessed no credentials as a practicing historian. He had never spent a day in the historical seminars at the Sorbonne, the Ecole Normale Supérieure, the Ecole Pratique des Hautes Etudes, or the Ecole des Chartes, which were being run by the scholars who had established history as an academic discipline during the last quarter of the nineteenth century.[3]

After his maiden foray into the realm of historical writing, Bainville returned to journalism, and remained in the newsroom until the outbreak of the First World War. In the midst of that conflict he reclaimed the title of historian with a series of penetrating analyses of the European past. He was never again to relinquish that claim. By the time of his death in 1936 he had amassed a personal fortune from the royalties of over forty books of popular history and had become one of the most widely read French historians of his time.[4] These writings, together with his daily newspaper columns on historical subjects, helped to burnish the reputation of the French monarchy that had been tarnished by the professional historians in the republican university. He left behind, in the person of Pierre Gaxotte, a disciple[5] who has carried on the tradition of royalist historical writing in France long after the demise of the royalist movement itself.

Despite Bainville's lifelong association with Maurras, his influence was felt most keenly outside the ranks of the Action Française. It was Bainville, much more than Maurras and Léon Daudet, the

tial publicists and public figures" (Weber, *Action Française*, p. x). My views on this matter more closely approximate those of Weber.

3. On the institutionalization of historical study in the French university system, see Keylor, *Academy and Community*.

4. See the Appendix for the number of printed copies of his most important works.

5. The two were not intimate friends, however. Gaxotte was never invited to the home of the royalist historian with whom he had been so closely identified. Interview with Pierre Gaxotte (1970).

two more narrowly partisan members of the royalist triumvirate, who constructed an intellectual bridge to the broader world of the respectable right in France. Maurras's and Daudet's anti-Semitic excesses, frequent brushes with the law, and outspoken advocacy of counterrevolutionary violence endeared them to many excitable young adventurers in the Latin Quarter. But the moderate tone and limpid style of Bainville's historical and journalistic writing rendered the royalist doctrine acceptable to nonroyalist members of the conservative intelligentsia who dominated the major newspapers, periodicals, publishing houses, and learned societies of Paris.

There was little in Jacques Bainville's familial background and upbringing that foreshadowed the ideological direction of his career. An exception is perhaps the fact that he was born in Vincennes, the Parisian suburb adjoining the capital city at its eastern limit with a famous château that had been a residence of French kings for centuries. Long considered the most royalist of French cities, Vincennes was where Charles V was born, where Mazarin died, where Louis XIII played as a youth. Here, at the Bainville house at 59 rue de Fontenay, the man who was to become modern France's preeminent monarchist historian was brought into the world on February 9, 1879.[6]

Jacques's father, Pierre Joseph Bainville, was a moderately prosperous distributor of coal who hailed from a long line of provincial bourgeois from Lorraine, near Nancy. The family was vociferously republican, and politics occupied an important place at the dinner table. The elder Bainville's republicanism was long standing and deeply felt. As a schoolboy he had participated in demonstrations against Louis Napoleon's coup d'état in 1851. Later he had attended meetings of the liberal opposition during the Second Empire.[7] Under the Third Republic he was an assiduous reader of *Le Temps* (the journal of the republican ruling elite), a close friend and

6. See Lyle E. Linville, "Jacques Bainville: His Political Life and Thought in the Era of the Great War" (Ph.D. dissertation, Kent State University, 1971), 30. Jacques was the third of four children. Interview with Hervé Bainville (1970).

7. See Bainville, *Histoire de trois générations: 1815–1918* (Paris: Fayard, 1918), 124–25, and Roger Joseph, *Qui est Jacques Bainville?* (Orléans: Lhermitte, 1967), 16.

political supporter of the future Radical minister Camille Pelletan, and an enthusiastic advocate of the policies of Jules Ferry.[8]

But as the political behavior of Maurice Barrès, Raymond Poincaré, and other transplanted Lorrainers was to demonstrate, the republicanism of the sons and even grandsons of France's lost provinces was influenced much more by memories of 1871 than of 1789. Young Jacques was subjected by his father to lurid tales of the hardship caused by Prussian pillaging, the siege of Paris, and the Commune. These bloodcurdling bedtime stories left a legacy of pessimism that was to remain with him all his life. "The child is always disposed to consider the things that he sees and hears around him as ordinary and normal," he later observed. "As for me, I was convinced for quite a while that invasion and revolution are a part of life, and I wondered during my early childhood when it would be my turn to eat rat pâté and horse stew and see Paris in flames."[9]

Upon completion of his primary education in 1895 (during which he established an early reputation for precocity[10]), Bainville enrolled in the prestigious Lycée Henri IV in Paris. There, in the hothouse atmosphere of the *fin-de-siècle* Latin Quarter, the impressionable young bourgeois acquired the intellectual proclivities that determined the character of his later writing. The pedagogical tradition of the Parisian lycées emphasized discipline, hierarchy, and order. The classical curriculum still held sway, dominated by the "morale antique." According to a noted alumnus who had preceded Bainville, the masters of the lycées rejected the "absurd sentimentality about the natural goodness of man" in favor of the pessimistic doctrine that civilization was a "thin varnish applied to

8. Bainville *père* allowed Pelletan to hold political rallies of the Radical-Socialist Party in one of his commercial warehouses. Interview with Hervé Bainville (1977); Georges Grappe, in Henri Massis, ed., *Le Souvenir de Jacques Bainville* (Paris: Les Amis des Beaux Livres, 1936), 76; Joachim Wieder, *Jacques Bainville: Nationalismus und Klassizismus in Frankreich* (Breslau: Priebatsch, 1939), 13–15.

9. Bainville, *Nouveau dialogue dans le salon d'Aliénor* (Paris: Lesage, 1926), 49–50. Interview with Madame Jacques Bainville (1970); Bainville, *Réflexions sur la politique* (Paris: Plon, 1941), 14.

10. Lucien Corpechot, in "Hommages à Jacques Bainville," *Revue universelle*, LXIV (March 1, 1936), 543.

human nature, which is rather fierce." The stylistic simplicity and rhetorical polish of the classics served as models of literary expression to be emulated by all lycéens. The concept of *la culture générale* determined what was taught and how, leaving little room for the specialization that had already invaded higher education by the 1880s. Taste, logic, and precise expression were regarded as prerequisites for confronting life.[11]

The intellectual inclination of the students coincided with the school's classical reputation. Literature enjoyed the greatest popularity, both inside and outside the classroom, while science, except for those students preparing for the military academy at Saint-Cyr, the Ecole Polytechnique, or the Faculty of Science, was of interest only in so far as it was necessary to prepare for the baccalaureate examination. But if science was consigned to the status of a bothersome obligation, "scientism" was anathema at this outpost of classicism. At Henri IV the philosopher Henri Bergson had set this tone of irreverence toward the cult of science, and it had begun to filter down to the student generation by the middle of the 1890s.[12]

But it was literary rather than philosophical studies that captured the minds of the students at Henri IV during this period, and Bainville was one of the most avid young *littérateurs* of his generation. His classmate Georges Grappe recalled that he and Bainville regularly attended the Thursday lectures of the critic Jules Lemaître that preceded the matinée performances at the Odéon Theater. They devoured literary works that were considered avant-garde even in the Bohemian milieu of the Latin Quarter. From Stendhal, Balzac, and Flaubert they graduated to Loti, Verlaine, and Rimbaud —potent antidotes to the staid classics which they were required

11. André Chaumeix, *Le Lycée Henri Quatre* (Paris: Gallimard, 1936), 158–59, 137. Chaumeix later became literary editor of the *Revue des deux mondes* and an intimate friend of Bainville.

The disparity between the pedagogical practices of higher and secondary education was to disappear in 1902, when the "modern curriculum" (which permitted specialization in such subjects as science and living languages) attained parity with the "classical curriculum" in the lycées. See John E. Talbott, *The Politics of Educational Reform in France, 1918–1940* (Princeton: Princeton University Press, 1969), 115–17.

12. Chaumeix, *Le Lycée Henri Quatre*, 126–27, 146.

to memorize and recite in the classroom. "We would have been astonished and even scandalized," Grappe later remarked, "to hear that one day we would adopt toward these thrilling delights the Maurrassian point of view."[13]

Indeed, Bainville's later literary preferences exceeded the narrow Greco-Latinism of his mentor. While his classical studies kindled in him a passion for Boileau[14] and caused him to consider a pilgrimage to Greece, "the place where perfection exists,"[15] Bainville also acquired an early taste for two writers who, by temperament, style, or national origin, were to prove anathema to the royalist movement. Grappe recalled that young Jacques often invited him to the family flat near the Boulevard Saint-Germain (where his father had retired early to live off his investments) for lengthy recitations from Heine, whose poetry had seduced him while at the lycée.[16] And Maurras himself later chided his younger associate for having acquired a predilection for Baudelaire that could best be cured by exposure to the verse of the Provençal poet Frédéric Mistral.[17]

It was this early infatuation with literature that diverted Bainville from the medical career that his father had carefully mapped out for him. At the end of his summer vacation in 1896 he wrote his classmate Grappe about his growing fascination with what he called "l'esprit littéraire." "Reading is so enjoyable," he exclaimed. "I always regret finishing the last page of a novel or a poem—it is like observing the death of one's friends."[18] The allure of a writing career became stronger as he approached the end of his studies. So did a brash confidence in his own literary merits. From his classroom desk at Henri IV he sent a letter to the eminent drama critic

---

13. Georges Grappe, in Massis, *Le Souvenir*, 73; see also Lazare de Gérin-Ricard, *L'Histoire de France de Jacques Bainville* (Paris: Editions Edgar Malfère, 1939), 12–13, and Grappe, in "Hommages à Jacques Bainville," 572–73.
14. Gérin-Ricard, *L'Histoire de France de Jacques Bainville*, 16.
15. Jacques Bainville, *Les Sept Portes de Thebes* (Paris: Les Editions du Cadran, 1931), 17–20.
16. Georges Grappe, in Massis, *Le Souvenir*, 76. Interview with Hervé Bainville.
17. Charles Maurras, *Poésie et vérité* (Lyons: H. Lardanchet, 1944), 141–42, 147.
18. Jacques Bainville to Georges Grappe, August 1896, in "Hommages à Jacques Bainville," 574.

of *Le Temps,* Francisque Sarcey, analyzing a recent performance of Molière's *L'Avare* at the Comédie Française. When Sarcey published the sixteen-year-old's comments in his column,[19] the letter was transformed from what Bainville *père* had originally condemned as an exercise in adolescent presumptuousness into the first overt indication of the precocity for which Bainville *fils* was soon to become famous.

These and other extracurricular preoccupations prevented young Bainville from compiling an oustanding scholastic record at Henri IV, but his undistinguished performance was also in part the result of his displeasure with certain features of the curriculum.[20] Of all the subjects that he was required to master in preparation for his baccalaureate examination, history proved to be by far the most distasteful. He later recalled the boredom and contempt that the study of history had inspired in him and many others in his class. He was disgusted with the reigning tradition of *histoire événemen- tielle,* which emphasized the compilation and narration of factual data, leaving the student with little more than vague memories of a few notable dates and events. He departed from the school with the impression that history was "a tissue of endless dramas, a mê- lée, a chaos in which the mind could discern nothing." The purely chronological recitation of unrelated facts struck him as insipid, as did his instructors' failure to explain their significance. Soon after his graduation he complained to his friend Grappe that he had been taught to think of history as "a collection of biographies, of news items, of drivel," adding that he was beginning to realize that he would be satisfied only if he could come in contact with real life beneath the "dry parchments and inflexible documents."[21]

19. *Le Fauteuil de Raymond Poincaré: Discours de réception de M. Jacques Bainville à l'Académie Française et réponse de M. Maurice Donnay* (Paris: Plon, 1935), 75–76; "Trois Nouveaux Académiciens," *Annales politiques et littéraires* (April 10, 1935), 347.

20. *Le Correspondant* (October, 1924), 91; *Le Fauteuil de Jacques Bainville: Discours de réception de M. Joseph Pesquidoux à l'Académie Française et réponse de M. André Bellessort* (Paris: Plon, 1937), 12.

21. *Les Nouvelles littéraires* (March, 1924); Jacques Bainville, *History of France,* trans. A. G. and C. G. Gauss (New York: Appleton & Co., 1926), v; see also *Le Divan* (1925), 52. Discontent with the event-oriented approach of professional history in France had already surfaced in the writings of Henri Berr and his collaborators at the *Revue de synthèse historique.* It later inspired the formation of Marc Bloch's

Still without concrete plans for the future, save a definite decision to renounce a medical career and an inchoate interest in literature,[22] Bainville enrolled in the Faculty of Law at the University
of Paris to accommodate at least the second choice of his father.
But his unsatisfying stay there merely strengthened his inclination
to pursue literary studies.[23] At this time a new preoccupation began to give a more definite form to his immediate plans. His youthful fascination with Heine had kindled an interest in the mysterious empire across the Rhine where he had spent most of his
summer vacations while a lycée student.[24] His discovery of the
novels of Maurice Barrès transformed this interest into an obsession. One novel in particular, *L'Ennemi des lois*, which describes
the journey of a Frenchman to the mountain castles of Ludwig II
of Bavaria, caused Bainville to surrender to the allure that Germany exercised upon so many young Frenchmen in the closing
years of the nineteenth century.[25] He joined a youth organization
devoted to the improvement of Franco-German cultural relations
and began to read every book on Germany he could get his hands
on. After working in a bookstore and translating books into French
for a German publisher to augment his allowance, he decided to
bring his formal academic training to an end. Bored with his
studies, his imagination fired by the torrent of picturesque literature about Germany that was saturating the Parisian literary land-
scape, he convinced his family to finance a trip to Munich where
he planned to sightsee, become fluent in German, and write up his
observations.[26]

---

and Lucien Febvre's *Annales*. See Lucien Febvre, "De *la Revue de synthèse aux Annales*," *Annales*, 7 (July–September 1952), 289–92, and "Sur une forme d'histoire
qui n'est pas le nôtre," *Annales*, 3 (1948), 21–24.

22. Henri Vidal, *La Pensée de Jacques Bainville en matière économique et sociale* (Paris:
Université de Paris, Faculté de Droit, Thèse pour le doctorat, Etablissements Busson, 1944), 89.

23. Grappe, in "Hommages à Jacques Bainville," 575.

24. Massis, *Le Souvenir*, 76; Linville, "Jacques Bainville," 50.

25. *Le Fauteuil de Raymond Poincaré*, 77–78; Wieder, *Jacques Bainville*, 17. For a
treatment of this phenomenon, see Digeon, *La Crise allemande, passim*.

26. Interview with Madame Jacques Bainville. Jacques Bainville, "Franco-allemand," *Revue universelle* (hereinafter cited as *RU*), (December 1, 1929), 611; Interview with Hervé Bainville; Linville, "Jacques Bainville," 51.

From the end of 1897 to the summer of 1898, Bainville toured the principal historical sites of Western Germany. After stopping off at Bayreuth, the Mecca of the Wagnerian cult then supreme in Paris,[27] he retraced the steps of Barrès's legendary André Maltère, marvelling at the eerie mystery of the palaces, gardens, and fountains that King Ludwig had constructed near Munich. The original attraction that the Bavarian monarch had exerted on Bainville was not due to the sentimental monarchism of a young royalist nostalgically yearning for his own nation's deposed dynasty, for Bainville was still very much under the influence of his parents' republicanism. He was primarily interested in explaining the enormous popularity that the dead king and his illustrious protégé Richard Wagner enjoyed in *fin de siècle* France.[28]

But in the course of his travels Bainville became increasingly attentive to the *political* realities of Germany, discovering that the homeland of Heine and Wagner was also the homeland of Bismarck and Wilhelm II. He visited Frankfurt and inspected the site of the revolutionary parliament of 1848.[29] While touring the castles of the Rhine, he bristled at the hostile glances of the guides as they pointed out ruins dating from Louis XIV's invasion of the Palatinate.[30] The spirit of order and discipline and the celebration of force and might that he observed everywhere contrasted dramatically both with the idealistic pronouncements of the liberals of the 1848 parliament and with the romantic reveries of the Bavarian king. The Francophobia that confronted him at every turn seemed to belie the presumption of cordiality between Southern Germany

27. Joseph, *Qui est Jacques Bainville?*, 16.
28. Louis Chaigne, *Histoire de la littérature française: les lettres contemporaines* (Paris: Editions Mondiales, 1964), 610. For differing views of Bainville's original attraction to Ludwig, see Robert Brasillach, *Les Quatre Jeudis* (Paris: Les Sept Couleurs, 1951), 91–92; Henry Bordeaux, *Quarante Ans chez les quarantes* (Paris: Fayard, 1959), 292 ff. and in *Ecrits de Paris* (April, 1958), 65–66; Edmond Pilon, *RU*, (June 1, 1924). Other future Action Française men who visited Ludwig's castles were Maurice Pujo (see *Revue bleue*, December 21, 1895), 786–89, Léon Daudet (see Charles Maurras, *Pour un Jeune Français* [Paris: Amiot-Dumont, 1949], 107), and Pierre Lasserre (see *Mercure de France*, [July, 1901], 71–94). In addition to Barrès's work on Ludwig II, Gustave Kahn's *Le Roi fou* and Catulle Mendès' *Le Roi vierge* introduced the royal legend to French readers.
29. Grappe, in Massis, *Le Souvenir*, 77.
30. *Le Fauteuil de Raymond Poincaré*, 83.

and her Catholic neighbor to the west. By the time he had settled
in Munich in the early summer of 1898 the young Frenchman had
come to view Germany as a land of contradictions and the per-
sonage of King Ludwig as the key that might unlock its mysteries.
This key furnished a suitable subject for a fledgling writer intent on
trying his hand at his chosen craft.

Reflecting the preferences that he had acquired during his formative years at the lycée, Bainville undertook his study of Ludwig
with the intention of writing a literary essay rather than a historical
treatise. "I now think that I will be able to put into literary form the
notes that I have been amassing for two months," he wrote to his
old classmate Grappe.

> I who, you will remember, was always a mediocre "historian" and who
> claimed only the title of "littéraire," have been overtaken with a pas-
> sionate interest in the history of contemporary Germany. And here I am
> engulfed in Ranke and Sybel. Who would have believed it? Certainly
> not old Lehugeur [his history instructor at Henri IV]. But set your mind
> to rest, I won't make my little book—if I write it—a little Michelet. It
> will be instead a study in "psychological biography." History will in-
> tervene only when Ludwig II will have acted upon it. And such cases
> are rare. I who used to belittle the scholars at the Ecole des Chartes—do
> you remember that too?—am busy determining how much Ludwig II
> ate for dinner and what kind of clothes he wore. Oh well, one may
> make sacrifices to other cults without destroying what one has adored.[31]

His plans for writing a literary, psychological biography were
foiled when he discovered that the royal archives were closed.[32]
Forced to rely principally on the memoirs of the king's entourage,
he came to place greater emphasis on the way that others saw and
were affected by the ruler. As it turned out, the inaccessibility of
the primary sources presented no serious problem, for it coincided
with the writer's growing interest in the political—as opposed to
the personal—implications of Ludwig II's reign.[33]

31. Bainville to Grappe, August 10, 1898, in the possession of M. Hervé Bainville.
32. *Le Correspondant* (March 25, 1900), 1239; Jacques Bainville, *Louis II de Bavière*
(Paris: Fayard, 1964), 13.
33. Pierre Gilbert, *La Forêt des Cippes* (2 vols.; Paris: Champion, 1918), I, 314.

While conducting his preliminary research, Bainville recalled the passages in Carlyle's *Heroes and Hero Worship* which extolled the virtues of absolute monarchy and the invaluable services that an authoritarian leader can render to his kingdom by promoting its prosperity and protecting its independence.[34] Expecting to discover evidence of such royal services as he examined the record of Ludwig's career, he was struck by the numerous occasions on which the king had failed to fulfill his royal obligations. He concluded that it was the monarch's lack of political realism that was primarily responsible for Bavaria's absorption by Prussia in 1871. Bainville attributed this political naïveté to the influence of Ludwig's romantic sensibility. "Isolated in his fantasy," he declared, "the king was no longer occupied with the details of public affairs except on occasion, and ended by completely losing interest in them." The Bavarian Nero, as Bainville was fond of dubbing him, had spent his time play-acting, writing mediocre poetry, and flattering Wagner at Bayreuth while the political independence of his kingdom was being destroyed.[35]

Since the days of Albert V (protector of Dürer, Peter Vischer, and Hans Sachs during the Bavarian Renaissance), the Wittelsbach dynasty had preferred the patronage of art to the conduct of politics. Bainville noted that this tendency to neglect its traditional responsibility alienated the ruling house from its subjects, whose principal concerns were understandably political. While Prussia was decimating Austria and Bavaria in the war of 1866, preparing the final push toward German unity under Hohenzollern auspices, Ludwig was in the company of Wagner in Switzerland, discussing plans for the construction of the Bayreuth theater. While the royal court vainly attempted to wean him away from his Wagnerian obsession by arranging a marriage with Princess Sophie of Austria (a wise policy from the standpoint of *raison d'état*), the virginal king

---

34. *Le Fauteuil de Raymond Poincaré*, 83. Reino Virtanen notes that Treitschke, Nietzsche, and Burke also contributed to his interest in an authoritarian state. See Reino Virtanen, "Nietzsche and the Action Française," *Journal of the History of Ideas*, XI, No. 2 (April, 1950), 194.
35. Bainville, *Louis II de Bavière*, 13–14, 12.

backed out at the last moment with a Parsifal-like declaration of the virtues of romantic chastity. He loathed the tedious burdens of diplomacy and administration and would frequently avoid having to receive royal visitors by escaping to one of his castles. In July 1870 he abandoned the capital for the solitude of his mountain retreat during the difficult negotiations over the impending war with France. Hence, in Bainville's eyes, this royal misanthrope's esthetic preoccupations and his distaste for state functions rendered him ignorant of the harsh realities of German politics in an age of blood and iron. The result was his kingdom's loss of independence.[36]

Bainville believed that he had discovered in the symbolic person of Ludwig II a phenomenon of universal significance: the secret of Germany's deceptive dual nature. The annexation of Bavaria by Prussia signified the victory of "realist" Germany over "romantic, idealist" Germany. The products of romantic genius that French observers since Madame De Staël had admired in the Germans— the poetry, the architecture, the drama, the music—were precisely those aspects of the German spirit that were being devalued in the empire of Bismarck. Wagner himself, a crafty agent of the military monarchy to the north, symbolized the new orientation of German *Kultur*: his Music of the Future was not a symptom of romantic nostalgia, as French observers erroneously believed, but rather was a celebration of the superiority of German power.[37]

But there were other lessons that the young French writer learned from the career of the accursed Bavarian ruler. Bainville observed with a touch of irony that Ludwig's passion for Wagner was rivalled only by his acquired taste for French customs. His lavish castles were intended to be perfect replicas of Versailles, complete with peasant cottages and trianons and gilded walls hung with pastiches of Watteau and Boucher. Bainville saw in Ludwig the perfect symbol of barbarian Germany embarrassed at its philistinism, perpetually seeking deliverance from its hereditary vulgarity through slav-

36. *Ibid.*, 15–16, 100–101, 110, 142–46, 181.
37. *Ibid.*, 225–26, 56, 187.

ish emulation of the French model. As the example of Nietzsche had proved, a strong Francophile element persisted in Germany after 1870, particularly in the south and west, an area which retained a stubborn feeling of resentment toward the Prussian dominator. Ludwig II appeared to Bainville as one of those aspirants of civilization who periodically emerged in Germany to be charmed by the superior culture of France.[38]

But if southern Germany had succeeded in preserving a modicum of cultural independence from its primitive neighbor to the north, its political servility to Prussia was an accomplished fact. What impressed Bainville most of all about the ruling elite of the German Empire was its signal success in imposing national unity upon the various German states, achieving the work of centralization and introducing the Prussian traditions of discipline and order in areas that had remained proudly independent for centuries. The impressionable young French visitor could not avoid contrasting this trend toward national unity and political stability with the deteriorating situation in France, where the Dreyfus Affair was generating political polarization, religious conflict, and antimilitarism.

Bainville's attitude toward the Dreyfus controversy was, at least at the beginning, painfully ambivalent. On the one hand, he declared to a friend, he found himself persuaded of Dreyfus's innocence and "dismayed by this violation of justice, this condemnation of a man whose guilt they cannot succeed in establishing." Yet on the other hand he admitted to feeling "joyful, jubilant, and triumphant at the defeat of the Freemasons, the radicals . . . and the libertarians, the old men of *Le Temps*," whom he accused of exploiting the cause of Dreyfus to further their own political ambitions. In a subsequent letter he proudly described himself as a "chauvinist" who deplored "the mud that they have thrown on the army and France."[39] This ambivalence remained with him for the rest of his life. In the mid-twenties he confessed to a friend

38. *Ibid.*, 195.
39. Bainville to Grappe (August, 1898); Bainville to Grappe, undated, both in the possession of M. Hervé Bainville.

that he never fully understood the issues involved in the Dreyfus case, and it received only cursory mention in his historical writings.[40]

Yet, as these statements suggest, the political views of the young writer were slowly moving away from the advanced republicanism that he had inherited from his parents.[41] The catalyst of this intellectual transformation was what he had come to regard as the threat posed by a militaristic, disciplined Germany to an increasingly impotent, politically divided France. This contrast could not be attributed to France's racial or cultural inferiority—Bainville was already too much of a French chauvinist and a cultural nationalist to entertain such an explanation for his nation's plight. Through the process of elimination, he gradually became convinced that the answer lay in the radically different political institutions of the two countries. By the time of his return to France, he had already begun to consider the possibility that the restoration of the monarchy was France's best hope of arresting the decline of her political vitality as well as of her international position, particularly vis-à-vis Germany.

Bainville's highly idiosyncratic religious views also began to take form during this period in his life. Indeed, he apparently experienced a spiritual crisis around the turn of the century that was promoted by an intense personal insecurity. "I have no confidence in myself," he complained to his closest boyhood friend. "No imagination, a mediocre, dull mind, and few ideas." But though the urge to escape this spiritual void by embracing a comforting faith was strong, the requisite ability to suspend disbelief was lacking. "I sense in myself a religious need that has not been satisfied," he candidly confessed.

40. Interview with René Wittmann (1970). However, later he did come to accept the Maurrassian doctrine of the patriotic lie—"An injustice is worth more than disorder, because disorder will one day be paid for by invasion and a million and a half deaths." Bainville, *Journal*, II (Paris: Plon, 1949), 134. See also his *Esquisses et portraits* (Paris: Wittmann, 1946), 39. The chapter on the Dreyfus Affair in his *La Troisième République* (Paris: Fayard, 1935), which represented his most extensive treatment of the subject, concentrated less on the issue of guilt or innocence than on the political consequences of the controversy.
41. Grappe, in Massis, *Le Souvenir*, 77.

It seems to me that the Catholic religion has not succeeded in satisfying it. . . . In any case, I may some day undergo a change of heart in favor of Catholicism, and that would not surprise me. I will perhaps be an independent, a detestable recruit without discipline, a wild sheep apart from the flock. What does it matter! My religion—if I have one some day—will be *for me*. No Church will have the right to claim it.[42]

Yet these free-thinking sentiments did not signify that he had succumbed to the anticlerical influences of his father. For like Voltaire, the agnostic Bainville recognized the importance of the church as an indispensable social institution which furnished a transcendent sanction for morality. He wrote Grappe that he had rediscovered the writings of Edmund Burke while in Germany and fully agreed with Burke's view that the spoliation of the property of the church during the French Revolution was a dastardly deed, remarking that "it is my bourgeois instinct speaking here."[43] In the midst of his adolescent agnosticism Bainville had concluded that the Catholic church was the sole guarantor of social order and must therefore receive the support of even those Frenchmen who were unwilling to apply its teachings to their own personal salvation.

While writing his biography of Ludwig, Bainville happened upon a work entitled *Trois Idées politiques* by Charles Maurras, a thirty-year-old writer who had migrated to Paris from the south of France in 1885. The book, a vitriolic indictment of the romantic movement in France, purported to demonstrate the natural affinity between the romantic mentality and eccentric political behavior; as such, it seemed to confirm Bainville's own analysis of the tragic career of Ludwig. Bainville wrote Maurras, displaying the same adolescent audacity that had prompted his earlier letter to the critic Sarcey. Introducing himself as a "young beginner in literature" who "regrets not having a voice," he thanked the elder writer for demonstrating to him the evils of French romanticism personified by Rousseau and Chateaubriand.[44]

42. Bainville to Grappe, undated; Bainville to Grappe, 1899, both in the possession of M. Hervé Bainville.
43. Grappe, in Massis, *Le Souvenir*, 76.
44. See Charles Maurras, *Trois Idées politiques* (Paris: Champion, 1898); Bainville to Charles Maurras, undated, in the possession of M. Hervé Bainville.

But certain aspects of Maurras's neoroyalist political sentiments (which he had acquired in 1896 and proceeded to propagate in the leading royalist journal subsidized by the pretender's Political Bureau, the *Gazette de France*)[45] proved less congenial to Bainville than his literary criticism. This was a circumstance that was probably attributable to the widely divergent origins of the two men. Maurras's nostalgia for his native province had inspired him to learn the Provençal language and eventually to join the *Félibres*, a tiny group of southern émigrés in Paris who sought to promote the Provençal renaissance inaugurated by the poet Frédéric Mistral.[46] From this provincial, back-to-the-soil milieu emerged the guiding principles of Maurras's peculiar brand of royalism: political decentralization, restoration of the pre-revolutionary provincial boundaries, opposition to statism, official recognition of Provençal.[47] Such doctrines hardly appealed to the cosmopolitan young Parisian who had recently observed the failure of Bavarian separatism and the enviable vitality of the unitary German Empire. In a subsequent letter Bainville declared himself in favor of centralization and accused Maurras of exaggerating the intelligence of France's rural population. Maurras kept the letter, planning to reply to it in print in order to respond to the objections that it raised.[48] Meanwhile, Bainville began to contribute articles to French periodicals which publicized his hostility to the republican regime at home and to its intellectual and literary defenders.[49]

As the young French traveler crossed the border into France in the late summer of 1898 with plans to revise his Ludwig manuscript for publication and seek a position with a newspaper, he rushed to the kiosk at the railroad station at Avricourt in Moselle

45. Weber, *Action Française*, 13–14, 49; Buthman, *The Rise of Integral Nationalism*, 235–52.
46. See Léon Roudiez, *Maurras jusqu'à l'Action Française* (Paris: Bonne, 1957), 148, 237ff.; Buthman, *The Rise of Integral Nationalism*, 185–98.
47. See Curtis, *Three Against the Republic*, 162–64; Nolte, *Three Faces of Fascism*, 61; Osgood, *French Royalism under the Third and Fourth Republics*, 55–56, 58.
48. Charles Maurras, *Au Signe de Flore* (Paris: Les Oeuvres Représentatives, 1931), 282.
49. See, for example, Bainville's articles in *La Critique* (August 5, 1898), 175ff. and in *La Plume* (June 15, 1899), 392ff.

and asked for the royalist papers. The *Gazette de France* was sold out, so he picked up *Le Soleil* and came across an article by Maurras.[50] In the following months he followed the writings and public activities of the royalist journalist with increasing interest and enthusiasm. In the winter and spring of the following year, Maurras and a group of writers who had joined the anti-Dreyfusard League of the French Fatherland[51] broke away to form a more militant cadre of nationalists which eventually became the nucleus of the Action Française.[52] But by the middle of 1899 Bainville's articles and his efforts to secure a publisher for his Ludwig book had caught the eye of Maurice Barrès, who, though willing to lend his name to the nationalistic cause of the new rump group, had kept his distance out of distaste for Maurras's royalism. The novelist invited the young writer to contribute articles to *Minerva*, one of his own intellectual mouthpieces, and Bainville later returned the compliment by dedicating his Ludwig biography to Barrès "in memory of *L'Ennemie des lois.*"[53] Thus it was Barrès rather than Maurras who introduced Bainville into the Parisian literary world.[54]

Barrès originally attracted Bainville's interest because of his devotion to nationalism and his antipathy for Germany, two sentiments that the younger man had recently acquired. It was Barrès who had first used the term "nationalism" in its modern, reactionary sense in an article, published in 1892, entitled "La Querelle des nationalistes et des cosmopolites."[55] The piece was a strident ap-

---

50. Maurras, *Au Signe de Flore*, 283.
51. See *Le Soleil*, December 31, 1898; Buthman, *The Rise of Integral Nationalism*, 95–96.
52. See AN, F⁷12862, "Notes sur l'Action Française"; Nolte, *Three Faces of Fascism*, 65–68.
53. Henry Bordeaux, *Quarante Ans chez les quarante*, 293–94. Interview with Madame Jacques Bainville. Bainville and Barrès were frequent travelling companions— see Jacques Bainville, *Tyrrhenus* (Saint-Félicien-en-Vivarais: Au Pigeonnier, 1925)— and their disagreement over the monarchy was always a friendly one. Once Barrès asked Bainville: "Without the Revolution what would you be?" Bainville, whose ancestors had moved from the peasantry to the bourgeoisie before 1789, replied: "Fermier-général." Cited in Henri Massis, *Maurras et notre temps* (2 vols.; Paris: La Palatine, 1951), I, 58.
54. See Charles Maurras, *Jacques Bainville et Paul Bourget* (Paris: Editions du Cadran, n.d.), 65.
55. *Le Figaro*, July 4, 1892.

peal to all Frenchmen to combat the influx of foreign ideas and preserve the purity of native French traditions. Nationalism was by no
means a new word in the vocabulary of French politics. Throughout most of the nineteenth century it was linked to the political
philosophy of the republican left, which promoted the cause of
parliamentary democracy in domestic politics and the principle of
national self-determination in foreign affairs.[56] But in Barrès's writings the nationalist creed underwent a major transformation which
rendered it increasingly hospitable to the reactionary principles of
the right. Anti-Semitism, anti-Germanism, and authoritarian Caesarism,[57] which had surfaced during the Boulanger crisis and resurfaced during the Panama scandal, were kept alive in Barrès's
political polemics until they acquired a new popularity during the
Dreyfus Affair.

Though the young Bainville hardly found these ideas unconge-
nial, he was not destined to remain very long under the tutelage of
Barrès. For despite his reservations about certain features of Maurras's royalism, it was the Provençal journalist rather than the Lor-
rainer novelist who captured Bainville's loyalty *in absentia*. Two
other right-wing intellectuals who had grown impatient with the
timidity of the League of the French Fatherland, Henri Vaugeois (a
lycée philosophy professor) and Maurice Pujo (a free lance journalist), had joined forces with Maurras in a schismatic group dedicat-

56. See John T. Marcus, *Neutralism and Nationalism in France* (New York: Book-
man Associates, 1958), 136–37; Henri Hauser, *Le Principe des nationalités* (Paris:
Alcan, 1916); René Johannet, *Le Principe des nationalités* (Paris: Nouvelle Librairie
Nationale, 1923).

57. Barrès's indictment of the Jews was thoroughly compatible with his exclusive
doctrine of nationalism. The Jews, he claimed, would inevitably be driven to exploit
France for their own profit since "their fatherland is not the French soil or the
French dead; it is the place where they find their greatest interests." Maurice Barrès,
Scènes et doctrines du nationalisme (2 vols.; Paris: Plon-Nourrit et c^{le}, 1925), I, 67. For
instances of Barrès's anti-Semitism, see Robert Soucy, *Fascism in France: The Case of
Maurice Barrès* (Berkeley: University of California Press, 1972), and Curtis, *Three
Against the Republic*, 212–14. Barrès preserved the spirit of hostility to Germany
that had characterized the first generation of republicans after Sedan, and it was
this conception of French history, which D. W. Brogan calls "a permanent watch
on the eastern frontier," that endeared Barrès to Bainville. D. W. Brogan, *French
Personalities and Problems* (New York: Knopf, 1947), 81. On Barrès's authoritarian
Caesarism, see Soucy, *Fascism in France*, 32.

ed to "French action," a catch-all term implying resistance to the leftward drift of the Republic. In July 1899 the new movement launched its first bulletin, which shortly became the *Revue de l'Action française*.[58] While the small group of dissident intellectuals was originally labelled by the police spies in its ranks as "nationalist and republican" in tendency,[59] it became obvious after the turn of the century that Maurras was succeeding in winning over several members of the organization to the royalist cause.

In the winter of 1900, after Bainville had mentioned his admiration for Maurras, Barrès introduced him to Vaugeois. Maurras's collaborator at the "little gray review" instantly recognized a kindred spirit whose precocious literary talents might prove useful to the new group and recruited Bainville to edit the book review section. His name was added to the official list of contributors on March 15, 1900, and his first article (an exposé of the subversive activities of French Protestants at home and abroad) appeared in the April 1 number.[60] Four days later, on April 4, Vaugeois invited the young writer, who had attained his majority only two months earlier, to accompany him to the Café Procope, where a number of neoroyalist intellectuals planned to debate the theory and practice of counterrevolution. After hours of heated discussion, the group moved on to the Café de Flore, where Maurras had spent the evening eagerly awaiting the opportunity to recruit new converts to the cause.[61] "Look, the young generation is joining us," Maurras exclaimed with delight as Bainville took his seat.[62] The elder man soon learned that the pale, thin lad across the table was the author of the penetrating letter that had so impressed him a few years earlier and the new contributor whose articles he had admired in

58. See Robert Havard de la Montagne, *Histoire de l'Action Française* (Paris: Amiot-Dumont, 1950), 13; Maurras, *Tombeaux* (Paris: Nouvelle Librairie Nationale, 1921), 153; Maurras, *Au Signe de Flore*, 90ff; Tannenbaum, *Action Française*, 28–35.

59. AN, F⁷12862, "Notes sur l'Action française," no. 1.

60. See Jacques Bainville, "Nos Calvinistes en Allemagne," *Revue de l'Action française* (hereinafter cited as *RAF*), (April 1, 1900), 553–64; Linville, "Jacques Bainville," 83–87; Wieder, *Jacques Bainville*, 24.

61. Maurras, *Au Signe de Flore*, 279–82; Linville, "Jacques Bainville," 70; Joseph, *Qui est Jacques Bainville?*, 29.

62. Interview with Madame Jacques Bainville.

the review. The two men immediately established a warm friendship that was to endure for thirty-six years. "I knew that he had
become a royalist," Maurras later remarked. "But he had assented
to the monarchy without having followed my catechism."[63] Within
a few months Bainville had completely forsaken Barrès's authoritarian Caesarism for Maurras's authoritarian royalism, though he
remained on excellent terms with Barrès until the latter's death in
1923.[64] Maurras arranged for Bainville to take a position at the *Gazette de France*, an organ of respectable royalist opinion to which he
became a regular contributor after his military service in 1901.[65] By
August 1900 Barrès was regretfully referring to Maurras and Bainville as his "two royalist adversaries."[66]

63. Maurras, *Au Signe de Flore*, 282–85.
64. Bainville, Maurras, and Barrès, despite their political differences, corre-
sponded and dined together frequently. See Barrès to Maurras, November 30, 1904;
Maurras to Barrès, December 1905; and Barrès to Maurras, October 15, 1916, in
*La République ou le roi: correspondance inédite de Maurice Barrès et Charles Maurras,
1888–1923*, edited by Hélène and Nicole Maurras (Paris: Plon, 1970), 432, 461, 566.
65. AN, F⁷13195, "Notes sur l'Action Française," no. 3.
66. Maurice Barrès, *Mes Cahiers* (14 vols.; Paris: Plon, 1929–57), II, 162.

CHAPTER TWO

The Shaping of the Royalist Program, 1900–1908

The false conception of the evolution toward liberalism and democracy in the world has resulted in very serious errors. That is why everything must always begin with the criticism of ideas and the refutation of prejudices.

Jacques Bainville

The modern French royalist movement was born with the twentieth century. During the year 1900 most of Maurras's nationalist colleagues at the Action Française succumbed to his argument that a monarchical restoration was the most suitable means of reestablishing domestic order and national security.[1] Since the founding of the fortnightly *Revue de l'Action française* in the summer of 1899, Maurras had been circulating among adherents and potential sympathizers alike a manuscript summarizing many of the royalist arguments that he had previously set forth in the pages of the *Gazette de France*. While preparing the manuscript for publication, he discovered in Bainville's biography of Ludwig II a splendid expression of his own literary and political sentiments. Taking note of the book's favorable reception in French literary circles,[2] he praised its brilliant unmasking of the psychological deficiencies of the idealistic monarch and its masterly indictment of the governing principles that had enervated the Bavarian kingdom to the profit of Prussia between 1866 and 1870. Maurras touted Bainville as a "rigorous, well-informed, scrupulously careful historian" who had avoided the errors of those neoromantic admirers of the colorful king who had celebrated his memory in recent years. He took great pleasure

1. See AN, F⁷13198, "Notes sur l'Action Française," no. 10; Nolte, *Three Faces of Fascism*, 66; Buthman, *The Rise of Integral Nationalism*, 257–68.
2. See, for example, *Le Correspondant* (March 25, 1900).

in pointing out that the young Frenchman had rallied to the cause
of royalist nationalism as a consequence of his exposure to the militarist traditions of Germany and his growing abhorrence of liberal
democracy in France.[3]

The publication of the manuscript in the form of an *Enquête*—a
statement of Maurras's political position followed by a number of
responses by hand-picked contributors—afforded Bainville the opportunity to announce publicly his conversion to the royalist cause.
He castigated the nefarious doctrines of revolutionary republicanism and parliamentary liberalism, both of which, he reminded
Maurras, constituted "two evils that you know I have abandoned."
He applauded Maurras's enunciation of the rigorous laws of "social physics" in his *Enquête sur la monarchie*, and contrasted the
logic and realism of the Maurrassian system with the "pitiful anarchy, fanaticism, and spiritual poverty" of the reigning ideology
of republicanism. Bainville contended that the type of consensus
that was necessary for political stability was an impossibility under
the Third Republic because of the inherent contradiction between
the requirements of social organization and the anarchical tendencies of democratic institutions.[4]

But Bainville's acceptance of the royalist solution to France's present problems was not entirely unqualified. He warned Maurras that
most Frenchmen were no longer enamored of the monarchy and
that few believed in the imminence of a restoration. The principal
obligation of French royalists was therefore not to engage in pre-
cipitous, premature agitation for counterrevolution, but rather to
disseminate information about the reforms proposed in the *Enquête
sur la monarchie*. He reiterated his earlier objections to Maurras's
emphasis on the necessity of political decentralization,[5] insisting
that the concept was likely to appear excessively abstract or anachronistic in the eyes of the large majority of people raised in the
tradition of the centralized state founded by Napoleon. The "naive

3. Maurras, *Enquête sur la Monarchie* (Paris: Nouvelle Librairie Nationale, 1909),
234.
4. *Ibid.*, 235. On the *Enquête* as a whole, see Weber, *Action Française*, 22, and
Tannenbaum, *Action Française*, 62.
5. See above, p. 18.

ignorance of the masses is limitless," he declared, while the enemies of the monarchy "excel in exploiting it."[6] The royalist movement should therefore concentrate on acquiring a following among the populace before endeavoring to launch a direct assault against the ideology of the Republic.

This tactical disagreement between the two men reflected their divergent intellectual tendencies. Maurras was a philosopher, a theoretician *par excellence,* who craved the perfection of a logically constructed system with little regard for its appeal to or effect on others. Perhaps the fact that he was almost totally deaf and an inveterate bachelor contributed to his insulation from external influences and responsibilities. What is beyond dispute is that Bainville was consistently more pragmatic, more sensitive to social realities. He was, as Ernst Nolte has accurately observed, "narrower than Maurras intellectually but broader in understanding."[7] His principal concern was the social utility of the philosophical system of royalist nationalism while Maurras's seems to have been its theoretical consistency. Bainville continually urged the new royalist intelligentsia to concentrate on proposing "particular and immediate reforms" that could be rendered "perceptible to the simplest mind," in order to broaden the base of support for the movement. These new royalists, as an intellectual vanguard of counterrevolution, should explain the royalist doctrine to "humble people who are poorly prepared for reflection and criticism, and who are convinced more by images than by the surest linkage of ideas."[8] Bainville suggested the adoption of a comprehensive program of specific social and political reforms that would appeal to a broad segment of the French public without running the risk of being co-opted by the republican regime.

Having thus unburdened himself of these minor criticisms of

6. Maurras, *Enquête sur la Monarchie,* 236.
7. Samuel Osgood, *French Royalism since 1870* (The Hague: Nijhoff, 1970), 65; Nolte, *Three Faces of Fascism,* 472n.
8. No statement more accurately explains the appeal of Bainville's later works of history, all of which avoided the scholarly apparatus and academic verbiage that had stood between the average reader and the works of the professional historians of the republican university. Maurras, *Enquête sur la Monarchie,* 236–37.

Maurras's program, Bainville proceeded to endorse the monarchical idea, appropriately presented, as the sole political principle "capable of satisfying the purest speculative intelligence" as well as "the most practical minds." More importantly, it was the only political creed left in France that could restore the indispensable consensus which the Third Republic, plagued as it was with religious quarrels and political polarization, had been unable to sustain. He concluded by insisting that all royalists should avoid the temptation to indulge in a narrow sectarianism and urging them to behave as representatives of national opinion rather than of a political party.

In his response Maurras commended Bainville's pragmatism, particularly his timely reminder that the French public had long ago lost its reverence for monarchical traditions and therefore had to be won over by persuasive arguments. Above all, he admired the tone of scientific detachment that informed his younger colleague's criticism of the established regime. He hailed Bainville's ideas as products of "the critical mind, the positive methods of science,"[9] echoing Bainville's profuse praise for the scientific, positivist features of Maurras's own political thought. On the thorny issue of political centralization versus federalism, Maurras later conceded that Bainville was "much more unitary than I, . . . more sensitive to administrative order, less interested in the free initiatives of our peasants and workers." While insisting that their disagreement was one of fine points rather than of principles, he reluctantly conceded that had they lived in medieval Italy "he would have been for the Emperor and the Ghibellines while I would have been for the communes and the Guelphs."[10]

A partial explanation of this cordial difference of opinion on the old question of Paris versus the provinces can be found in the radically dissimilar backgrounds and temperaments of the two men. Though Maurras had left his native Provençal city of Martigues for Paris while still a teenager, he had never shed his provincial re-

9. *Ibid.*, 237–38.
10. Maurras, *Jacques Bainville et Paul Bourget*, 62–63.

pugnance for the complexities of urban society. From the time of his conversion to the cause of the Provençal renaissance, he had exhibited in his own personality the unrestrained enthusiasm and *élan* that the *Félibres* had been advertising as the distinctive qualities of the Mediterranean mind. Bainville, by contrast, regardless of how hard he tried to share the rustic enthusiasm of his southern mentor,[11] remained a model of Parisian urbanity and cosmopolitan finesse.

This temperamental difference between the two men was further highlighted by a mild dispute over the function of poetry that took place in the editorial offices of the *Gazette de France* in November 1901. Bainville acclaimed Heine's verse along with Voltaire's tales as the finest efforts of satire and irony to counteract the poisonous influence of romantic lyricism. Maurras countered with the charge that irony was the most despicable of all literary devices because it was of "the earth" while poetry was of "the sky." Maurras regarded poetry's proper goal as the attainment of the purest expressiveness. In his view, Heine's brand of irony was insipid, ponderous, and dull, preventing his poetry from expressing the ultimate sentiments. Bainville gently accused Maurras of embracing the very romantic temperament that both had condemned in their writings. "You detest the pedestrian muse," he declared, "and I have just discovered in you an annoying taste for the summits." Bainville preferred the "moderate slopes." When Bainville began to recite a passage of Heine's works in the original to persuade his interlocutor of its merits, Maurras resisted vigorously. When Bainville again lapsed into the original and then suddenly remembered that Maurras did not understand the language, Maurras remarked that Bainville understood it "perhaps too well."[12]

---

11. Bainville often waxed lyrical about the bucolic life of the Provençal countryside. See, for example, his *Les Sept Portes de Thebes*, 43ff. But on other occasions he declared that he was bored with *la campagne* and preferred the sociability of urban life. See Massis, *Le Souvenir*, 20–21.

12. Charles Maurras, *Ironie et poésie* (Saint-Félicien-en-Vivarais: Au Pigeonnier, 1923), 10, 13–14, 15, 17, 18, 31. Jacques Bainville, *Filiations* (Paris: A la Cité des Livres, 1923), 11, 12.

Bainville, the well-traveled, multilingual Parisian,[13] labored to reconcile himself with the parochial son of Provence. He thanked Maurras for demonstrating the importance of meridional poetry, but regarded it as a domain which a man of the north could approach but never enter. Bainville conceded that in the early years of their friendship he had failed to penetrate the mystery of his mentor's Mediterranean mind. It required prolonged visits to the Maurras house in Martigues to convince him that he had "perhaps advanced yet a little more in the comprehension of your principles."[14] Both men were staunch defenders of the royalist cause. But Maurras, ignorant of Germany as well as other nations beyond the borders of his one and only France, had become a monarchist for domestic reasons. The Dreyfus Affair had convinced him of the decadence of republicanism and the necessity to revivify the monarchical traditions of the prerevolutionary period.[15] Bainville, on the other hand, had been rescued from the republican influences of his family and transformed into a devotee of the royalist idea through his contact with Germany, whose political power and military might he had learned to envy and to fear.[16]

The passionate Germanophobia that gripped Bainville in these

13. Unlike Maurras, Bainville was to travel extensively in Germany, England, Eastern Europe, Scandinavia, and Russia. Also unlike Maurras, he read German, English, and Italian. See Joseph, *Qui est Jacques Bainville?*, 17–18; Szekeley de Doba, et al., *Jacques Bainville*, 139–47; interview with Madame Jacques Bainville; André Rousseaux, "Jacques Bainville," *Vient de Paraître* (April, 1924), 197.

14. Bainville, *Filiations*, 13–15. Much later, Maurras in turn acknowledged his own desire to fathom his younger friend's northern and urban mentality. He placed Bainville in the company of "all the natives of your *Ile de France*," such as Villon, Boileau, Molière, and La Bruyère. The Western world must recognize in Paris, he conceded, the "*ville mère*" of its thought." He could not stop worrying, however, about the tyranny that the French capital exercised over "cities and regions that are perfectly capable of discovering their own destiny" and suspected that Bainville would "recognize my obstinate federalism here." Charles Maurras, *L'Allée des philosophes* (Paris: Editions Crès, 1924), xiv–xvii.

15. Though Maurras had first sensed the weaknesses of France's democratic system and felt the first stirrings of monarchist sentiments in 1896 while attending the first Olympic Games in Athens as a reporter for the *Gazette de France*, it was the Dreyfus Affair which, two years later, launched him on his ideological crusade against the Republic. See Buthman, *The Rise of Integral Nationalism*, 102ff., 235ff.; Weber, *Action Française*, 13, 16–18; Nolte, *Three Faces of Fascism*, 56.

16. Maurras, *Au Signe de Flore*, 282–83.

early years reflected a growing hostility toward the Second Reich that was felt by many French literati of his generation. Even as late as the 1890s, a number of French writers were still expressing the hope that a cordial intellectual interchange with their German counterparts could be established to supplement the temporary diplomatic détente that had been forged by foreign minister Gabriel Hanotaux. A majority of the respondants to a questionnaire on Franco-German cultural relations sponsored by the *Mercure de France* in 1895 went on record in favor of the establishment of closer intellectual ties between the two nations.[17] But a similar inquiry conducted in 1902 by the same periodical revealed that the intervening seven years had brought a dramatic change in attitude which culminated in a widespread resistance to German cultural influences in France.[18] Claude Digeon has noted that by 1902 many French writers who were hardly nationalists in the Barrèsian sense of the term were beginning to proclaim the superiority of French spiritual values and the need to protect them from the corrosion of German thought. The advent of the German naval program, the Kaiser's declaration of his new "world policy," and the replacement of Hanotaux by the less conciliatory Delcassé at the Quai d'Orsay all contributed to this reaction against the incipient Franco-German rapprochement of the mid-nineties. Accordingly, with the notable exception of Romain Rolland, the respondants to the second inquiry collectively sounded the alarm against the German threat to French national security.[19]

Bainville's response to the *Mercure de France* questionnaire supplied further confirmation that he was far more interested in the developments across the Rhine than was Maurras, who remained preoccupied with domestic matters. It had already become evident that Maurras and most of the other members of the Action Fran-

17. Alfred Vallette, "Une Enquête franco-allemande," *Mercure de France* (April–June, 1895), 1–65.
18. Jacques Morland, "Enquête sur l'influence allemande," *Mercure de France* (November–December, 1902), 289–382, 647–95.
19. See *ibid.* and Digeon, *La Crise allemande*, Chap. IX. Rolland was to become one of the few French intellectuals to oppose France's participation in the First World War.

çaise "hated French 'Germanism' and internationalism more than German 'Germanism' and nationalism."[20] But in his response, Bainville, whose biography of Ludwig II and numerous articles on Germany in the *Revue des revues* had already established his reputation as an expert on German affairs, proved to be something of an exception to this generalization. He emphasized "the superiority of our literary tradition and the wretched poverty of contemporary German literature." He denounced as illusory the notion that French *civilisation* had anything to fear from the threat of German *Kultur*. He had observed at first hand the extent to which one German writer or artist after another slavishly imitated French forms in recognition of their indisputable superiority.[21] The German language itself was "more bizarre and more complicated than Sanskrit or Chinese," wholly unsuitable to the requirements of logic and clarity of expression. Frenchmen therefore must strive to "rediscover the natural current of our idiom," which is entirely free of the "pedantry" and "opacity" that characterizes German language and thought.[22]

But Bainville's condescending attitude toward German cultural achievements did not prevent him from expressing profound admiration for the political traditions that he had observed during his youthful sojourn. On the contrary, he discovered certain political principles that he considered worthy of adoption by France. Herein lay the ambivalence toward Germany that characterized so many French intellectuals during this period. Nietzsche headed his list of good Germans because of the newly renowned philosopher's devastating onslaughts against the moralistic humanitarianism of liberal democracy. Bainville noted that an increasingly large number of Frenchmen had taken an avid interest in the antidemocratic theories of this Francophile iconoclast. Indeed, his ideas seemed more applicable to republican France than to imperial Germany.

The French writer also praised the anti-Semitic, antiliberal doc-

---

20. Digeon, *La Crise allemande*, 448.
21. Bainville response, in Morland, "Enquête," 299.
22. Bainville, *Journal*, I, August 1, 1903.

trines of Dühring and von Hartmann as admirable principles which French reactionaries would do well to employ in their ideological confrontation with Dreyfusard radicalism. And whereas professional historians in France had learned from their Germanic counterparts the virtues of critical scholarship, Bainville acquired from the writings of Mommsen and Treitschke an appreciation of national grandeur and its prerequisites, domestic order and authority. The spectacle of the Hohenzollern monarchy and its achievements taught him a valuable lesson in political philosophy. When a Frenchman who is perceptive in political matters observes events in Germany, he exclaimed, he rapidly "becomes a nationalist and ceases to be a republican."[23] Once again, he discovered intellectual support for his antidemocratic views in the writings of Carlyle, the British admirer of Prussian authoritarianism whom Bainville later credited with helping to inspire the growth of reactionary political thought in France toward the end of the nineteenth century.[24]

But no writer in France, least of all one who fancied himself a nationalist, could expect to acquire a respectable reputation in the eyes of his compatriots by attributing his intellectual formation to German and Anglo-Saxon influences alone. Bainville therefore dutifully recorded his debts to his French intellectual godfathers, many of whom, interestingly enough, did not occupy a prominent place in the Maurrassian pantheon. In addition to Heine, it was Renan and Voltaire who had provided him with the "precious gift of irony" that he employed in his writings to puncture what he regarded as the illusions of romanticism and revolutionary idealism. He admired the "skeptical good sense" of these two *bêtes noires* of French Catholicism as a characteristically Gallic trait that had enabled Frenchmen to resist the attraction of the "visionaries and emancipators who want to spread their anarchistic sickness on the pretext of abolishing human suffering." He also invoked the

23. Bainville response, in Morland, "Enquête," 300. See also Digeon, *La Crise allemande*, 472–74.
24. Jacques Bainville, *Le Vieil Utopiste* (Paris: Les Cahiers d'Occident, 1st year, no. 3, 1927), 15.

heritage of Montesquieu, Pierre Bayle, and the Encyclopedists for similar reasons.[25]

This declaration of kinship with the men of the Enlightenment represented a radical departure from the dominant tradition of French counterrevolutionary thought. Bainville decisively rejected the view, popularized by Taine in his *Origines de la France contemporaine*, that the classical spirit of the eighteenth-century philosophers had prepared the way for the triumph of the principles of 1789 by preaching resistance to established authority and postulating theoretical schemes for political and social utopias. The "materialists and libertines of the classical age," Bainville claimed, "thought themselves no more authorized to revolt against the spiritual traditions of their country than against the temporal authority." He accused Taine of confusing the influence of the native French classical writers with that of the protoromantic half-breed Rousseau, who was simultaneously infecting France with his noxious doctrines. While it was true that the philosophes encouraged disrespect for existing social institutions and frequently engaged in indiscriminate criticism, they nevertheless intended

> only to reform a limited number of abuses. The Revolution that was accomplished by Montesquieu, Voltaire, and the Encyclopedists would have been a limited revolution and would have established a clearly defined political state. But the Revolution accomplished by Rousseau was "the Eternal Revolution," the Revolution that must always be spelled with a capital R, the unlimited, infinite Revolution, the universal subversion.[26]

It was thus possible for Bainville, a fervent defender of the *ancien régime*, to herald the return to the spirit of the true philosophes of

25. Jacques Bainville, *Le Critique mort jeune* (Paris: Editions du Monde Moderne, 1927), no pagination.
26. *Ibid.* Yet Bainville did not hesitate to hold the philosophes responsible for the intellectual errors that contributed to France's present predicament. As Germany prepared for the centennial of Frederick the Great in 1912, he observed with regret that "It is we, my God, yes it is we who made Frederick the 'Great,' It is we who admired him, exalted him." He noted that while "the salons, the cafés, the street" indulged in the supreme luxury of "loving everyone, even enemies," the French monarchy, "more clairvoyant than public opinion," made war on the Prussian monarchy, "whose nascent power worried it." *AF*, January 22, 1912.

the eighteenth century and to identify himself with that classical renaissance. He detected in twentieth-century France the rebirth of a healthy political skepticism, which was reflected in the tendency to respect the established traditions of one's country while refusing to surrender to the seductive appeals of metaphysical, religious, esthetic, and political ideologies. "The atheism of cultivated Frenchmen, classical atheism, was conservative," Bainville reminded his readers, whereas Rousseau, "nourished on the Bible, raised in a Bible-ridden city, penetrated with Protestantism," introduced a foreign way of thinking that seduced Frenchmen of the eighteenth century who were susceptible to the appeal of a new faith.[27] It was during the intervening century—the Romantic nineteenth—that the revolutionary doctrines of Rousseau had begun to unravel the loose fabric of French society. A modern advocate of classicism and monarchism need not, therefore, shrink from identifying himself with the heritage of the Enlightenment. As Maurras had demonstrated, romanticism rather than classicism was the intellectual accompaniment of political revolution.[28]

Bainville proceeded to trace the line of thought that linked the counterrevolutionaries of the twentieth century to the protocounterrevolutionary thinkers of the eighteenth. This clearly represented an effort to establish for the modern French royalist movement a respectable niche in his country's conservative intellectual tradition. Though this ambitious task was soon to be undertaken in a more systematic manner by his colleague Louis Dimier,[29] Bainville himself began to dredge up evidence of an intellectual counterrevolution in the works of some of the major theoreticians of nineteenth-century France. He resumed his earlier effort to appropriate for the royalist cause intellectual precursors for whom more orthodox royalists had little love. Maurras had denounced Stendhal, for example, as an enemy of Racine, an admirer of Shakespeare, and a spiritual brother of the despicable romantic, Victor Hugo. Bainville

27. Bainville, *Le Critique mort jeune.*
28. See Charles Maurras, *Romantisme et révolution* (Paris: Nouvelle Librairie Nationale, 1925).
29. See below, 43–4.

forgave the esteemed novelist for these lapses in literary judgment and sought to rehabilitate him as one of the leading opponents of democracy of his time. He praised Balzac for his royalist sympathies and his opposition to popular sovereignty.[30] He aligned himself with Anatole France, whose Voltairian skepticism had served as an effective antidote to the nonsensical mysticism of Zola and the naturalists. The secret of Anatole France's art, Bainville observed, was realism and a sense of irony. He noted with regret that an untimely lapse into "religiosity" was responsible for the celebrated writer's momentary outburst of "democratic fervor and Dreyfusard zeal" at the turn of the century.[31]

During the first decade of the twentieth century the leaders of the Action Française took up Bainville's suggestion in the *Enquête sur la monarchie* that the movement strive to disseminate the royalist message in its simplest and most attractive form to a general public whose attitude toward a prospective restoration was likely to be hostile or, at best, indifferent. To endow their apparently anachronistic political program with a broader appeal, the royalist intellectuals continually emphasized the nationalist aspect of the Maurrassian program and de-emphasized the royalist terminology. This policy embodied Bainville's conviction that the movement would do well to concentrate on promoting an eclectic brand of patriotism rather than engaging in narrow ideological sectarianism. By playing on the twin fears of a decline of French and the rise of German power and prestige in the world, the Action Française was able to acquire for itself a preeminent position in the nationalist revival that swept France in the prewar decade.[32]

The royalist indictment of the Republic was cast in an unmistakably nationalist mold. The educational policies of the regime had imposed "Germanic" methods of pedagogy and scholarship upon the unsuspecting youth of France at the expense of the tradition-

---

30. Bainville, *Le Vieil Utopiste*, 25, 53, 59, 93.
31. Jacques Bainville, *Au Seuil du siècle* (Paris: Editions du Capitole, 1927), 138, 147, 132, 146.
32. See Eugen Weber, *The Nationalist Revival in France: 1905–1914* (Berkeley: University of California Press, 1959), 55–56.

alist approach to higher learning. The Republic's foreign policy was a hodgepodge of failures and missed opportunities which had permitted the victor of 1870 to pose a renewed threat to French security. Religious division and class conflict were ripping apart the consensual bonds of French society. These festering sores on the body politic—the educational decadence of the lycées and universities, the diplomatic bumbling of the Quai d'Orsay, and the political polarization and social disruption caused by the Dreyfus Affair— supplied ideological ammunition for the royalists' campaign to discredit the Republic in the name of integral nationalism.

The dissemination of such antirepublican ideas was rendered particularly difficult by the republican government's firm grip on the principal channel of public communication, the school. The series of educational laws enacted between 1880 and 1905 had extirpated the remnants of clerical influence and established a centralized, standardized educational system under the jurisdiction of the Ministry of Public Instruction, which maintained tight control over the curricula, textbooks, and appointment and promotion of teachers. The ideals of the Republic were inculcated in French youth through the civic education program of the primary schools, presided over by a teaching corps described by one of its most ardent defenders as "the militia of the republican party."[33] The institutional structure of the French *Université*, which linked primary, secondary, and higher education in a vast, monolithic apparatus directed by the government, could not have been less hospitable to the massive campaign of political reeducation which the leaders of the Action Française planned to mount in an effort to win over French youth to the royalist cause.

But once the royalists determined that they could not penetrate the protective shield that the Republic had erected around its younger citizens, they decided to circumvent it instead. In the years 1905–1908 Maurras and his disciples created a number of pedagogical institutions designed to counteract republican teach-

33. Ferdinand Buisson, in *La Grande Revue* (November 10, 1909), 26; Stock, "New Quarrel of Ancients and Moderns," 118–34; Keylor, *Academy and Community*, chaps. III and V.

ing and communicate the royalist doctrine to the rising generation. In January 1905 a Ligue d'Action Française was established to raise funds for the purpose of extending the *Revue*'s propaganda activities among French youth. In December Lucien Moreau founded the movement's first student group, which met twice a week to study and discuss royalist ideas. Early in 1906 a royalist "Institute," financed by private donations, began to sponsor public lectures by members and eminent sympathizers.[34] During the same period the movement's unofficial publishing house, the Nouvelle Librairie Nationale, commissioned a number of historical works with the aim of exposing the partisan nature of academic historical scholarship. Soon thereafter a steady stream of royalist propaganda flowed from the Institute and the Librairie. The outpouring was to continue for decades.

The campaign to acquaint the intellectual elite of the French nation with the twin dangers of republicanism at home and Germanism abroad was officially launched in March 1905, on the occasion of the seventy-fifth anniversary of the birth of the late historian Fustel de Coulanges. The fact that Fustel had not been a royalist did not deter the Maurrassians from publicly touting the illustrious scholar as a forerunner of their movement. After all, the noted medievalist had established a reputation as a critic of "Germanic" methods of historical research as well as of the doctrine of the Germanic origins of French political institutions. What was more, though he had taught in the university and held high administrative posts, he was not a member of the despicable Sorbonne clique that had seized control of French higher learning at the end of the nineteenth century and radically transformed its institutions and functions. Louis Dimier, a former lycée professor and art historian who had recently left the *Université* to join the Action Française in reaction against the invasion of the educational system by "Dreyfusard propaganda,"[35] formed a committee to commemorate Fus-

---

34. See Tannenbaum, *Action Française*, 89–91, and Louis Dimier, *Vingt Ans d'Action Française* (Paris: Nouvelle Librairie Nationale, 1926).

35. Louis Dimier, *Souvenirs d'action publique et d'université* (Paris: Nouvelle Librairie Nationale, 1920), 242–43.

tel's birth after securing the permission of the widow. Madame Fustel had stipulated that the celebration be faithful to her husband's memory, and was assured that men of various political persuasions would be included on the organizing committee. But the membership list, though distinguished, was heavily stacked with anti-Dreyfusards, republican nationalists such as Gustave Schlumberger of the Acádemie des Inscriptions, Alfred Rambaud (the Sorbonne historian and noted academic reformer), Barrès, and his fellow novelist and critic Paul Bourget.[36]

When the nationalist, anti-Dreyfusard character of the group began to become apparent, a number of Fustel's former students jumped to the offensive. Assailing the ideological narrowness of the committee's membership, which was bound to turn the celebration into a partisan polemic, they reminded the organizers that their mentor had been thoroughly apolitical.[37] One of the most vocal participants in the dispute was Gabriel Monod, the editor of the *Revue historique* and custodian of Fustel's papers. Monod's intervention in behalf of the dead historian infuriated Maurras and his fellows, who regarded Monod as France's foremost symbol of pro-German, Protestant, Dreyfusard sentiment.[38] Subsequent attacks by Jean Jaurès in *La Petite République* and Albert Petit in *Le Journal des débats* sealed the fate of the event. Fustel's widow withdrew her permission and several members resigned from the committee. Undaunted by this rebuke from men they detested, the royalists proceeded to hold their own celebration on March 18, at which the memory of the old historian was invoked against his successors and their alleged betrayal of the historical tradition that he embodied.[39]

36. Dimier, *Vingt Ans*, 87–88. See also Weber, *Action Française*, 36–38.
37. Maurras, *Devant l'Allemagne éternelle*, 159–61. Maurras himself had never met Fustel, though his associate Frédéric Amouretti had known the celebrated historian in his later years. See Jane Herrick, *The Historical Thought of Fustel de Coulanges* (Washington, D.C.: The Catholic University of America Press, 1954), 111. Stephen Wilson, "Fustel de Coulanges and the Action Française," *Journal of the History of Ideas*, XXXIV (1973), 123–34.
38. See Maurras's attack on Monod's "Germanic" character in his *Quand les Français ne s'aimaient pas* (2nd ed.; Paris: Nouvelle Librairie Nationale, 1926), 62; *Gazette de France*, March 20, 1905.
39. Dimier, *Vingt Ans*, 88.

The royalists' commemoration of Fustel's birth deserves an extensive examination here because it represented their first major attempt to employ history for their own political purposes—that is, to challenge in the public arena the historical doctrines of the republican university. Dimier opened the session by taking note of the widespread misunderstanding regarding France's past and citing the need to rectify the errors perpetuated by the university historians. The Sorbonne scholars were guilty of two principal sins. The first was pedantry. Most historical research conducted at the university was a colossal waste of time and effort which produced no general conclusions that could be useful or instructive. The historians' distrust of philosophy and their obsession with factual documentation prevented them from grasping the interconnection of historical events, which in turn precluded the development of useful prescriptions for action. Unlike the modern mandarins of the Sorbonne, Fustel had recognized that the facts of history contain "the lesson for some line of conduct, the repudiation of some prejudice, the solution of some problem."[40]

But lurking beneath the university historians' pedantic preoccupation with the documents, Dimier charged, was a penchant for committing the opposite sin of political partisanship in their historical writings. Fustel had recognized the important role that historical consciousness must play in the encouragement of patriotic feeling. But the republican historians in the university, for all their professed objectivity, produced works that sowed disrespect for the traditions and institutions of the glorious centuries of monarchical rule, matters which should be the subject of patriotic pride rather than ideological criticism. Dimier assailed the self-proclaimed "scientific" historians for perpetuating the practices of their romantic predecessors, whom Fustel had denounced for placing their scholarly talents at the service of their political cause.[41]

Frédéric Amouretti, the only member of the Action Française's inner circle who had known Fustel personally, followed with a blistering indictment of the methodological practices of the aca-

40. Maurras, *Devant l'Allemagne éternelle*, 186–88.
41. *Ibid.*, 189–91.

demic historians. He mercilessly chided Charles Seignobos and Charles Victor Langlois, co-authors of the standard textbook of historical methods in France,[42] who jointly taught the historiography course at the Sorbonne. These two despicable pedants, he suggested, fired by an indiscriminate fascination with every moldy manuscript they could lay their hands on, were quite capable of compiling a historical treatise from a telephone book. He ridiculed Ernest Lavisse's pretensions of producing an impartial history of France by assembling a team of collaborators to divide up the task. Such an enterprise was comparable to workers in heavy industry attempting to turn out finished products without the guidance of foremen. Fustel de Coulanges, he confidently asserted, would have recoiled in disgust at this perversion of the historical method.[43]

Such criticism of the university historians was nothing new. The debate within the profession itself regarding the nature and goals of historical study had already begun to spill over into the public arena during the last decade of the nineteenth century. Sociologists, philosophers, and men of letters all harbored grievances

42. See Charles-Victor Langlois and Charles Seignobos, *Introduction aux études historiques* (Paris: Hachette, 1898).

43. Maurras, *Devant l'Allemagne éternelle*, 184–85. Lavisse and Alfred Rambaud had co-edited the collaborative series *Histoire générale du IVᵉ siècle à nos jours* (12 vols.; Paris: Colin, 1892–1901) and Lavisse edited the *Histoire de France depuis les origines jusqu'à la Révolution* (9 vols.; Paris: Colin, 1900–1911). Another important reason that the royalists adopted Fustel as one of their own was his advocacy of the "Roman thesis" in the continuing debate among historians over the question of the origins of the French national character. The ancient controversy over the predominance of Germanic (Frankish) or Latin (Gallo-Roman) influences in France assumed the form of a bitter polemic in the years after the disaster of 1870. After Fustel published a manifesto denying Germanic origins in the formation of France (see *Revue des deux mondes*, May 15, 1872), he was stigmatized by his academic detractors as the modern champion of "l'école romaniste." (See for example Gabriel Monod, "Historiens Contemporains," *La Revue politique et littéraire* [May 15, 1875], pp. 1077–83). Hence the royalists were able to attack the "Germanic professors" at the Sorbonne while lionizing Fustel as "the master of anti-German prophylaxis." They meant this in a double sense. They attacked Monod and his colleagues for reintroducing the "Germanic doctrines that Fustel had fought all his life" as well as for introducing Germanic *methods* into the academic curriculum. (See Octave Martin [pseud. Charles Maurras], *Le Parapluie de Marianne* (Paris: Editions de 'La Seule France,' 1948), 11, and Charles Maurras, *Devant l'Allemagne éternelle*, 145. Monod, Maurras observed, regarded Germany as his "second fatherland," and was busy "organizing the world of our history professors against the method and doctrine of Fustel." Octave Martin [pseud. Charles Maurras], *Le Parapluie*, 11.)

against the modern historical school of the French university. The complaints followed a consistent pattern, depending on the methodological or ideological predisposition of the critics. Some bemoaned the academic historians' alleged betrayal of the literary and philosophical tradition of France in favor of historical methods imported from Germany. Others, most of whom were spokesmen for the old order, railed against the partisan intervention of the university historians in the public disputes during the Dreyfus Affair and the subsequent campaign against the Church.[44] But whatever the source of such criticism, the royalists did not have to invent a case against the historical profession. They were simply able to repeat, in a less balanced form, the allegations that had originally emanated from more respectable critics.

Maurras's subsequent description of the Fustel celebration as the official launching of the Ligue de l'Action Française was no exaggeration. The League and its youth group both owed their early successes in enlisting young recruits to the excitement engendered by Dimier and his associates in the spring of 1905. The campaign's effectiveness in publicly embarrassing the historians of the republican university convinced the Maurrassians of the need to institutionalize their efforts to win support for their political program among students.[45] This single spectacular success also gave them confidence in their ability to succeed at such an ambitious task. Dimier recalled that the most valuable lesson he and his friends had learned at the celebration was how easy it had been "to inspire passion in the crowds, provided that we got them to seize the idea that we were trying to get across. . . . Not one in fifty of the listeners had ever read Fustel; we taught him to them, and in an instant we rendered him interesting . . . the citations that we gave from his works produced an ovation." In order to expand and regularize such contact between the intellectuals of the Action Française and

44. See William R. Keylor, "Clio on Trial: Charles Péguy as Historical Critic," in Keylor and Dora B. Weiner, *From Parnassus: Essays in Honor of Jacques Barzun* (New York: Harper & Row, 1976); Keylor, *Academy and Community*, pt. II.

45. The chapter in which Maurras described the incident was entitled "La Bagarre de Fustel ou les Débuts de la ligue d'Action Française." See Maurras, *Devant l'Allemagne éternelle*, 95–212.

its potential audience in the Latin Quarter, all that would be required were "teachers, a role that we could play, a classroom, which we could rent, and money, which was ultimately found."[46]

Dimier's stellar performance at the celebration, together with his impressive academic credentials, made him the logical choice to organize the intellectual counteroffensive of the royalist movement. A few months later he began preparing the groundwork for what was to become the Institut d'Action Française, a private center of higher learning dedicated to combatting the subversive doctrines of the university by offering alternative courses to the Parisian student community. By the end of 1905 he had put together the rudiments of a full-fledged academic organization. A committee set up by several respectable members of the old nobility and *haute bourgeoisie* served as a conduit for funds that were used to rent classrooms at the headquarters of Les Sociétés Savantes (the site of the Fustel celebration) in the heart of the Latin Quarter.[47]

In mock emulation of the Sorbonne, the royalist Institute retained much of the traditional academic paraphernalia. A formidable list of alternative courses was drawn up. A number of "professorial chairs" were established, which were named after the various political and social theorists in French history whom the modern royalists regarded as forerunners; the chairs were occupied by the leading members of the Action Française. Bainville was awarded the Fustel de Coulanges chair in foreign affairs and despite his aversion to public speaking was to become what Ernst Nolte has called "the most brilliant lecturer of all." Eminent men of letters who sympathized with the conservative, nationalist objectives of the movement, such as Maurice Barrès, Paul Bourget, and Jules Lemaître, were invited to supplement the regular programs with occasional guest lectures to which students were admitted free of charge.[48] Two promising young historians who had been attracted to the movement during the Fustel incident, Franz Funck-

46. Dimier, *Vingt Ans*, 93.
47. Weber, *Action Française*, 38; Nolte, *Three Faces of Fascism*, 90–91; Tannenbaum, *Action Française*, 90–91.
48. Dimier, *Vingt Ans*, 93–98; Nolte, *Three Faces of Fascism*, 90–91. See also AN, F⁷12862.

Brentano and Eugène Cavaignac, were recruited for service in the pedagogical campaign. Soon after the inauguration of the Institute in February 1906, the movement's leadership was hailing it as "our royalist Sorbonne." Daudet boasted that its "campaign of intellectual rectification" furnished Parisian students with a patriotic alternative to the subversive doctrines embedded in the curricula of the republican university.[49]

This declaration was more than mere idle boasting. The Institute unquestionably afforded the royalist intellectuals, particularly those who thought of themselves as gifted amateur historians, an influential public forum for the dissemination of their views among students. "People stopped thinking that we were kidding around," Dimier observed. "We enjoyed the prestige of having, as they began to say, 'a doctrine.'" Though he was well aware that it was not customary for "political parties to become schoolmasters," he and his colleagues fully appreciated the potential advantages of such a status.[50]

This concern for ideological reeducation signified a fundamental shift in strategy for the new movement. Since the public could be reached by intellectual argument (as the Fustel celebration, with its packed lecture halls, had clearly demonstrated), street fighting and *coups de force* no longer were seen as the only means of toppling the despised regime. The royalist theorists gradually began to believe that by undermining public confidence in the Republic they might achieve their objective peacefully. While hotheads in the movement continued to call for violent action, Bainville, Dimier, Lucien Moreau, and others exerted a restraining influence—less for reasons of timidity than from the conviction that the pen and the lectern were more effective means of persuasion than the blackjack and the paving stone.[51] In a speech to the closing meeting of the Institute in 1906, Dimier, according to the movement's resident police informer, announced that "it is by the instruction of the

---

49. Léon Daudet, *Vers le Roi* (Paris: Grasset, 1934), 228–29.
50. Dimier, *Vingt Ans*, 98, 84.
51. Archives de la Préfecture de Police, Département de la Seine (hereinafter cited as APP), A31805, 24E (June 17, 1906 and December 18, 1907).

masses that the monarchist party plans to defeat the present government and restore prosperity, peace, and tranquility to France." Students and intellectual leaders right up to the Cardinal crowded into these lectures,[52] and, as Ernst Nolte has observed, the Institute's "influence on the nation's educated class, and through many ramifications, on the *réveil de l'orgueil français*, was considerable."[53]

One notable achievement of the Institute was its success in demonstrating that important and influential works of history could be produced without the benefit of years of patient archival research and criticism by scholarly specialists in graduate seminars. A number of historical studies which contributed greatly to the elaboration of French royalist doctrine were first presented at the Institute in the form of the public lecture, an institution that had come under attack by professional historians for its unscholarly character. Bainville's lectures on "La Politique Réaliste" during the 1906–1907 academic year alerted his audience to the menace of the virulent brand of nationalism that had taken hold in Germany and Italy. In the following year his course on "The Formation of German Unity" (which was later published in revised form as *Histoire de deux peuples*) warned of the unavoidable conflict between the two Rhine powers and first expressed the Bainvillian doctrine of the incompatibility of German unity and French security. During the 1908–1909 academic year he used the history of Poland as a means of demonstrating the dangers of an elective monarchy and, by implication, the superiority of a hereditary one.[54]

Other royalist "professors" made important contributions to party doctrine from the podium of the Institute. Dimier's lectures on the historical origins of French reactionary thought (later to appear in print as *Les Maîtres de la contre-révolution*) assured conservative nationalists that their ideology was firmly rooted in the finest traditions of French thought. The public attacks on the academic his-

---

52. *Ibid.*, Dimier, *Vingt Ans*, 100.
53. Nolte, *Three Faces of Fascism*, 91. See also Arno J. Mayer, *Dynamics of Counterrevolution in Europe, 1870–1956* (New York: Harper Torchbooks, 1971), 38ff.
54. See Keylor, *Academy and Community*, 62, 71–73; see Jacques Bainville, *Histoire de deux peuples* (Paris: Nouvelle Librairie Nationale, 1919); see *RAF*, (February 1, 1908), 192; (March 1, 1908), 705; Linville, "Jacques Bainville," 114.

torical profession by Dimier and his former classmate and fellow *universitaire* Pierre Lasserre (later to appear, respectively, as *Les Préjugés Ennemis de l'histoire de France* and *La Doctrine officielle de l'université*) fueled the already rampant dissatisfaction with French higher education in student circles.[55] Historical lectures on Rivarol, de Maistre, and Joan of Arc by various other self-appointed experts in the movement reminded French youth of past national heroes and heroines whose memory had been tarnished by the republican historical school.[56]

Efforts were also made to supplement the spoken with the written word. The idea of rewriting the history of France from a systematically royalist viewpoint had first been broached in the public lectures of March 1905 by Dimier. He recalled that Fustel de Coulanges's propensity for drawing general conclusions of a philosophical nature from his research had elicited rebukes from the university historians, who insisted upon a scrupulous devotion to the accumulation of historical "facts." The old historian had recognized that the "facts" of the past were worthy of the scholar's concentration only if they yielded a general type of historical knowledge that might contribute to a better understanding of the present and the future. Dimier accused the republican historians of hypocrisy in this regard. For all their professions of objectivity, they persisted in viewing history through the tinted glasses of their own philosophical prejudices. They did not hesitate to recommend future courses of action based on the lessons that they had learned from their study of the past. It seemed to him quite understandable that royalist historians should wish, and be entitled, to do the same.

In line with this objective, the 1907 annual congress of the Action

---

55. See Louis Dimier, *Les Maîtres de la contre-révolution* (Paris: Librairie des Saints-Pères et Nouvelle Librairie Nationale, 1907); Louis Dimier, *Les Préjugés Ennemis de l'histoire de France* (Paris: Nouvelle Librairie Nationale, 1917); and Pierre Lasserre, *La Doctrine officielle de l'université* (Paris: Mercure de France, 1912). See also Jean de Fabrègues, *Charles Maurras et son Action française* (Paris: Librairie Académique Perrin, 1966), 191.

56. Fabrègues, *Charles Maurras*, 193. Also see *Action Française* (hereinafter cited as *AF*), September 1, 1909.

Française passed a resolution calling for the publication of a history textbook presenting the monarchist version of the French past. During the 1908–1909 academic year the royalist organization sponsored a contest in which sympathetic historians were invited to submit manuscripts of a prospective history manual purged of republican prejudices. The goal was to produce a textbook on the history of France suitable for adoption in the Institute's history courses. The Action Française would thereby be able to counter the calumnies that had been directed at the prerevolutionary past by the likes of Lavisse, Aulard, and Seignobos in the university. Several amateur writers entered the competition, which was eventually won by Eugène Cavaignac, a scion of a respectable republican clan who had been converted to the Maurrassian cause during the Fustel celebration.[57] His *Esquisse d'une histoire de France*, awarded the Institute's Fustel prize for history, was published in 1910 and became a major weapon in the royalists' arsenal of historical revisionism. Another history text of royalist inspiration was produced by the Catholic journalist Jean Guiraud in 1914, after the French episcopate had condemned several public school textbooks in 1908 and 1909. In the meantime, the Action Française produced blistering critiques of the historical texts used in the public schools which focussed on their alleged republican biases. Finally, the royalist intellectuals formed a Fustel de Coulanges Society to "encourage the production of works according to his philosophy and methods."[58]

The success of this series of enterprises exceeded even the most optimistic forecasts of the Action Française leadership. Maurras later lamented that the extensive political activity of the league had prevented it from devoting sufficient attention to the production of such history books. But this early campaign of historical revision

57. *Action française mensuelle*, July 15, 1908, "Chronique"; *AF*, June 18, 1909; AN, F⁷12862, Notes sur l'Action Française, no. 4.

58. Weber, *Action Française*, 25, 36, 523; Jean Guiraud, *Cours d'histoire de France pour les écoles primaires* (Paris: Girord, 1914); Wilson, "A View of the Past," 137; Jean Guiraud, *Histoire partiale, histoire vraie* (4 vols., Paris: Beauchesne, 1911–1917); Georges Valois and François Renié, *Les Manuels scolaires* (Paris: Nouvelle Librairie Nationale, 1911); Maurras, *Devant l'Allemagne éternelle*, 210.

nevertheless represented in the leader's eyes an important first
step that rapidly led to the publication of several works of historical
synthesis written from a royalist perspective. These, he affirmed,
helped to transform the thinking of the French elite (presumably in
the direction of greater tolerance of royalist ideas), thereby paving
the way for the historical works of Bainville during the interwar
period.[59] Near the end of his life Maurras boasted that though his
movement had suffered a political setback at the conclusion of the
Dreyfus Affair, it had become the intellectual conquerer of the Latin Quarter by the outbreak of the war. He supported this grandiose
assertion by citing the immense popularity of Bainville's lectures
and writings and crowed that the students who were being misled
by their professors in the university "met in the street and in the
classrooms other students whom the Action Française had instructed and armed with ideas and rectifying documents."[60]

Jules Lemaître lent the prestige of the French Academy and the
world of higher criticism to the Institute courses, inviting Parisian
students to attend "the only place where true history is taught with
impartiality, discipline, and exactitude." At the opening of the
1908 academic season, he quoted Fustel on the importance of history to a nation's well-being:

> History forms our opinions. While it is true that the *ancien régime* no
> longer governs us, at least the idea that we have of it dominates and
> governs each one of us. . . . As many ways as there are of envisaging
> the Middle Ages, as many parties as there are in France, it is our his-
> torical theories that divide us the most; they are the starting point where
> all our factions have originated, they are the terrain from which all our
> hatreds have sprung.

Ever since the French Revolution, Lemaître declared, historical writing in France had been dominated by scholars and publicists who
were prejudiced enemies of the social forces that had formed the
French nation under the *ancien régime*. The task of the royalist his-

59. Maurras, *Devant l'Allemagne éternelle*, 201–202.
60. Octave Martin [pseud. Charles Maurras], *Le Parapluie*, 14. This evaluation of
the Action Française's influence on the Parisian students is shared by André Malraux. See his *Felled Oaks* (trans. Irene Clephane, New York: Holt, Rinehart and
Winston, 1971), 103.

torians, therefore, was to "rip apart this network of errors," and "re-form the minds of young Frenchmen by beginning with the student elite. For if we could render our history more intelligible and re-establish it in its full truth, that would be, believe me, a very efficacious preparation for the restoration of the monarchy."[61]

Yet neither Maurras nor Lemaître envisioned the goal of the Institute's teachings as intellectual persuasion alone. They hoped and expected that their students would leave the classes armed with "ideas and documents" not merely for the purposes of sterile intellectual debate, but for combat as well. Lemaître urged the young royalists returning to their university classrooms to "listen to your true professors" at the Institute, for they will prepare you "for new struggles. Intellectual struggles—and others, if necessary."[62]

The provocative language of the Institute's "professors" soon exercised its intended influence on the student generation. In the autumn of 1908 a special youth section of the Action Française was constituted, choosing for itself the rather presumptuous title *Camelots du Roi* (news vendors of the king). In the beginning the principal occupation of the *camelots* was, as their name implied, hawking royalist newspapers on street corners. But they soon became, with the leadership's blessing, the official emissaries of the royalists to French youth, charged with enlisting new members and soliciting politically uncommitted students and café sitters to attend the Institute lectures. But the youthful exuberance and crusading zeal of the *camelots* rapidly developed into a taste for the other struggles of which Lemaître had spoken. They were soon demolishing statues of despised historical figures, disrupting theatrical performances of works by "subversive" dramatists, intimidating unfriendly professors, and clashing in the streets of the Latin Quarter with their counterparts in the Socialist youth movement.[63]

The first important manifestation of the new spirit of political activism characteristically involved a historical subject. After a series

61. APP, A31805, 24E, November 21, 1908.
62. *Ibid.*, A31950, 77E, November 13, 1909.
63. See Maurice Pujo, *Les Camelots du roi* (Paris: Flammarion, 1933); *L'Humanité*, May 15, 1908; Weber, *Action Française*, 53; Nolte, *Three Faces of Fascism*, 91–93; Tannenbaum, *Action Française*, 95–96.

of public lectures by a lycée professor of history named François Thalamas was announced at the Sorbonne for the winter of 1908–1909, the *camelots* discovered that the lecturer had insulted the memory of Joan of Arc in his classes at the Lycée Condorcet four years earlier. Since the royalist Institute had been bombarding its students with allegations that the republican university was engaged in a conspiracy to defame the heroes and heroines of French history, the leaders of the youth movement seized upon the Thalamas lectures as an ideal occasion to apply the lessons they had learned at the Institute. Throughout the winter term the hapless lecturer was prevented by catcalls from speaking, bombarded with objects, and physically assaulted until the university was compelled to suspend the series before its completion.[64]

That such outrages could be committed in the name of a historical symbol was an indication of the importance of historical consciousness in the ideological system of the Action Française. And the publicity it acquired from such antics served to inflate the royalist movement's reputation as a staunch defender of French national traditions far out of proportion to the length of its membership list. These and other such events suggested that the royalist program that was first developed in the *Enquête sur la monarchie* and subsequently communicated to the public by means of the fortnightly review, the Institute, and the publishing house was beginning to gain widespread popular support, particularly among Parisian students. In the decade before the First World War, the Latin Quarter became a veritable battleground of political ideologies. Among the most prominent doctrines competing for public favor was the idea launched by Maurras and Bainville at the turn of the century: that France's only hope for restoring national grandeur and prosperity lay in the restoration of her banished monarchy.

---

64. APP, A31805, 24E, May 23, 1908. See Buthman, *The Rise of Integral Nationalism*, 301–304, for a lengthy description of the Thalamas episode.

CHAPTER THREE

Polemics Against the German Empire and the French Republic, 1908–1914

Electoral victories are the only victories that the republican government ever wins.

Bainville

The campaign to convert the educated elite of French youth to the royalist cause did not signify any desire on the part of the Action Française leadership to neglect the adult generation. Maurras and his associates harbored the hope that their counterrevolutionary program could be implemented forthwith, not in some distant future. But their experience during the Dreyfus Affair had demonstrated that the most effective medium for attracting and retaining the attention of the general public was the daily press. The fortnightly review through which the modern royalists had been publicizing their program never achieved a wide circulation. The *Gazette de France*, the well established monarchist daily to which both Maurras and Bainville had contributed articles in the early years of the movement (and which received funds from the pretender's political bureau), remained firmly in the hands of Gustave Janicot, an aging journalist whose anachronistic ideas and tame tactics had little in common with the more militant royalism of the Action Française. For years the Maurrassians had talked about establishing a daily newspaper of their own in order to disseminate the ideas of integral nationalism to a wider public.

Such an opportunity fortuitously arose in early 1908. Madame Léon Daudet, who had successfully urged her famous husband to join the Action Française four years earlier, received 200,000 francs bequeathed to her by the Comtesse de Loynes, a socially prominent hostess during the early years of the Third Republic. The

Daudets were only too happy (and secure enough financially) to donate the proceeds from this unexpected legacy, together with several thousand francs from their own funds, to underwrite the publication of a daily newspaper bearing the title of the movement itself.[1] In March 1908 Maurras and Bainville left the *Gazette de France* and joined forces with Daudet and other converts to the cause to found the *Action Française* as a daily organ of royalist opinion.

Within a month of the daily's appearance on March 21, 1908, the ubiquitous police informer in the editorial offices was reporting that the Action Française leadership was already making plans to broaden the new paper's base of support. According to this source, plans were being laid for a vast journalistic enterprise that would capture the readers of *Le Soleil*, *Le Gaulois*, *L'Echo de Paris*, *La Croix*, and other established rightist journals.[2] Though this project was to fall short of such an ambitious objective, it was symptomatic of the Maurrassians' increasing desire to attract the patrons of the more respectable organs of conservative opinion.

A year later the Maurrassians attempted by more devious means to wrest control of the *Gazette de France* from its doddering septuagenarian editor, Janicot. Maurras first proposed that he and Bainville (as well as the crack team of writers that he had assembled at the *Action française*) be allowed to assume *de facto* control of the old daily, with the ultimate purpose of rejuvenating it and increasing its circulation. When Janicot rejected this presumptuous proposition and alerted his subscribers and advertisers to the incipient insurgency, Maurras apparently hatched a bizarre scheme to marry off the eligible bachelor Bainville to one of Janicot's grandnieces, whose financial interest in the paper would strengthen the hand of her new husband and his allies. Had this plan proved successful it would have catapulted the *Action française* to the head of the royalist forces in France, but Janicot steadfastly refused to give his blessing to the match and the plot was nipped in the bud.[3] The

1. Weber, *Action Française*, 47–48; Osgood, *French Royalism since 1870*, 80; Tannenbaum, *Action Française*, 92.
2. APP, A31805, 24E.
3. AN, F⁷12862, "Notes sur l'Action Française," (September 25, 1909), no. 4. A slightly different version of this abortive courtship is supplied by François Leger,

new daily had nevertheless begun to attract a loyal readership of its own, and soon the Maurrassian newspaper was luring readers away from the *Gazette*, as well as from other stodgy mouthpieces of the royalist cause such as *Le Soleil* and *Le Gaulois*.[4] For his part, Bainville married Jeanne Niobey, an attractive socialite from an old Norman family, in 1913.

Maurras had recruited a talented group of young journalists for his new daily, imperiously assigning editorial tasks on the basis of his intuitive evaluation of each man's abilities. He reserved for himself the daily commentary on public affairs (which he wrote under the classical *nom de plume* Crito). The topics education and the arts were claimed by the two members of the editorial staff who possessed solid literary and pedagogical credentials, Dimier and Pierre Lasserre. One day in the spring of 1908 Maurras summoned Bainville to his office and asked him to write a daily column on foreign affairs, a subject totally outside his sphere of competence to date—most of his articles in the fortnightly review had dealt with literary topics. Bainville acceded to his master's peculiar request, but not before expressing his distaste at being asked to undertake an assignment for which he had so little preparation. "I didn't like it one bit," he later confided to an interviewer. "If I did it, it was at the express request, I could almost say at the behest, of Maurras." Bainville's greatest cause for dismay was his premonition that the new assignment would make it virtually impossible for him to continue to pursue his first love, literary criticism. Maurras noticed the flash of reluctance, and replied: "I have your grimace in my pocket."[5]

Bainville's prodigious energy and versatility could not be harnessed to a single preoccupation, even one as broadly defined as foreign affairs. He wrote a daily column on general subjects under the pseudonym "Léonce Beaujeu," a Sunday financial report as

---

who claims that Janicot refused Bainville's request for his grandniece's hand because he could not foresee a promising future for the young journalist. François Leger, "Le Dessein de Jacques Bainville," *L'Ordre français*, no. 19 (November, 1964), 48.

4. *Ibid.*; Weber, *Action Française*, 49.

5. Dimier, *Vingt Ans*, 15. See also *Les Nouvelles littéraires*, July 21, 1923.

"Jean Cotteret," an occasional article on literary subjects signed "Henri Dartevel," and frequent pieces on parliamentary news and the theater. A single issue of the paper would often contain four or five articles by the Action française's resident jack-of-all-trades. But his new assignment inevitably compelled him to put aside most of his projects of literary criticism—he later referred to himself as "le critique mort jeune"—in order to devote the bulk of his intellectual energies to the two topics that were to dominate his thinking for the remainder of his career: history and foreign affairs.[6]

These new preoccupations were not as unrelated as they might appear to the modern reader. In the years between the fall of Napoleon I and the outbreak of the First World War, the pronouncements of historians were received by diplomats and policy makers in France with the same attentiveness that has been accorded the theorists of international relations in recent times.[7] As the young royalist journalist began to study the development of French foreign policy, he increasingly came to rely on historical evidence to trace the roots of the international problems that confronted French policy makers in the decade before the war. His daily column bristled with pessimistic predictions of an approaching Franco-German conflict whose inevitability he believed to be guaranteed by the numerous blunders that had been committed by French diplomats and statesmen since 1789. This pessimism contrasted sharply with the confident tone of his response to the 1902 enquiry on German influences in France. His writings during the prewar years reflected a mounting skepticism about France's prospects for surviving the inevitable German drive to establish hegemony on the continent.[8] These analyses of French foreign policy characteristically assumed the form of a political polemic. He unceasingly attributed France's military and diplomatic problems during the past century to republican and Bonapartist mismanagement, while ascribing

6. Linville, "Jacques Bainville," 136; Szekeley de Doba, et al., Jacques Bainville, 77; Bainville, Le Critique mort jeune.

7. Indeed, several notable French historians—Guizot, Tocqueville, Thiers, Lavisse, Rambaud, Hanotaux, and Albert Sorel, for example—combined public careers in politics or diplomacy with scholarly vocations.

8. See, for example, Bainville, Journal, I, November 8, 1906.

the few manifestations of diplomatic foresight to the shrewdness of Bourbon or Orleanist statesmen.[9]

Bainville's indictment of the Third Republic for what he alleged to be its suicidal lack of preparedness represented an important component of the Action Française's ideological campaign against the regime. A number of polemical works rolled off the movement's presses purporting to expose a series of sinister conspiracies linking various members of the republican elite with the leaders of the German Empire. Typical of these was Maurras's *Kiel et Tanger*, which blamed the declining international position of France on the sinister unwillingness of republican politicians to take measures to halt Germany's new world policy in its tracks. Léon Daudet's vicious diatribe, *L'Avant-Guerre: études et documents sur l'espionnage juif-allemand en France depuis l'affaire Dreyfus*, rehashed old arguments that France was being betrayed by French Jews and their political accomplices.[10]

The most noteworthy royalist critique of the foreign policy of the Republic was Bainville's *Bismarck et la France*,[11] which he published less than a year before the *Action française* daily was founded. In this work, which comprised a collection of articles on Germany that he had written for the *Gazette de France* between 1900 and 1905, he purported to present irrefutable historical evidence demolishing the Republic's reputation as the regime that had saved France from total destruction after Sedan and protected her from subsequent invasion. The real bombshell that emerged from this work was a series of carefully selected excerpts from the memoirs of Count Hohenlohe-Schillingsfürst (the Bavarian statesman who cooperated with Bismarck to smooth the path toward German unification before 1871) as well as selections from those of the French Am-

---

9. The image of Bainville as a foreign policy critic was perfectly captured by a cartoon accompanied by the caption: "The fleur-de-lys [the coat-of-arms of the French royal family] mounted on the roof of the Quai d'Orsay." Léon Treich, ed., *Almanach des lettres françaises et étrangères* (Paris: Crès, 1924), 257.

10. Maurras, *Kiel et Tanger* (Paris: Nouvelle Librairie Nationale, 1916); Léon Daudet, *L'Avant-Guerre: études et documents sur l'espionnage juif-allemand en France depuis l'affaire Dreyfus* (Paris: Nouvelle Librairie Nationale, 1913).

11. Jacques Bainville, *Bismarck et la France* (Paris: Nouvelle Librairie Nationale, 1907). Henceforth the 1918 edition will be used in this book.

bassador in Berlin during the early years of the Third Republic, the Vicomte de Gontaut-Biron.[12] The documents, which Bainville had happened upon during his research for the Ludwig biography, were presented as evidence supporting two themes which would continually reappear in his writings: the collusion between Bismarck and the leaders of the French left after Sedan to create the Third Republic in order to forestall a monarchical restoration, and the decisive role played by the "principle of nationalities" in weakening France while strengthening her real and potential enemies.

The crucial political lesson to be drawn from these historical revelations was obvious, at least to Bainville. The growth of republicanism in France after 1871 was intimately associated with the rising fortunes of the German Empire. The French regime therefore did "not merit the confidence of true patriots." Once the political system installed in the 1870s began to pursue a foreign policy that was directly "contrary to the national interest," Bainville declared, "the divorce between the Republic and the fatherland" had been completed.[13]

The task of saddling Gambetta, generally revered as the organizer of national defense and the foremost advocate of *revanche*, with the responsibility of doing the bidding of the enemy required a monumental exercise in historical revisionism. Bainville was given the assignment by the royalist leadership because he was thought to possess the greatest credibility. He alone among the leading members of the Action Française had already established a certain

12. See *Polybiblion*, 78 (July, 1913), 79, and *Le Dictionnaire de bibliographie française* (Paris: Librairie Letouzey et Ane, 1941), no pagination. In 1905 Bainville had edited a series of speeches delivered by the Marquis de Roux (an attorney from Poitiers who subsequently defended many Action Française leaders in their legal battles with the courts) which were published under the title *La République de Bismarck, ou origines allemandes de la Troisième République* (Paris: Nouvelle Librairie Nationale, 1905). This work, which drew upon the recently published correspondence between Bismarck and Gambetta during the 1870's, argued that a secret pact signed in the summer of 1877 by Gambetta and Count Henckel, Bismarck's representative, arranged for an end to the campaign of *revanche* in return for German support for Gambetta against MacMahon and the monarchists. For a more balanced, less polemical study of Franco-German relations after Sedan, see Allan Mitchell, *Bismarck and the French Nation* (New York: Bobbs-Merrill, 1971), 73–88.
13. Bainville, *Bismarck et la France*, vii, xv.

reputation as a well-informed expert on German affairs that was to grow steadily for the rest of his career. "Germany never let him go," Ernst Nolte has observed. "In contrast to Maurras, he was acquainted with Germany through observation and wide knowledge of its literature." Maurras did not read German and took his only trip to Germany in 1910. While Maurras was "enclosed in his meditation on *la seule France*," Claude Digeon has noted, Bainville "anxiously observed the Empire of William II" and became a nationalist "through consciousness of the threat and example of the Germans."[14]

Lest it appear paradoxical that an inveterate traveler whose daily reading included a dozen newspapers in four languages would succumb to a narrow, inward-looking nationalist doctrine, Digeon reminds us that in the late nineteenth and early twentieth century "to travel frequently meant to become conscious of national particularisms and to become fond of exalting them."[15] Another attentive observer of Bainville's career later explained that the royalist writer never permitted his own worldly experience to alter his political judgments. Bainville recognized that while he and others like him had been privileged to have the opportunity to sample the delights of foreign cultures, cosmopolitanism was a luxury that was beyond the means of the average Frenchman, whose principal concern was the preservation of his nation's security from external invasion, the maintenance of domestic order, and the encouragement of economic prosperity.[16]

"Everything that is national is ours," proclaimed the masthead of the *Action française*, quoting the pretender, and much of the journal's propaganda was aimed at wresting from the republicans their historic claim to the mantle of patriotism. The conventional historical interpretation regarded French nationalism as a product of the Revolution, a view that was nurtured by the early romantic writers and historians and perpetuated throughout the nineteenth

14. Nolte, *Three Faces of Fascism*, 472; Digeon, *La Crise allemande*, 473–74.
15. Digeon, *La Crise allemande*, 473–74.
16. Rousseaux, "Jacques Bainville," 197; see also Szekeley de Doba, *et al.*, *Jacques Bainville*, 142.

century by the parties of the left. The monarchist right, on the
other hand, beginning with the departure of the first aristocratic
émigrés in 1789, had consistently rated the solidarity of thrones
above the security of the fatherland. It was this stigma that Bainville strove to erase in his *Bismarck et la France* and subsequent writings. The objective was absolutely crucial to the success of the
royalist cause: to sever the link between nationalism and republicanism in the popular imagination and to identify the royalist tradition with the cause of national regeneration.[17]

To accomplish this feat Bainville emphasized the distinction between nationalism in the modern, conservative, Barrèsian sense,
and the "principle of nationalities," the doctrine of national self-
determination developed during the Revolution and disseminated
during the nineteenth century. He blamed the latter concept for
inspiring the movements that destroyed the Vienna settlement and
brought about the unification of Germany and Italy, two nations
that were currently allied against France. The right of national
self-determination had been proclaimed by the French revolutionaries in the name of "the people," only to redound "to the profit of
two monarchies." The Habsburgs, the Romanovs, and the Bourbons had served as the guarantors of the post-Napoleonic system
by virtue of their devotion to historical tradition and monarchical
legitimacy. But the parvenu monarchies of Germany and Italy,
under the influence of two shrewd statesmen (Bismarck and Ca-
vour), had appropriated the revolutionary program of cultural nationalism in order to ensure the preservation of their authority in
the newly united states. "Applied to Italy and Germany," Bainville observed, "the principle of nationalities has already caused
blood to flow, and . . . produced the system of the armed peace
that currently oppresses the European world."[18]

What most displeased Bainville was France's failure to take the

17. On the beginning of the evolution of French nationalism from left to right
toward the end of the nineteenth century, see Herbert Tint, *The Decline of French
Patriotism: 1870–1914* (London: Weidenfeld & Nicolson, 1964), 70–114.
    18. Bainville, *Bismarck et la France*, xii; *AF*, July 3, 1913.

necessary precautions to prevent the consolidation of the German national state. He attributed this egregious display of impotence to residual sympathy for the discredited ideals of France's own national revolution, which French liberals incorrectly believed Germany to be pursuing. Only too late, and to her own peril, did France discover that her powerful neighbor had employed those ideals as a smoke screen while achieving national unification and military superiority. Bainville called on all French patriots to discard their ideological blinders and recognize that French nationalism derived its justification not from some vague revolutionary principle, but rather from "the centuries of civilization and culture that it represents." From this discovery, he believed, would follow the realization that "democracy, liberalism, and the republican ideal," far from representing the source of French nationalism, had set in motion the diplomatic and military assaults on the settlement of 1815 that culminated in the debacle of 1871.[19]

Bainville's criticism of the Bismarckian international system was less the vengeful protest of a bitter citizen of humiliated France than the lament of a theorist of the balance of power alarmed at the disappearance of the safeguards against international anarchy that had been erected at Westphalia and then Vienna. Whereas the settlements of 1648 and 1815 had harmonized the relations among the great powers and regulated the activities of the lesser states, the Treaty of Frankfurt contained the seeds of ferocious national antagonisms. He believed the failure of the European system established after the Franco-Prussian War to be preordained, because it rested on "the barbarous principle of the arms race" rather than on a broader principle such as that which had operated at Vienna in 1815.[20] The balance of power during the armed peace constituted a totally unstable system, he later observed, because Germany, its organizer, was capable of achieving her objectives in the world arena only by "intimidation."[21] Part of the reason for

19. Bainville, *Bismarck et la France*, xviii.
20. *AF*, July 2, 1911, quoted in Bainville, *L'Allemagne*, I (Paris: Plon, 1939), 16.
21. *AF*, September 24, 1921.

this pessimism was his Malthusian fear that the pressure of population on the food supply in *Mitteleuropa* represented a perpetual source of national conflict.[22]

Having unmasked the iniquitous principle of nationalities, Bainville proceeded to defend the proposition that the only durable basis for French nationalism was to be found in the person of the king. It was under the auspices of the hereditary monarchy that France had enjoyed centuries of national unity and security while her eastern neighbor remained a disjointed mosaic of feudal fiefs. Conversely, it was the absence of that strong royal authority in postrevolutionary France that had enabled Germany to achieve national unification and European hegemony at France's expense. Obsessed with what he regarded as the risks of liberty in a republican France confronted with an authoritarian regime across the Rhine,[23] he argued that the power relationship between the two rivals had varied historically according to the strength of their respective monarchies.

At this point in his argument Bainville introduced the "evidence"[24] contained in the Hohenlohe memoirs establishing a link between the foundation of the Third Republic and the objectives of German foreign policy. According to the documents, Bismarck's principal concern throughout the early 1870s had been to drive a wedge between France and the rest of Catholic, monarchical Europe in order to prevent the formation of a "white coalition" that could conceivably dismantle the fragile unity of the Second Reich. The German chancellor accomplished this feat by tacitly supporting the republican movement in France in its campaign against the monarchist majority in the National Assembly. Bismarck, the master practitioner of *Realpolitik*, conspired to impose upon France "a Republic and its civil discords," the surest guar-

22. See below, 78–79.
23. Henri Clouard, "Jacques Bainville," *Mercure de France* (February 15, 1936), 266.
24. Bainville's selective, highly interpretive use of the documents failed to prove the case against Gambetta and the first generation of republicans after 1870. But it made exciting reading and played its role in the Action Française's campaign to expose the "pro-German" tendencies of French republicanism in the years before the First World War.

antee of domestic weakness and diplomatic isolation. The Republic would institutionalize social unrest and political instability in France, thereby deterring European royalty from seeking diplomatic contacts with the pariahs in control of the new regime.[25] The consequence of this European transformation was "anarchy in France, a king in Rome, and an emperor in Berlin."[26]

In a later work, Bainville credited Bismarck with having successfully quarantined the Third Republic during the first decade of its existence. The meeting of the crowned heads of Germany, Russia, and Austria in 1872 was a crafty Bismarckian scheme to drive French citizens into the hands of the French left by making them fear that a league of foreign monarchies had been formed to "threaten the Republic." In reality, of course, the *Dreikaiserbund* was in no sense an attempt to resurrect the principle of monarchical solidarity established at Vienna in 1815. The Iron Chancellor knew full well that any updated version of the Concert of Europe was likely to be directed at the German Empire, which had succeeded Napoleonic France as the "violator of European order." But the deception was successful in France, where the leftist parties supplanted the monarchists in the legislative elections between 1873 and 1877 by reviving the specter of the Republic endangered by the autocratic powers to the east and their domestic accomplices. By thus surreptitiously abetting the victory of the republican, anticlerical forces in France, Bismarck was able to prevent the formation of "a coalition of Catholic countries" (France, Austria, and Italy) against Protestant Prussia. He also thereby succeeded in dashing the hopes of the last remaining domestic opponents of his policy of German unification under Prussian auspices, the Catholics of the south and west, who might have been susceptible to overtures from their co-religionists in France. The result was that the German chancellor acquired "a free hand on the continent."[27]

The Third Republic's "complicity" in this Bismarckian design was viewed by Bainville as a variation of the disastrous Italian policy of

25. Bainville, *Journal*, I, June 28, 1907; Bainville, *Bismarck* (Paris: Editions du Siècle, 1932), 62ff.
26. Bainville, *Bismarck et la France*, xii.
27. Bainville, *Bismarck*, 67, 84–88, 108.

its predecessor, the Second Empire. Napoleon III's sponsorship of Italian unification, the "Carbonarist reveries" that led him to support the liberal, anticlerical campaign against the Papacy and Catholic Austria, were patently self-defeating. Bainville considered it a rule of thumb that "everything that is directed against Catholicism is directed against France, and vice versa," and even ventured the dubious proposition that "if Rome were still a pontifical city, the French flag would still be flying at Strasbourg." Rather than seeking an alliance of Catholic powers, the Emperor committed the fatal error of creating "a united kingdom, a possible enemy, a certain rival" in an area where the territorial and political settlement of 1815 had assured the preservation of French influence and forestalled the appearance of Francophobic sentiment.[28] The ultimate proof of the bankruptcy of the Napoleonic policy was the anti-French military alliance forged in 1882 by Germany and Italy, the two nations that had achieved their unification with French encouragement.

This identification of French national interests with European Catholicism that appears throughout Bainville's writings was based not upon personal religious affinity, but rather on what he believed to be the rigorous requirements of *raison d'état*. In his frantic search for methods of reestablishing the balance of power that had been upset in 1871, he seized upon religion and culture as unifying principles with which to forge a coalition of European states friendly to France. During his extensive travels in Central Europe, a recurring theme that he encountered in Catholic and non-Catholic countries alike was a pervasive sympathy for French customs coupled with its natural converse, a profound antipathy for Germanism. During a trip to Bohemia in April 1907, he observed with approval the hatred that Germany inspired among those "upon whom it is attempting to impose its *Kultur*." On a sojourn to Vienna in the summer of 1905 he had marvelled at the extent to which life in the ancient imperial city resembled that of Paris in its pleasantness and

28. *Ibid.*, 211, 200.

spirituality. "Can we count the Viennese among the civilized peoples?" he exclaimed with incredulous delight. "Are we no longer in Germany?" In Hungary he saw evidence everywhere of the traditions of "Latinity" which distinguished the Magyars from the Germans and bound them to France.[29]

Traces of Francophilia had once existed even in many areas of Germany itself. "If the upheavals of the Revolution and the Empire had not metamorphosed Central Europe," Bainville declared, "France would have discovered in Franconia, in the person of these little autonomous princes, if not sure allies, at least protégés whose friendship could be purchased." Unfortunately, Napoleon's German policy after 1806, which discouraged particularism and stimulated nationalist sentiment, had destroyed the possibility of such an alliance between France and German Francophiles.[30]

But what was the alternative to German hegemony and French isolation in the early years of the Third Republic? Bainville's retrospective scenario of the policy that France should have pursued in order to ensure her security, however unrealistic it may have appeared to contemporary opinion, was a deceptively simple and appealing one. It was, of necessity, composed of several conditions that had long ago become missed opportunities. If the South and West German states, which he liked to call the "meridional kingdoms,"[31] could have been split off from their Prussian oppressors, if Austrian autonomy could have been guaranteed, and if Italy had remained under the tutelage of the Habsburgs, the Bourbons, and the Papacy, a Rome-Munich-Paris-Vienna axis could have conducted a conservative Catholic policy of encirclement against revolutionary, Protestant Prussia. But Bismarck had precluded such a diplomatic constellation by absorbing the Catholic powers to the south, neutralizing Austria, supporting Italian unity at the expense of the Church, and favoring the establishment of an anticlerical,

29. Jacques Bainville, "Notes de voyages," reprinted in Szekeley de Doba *et al.*, *Jacques Bainville*, 29–30, 38, 51–58.
30. Bainville, *Bismarck*, 42–44.
31. *AF*, May 11, 1911.

republican regime in France. The German Chancellor, in short, was a Germanic Richelieu, who divided his enemies while promoting the unity of his own nation. The Germanic Richelieu had reversed his French counterpart's policy of "Kings for France, anarchy for Germany," and the French government lamely acquiesced in this historic reversal.

France's lonely position after 1871 as the only major European power with a republican government and without allies rendered the regime particularly vulnerable to the antirepublican allegations of diplomatic impotence and incompetence. Moreover, the lingering problem of political polarization bequeathed by the Dreyfus Affair, the labor unrest, and the church-state controversies of the same period proved to be continuous sources of embarrassment to those republican patriots who argued that a democracy was capable of preserving domestic order and national independence as effectively as the authoritarian monarchies to the east.

Voices of doubt and despair on this score began to emanate from the ranks of the foreign service itself. In the same year that Bainville published his study of Bismarckian diplomacy, Alcide Ebray, the resident minister of France in Bolivia, resigned his post to protest the dismissal of his patron, Foreign Minister Théophile Delcassé, who had been sacrificed to the whims of parliamentary opinion and German pressure during the Tangier crisis of 1905. Ebray accompanied his resignation with the allegation that "there is an absolute incompatibility between our political regime and . . . the maintenance of whatever influence and consideration we have left in the world." He blamed the republican system for what he regarded as the decline of French security, charging that internal dissension and parliamentary instability had inhibited the conduct of a consistent, stable foreign policy. If public or parliamentary opinion had been omnipotent under the *ancien régime,* he charged, Richelieu would have met the same fate as Delcassé, and France would never have achieved her prominent position in the world. While French foreign policy shifted with the vagaries of public sentiment, the German government enjoyed the advantage of untrammeled freedom of action. This enabled it to base its diplomacy on rational calculation rather than political expediency.[32]

Such sentiments were unmistakable echoes of Bainville's daily warnings that the republican government was rapidly leading France down the path of national self-destruction. Over and over again he complained about the tendency of obscure, anonymous politicians to inaugurate a particular foreign policy and then, "when the operation has taken a bad turn, vanish into thin air, letting forty million people fend for themselves." The absence of legitimate executive authority appeared to Bainville as the most serious defect of a parliamentary system; the ruling elite of a republic could easily evade responsibility for its policies, while hereditary monarchies were held accountable for their actions by virtue of the principle of dynastic continuity. "Since a government must be in the hands of someone," he remarked, "it is important that that person [be able to] offer guarantees. You decide if Edward VII, son of Victoria I and father of George V, offers more or less of them to his subjects than M. Joseph Caillaux offers to us."[33]

What particularly alarmed Bainville about the Third Republic's distrust of personal power was that it coincided with the regeneration of monarchical authority in the other major nations of Europe. At the time of the revolutions of 1848 most observers had believed that the institution of hereditary monarchy was on the verge of extinction, destined to be replaced by parliamentary rule. But events since midcentury had convinced Bainville that the course of history was evolving in precisely the opposite direction. In England the trend toward parliamentary sovereignty, set in motion at the end of the seventeenth century, had been reversed by Queen Victoria. Her lengthy reign constituted a "continual rehabilitation of monarchical authority" which was pursued by her son Edward VII after the turn of the century. The English people had evidently learned that an

32. Alcide Ebray, *La France qui meurt* (Paris: Société Française d'Imprimerie et de Librairie, 1910), x–xi, 216, 260, 303.

33. Jacques Bainville, *Le Coup d'Agadir et la guerre d'orient* (Paris: Nouvelle Librairie Nationale, 1913), 31–32; see also *AF*, August 15, 1910, March 25 and October 5, 1912.

independent executive was best suited to the preservation of national security in the hazardous world of power politics.[34]

Further evidence of the mounting prestige and power of hereditary monarchy was to be found in the process of national unification in Belgium, Italy, Germany, and the fledgling states in the Balkans. All these nations had achieved and preserved their national
unity under the auspices of royal houses rather than parliamentary
republics. There were more "elective" regimes in the "monarchical" seventeenth century—Cromwellian England, Holland, Venice,
Bohemia, Poland—than there were in the "democratic" twentieth.
There was "nothing more antique, more out of style" than democracy in the modern world, for the lessons of its weaknesses
had been learned outside of France.[35] Everywhere in Europe people were searching for the stability, disinterested authority, and
effective leadership that only a hereditary monarch could supply.
Yet France clung to the outmoded institutions of parliamentary
sovereignty that had been wisely abandoned or avoided altogether
by her competitors in the international arena.[36]

Unlike many of his fellow royalists, Bainville harbored few illusions about the likelihood that his country would jettison its republican institutions in the immediate future. He knew democratic
prejudices were too ingrained for that. But this realistic assessment
did not impede his determination to warn all who would listen
that French security would remain in grave danger so long as the
governing elite of the Third Republic failed to comprehend the true
nature of the German menace. Germany was "drunk with imperialism." The slightest evidence of French weakness would therefore encourage her to become intolerably "demanding, arrogant,
and provocative" on the world stage. Yet French democrats continued to entertain the comforting illusions of nineteenth-century
liberalism with regard to European peace. The most notorious of
these was the widespread conviction that "the horrors of modern

34. Bainville, *Le Coup d'Agadir*, 190; *Journal*, I, May 8, 1910.
35. Bainville, *Le Coup d'Agadir*, vi, 130, 276, 279–81.
36. Bainville, *Journal*, I, September 14, 1908.

war constitute an insurmountable obstacle that would always re-
strain statesmen before the opening of hostilities." Hence, France
ignored the recent German advances in naval construction and
armaments production, preferring to place its faith in the underlying good will of humanity.[37] If French democracy's manifest inferiority vis-à-vis Germany in matters of foreign policy and national
defense were ever to be rectified, Bainville insisted, Frenchmen
would have to abandon the pipe dream of a peaceful world order
based on the assumption of good intentions in favor of a realistic
assessment of the continually evolving requirements of the balance
of power.

In Bainville's view the danger of permitting public or parliamentary opinion to influence the formulation of diplomatic and military
policy was twofold: uncontrollable public pressure was likely to
stampede governments into abject submission to foreign intimidation in order to avoid bloodshed or, conversely, to compel the ruling elite to undertake illconceived military adventures in the name
of some vague popular principle. The dismissal of Delcassé during
the Moroccan crisis of 1905 was an instance of the former phenomenon. The architect of an effective foreign policy was hounded
from office by petty politicians who feared that his belligerent
stance toward Germany would provoke armed conflict.[38]

Instances of the opposite danger abounded in modern Europe.
"Nothing is more false," Bainville declared, "than the axiom that
governments are belligerent and peoples are pacific." Had it not
been the Russian Tsar who restrained the popular movement of
Pan-Slavism, "burning with the desire to rush to the aid of the
Balkan brothers?" Was it not the "tenacious resistance" of the profoundly conservative William I of Prussia that represented the only
(albeit unsuccessful) opposition to Bismarck's bellicose policy of
national unification, a movement which had "the most unmistakable democratic and liberal origins?" Was it not the "commendable
moderation" of the Habsburgs that was helping to prevent Pan-

37. *AF*, September 24, 1912 and April 17, 1913.
38. Bainville, *Le Coup d'Agadir*, 48; *AF*, February 15, 1911.

German agitators in Vienna from provoking a confrontation with the Southern Slavs?[39]

The principle of monarchical legitimacy represented for Bainville the only remaining safeguard against the outbreak of a European war. "In the great European crises that we are experiencing," he announced during the Second Balkan War in the summer of 1913, "we will have owed the maintenance of peace much more to what is lately being called the 'forces of the past,' that is, authority, aristocracies, and hierarchies, than to the good will of peoples." The principal menace to world peace, declared this latter-day Metternich, was the liberal principle of national self-determination, a "powder keg" that could at any moment explode the tranquility of the European continent. Unfortunately, dozens of dangerous outbreaks of popular agitation in the name of that vague principle were already "bursting the dam erected by the traditional authorities."[40]

But in the case of France, Bainville feared that the danger of democratically inspired belligerence was currently outweighed by the opposite menace of idealistic pacifism. He considered it typical of democratic societies that the pendulum of public opinion should shift from one extreme to the other at precisely the most inopportune moment. In the early 1870s, for example, when France was a vanquished nation in need of peace and tranquility to heal her wounds and enable her to rebuild for the future, the liberal republicans mouthed such slogans as "revenge" and "return of the lost provinces," both totally unrealistic goals during a period of French military weakness and diplomatic isolation. After the turn of the century, on the other hand, when France had recovered from the defeat, rebuilt her army, and acquired allies in her continual confrontation with the German Empire, the new republican watchwords were "peace," "international solidarity," and "the United States of Europe."

The only hope for a secure European peace, in Bainville's eyes,

39. *AF*, July 3, 1913; January 29, 1914.
40. *AF*, July 3, 1913.

was the maintenance of a stable equilibrium on the continent. Such a strategy implied the need to preserve the Austro-Hungarian and Turkish Empires as obstacles to German expansion to the south and as federators of the competing ethnic minorities in the region (whose quest for national independence threatened to embroil the great powers in a senseless war). The maintenance of these two multinational empires, together with the strengthening of the Anglo-French-Russian alliance system, represented the best mechanism for averting the catastrophe that loomed on the horizon.[41] French liberals' proposals for the partition of the Habsburg Empire in the name of national self-determination for its subject nationalities prompted an outburst of irritation from the usually mild-mannered royalist writer. "These peoples are not living so badly under the scepter of the Habsburgs," he remarked. In any case, the dissolution of that ancient state would tilt the European balance in such a way as to produce a diplomatic nightmare for France. "Oh, what a political masterpiece!" he sarcastically exclaimed. "An Italian kingdom without counterweight and master of an entire sea; a German Empire with nearly eighty million inhabitants, both facing a powder of small and middle sized Czech, Magyar, Serbian, Greek, and Rumanian states." The very thought should persuade Frenchmen to acknowledge the obvious: "the existence of Austria-Hungary is indispensable to France."[42]

Yet Bainville was never entirely comfortable with the existing alternative to such a partition: the bipolar system of early twentieth-century Europe that had cleaved the continent into two armed camps prepared to transform the most minor of localized incidents into a Europe-wide conflagration. What bothered him most about the putative balance established by the Triple Alliance and the Triple Entente was that that equilibrium was a smokescreen that concealed grave continental instability. The practice of diplomacy based on traditional balance-of-power principles was in reality endangered by the growth of political parties and pressure groups in-

41. *AF*, November 28, 1912; October 9, 1913.
42. Bainville, *Journal*, I, November 28, 1912.

tent on injecting ideological issues into international politics; such
a development threatened to produce great uncertainty and impede efforts to conduct foreign policy in a rational manner.[43]

Furthermore, the introduction of universal military conscription
placed the ultimate power to defend the fatherland and deter aggression by others in the hands of the masses, a potentially unstable if not disastrous circumstance. Bainville longed for the return to the prerevolutionary era, when monarchs and professional
diplomats who were insulated from popular pressures conducted
diplomacy according to the tested axioms of statecraft and when
professional armies of trained mercenaries constituted a depend-
able, obedient source of military might.[44]

But if the manifest shortcomings of republican diplomacy supplied Bainville with a number of themes for his ideological critique
of the regime, the instances of indisputable success demanded an
explanation consistent with Maurrassian principles. The most conspicuous achievement of the Quai d'Orsay, the formation of the
Triple Entente itself, had reached its climax less than a year before
Bainville's debut as a foreign policy analyst with the French-
sponsored colonial settlement between England and Russia. The
Anglo-Russian agreement of 1907, following the Franco-Russian
alliance of 1894 and the Anglo-French entente of 1904, gave the
appearance of that "nightmare of coalitions" that Bismarck had
labored so earnestly and so effectively to prevent during his career. The obligation to account for this happy turn of events elicited from Bainville an analysis that further revealed the royalist
writer's skill at interpreting historical events to meet the requirements of political doctrine.

The Anglo-Russo-French diplomatic constellation struck Bainville as "entirely called for by the circumstances." It represented
the best available instrument for deterring German aggression on
the continent because it presented the Kaiser and his military strat-

43. Bainville, *Journal*, I, July 27, 1914; *AF*, December 5, 1912.
44. *AF*, December 5, 1912. Bainville objected to compulsory military service as an
unbearable "tax" imposed upon the citizenry by the republican government, a
burden that would have been unthinkable under the monarchy; *AF*, February 6,
1912; December 5, 1912.

egists with the prospect of a two-front war and a crippling naval blockade. But he stoutly refused to recognize this masterly achievement as a product of republican diplomacy. The alliance of 1894 was instead a timely return to the policy of Franco-Russian friendship established under the Bourbon Restoration. The Russian connection had first been proposed by an aristocratic advocate of *ancien régime* diplomacy, the Comte de Chaudordy, and was forged in spite of intense ideological hostility toward the Russian Empire on the part of French republicans. Similarly, the Anglo-French entente was the work of a king and a Tory aristocrat, Edward VII and Lord Lansdowne, and French Foreign Minister Delcassé, who had been imbued with the concepts of balance of power diplomacy and achieved a high degree of independence from parliamentary interference during his long tenure at the Quai d'Orsay.[45]

But the entente formed by an English king, a Russian emperor, and a French diplomat of the old school was gravely weakened after 1905, Bainville complained, by a succession of ominous domestic developments. The revolution in Russia had saddled the Tsar with a parliament and a constitution, both of which limited his freedom and placed Russian foreign policy at the mercy of a public opinion that was abominably ignorant of world affairs. "How to convince the Moujik that he has an interest in France's position in Morocco" represented in Bainville's eyes an impossible task. In the same year Delcassé was overthrown as a consequence of German intimidation in Morocco, while France's Russian ally lent little support. The man who had conducted a consistent, effective foreign policy between 1898 and 1905 amid terrible domestic convulsions was succeeded by a series of weak foreign ministers who bent with the wind of parliamentary and public opinion.[46]

Meanwhile, across the channel, the electoral victory of the British Liberals in 1905 replaced the Conservative architects of the *entente cordiale* with men driven by radical, pacifist prejudices and

45. *AF*, July 30, 1908; October 5, 1912; *AF*, December 5, 1912; Bainville, *Le Coup d'Agadir*, 21–22, 5, 21, 30–31. For the standard study of Delcassé's role in promoting the Anglo-French entente of 1904, see Christopher Andrew, *Théophile Delcassé and the Entente Cordiale* (New York: St. Martin's, 1968).
46. *AF*, December 5, 1912; Bainville, *Le Cour d'Agadir*, 95, 48, 61–66.

"Puritan rancor against Catholic France." Asquith, Lloyd George, and Morley were the successors of the Cobden-Bright-Gladstone clique that had abandoned France to its terrible fate in 1870. Fortunately, the Liberal government was persuaded by the king to discard its ideological prejudices and support France against Germany at the Algeciras conference on Morocco in 1906, and to join Tsarist Russia in the anti-German entente a year later. But the English Liberals thenceforth launched a domestic program that produced political division, social unrest, and economic catastrophe. The fiscal assault on inherited wealth, the campaign against the House of Lords, and the support for Irish Home Rule threatened to remove the oligarchic safeguards against pure democracy, plunge the British Isles into social and ethnic conflict, and therefore destroy the national unity of France's ally during Germany's drive for European domination.[47]

For Bainville, the great tragedy of the Triple Entente was its inability to capitalize on what should have been an advantageous situation. The Central Powers suffered a number of disabilities that should have rendered them inferior to the combined forces of Russia, France, and England. Not the least of these internal defects was a heterogeneous population of disruptive ethnic minorities whose loyalty to their Germanic oppressors was problematical: "Without exaggeration, one can say that Germany, with its two religious traditions, at bottom still hostile to each other, its socialists, its Alsatians, its Poles, its eternal concern about particularism, and that Austria, with its rival nationalities, are the two states in the world that are not only the most difficult to govern well, but even to govern at all." The entente powers, on the other hand, were blessed with comparatively homogeneous populations and superior resources, both natural and human.[48]

But these considerable social and economic advantages were

47. Bainville, *Le Coup d'Agadir*, 20, 78; *AF*, April 25, 1914.
48. *AF*, December 23, 1912. This critical reference to Austrian instability clashes with his frequently expressed belief in the importance of preserving the multinational Empire. See below, 127.

squandered owing to a defective political machine, which Bainville regarded as the engine of a nation's power and influence in
the world:

> There are cooks to whom one can give the most succulent meats, the
> richest butter, and the most savory spices, and who will create only vile
> stews. Bad governments resemble these incompetent cooks. With all
> the resources of a great country, a diligent elite, [potentially effective]
> methods of action, and all the trump cards in the game of international
> politics, they stumble along from setback to setback.

So long as "France is republican, England is governed by liberal-
radicals, and Russia is sick with a parliament and pregnant with a
constitution [en mal de Duma et en génèse de constitution]," Bainville complained, Germany retained the potential for overcoming
hostile circumstances and imposing her will on the continent. The
ancien régime policy of forging an entente with Russia and England
to counterbalance the Triple Alliance was severely weakened by
the absence of the political institutions of the ancien régime in Paris
and the weakening of the traditional authorities in London and
Saint Petersburg.[49]

The first significant test of the solidity of the anti-German alliance
system came in the autumn of 1908, when the Austrian government
proclaimed the annexation of the Balkan provinces of Bosnia and
Herzegovina. Russia's vehement protests and frantic appeals for
the convocation of an international conference to discuss the Austrian action fell on deaf ears in France and England. Bainville interpreted this failure of nerve on the part of the Tsar's two allies
as dramatic confirmation of his fears about the viability of the entente. Berlin had issued a blank check to Vienna, and the gamble
had paid off. At one fell swoop the Kaiser had regained the prestige
and diplomatic momentum that he had temporarily lost at the Algeciras Conference in 1906, where the great powers had supported
France's claims in Morocco. Within two years Russian interests in
the Balkans were severely threatened by a resurgent Austria. Once

49. *AF*, September 26, 1910; December 23, 1912. Bainville, *Le Coup d'Agadir*, 20,
22, 77–78.

again, by failing to come to the assistance of their beleaguered ally, "the liberal powers have given in to two military and authoritarian monarchies."[50]

A few years later it was France's turn to experience the agony of abandonment and humiliation. The English government's failure to support France during the second Moroccan crisis of 1911, together with the French government's eagerness to appease the German hunger for diplomatic triumphs, further revealed the weakness of the anti-German coalition. Bainville denounced the Franco-German agreement of November 1911 (negotiated by the notorious Germanophile Joseph Caillaux, after the German gunboat *Panther* arrived at Agadir on the coast of Morocco to press Germany's claims in the area.) The transfer of territory in "our Congo" to Germany in return for German recognition of French hegemony in Morocco—the "Agadir coup" as Bainville contemptuously called it—was a spineless concession to Teutonic blackmail reminiscent of the cashiering of Delcassé in the aftermath of the first Moroccan crisis six years earlier. Once again, republican France and liberal England (controlled by the likes of "the Quaker, Puritan, pro-German Lloyd George") had collapsed before the diplomatic juggernaut of autocratic Germany.[51]

But Morocco was now French, a circumstance which called attention to the one achievement in foreign policy that indisputably belonged to the Third Republic: its acquisition of a vast colonial empire in Africa and Southeast Asia. Yet even that success failed to moderate Bainville's critique of republican foreign policy. On the contrary, he denounced it as a serious mistake replete with grave consequences for the future. Imperialism was a costly enterprise which squandered French men and money on ventures that promised to bring few benefits to the metropole, created new frontiers to defend, and embroiled France in unnecessary colonial disputes

50. *AF*, October 19, 1908, February 15 and July 23, 1911.
51. *AF*, July 23, November 6, 1911, February 26, 1912; Bainville, *Le Coup d'Agadir*, 27. For an analysis of the causes of Delcassé's controversial fall from power, see Charles W. Porter, *The Career of Théophile Delcassé* (Philadelphia: University of Pennsylvania Press, 1936), 229–60.

with friends such as England and potential friends such as Italy. Most important of all, Bainville recalled Chaudordy's warning that the "unlimited expansion of our colonies" would result in the "dispersion of our energies," diverting attention from the much more critical problems in Europe. By acquiring territory from Senegal to Saigon, the Third Republic had merely played into Bismarck's hands by averting its attention from the Vosges.[52]

Even the most clear-cut diplomatic triumphs of the Triple Entente and its client states provided grist for Bainville's ideological indictment of the French Republic. The defeat of the Turkish Empire by the Balkan League in 1912–1913, universally recognized as a victory for the Entente and a rebuff for the Central Powers, did nothing to allay Bainville's fears of French diplomatic weakness. On the contrary, the outcome of the Balkan Wars merely confirmed his previous analysis of the entente's endemic disability. France had gained nothing in the way of concrete commitments from the victorious nations of Southern Europe, while Germany used the defeat of her client state Turkey as a pretext for increasing the size of her army at France's expense. The royalist writer even managed to extract an ideological lesson from the Balkan events that could be applied to Western Europe: the triumph of the Bulgarian, Serbian, and Greek monarchies over a Young Turkey recently plunged into "parliamentary anarchy" further demonstrated the superiority of the hereditary principle and the inferiority of popular regimes.[53] The Ottoman Sultan, as "detestable" a dictator as he was, had at least delayed the process by which the sick man of Europe expired. Within a few years of the Young Turk revolution of 1908 and the advent of a parliamentary regime, Turkish sovereignty in Southern Europe and North Africa had disappeared.[54]

But the period which Gordon Wright has described as the nationalist revival of 1911–1914 in France produced a series of events

52. Bainville, *Le Coup d'Agadir*, 22–26; *AF*, October 26, 1911; Bainville, *Chroniques* (Paris: Plon, 1938), 122.
53. *AF*, December 15, 1912; March 6 and March 13, May 29 and November 20, 1913.
54. Bainville, *Le Coup d'Agadir*, 97–98; *AF*, March 6, 1913.

which elicited from Bainville a momentary feeling of optimism. In January 1912 the Radical government of Joseph Caillaux that had sought an accommodation with Germany was swept out of office and replaced by a "republican nationalist" government led by Raymond Poincaré. In January of the following year Poincaré acceded to the presidency with the support of the conservative parties, and in August the term of military service was extended from two to three years despite fervent accusations of militarism from the left. These developments suggested to Bainville that certain sectors of French republicanism were gradually turning away from the liberal faith in international reconciliation and adopting a more realistic attitude toward the requirements of national security.[55]

Poincaré was unquestionably the ablest and most strong-willed statesman to occupy the Elysée Palace since Thiers.[56] But what endeared him to Bainville above all was his attitude in matters of foreign policy and national defense. His Lorraine origins rendered him implacably antagonistic to Germany, his bourgeois good sense inoculated him against the disease of idealistic pacifism, and his public declarations in favor of strengthening the power of the executive suggested a desire to rescue France from the evils of legislative omnipotence (and incompetence) that Maurras and his associates had been denouncing. It appeared that France had, by some miracle, acquired a president who possessed "all the powers of a king" and was prepared to use them.[57]

It has been claimed that Poincaré was an admirer of Bainville's abilities as an analyst of political affairs.[58] Though he never public-

55. Gordon Wright, *France in Modern Times* (Chicago: Rand, McNally & Co., 1960), 339. See also Tannenbaum, *Action Française*, 140–42 and Buthman, *The Rise of Integral Nationalism*, 311–17; *AF*, October 29, 1912.
56. See Gordon Wright, *Raymond Poincaré and the French Presidency* (Stanford, Calif.: Stanford University Press, 1942).
57. *AF*, January 23, 1913.
58. Weber, *Action Française*, 121. The conservative American writer Stanton Leeds claimed that Poincaré had once, in a private conversation, summed up his impression of Bainville thus: "Like Maurras he sees clearly, but unlike Maurras and Daudet, he does not provoke controversy. This is an advantage. . . . He is above party. In the world of thought Bainville is above dispute. You will see, he will become a criterion." Stanton Leeds, *These Ruled France* (Indianapolis: Bobbs-Merrill, 1940), 146.

ly acknowledged his debt to the royalist writer, Poincaré's behavior as president was remarkably consistent with the type of executive statesmanship that Bainville was calling for in his daily articles. But Bainville's high hopes that the new leader would provide a welcome antidote to republican weakness and mismanagement were disappointed within a year of Poincaré's election. The new leader had promptly begun to "squander the greatest amount of authority that public favor has put in the hands of a politician for a long time." After the fashion of an earlier aspirant to executive power, Bainville complained, "this civilian Boulanger is losing precious time, every day using up a little more of the credit and prestige with which he is doing nothing."[59]

Bainville attributed Poincaré's disillusioning performance to the interplay of two incompatible instincts in the mentality of the new president, a personal conflict which he described metaphorically as "the dialogue carried on between the eternal Don Quixote and the eternal squire":

> You have the power, the prestige, the popularity, use it, suggests Don Quixote—Don't risk them in a brawl, replies Sancho—Dissolution, revision of the constitution, we will cut a grand figure before the country and before history by resorting to heroic means, advised chivalry. And prudence immediately retorted: Try for an accommodation, a deal, instead. Temporize, experiment with a Briand ministry, a Barthou ministry, try one and then another.

Poincaré, the patriotic son of the lost province who recognized the necessity for a strong executive and an imaginative, vigilant foreign policy, was inhibited by Poincaré, the loyal servant of parliamentary democracy. By refusing to break with the republican tradition, Bainville lamented, this latter-day Boulanger was betraying the trust of those supporters who had awaited his election with anticipation.[60]

For his own part the new president was careful to maintain a certain distance from his potential supporters in the royalist movement. He had kind words for the "patient work of the ancient

59. Jacques Bainville, *Esquisses et portraits* (Paris: Wittmann, 1946), 17. This selection was written in 1913.
60. *Ibid.*

monarchy" in centralizing the French state, and observed that the Republic had merely appropriated the results of that beneficent policy. He even went so far as to discuss with equanimity the pros and cons of the monarchical form of government and candidly expressed his reservations about certain aspects of the democratic system. He severely criticized the notion that public opinion deserved a voice in the formation of foreign policy, suggesting that the Russian alliance would have been blocked for domestic political reasons had the president publicized the preliminary negotiations. But in the end he remained securely wedded to the republican tradition, concluding that "in any case, we shall not return to the past; the bygone centuries are dead, and we have to live in the present."[61] He was satisfied to operate within the framework of the existing system, despite the limitations that it imposed upon the independence of the chief executive.

But Poincaré was nonetheless viewed with increasing suspicion by the French left. The Socialist Party hastened to denounce the belligerent turn in French foreign policy after 1912, particularly since it was directed at the nation in which its ideological allies, the German Social Democrats, had recently become the largest political party. The Socialists' dissatisfaction with the rightward drift of French diplomacy reached its apex during the campaign for the three-year law of military service in 1913. In that year Marcel Sembat, one of the party's parliamentary leaders, published a book entitled *Faites un roi, sinon, faites la paix* ("either make peace or bring back the king"), in which he bluntly accused the "nationalist" republicans associated with Poincaré of conducting a foreign policy that was indistinguishable from that advocated by the royalists. The old revolutionary doctrine of the "Universal World Republic," he observed, was rapidly giving way to new sentiment for "a nationalist, militarist, and warlike republic."[62]

Sembat denounced the Triple Entente, especially the Russian

61. Raymond Poincaré, *How France is Governed*, trans. Bernard Miall (London: Unwin, 1913), 93, 130, 181–82.
62. Marcel Sembat, *Faites un roi, sinon, faites la paix* (Paris: Figuière, 1913), xi, 63. See also Tannenbaum, *Action Française*, 142.

connection, as both a provocation against Germany and a repudiation of republican principles. He called for the revival of the
Hanotaux-Caillaux policy of Franco-German rapprochement,
which he defended as the surest road to European peace. The dilemma that the French government now faced, Sembat announced,
was whether to continue pursuing the policy of the Action Française by maintaining a belligerent posture toward Germany or to
return to the revered republican ideals of peace, brotherhood, and
international cooperation. The choice was between the perpetua-
tion of a strident nationalism that played into the hands of the
Maurrassians or the advent of a genuine republican internationalism.[63]

This evolution of French foreign policy away from the pacific
program advocated by the Socialists and the Caillaux branch of the
Radical party was temporarily interrupted in the last prewar elections held in the spring of 1914. The voters had returned a majority
to the Chamber of Deputies that was committed to the reduction of
the term of military service and a more flexible policy toward Germany. Bainville was so alarmed at this public repudiation of the
vigilant defense policy which he had been advocating (and Poincaré had been pursuing) that he accepted Daudet's invitation to
accompany him on a speaking tour of the provinces to drum up
public resistance to the strategy of détente.

Such an undertaking represented a major departure from previous practice. Bainville's hatred of crowds and public speaking
was well known among his colleagues in the movement, and his
passion for privacy was usually respected. Aside from his lectures
at the Institute, he was seldom asked to participate in the public
activities of the League and was scarcely ever mentioned in the
daily reports of the police informers. But the combination of the
increase in pacifist sentiment in France and the impending menace
of German aggression forced him to overcome his reticence. He

63. Sembat, *Faites un roi*, xiii, 75ff., 212–13, 262. See Osgood, *French Royalism Since 1870*, 24, and Tannenbaum, *Action Française*, 140–42 for discussions of the similarity between the foreign policy goals of the royalist movement and the activities of the conservative republican governments after 1912.

traveled with Daudet from city to city repeating his warning that the policies of the Radical Republicans and their Socialist friends were gravely endangering French security, marshalling historical analogies and arguments to support his claims.[64]

Daudet later described Bainville's daily address in the provinces as "less a speech than a rigorous demonstration" of the danger that awaited France if she lowered her guard. Nor could Daudet help but notice the marked difference in style between himself and his less bombastic colleague. "Coming after him, with my hodge podge of [warnings about] Boche spies and plots," Daudet observed in a rare expression of self-deprecation, "I seemed like a bear adding his explanations to those of a professor from the Collège de France."[65] The two illusory ideas that Bainville strove to refute on this speaking tour were the French liberals' optimistic faith in the power of reason as a restraining influence on the German policymakers and the Socialists' conviction that their German equivalents would prevent the Kaiser from launching a war of aggression.

In a series of prophetic articles published in July 1913,[66] after the Socialist deputies in the Reichstag had supported an increase in the defense budget, Bainville had predicted that a future war between France and Germany would receive the unconditional support of the German Socialists. "Monarchist or collectivist," he had warned eight years earlier, "Germany will not change its nature," and its nature is to detest France.[67] He was afforded the opportunity to repeat this warning at a public gathering in Nantes, when a Socialist in the audience loudly proclaimed that the German Social Democratic party (SPD) had the Kaiser in the palm of its hand. Later in the same evening, during a gourmet meal at an inn on the Loire which featured the finest wine and cuisine of La Touraine, Bain-

64. Interview with Madame Jacques Bainville; Linville, "Jacques Bainville," 114; Daudet, in *AF*, July 11, 1915.
65. Léon Daudet, *Souvenirs des milieux littéraires, politiques, artistiques, et médicaux* (Paris: Nouvelle Librairie Nationale, 1926), 311ff.
66. See in particular *AF*, July 1 and 3, 1913.
67. Jean-Marie Carré, *Les Ecrivains français et le mirage allemand* (Paris: Bouvin, 1947), 144; Bainville, *Journal*, I, January 22, 1906.

ville remarked that while he and Daudet enjoyed the produce of the fertile French countryside, some penniless German peasant was "drinking a glass of sour beer and chewing a tough sausage. Six million men, armed and destitute, live some five or six hundred kilometers from this repast. Such a situation cannot last."[68] The pressure of Germany's excess population against her inadequate food supply would rapidly destroy the hopes for either proletarian solidarity or the brotherhood of man. And *la douce France* would be the loser for it.

The plausibility of Bainville's ominous prophecies was strengthened by his serene air of certainty, punctuated by his morose sense of the repetition of historical tragedy. He conveyed the impression of a perceptive historian experiencing *déjà vu*, a clairvoyant whose grasp of the recurrent patterns of historical development empowered him to predict the future. Even the most fortuitous of events appeared to fit into a vast historical continuum leading toward doom. When the news of the assassination of the editor of *Le Figaro* by Joseph Caillaux's wife in March 1914 reached the newsroom of the *Action française*, Bainville's mind raced back to an analogous occurrence prior to the war of 1870. He looked at his colleagues, lowered his head, and murmured laconically: "Victor Noir." This reference to the pseudonym of the journalist who was shot by Prince Pierre Bonaparte, a cousin of the Emperor, six months before the outbreak of the Franco-Prussian War, reflected Bainville's fear that Madame Caillaux's evil deed was an analogous omen of disaster.[69]

In a speech in Bordeaux on June 20, 1914, eight days before the assassination in Serajevo, Bainville's pessimism about the international situation reached its peak. Only two currents of opinion remained in Germany, he warned. "There are those who are content to eat the French artichoke leaf by leaf," wresting debilitating concessions from fainthearted French leaders through diplomatic pressure, such as the acquisition of French territory in Africa after

68. Daudet, *Vers le Roi*, 262 and *Ecrivains et artistes* (Paris: Editions du Capitole, 1927), 98–100.
69. Daudet, *Souvenirs*, 339.

the Agadir crisis. And there are "those who want to consume it in one gulp" by means of military aggression. He noted that the proponents of the latter strategy were rapidly gaining control.[70]

But despite his pessimism, Bainville scarcely relished his role as a Cassandra. "It is not always agreeable to be right," he remarked. "It is particularly cruel to be right against [the popular opinion in] one's country."[71] It was probably in the interests of national morale that he avoided indulging in the expression of self-congratulation that may have been his due as his predictions of a Franco-German confrontation came true in the summer of 1914.

70. Bainville, *Journal inédit: 1914* (Paris: Plon, 1953), August 1–2, 1914.
71. Bainville, *Le Coup d'Agadir*, 236.

CHAPTER FOUR

The Sacred Union,
1914–1918

For six years I have been writing . . . that the division of Europe into two
camps armed to the teeth, one of which, the Triple Alliance, constantly
resorts to intimidation, is bound to lead to the greatest European war since
the revolutionary period. Well here it is.

Bainville (August 1914)

Upon learning of the Austrian ultimatum to Serbia on July 23, 1914,
Bainville publicly urged the Quai d'Orsay to pressure Belgrade
into accepting its terms. A Pan-Slavist crusade against an Austrian
Empire whose existence he deemed essential to European equilibrium hardly seemed worthy of French support, particularly in
view of the risks involved. As the Balkan situation deteriorated
throughout the remainder of the month of July, Bainville's response
was initially one of bitterness toward French diplomatic mismanagement rather than patriotic fulminations against the Central
Powers:

> What madness it was to believe that a Europe composed of two alliances
> of formidably armed powers furnished a solid basis of peace! It appears
> today, and perhaps too late, that the balance of power between the Triple
> Entente and the Triple Alliance was nothing but a word, a word that
> concealed the real situation, a word which the ministers and orators of
> the Republican government have dangerously abused.[1]

But the simultaneous mobilization of the French and German armies on August 1 compelled Bainville to bury his recriminations
and regrets. Thenceforth, he remained an unswerving supporter
of his government's belligerent posture toward the Central Powers.

1. *AF*, July 25, 1914; Bainville, *Journal*, I, July 27, 1914.

Though hardly at the most opportune moment, the time to settle accounts with the Hohenzollern Empire had arrived.

The advent of the Great War came as no surprise to Bainville, who had been heralding the inevitability of armed conflict between the two belligerents of 1870 since the turn of the century. But what did take him unawares was the rapidity with which the parties of the French left jettisoned their pacifist program to become loyal members of the *union sacrée*. Equally as surprising (and encouraging) was the effectiveness with which the republican government, led by the former Socialist René Viviani, took the precautions that were necessary to forestall the execution of the German war plan for a lightning victory in the west.

Bainville had long despaired of the ability of the parliamentary regimes of the western alliance to contend with the military might, diplomatic skill, and domestic unity of the autocratic empires of Germany and Austria. As late as April 1914 he was expressing grave misgivings about France's ability to count on the British Liberal government to sustain the *entente cordiale* were Germany to put it to the ultimate test. "Throughout history, and whatever the appearances, a party is always controlled by its origins," he declared. "The men that it brings together always share the same fund of ideas, the same intellectual tendencies, the same instincts, the same reactions."[2] If Gladstone could remain idle while Prussia decimated France in the summer of 1870, could not his ideological heir, Asquith, be expected to do the same in the summer of 1914?

The royalist writer gloomily recalled Metternich's memorable declaration: "I have no fear of an alliance between two liberal administrations," which he took to mean that such a coalition was incapable of coordinating defense policy owing to political interference from parliament, press, and people. He fully expected to witness a Socialist-led general strike to prevent mobilization and parliamentary attempts to forestall the provision of war credits. Learning of Jaurès's assassination on the evening of July 31, he

2. *AF,* April 13, 1914.

worried that sympathy for the felled tribune of the workers would produce a domestic revolution in France. "Are we going to see a Commune before the war?" he asked in desperation. "Will the enemy have this satisfaction?" As late as December, when the French government returned from its temporary flight to Bordeaux, he still wondered whether the future would bring "interpellations, speeches, parliamentary maneuvers, or whether, as in the Reichstag, they [the deputies] will be content to vote the credits requested by the government."[3]

But events had by then dispelled Bainville's worst fears of domestic subversion. At the beginning of August he was already recording in his diary his delight at having been proved wrong this time. He hailed the "enthusiastic reconciliation, the communion of all parties," and noted with satisfaction that "the antimilitarists of yesterday are the first to ask for a rifle." The most pleasant surprise of all was the sudden metamorphosis of the French and English left, two groups which he had expected to undermine the war effort. The patriotic, indeed jingoist, stance of the leftist parties led him to conclude that democracy was susceptible to transformation through the influence of an external threat. He became convinced that the German menace alone was capable of lifting the French political system out of the swamp of anarchy and pacifism. Temporarily suspending his skepticism about the ability of a democratic government to wage war, he conceded that "present events will change many points of view."[4]

He did not hesitate to exploit the unexpectedly swift British intervention for his own ideological purposes. Through the multilateral guarantee of Belgian neutrality in 1839, Bainville argued, the July Monarchy had "saved the France of 1914" by ensuring the entry of "Radical and pacifist England" into the war.[5] The Anglo-French entente, he never ceased to remind his readers, was also a

3. Bainville, *Journal inédit: 1914*, introduction, 9; December 16, 1914.
4. Bainville, *Journal inédit: 1914*; August 5, 1914; August 7, 1914; August 9, 1914. See also Jacques Bainville, *Angleterre*, ii.
5. Bainville, *Journal*, I, October 13, 1914.

product of royal foresight and was sustained in spite of public opposition.[6] But such a policy had not been accomplished without difficulty. As he had sadly remarked so many times before, the English Liberals' preoccupation with such domestic issues as Irish home rule and fiscal reform had blinded them to the growing German threat, and their "Puritan" prejudices caused them to disdain their Catholic ally across the Channel.[7]

It was one thing to account for "Radical, pacifist" England's laudable performance in the early months of the Great War; she, after all, had a hereditary monarch to guide her and curb her political excesses. It was much more difficult for Bainville to furnish a plausible monarchist explanation for his own country's prompt and effective response to the German declaration of war; for France had been without the services of a monarchical guiding hand for sixty-six years. Nor was it an easy matter to explain why the deep ideological fissures that had crippled French political life since the Dreyfus Affair had instantaneously disappeared in the summer of 1914, enabling the Viviani government to herd the orthodox Marxist Jules Guesde and the fanatical antimilitarist Gustave Hervé into the same corral with royalists and conservative nationalists. Taking this development as unexpected but welcome testimony to the strength of French patriotism, Bainville later accepted with equanimity the entrance of Socialists and former pacifists into the wartime cabinet, interpreting it as a guarantee against the outbreak of a crippling domestic insurrection such as France suffered during her last war with Germany.[8]

The Action Française declared an immediate armistice in its political campaign against the republican government, and the bulk of the movement's leadership rallied to the colors. Bainville was

6. This view was generally supported by Paul Cambon, the French ambassador to London during the entente negotiations. London *Times*, December 22, 1920.

7. *AF*, April 13, 1914. France was also immersed in domestic squabbles during the first six months of 1914. Eugen Weber remarks that Bainville was one of the few Frenchmen who recognized the absurdity of this preoccupation with internal affairs (such as the proposed income tax) in a period of mounting international tensions. Weber, *The Nationalist Revival in France*, 122.

8. Bainville, *Journal inédit: 1914*, August 28, 1914.

proud of the contribution to the national cause of those very royalists who had been warning of the imminence of war and urging the necessary precautions. On the anniversary of the French defeat at Sedan (September 1), he observed that "for the fourth time in a century, the foreigner has invaded France, and this year is the centenary of 1814. The French people will not be able to avoid learning the terrible lesson. Those who had already learned it, those who knew that it was democracy and the principles of the Revolution that led us to defeat, have been the first to march."[9]

As for Bainville himself, a recurrent heart ailment rendered him exempt from service.[10] Experiencing understandable guilt feelings at not serving beside the defenders of Paris, he proceeded to demonstrate that his loyalty to the fatherland outweighed his distaste for its political regime. After returning from a two-week retreat in Bordeaux, to which he and other Parisian journalists had fled (along with the government) in the first week of September to escape the anticipated German assault on the capital city, he immediately placed his pen at the service of the national cause. His wartime articles in the *Action française* and other journals were conspicuously lacking in the mordant political criticism that had informed his writings in the prewar years, a change that reflected not only the success of wartime censorship but also his desire to support the war effort.[11] These articles were models of patriotic, anti-German propaganda, whose moderate tone and polished

9. See Osgood, *French Royalism Since 1870*, 96–97, and Tannenbaum, *Action Française*, 145–49; Bainville, *Journal inédit: 1914*, September 1, 1914. For a list of the leading members of the movement who served, see Louis Rambert, *L'Action Française pendant la guerre* (Paris: L'Action Française, 1919), 47–48.

10. Interview with Madame Jacques Bainville and Hervé Bainville. Ernest Renauld also attributes his exemption to a foot injury. Ernest Renauld, *L'Action Française contre L'Eglise Catholique et contre la monarchie* (Paris: Tolra, 1936), 188. See also François Leger, "Le Dessein de Jacques Bainville," *L'Ordre française* (November, 1964), 48.

11. Bainville, *Journal inédit: 1914*, September 18, 1914; September 7 and 22, 1914. Bainville was eventually mobilized in the auxiliary service in February 1915 and worked for a few weeks in a hospital behind the lines. But his cardiac problems led to his demobilization on March 5 of the same year. Interview with Madame Jacques Bainville and Hervé Bainville; Leger, "Le Dessein de Jacques Bainville," 48. For a collection of wartime articles by Bainville, Maurras, and Daudet during the first two

style set them apart from the jingoist fulminations that were emanating not only from his less restrained colleagues at the Action
Française, but also from republican historians such as Ernest Lavisse and Alphonse Aulard.[12]

But this new policy of support for the Republic did not prevent
him from viewing the events following the declaration of war as
symptoms of the bankruptcy of democracy. He crowed at the
weakening of liberal principles and the reinforcement of the principle of authoritarian leadership in the heat of combat. "The hour
of the *chef unique* has arrived," he announced as the French armies
prepared for the First Battle of the Marne. He scanned the ranks of
the republican politicians for a potential leader strong enough to
serve as the organizer of victory. First he favored Viviani, and later
Millerand. The latter he briefly hailed as a new "Carnot."[13] But he
could never quite swallow the notion of two former Socialists at the
helm and soon began to revive his dormant royalist hopes. The
unavailability of the French pretender forced him to look else-
where. He noted with what can only be described as wishful thinking that people everywhere were hailing King Albert of Belgium as
"consul, protector, or adviser" of the French Republic, and that
many Frenchmen were seriously considering the possibility of installing him on the throne of Louis Philippe.[14]

It was a great source of satisfaction to Bainville to learn that the

---

years of the war, see Jacques Bainville, *La Presse et la guerre: choix d'articles* (Paris:
Bloud et Gay, 1915). His public statements did not reflect his private misgivings
about the strategy and tactics of the French government during the war. He privately criticized the cabinet for deficiencies in the production and distribution of
clothing, equipment, and weapons to the soldiers on the front, and for having
ignored the warnings of diplomats such as Jules Cambon about the progress of the
war party in Germany. He attributed this latter blindness not only to the ineptitude
of the politicians, but also to the *"ignorantia democratica"* of the voters, whose "mind
is naturally limited to the preoccupations of their *métier*, of their town or village."
Bainville, *Journal inédit: 1914*, November 30, 1914.

12. See Harry Elmer Barnes, *A History of Historical Writing* (2nd rev. ed.; New
York: Dover Publications, 1962), 278ff., and Georges Demartial, *La Guerre de 1914:
Comment on mobilisa les consciences* (Paris: Editions des Cahiers Internationaux, 1922).

13. Bainville, *Journal inédit: 1914*, September 10, 1914; Bainville, *Angleterre*, iii.

14. Bainville, *Journal inédit: 1914*, September 15, November 15, 1914.

liberal infatuation with Germany was an early casualty of the war. He savored the irony of the report that the rue de l'Humanité in Armentières had been put to the torch by "the bearers of Kultur" who had been lionized by the liberal writers of the nineteenth century. Frenchmen would soon witness the spectacle of German soldiers marching down the various rues Michelet that several French cities had named in honor of the French historian who had once exclaimed: "May God permit us to see a greater Germany!"[15]

As the months of stalemate warfare wore on, mocking the confident predictions of many liberals that the *poilus* would be home in time to celebrate Christmas because mankind would not support a long, bloody war, Bainville could realize how perceptive was his observation at the beginning of hostilities: "It took a war of thirty years to subdue the Germany of yesteryear. How can we hope to defeat in a few months an Empire that is much better prepared for war than any other modern state?" Along with liberalism's faith in the decency of humanity, the Marxist illusion of the international peace that was to result from the simultaneous revolution in all industrial countries was dispelled in the autumn of 1914. Bainville had long considered this doctrine intrinsically flawed because Marxism contained two irreconcilable principles: the belief in the predominance of material interests and the doctrine of the international brotherhood of the proletariat. Marx's "workers of the world, unite" had become "workers of the world, shoot each other," he observed, because the material interests of the German proletariat collided with those of the French working class.[16]

Bainville's accurate predictions of Germany's bellicose intentions and their terrible consequences rapidly earned for him a reputation of clairvoyance in foreign affairs. The lucid wartime articles that appeared in his daily column attracted the attention of readers of all political persuasions. His growing reputation for sagacity set the stage for the extraordinary popularity of the historical essays that

15. *Ibid.*, December 29, 1914.
16. *Ibid.*, September 14; December 31, 1914; August 29, 1914; and *AF*, November 17, 1914.

he produced during the war years. The first of these, *L'Histoire de deux peuples*, which appeared in 1915, comprised the lectures on the origins of German unity that he had delivered at the Action Française Institute. The public appeal of this work derived from the simple, if not simplistic, explanation it offered for the historical causes of the present holocaust. It expanded on the general themes that underlay his two earlier studies of Ludwig II and Bismarck. But whereas these earlier pieces were modest monographic forays into particular episodes in recent German history, his wartime work was a vast synthesis of three hundred pages which recapitulated the historical interrelationship of the two hereditary enemies from Gallo-Roman times to the present. The book also represented Bainville's first major effort to peddle oversimplified but plausible historical explanations as a means of disseminating the royalist critique of democracy in the guise of serious historical analysis. Barred by the censor from denouncing directly the republican system of the present, Bainville reached into the past to achieve the same result in an indirect fashion. Since it established many of the themes that were to recur continuously in his subsequent historical writings, an extensive summary and analysis of his *Histoire de deux peuples* is in order.

The central argument of the book was the historical inevitability of Franco-German conflict. This hereditary antagonism had originated in ancient Gaul, where it had already become obvious that the necessity of providing security against the Germanic hordes outweighed all other political considerations. As the Capetian monarchy began to unify and centralize the French nation during the Middle Ages, one of its principal concerns was the surveillance of the eastern frontier. The threat from England was attenuated by the Channel, which served as an effective buffer and contributed to England's penchant for isolation from continental affairs. The absence of "natural frontiers" between France and Germany, on the other hand, guaranteed a "permanent rivalry" between these two continental powers over the territory between them. "All attempted solutions, all political combinations brought into play," he reminded his wartime audience, "have failed to resolve the conflict."[17] The implication of this deterministic analysis of the problem was clear to any Frenchman in 1915: the need to establish a permanent Franco-German border at the only natural frontier, the Rhine.

Here again Bainville displayed the propensity for selectivity and oversimplification that occasionally strained the credibility of his historical writing. His preoccupation with the eternal conflict between the two Rhine powers caused him to neglect the Hundred Years War, during which the two Channel powers engaged in mutual destruction.

The ideological flavor of the study was apparent from the beginning. The source of the French state's success in its continual confrontation with German expansionism was its superior political institutions. By the late Middle Ages the Capetians had succeeded both in acquiring hereditary authority and in forging a durable alliance with the Papacy, which shared the French monarchy's interest in restraining the power of the Holy Roman Empire. Furthermore, the strength of particularism, the "infinitely diverse pieces of the German mosaic," contributed to the weakness of Germanic central authority (and to France's strength). The imperial electoral system enabled the feudal interests to preserve their independence from the Emperor, thereby preventing him from creating a unified, powerful Germany under a single scepter. Consequently, "this conspiracy of the internal and external enemies of a stable and strong [centralized] power in Germany successfully crystallized the Empire for many years in an anarchy with a pompous appearance."[18]

Bainville credited the authors of the Treaty of Westphalia, "the model for any serious and durable treaty with the Germanic countries," with having institutionalized this structural weakness of the Germanic Empire in order to enhance the security of France and the rest of Europe. The political and territorial divisions dictated by that treaty guaranteed a continuation of the internecine rivalries that prevented the unification of the German lands under Habs-

---

17. Bainville, *Histoire de deux peuples*, 11–14.
18. *Ibid.*, 21ff., 45.

burg auspices. He recalled with great satisfaction that cartographers in the seventeenth century "did not have enough colors to distinguish all those little territories from one another." The electoral principle permitted the French monarchy to influence the imperial succession by withholding and granting favors to the various feudal electors. The Imperial Diet limited the independence of the Emperor by reproducing "all the territorial, political, and religious divisions of Germany and heating them up in a closed vase." Finally, the resolve of Sweden (which played the role assumed by Russia in the modern world) and France to erect an effective barrier to German expansionism on two fronts preserved the balance of power in Europe.[19]

Bainville credited the diplomatic foresight of Richelieu and his pupil Mazarin with having enabled Louis XIV to inherit a kingdom that supervised a French-dominated Europe. But unlike Germany after 1871, which sought to exercise hegemony through intimidation, the France of the Sun King proceeded to extend its influence by "persuasion" and peaceful means. France became the regulator of European affairs during the seventeenth century by virtue of the "seductive force of our ideas and customs," Bainville declared, conveniently forgetting the role played by the marauding French troops in Western Germany during the Thirty Years War in the extension of French "influence." By the middle of his reign, Louis XIV recognized that the Prussian Hohenzollerns were rapidly becoming the principal threat to European stability at the very moment that the Habsburgs were abandoning all hopes of presiding over a united Germany. Through his royal "clairvoyance," the Sun King had "left France warned of a new peril."[20]

Louis XV continued the realistic policy of his illustrious predecessor, moving closer to the Holy Roman Empire while maintaining a safe distance from the parvenu monarchy to the north. Unfortunately, public opinion compelled the French monarch to acquiesce in Prussia's "rape of Silesia" in the winter of 1740–1741 and to reward that transgression with the offer of an alliance. This self-

19. *Ibid.*, 82ff., 89.
20. *Ibid.*, 110, 112, 120, 140.

defeating behavior reflected the influence of the Parisian publicists who execrated Catholic Austria and adored Frederick the Great, "the idol of liberal minds," the enlightened despot who justified his acquisition of territory as Prussia's "natural right." French public opinion, formed by the habitués of Parisian salons, was ignorant, rooted in tradition, incapable of recognizing that changed circumstances had produced a new menace to French security. Whereas the vigilant monarchy perceived that "the threat had begun to emanate from Berlin," the masses "continued to see it in Vienna."[21]

The assertion that public sentiment determined the course of French foreign policy under a regime which had no representative assembly to contend with and could (and did) muzzle the press at will was historically inaccurate. It also was another instance of Bainville's tendency to apply concepts appropriate to the twentieth century to events of the eighteenth, as though nothing had transpired in the interim.

In this same vein, Bainville defended the Bourbon monarchy's détente with Austria in 1756 as the triumph of royal realism over popular sentimentality, which favored Prussia over Austria for ideological reasons. But the royal house of France was to pay dearly for its courageous action. Totally ignoring the social and economic causes of the French Revolution, Bainville contended that it was that wise but unpopular diplomatic reversal of 1756 that was responsible for generating the public resentment against the monarchy which culminated in the social upheavals of 1789–1793. By portraying the French monarchy's pro-Austrian posture as a "betrayal" of the liberal principles of the Enlightenment (personified by Frederick the Great) in favor of "clericalism and reaction" (represented by the House of Habsburg), Parisian publicists had fanned the flames of popular discontent that eventually dethroned Louis XVI and his Habsburg spouse. The attempt by the innovative, pragmatic, and flexible monarchy to adapt the Westphalian policy to "the new circumstances and requirements" of the eigh-

21. *Ibid.*, 135–37.

teenth century was misinterpreted by the ignorant populace as a conspiracy of Catholic fanaticism against the forces of enlighten-ment and progress.[22]

The French Revolution brought to power men who were imbued with this archaic preference for Prussia over Austria. As a result, the "barriers" to German unification that had been erected at West-phalia and propped up by the French monarchy in the eighteenth century were rapidly "dismantled." In this sense the Revolution was "reactionary," for it revived the anti-Habsburg policy that had been wisely abandoned by Louis XV. It is important to note here that Bainville defended the French monarchy's pro-Austrian posi-tion between 1756 and 1792 not on the basis of Catholic solidarity or monarchical legitimacy, but rather because he was convinced that Prussia posed the principal threat to French security even at that early date. He denounced the revolutionary government's re-pudiation of the Austrian connection and subsequent declaration of war on the Empire in 1792 as an ideologically-inspired policy that was inimical to the French national interest. He characteris-tically relied on analogical reasoning to drive home his message. Imagine the potential consequences, he declared, "if a Chamber animated by subversive passions had wanted to destroy the Franco-Russian alliance in April 1914 and decreed a war of principle against autocratic Russia."[23] The mere mention of such a prospect in 1915 must have caused more than one French patriot to shudder.

For all his reservations about the foreign policy of the First Re-public, Bainville was no less hostile to that of the First Empire. In-deed, he blamed Bonaparte for pushing the dangerous policies of the Revolution to the extreme by extending the disruptive principle of national self-determination to the unstable heartland of Central Europe. A child of the Enlightenment, Napoleon saw in a Balkan-ized Germany not the "anarchical dispersion" that the peacemak-ers at Westphalia had thought necessary to continental stability, but rather the "odious remnants of feudalism" to be extirpated in the name of the revolutionary principle. By his "brutal and immod-

22. *Ibid.*, 149, 154–55.
23. *Ibid.*, 167, 177, 189.

erate annexations," the Emperor provoked irredentist sentiment against France, which had exercised an indirect and benevolent influence on Central Europe under the Bourbons. By destroying the autonomy of the minor principalities, ecclesiastical domains, and free cities of Western and Southern Germany, he strengthened the centralizing tendencies that later produced national unity at France's expense. Most importantly, Bonaparte's destruction of the Holy Roman Empire abolished "one of the principal guarantees of French security" in the face of the rising menace of Protestant Prussia.[24]

Bainville's treatment of the Bourbon Restoration in his *Histoire de deux peuples* was a model of didactic historical writing. Viewed through his narrow ideological perspective, the post-Napoleonic regime succeeded against intense domestic opposition in rectifying all of the evils that had been inherited from the recent past. In the face of a hostile public still suffering from the delusions of grandeur fostered by Bonaparte, the French government was able to negotiate a settlement at Vienna which preserved French economic prosperity, territorial integrity, and national independence. Moreover, the legitimate sovereigns of Europe succeeded in forestalling the formation of a greater Germany under the leadership of Prussia and created an "international police force" to maintain the balance of power on the continent. Had the Concert of Europe, which restored the principle of German disunity that had been proclaimed in 1648, endured until 1871, the twin disasters of German unification and French military humiliation would never have occurred. Whatever "order, repose, and prosperity" France (and Europe at large) enjoyed in the years after 1815 would have been unthinkable without the French Bourbon regime, which reconciled *la grande nation* to its loss of empire, reintegrated her into the international system, and revived her wartorn economy.[25]

Yet it was this very policy of returning France to a situation of peace and tranquility, Bainville argued, that undermined the prestige of the monarchy in the eyes of the French public. Though

24. *Ibid.*, 197, 200–203.
25. *Ibid.*, 224, 229.

France prospered economically under the Restoration and her people enjoyed a rare period of peace, these successes failed to quench the public's thirst for glory and liberty, ideals that were associated with the memories of the Revolution and the Empire. Spurred by the writings of the Romantic poets and publicists, the Parisian mob that expelled Charles X was dreaming "less of acquiring political liberty than of resuming the revolutionary and Napoleonic foreign policy." The July Monarchy was to meet a similar fate once it began to conduct the cautious diplomacy that French national interests required at the time. Louis Philippe patiently tried to assure the autocratic empires to the east that the accession of a French monarch who sang the Marseillaise and saluted the Tricolor did not signify a revival of revolutionary interventionism. His efforts merely elicited charges from republican and Bonapartist quarters that France stood "inactive and humiliated in Europe." These allegations helped to bring about the collapse of public support for the regime.[26] The advocate of the Maurrassian maxim *politique d'abord* characteristically ignored the broader social causes of the Revolution of 1848 in order to present a purely political explanation designed to support his ideological view of the French past.

Bainville's opinion of the Second Empire resembled in many respects his evaluation of the First: even before Bismarck began to lay the groundwork for a united Germany under Hohenzollern auspices, Napoleon III had started to undermine the international political system which had been so loyally supported by the French Bourbons and Orleanists as the best means of preserving the European status quo. His Crimean expedition was the "first step" of a policy aimed at "abolishing the treaties of 1815." This policy succeeded in alienating Russia, as did the French Emperor's verbal

26. *Ibid.*, 235–37, 247. Though Louis Philippe's was a constitutional monarchy whose power was restricted by parliament, Bainville credited the king with the responsibility for these wise policies. When Prime Minister Thiers set France against the entire Concert of Europe to support the Egyptian leader Mehemet Ali, for example, Louis Philippe "saved France from a disastrous war, a Waterloo or Sedan," into which "the blindness of public opinion, aggravated by the vanity of the parliamentary leaders, . . . had precipitated it."

support for the Polish rebellion of 1863. His sponsorship of Italian unification, together with his benevolent neutrality during Prussia's lightning military victory of 1866, contributed to the displacement of Austria as a counterweight to Prussian power in Central Europe. As a result of these military and diplomatic blunders, Prussia was able to face a France that was isolated and vulnerable in a Europe whose traditional balance of power had been upset with French acquiescence. But France's effort to recover from the third invasion that she had suffered in sixty years was doomed to fall far short of her successes at Vienna. When the Duc de Broglie left for the Conference of London after Sedan, this latter-day Talleyrand intended to "achieve for France through diplomatic means what she had lost in war." He failed, Bainville noted, because, unlike Talleyrand, he had no Louis XVIII waiting in the wings.[27]

The date 1870 represented for Bainville a critical turning point in European history, for it signified the "advent of international anarchy." The carefully constructed system of international safeguards and reciprocal guarantees that had been devised at Westphalia, readjusted and updated at Vienna, and supported by the French monarchy in the first half of the nineteenth century, had collapsed before the rising tides of "national egoism." The lessons of the past had been ignored and the valuable services rendered to France by her forty kings went unrecognized by the modern world. "It is the mistakes of our fathers that are killing us today," Bainville proclaimed to the generation in the trenches. In October 1915 he learned of an event that struck him as the perfect symbol of this tragic legacy: the death in battle of a Lieutenant Gladstone, the grandson of the man who had masterminded Britain's neutrality while Bismarck created German unity over the battered body of France in 1870–1871.[28]

The commercial success of *L'Histoire de deux peuples* established Bainville's reputation as a popular historian of the first order. Moreover, as Ernst Nolte has observed, the book "contributed almost

27. *Ibid.*, 264–76, 284.
28. *Ibid.*, 281, 278; Bainville, *Journal*, I, October 15, 1915.

more than any other work to the undermining of the revolutionary-
democratic-socialist viewpoint and to the strengthening of the conviction that the dismemberment and impotence of Germany were
indispensable to France's peace and greatness."[29] But it understandably marked him as an object of derision in the eyes of the
professional historians in the republican university, who could
hardly have been expected to ignore a historical best seller which
attributed France's wartime agony to the absence of a monarchical
guiding hand. An official reply was unmistakably called for, and
appeared in early 1917. Albert Mathiez, erstwhile disciple of the
distinguished Sorbonne historian Alphonse Aulard, published a
point-by-point rejoinder to the Bainvillian thesis regarding the historical antagonism of France and Germany. After acknowledging
that the "lively and alert style" of the work had achieved for it a
great literary success, he proceeded to dismiss its claim to the title
of a serious contribution to historical scholarship. Ignoring its manifest methodological deficiencies (save a contemptuous reference to
the author's exclusive reliance on secondary sources), Mathiez preferred to dwell on its narrow, ideological focus. Despite his attempt
to become a historian, Mathiez declared, "the author has remained
a journalist and a propagandist." He ridiculed the principal theme
of the work: the assertion that the policies of the French monarchy
had historically served the French national interest.[30]

Mathiez went on to assert that the evidence marshalled by professional historians led to precisely the opposite conclusion, namely, that the policies of the Bourbons had served to weaken France
while strengthening the power of the Germanic empires to the east.
From the reign of Louis XIV onward, the French monarchy became
less and less national and increasingly devoted to the international
interests of royalty. He chided Bainville for tempering his anti-
German ardor with a tenderness for Austria (also an enemy of
France in 1915), a predilection which caused him to underestimate
the continual menace posed by the Habsburg monarchy. Moreover,

---

29. Nolte, *Three Faces of Fascism*, 73. For the number of printed copies of *L'His-*
toire de deux peuples, see Appendix below.
30. Albert Mathiez, *La Monarchie et la politique nationale* (Paris: Alcan, 1917), 1–2.

Bainville was wrong to defend the Congress of Vienna from the standpoint of French national interest. Had it not delivered the Rhineland to Prussia, thereby exposing France to invasion? The academic historian concluded his polemical response to Bainville's royalist apologia with the ringing plea: "If you want Victory, support the Republic!"[31]

Bainville's only public rejoinder to Mathiez's criticism appeared during the preliminary negotiations between the new Russian Bolshevik government and the German high command at Brest-Litovsk in December 1917. He reciprocated the republican historian's indictment brickbat for brickbat. By focussing on the alleged "pedantry" of the academic historical profession, he was reaching for the same sensitive nerve that had been touched by prewar critics such as Charles Péguy, Pierre Lasserre, and Henri Massis. He patronizingly observed that his recent book had been unfavorably received by "a professor who has been initiated into the philosophy of history by research in the various domiciles of Robespierre." He noted that Mathiez's principal objection to his work concerned its emphasis on European revolutionaries' tendency "to regard Prussia as a 'natural ally'," a tendency which Bainville had described as a manifestation of the historical mutuality of interests between the forces of revolution and German autocracy. What better confirmation of that theory could there be, he asked, than the present spectacle of Russian Marxists and German imperialists negotiating a separate peace at France's expense? Such an oversimplification of the Brest-Litovsk discussions again served the function of lending credence to the conception of a continuous, interconnected chain of historical events with a logic of its own, linking eighteenth-century liberals to the Bolsheviks, Frederick the Great to William II.[32]

Mathiez's effort to identify the republican tradition with the de-

---

31. *Ibid.*, 8–9, 14–15, 25–29, 33, 37–38, 77–81, 100.
32. See Charles Péguy, "De la situation faite à l'histoire et à la sociologie dans les temps modernes," *Cahiers de la quinzaine*, 8th ser. (1906), 11–14; Pierre Lasserre, *La Doctrine officielle de l'université* (Paris: Mercure de France, 1912); Henri Massis and Alfred de Tarde (pseud. Agathon), *L'Esprit de la Nouvelle Sorbonne* (Paris: Mercure de France, 1911). See also *AF*, December 21, 1917.

fense of the Fatherland was part of a general campaign on the part of the professional historians to lay to rest once and for all the old allegations of pacifism and Germanophilia that had been raised against them during the prewar years. The same members of the French academic intelligentsia who had promoted the cause of Franco-German reconciliation and international peace before 1914 executed an abrupt *volte face* after the outbreak of war. One historian later compared this development to an earlier transformation at the outbreak of the last Franco-German conflict:

> Just as in 1870 the idealists put their house in order, the pacifists recognized their error, and those "Sorbonnards" whom Péguy, in a fit of anger, had unjustly labelled Pan-Germanists, those good and honest men with their utopian rectitude and limited clairvoyance, torn apart and upset, cast all of their work . . . into the abyss . . . in the service of the Fatherland.[33]

Noted academic historians in France, as we have seen, took pains to demonstrate the sincerity of their newly discovered hatred of everything German and glorification of everything French. The old ideal of the United States of Europe, the Kantian reveries of universal peace, the fond hopes for détente with Germany, were consigned to the dustbin of dispelled illusions, where they remained until they were later to be revived in the midtwenties.

In the meantime Bainville's vigorous defense of the cause of French patriotism, together with his condemnation of Germany's historical role in the world, won him a large circle of admirers in war-torn France. Most of these were willing to forgive him his royalism. He began to receive solicitations for contributions to newspapers and periodicals that had never been well disposed to the ideology of the Action Française. His wartime analyses of the Italian intervention and the Mexican Revolution were published in the eminently respectable *Revue des deux mondes*, an honor that had eluded even Maurras himself.[34]

Bainville's mounting prestige in journalistic circles outside the

---

33. Carré, *Les Ecrivains français*, 147.
34. See *Revue des deux mondes*, XXIX (1915), 559–88; XXXIV (1916), 778–815; XXXVII (1917), 622–39; and XXXVIII (1917), 869–94.

royalist movement precipitated occasional outbursts of resentment from within. The Sûreté's informer at *Action française* headquarters reported that Bainville, for a variety of reasons, seriously considered breaking with the movement during the war. The commercial success of his *Histoire de deux peuples*, his frequent collaboration with nonroyalist journals, and the financial rewards that resulted from these endeavors progressively lessened his dependence on the movement for fame and fortune. Moreover, as a confirmed anticlerical, Bainville occasionally quarrelled with Maurras (though never publicly) over the latter's enthusiastic (if agnostic) Papism. Maurras, in turn, had expressed irritation at Bainville's tolerant attitude toward various republican statesmen.[35]

But perhaps the most compelling reason for the younger writer's restlessness, according to the police informer, was the sense that his prospects for personal advancement were being thwarted by a movement from which he had little more to gain. He was now mature enough to abandon whatever hopes he may have harbored of becoming minister of foreign affairs under a restored Philip VIII. Unwilling to spend the rest of his life in Maurras's shadow promoting a lost cause, he eagerly sought an escape route. Sensing their colleague's dissatisfaction, Maurras and Daudet heaped praise upon him for his recent writings. Such flattery was probably prompted, the spy speculated, by the realization that Bainville was one of the few members of the royalist general staff who had acquired sufficient prestige in the eyes of Frenchmen outside the movement to enable him to launch an independent career should he choose to do so.[36] This private dispute between Bainville and his two associates was resolved by the end of 1915, largely owing to the efforts of Maurras and Daudet to keep their discontented colleague within the fold.

In any case, the doctrines formulated by Bainville in his wartime writings began to find their way into the public pronouncements of certain politicians of the Republic. In September 1915 Paul Deschanel, the president of the Chamber of Deputies, published an

35. AN, F⁷12863, "Notes sur l'Action Française," no. 5.
36. *Ibid.*

article in the *Manuel de l'instruction primaire* that surveyed the general development of French foreign policy since 1789. He observed that France had been invaded five times since abandoning her absolute monarchy (a theme reiterated *ad nauseam* in Bainville's writings) and conceded that she had made a grave mistake in remaining inactive during Germany's march toward national unification between 1864 and 1871 (another Bainvillian theme). Deschanel urged French schoolteachers to remind their students of the "clever, prescient policy of the ancient monarchy" that had kept Germany divided and weak and protected the smaller German states against the encroachments of Prussia. Ferdinand Buisson, the editor of the *Manuel* and the universally acknowledged authority on French primary education, endorsed these instructions, thereby placing the imprimatur of the academic establishment on this striking piece of historical revisionism.[37]

In a tongue-in-cheek article playfully entitled "Un Accord National: Buisson, Deschanel, et Bainville," Maurras enthusiastically endorsed his former adversaries' change of heart. He speculated that the republican pedagogue and republican politician must have been converted to these sentiments by Bainville's *Histoire de deux peuples*. The royalist Institute had long been teaching this realist method of diplomatic history, and any student (or professor, for that matter) whom the state university might wish to send to the Action Française would be welcomed with open arms and given the same lessons in "intellectual patriotism" that the royalist youth had received. Maurras wondered whether Deschanel's allegation that the historical facts of the defeat of 1870 had been "artfully and artificially covered over by a wave of self-serving lies" constituted a veiled indictment of the late Gabriel Monod, founder of the *Revue historique* and frequent object of Maurras's scorn.[38]

The royalist movement's attempt to take credit for the increasingly bellicose character of the successive wartime cabinets continued unabated for the balance of the war. When Denys Cochin, an avowed royalist who joined the government in the fall of 1915,

37. *Ibid.* See also Havard de la Montagne, *Histoire de l'Action Française*, 91.
38. *AF*, September 21, 1915.

was dispatched to Greece to gather information about the deteriorating Balkan front, Maurras saw this as further evidence that the republican leadership was heeding the advice and tapping the resources of the royalist movement to formulate its war policy.[39]

But the most dramatic instance of the government's willingness to rely on the royalists came at the beginning of the following year. In early January Premier Aristide Briand expressed to his private secretary his dissatisfaction with the confusing reports on the domestic situation in Russia that he had been receiving through normal diplomatic channels. He wondered aloud whether there existed a well-informed private citizen who could be entrusted with a fact-finding mission to probe the internal difficulties of the eastern ally. The secretary, who had met Bainville while the latter was covering the Quai d'Orsay before the war, suggested the royalist writer as the perfect man for the job, his unacceptable political views notwithstanding. If the royalist Cochin could be sent to observe the collapsing front in the south, could not Bainville be trusted to report on the problems in the east?

Though Briand was a determined enemy of the Action Française, he read Bainville's column daily and the two often met at dinner parties given by mutual friends.[40] Bainville, for his part, nurtured a grudging admiration for the new premier ever since he had suppressed the railway workers' strike in 1910. During the early stages of the war, he had hailed Briand as the most vigorous opponent of the remnants of weak-kneed pacifism in the republican ruling elite. In any event, the former socialist lawyer summoned the royalist writer to his office and commissioned him to undertake an unofficial mission to Russia and report his findings.[41]

Bainville and his wife embarked in late January 1916 on a four-month tour of several important Russian cities, including Petrograd, Moscow, and Kiev. Armed with an official letter of intro-

---

39. AN, F⁷12863, "Notes sur l'Action Française," no. 5, and *AF*, November 22, 1915.
40. Interview with Madame Jacques Bainville; Linville, "Jacques Bainville," 258.
41. Bainville, *Journal inédit: 1914*, October 11, 1914; interviews with Madame Jacques Bainville, Charles Popin, and Hervé Bainville.

duction (though travelling in the capacity of a private citizen), he obtained audiences with several prominent Russian politicians, including Prince Lvov (who was to become the head of the Provisional Government after the March Revolution), and attended several sessions of the Duma. He returned to Paris during the failure of the Russian army's spring offensive. His publicly expressed confidence in the future of the Tsarist regime was offset by private misgivings. These he confided to the government. The false optimism was conveyed to the French public in a number of articles which he was invited to contribute to the influential *Revue des deux mondes* as part of a campaign to inspire faith in France's faltering ally.[42]

On the positive side, Bainville was highly impressed by the "spirit of moderation" displayed by the Russian liberals, who seemed willing to tone down their ideological opposition to the regime in the darkest hours of national combat. "Holy Russia found liberal Russia at its side in the war just as the 'two Frances' . . . joined forces" in the summer of 1914. He considered Nicholas II a master at making the best of a bad situation. Compelled to share power with a parliament, he won the respect of the Duma by presiding at its opening session "dressed in a simple country uniform, with a small entourage," disarming potential opponents with expressions of good will. Bainville was also pleased to report that French influence still predominated among the Russian upper classes, serving as a guarantee that "Frenchified Russia" would remain a loyal ally of France. He considered it a good sign that the two remaining bulwarks of the social order, the monarchy and the church, continued to play an important role in the war effort.[43]

42. Interview with Madame Jacques Bainville and François Leger (1970); Linville, "Jacques Bainville," 260–61. Like Mr. Linville, I have been unable to locate any official reports on Bainville's Russian mission in the archives of the Quai d'Orsay. It is possible that they were destroyed during the Second World War. Neither President Poincaré nor Ambassador Paléologue mention the visit in their memoirs or writings. Briand's papers are closed. For the first of Bainville's articles describing his Russian sojourn, see "Quatre Mois en Russie pendant la guerre," *Revue des deux mondes*, XXXIV (August 15, 1916), 778–814.

43. Jacques Bainville, *Petit Musée germanique, suivi de la Russie en 1916* (Paris: Société Littéraire de France, 1917), 272–74, 268–70, 286, 306–307.

What impressed Bainville above all was the Tsar's ability to re-
strain the excessive zeal of the Pan-Slavist movement, which enjoyed support among the liberals and had been acquiring sympathizers in the Duma. He credited Nicholas with having coaxed
Russian patriots away from the revolutionary doctrines of liberal
nationalism and Pan-Slavism, which would inevitably complicate
the postwar territorial settlement, and with having won them over
to sensible policies calculated to restore the European balance of
power. Under the watchful eyes of the Tsar, the Russian war effort
was designed to repel the onslaught of Pan-Germanism rather
than to further the interests of Pan-Slavism, which in Bainville's
eyes represented an equally repugnant doctrine.[44]

But between the lines of this generally favorable account of Russian robustness appeared faint glimmerings of alarm at the deteriorating political situation that Bainville had witnessed during his
brief sojourn. He noted that certain segments of the intelligentsia
had begun to question the wisdom of continuing the war and that
several "regrettable strikes" had occurred at the instigation of proletarian organizations. These ominous signs of social unrest reminded him of similar occurrences in the history of his own country that were "fatal to the fatherland and gave secret joy to the
enemy." He remarked that a significant segment of Russian socialism had been "Germanized through the influence of Karl Marx"
and that "people speak of revolution every day."[45] Barred from expressing in public his misgivings about the domestic situation of
the wartime ally, he offered a private evaluation that betrayed a
gloomy pessimism about the future of the Romanov dynasty. "In
six months," he confided to a friend shortly after his return in the
spring of 1916, "there will no longer be a Russian Empire."[46]

Less than a month after the March Revolution toppled the Tsar,
Bainville strove to explain to his compatriots why the ancient dynasty of France's eastern ally had collapsed so suddenly. His ac-

44. *Ibid.*, 295–301.
45. *Ibid.*, 261, 272, 292.
46. Lucien Dubech, *Les Chefs de file de la jeune génération* (Paris: Plon, 1925), 28.
See also *Candide*, April 10, 1924.

count, given wide circulation in the *Revue des deux mondes*, drew upon his personal observations as well as his knowledge of Russian history. Its conclusions marked the beginning of an important modification of his political attitudes: the growing recognition of the value of political liberalism as a potentially useful ally of a modern national monarchy. He had come to believe that the principal cause of the Romanov dynasty's precipitate downfall was its inability to retain the loyalty of the liberal majority in the Duma. And he did not hesitate to place the primary responsibility for this failure squarely upon the shoulders of the deposed ruler himself.

To buttress his argument of royal culpability, Bainville again reminded his readers that the liberal members of the Duma had postponed their demands for domestic reform once the war had broken out and had become loyal supporters of the Tsar's war policy. The war continued to enjoy widespread public and parliamentary support; indeed, "it would hardly be an exaggeration to say that it was the war of the Duma," a body "whose dominant tendency was nationalism." But the Tsar proved incapable of recognizing that Russian liberalism had been converted to the national cause. He failed to learn from the history of the monarchies of Germany and Italy, which had "renovated their traditions and broken with their conservatives," forging a *mariage de convenance* with the liberal bloc on the basis of a shared commitment to nationalism. Nicholas II had mistakenly lumped his "national liberals" together with the revolutionary socialists as threats to national security, and furnished the pretext for revolution by proroguing the Duma on March 11. The Tsar was unable to distinguish between the liberals, who were "prepared to make generous concessions" in the interests of the national cause, and the revolutionary elements, smarting from their defeat in 1905, which were "awaiting the occasion to take their revenge."[47]

Moreover, the last of the Romanovs stood condemned in Bain-

---

47. Jacques Bainville, *Comment est née la révolution russe* (Paris: Nouvelle Librairie Nationale, 1917), 23–24, 27–28, 59–61. This work was originally published in article form less than a month after the overthrow of the Tsar. See Bainville "Comment est née la révolution russe," *Revue des deux mondes* (April 15, 1917), 869–93.

ville's eyes not only of ignorance of the successful precedent set by the houses of Hohenzollern and Savoy of how to tame and co-opt the forces of liberal nationalism, but also of a failure to learn from the experience of his own ancestors. For there was ample evidence of such mutually beneficial alliances of ruler and people in Russian history. He recalled that Michael Romanov, the founder of the dynasty, had been "elected" by a popular assembly in 1613 in order to provide Russia with a leader capable of "saving her from the menace of the foreigner."[48]

But how to account for this disastrous failure of royal responsibility? The French monarchist attributed the Russian monarch's fatal misreading of popular sentiment to the nefarious influence of the imperial bureaucracy. The Tsar's counsellors and courtesans continually hampered him whenever he "displayed the slightest inclination to accommodate the legitimate demands of public opinion." Moreover, the civil service had opposed Russian intervention from the beginning because of its fear that the war would strengthen those social forces which threatened its monopoly on influence and power. The complete "absence of patriotism" among this conspirational coterie, preoccupied with protecting its "parochial interests" to the detriment of the regime, might have been detected and dealt with by a "stronger and more clairvoyant sovereign." But much of his power had by then been usurped by the imperial bureaucracy itself. Transforming itself from an administrative organism into a political institution at the expense of the monarchy, the Russian bureaucracy mistakenly accepted the dictum that "to make a counterrevolution, one must make a revolution first." And like the aristocratic rebels of 1789 in France, those Russian functionaries who managed to escape lived to regret that miscalculation.[49]

In view of the French royalists' previous analyses of the causes of political decadence in their own country, it was predictable that Bainville's quest for the source of this bureaucratic treachery in wartime Russia would lead across the German frontier. The Rus-

48. Bainville, *Comment est née*, 63.
49. *Ibid.*, 36–40, 32, 57–58.

sian civil service, established by Peter the Great as an "instrument of progress" and modernization, had fallen under the influence of the Prussian model in the nineteenth century. By the middle of the war it had become a hotbed of "German intrigues for a separate peace." Similarly, the persistence of Teutonic traditions in the foreign service and the officers' corps continued to pose serious problems for the durability of the Franco-Russian alliance. Added to these problems was the failure of the Father Tsar to retain the support of his traditional allies among the peasantry. Rural Russia had been turned against the royal house by the clergy, alienated from the regime on account of the Tsarina's relations with Rasputin. This decisive split between throne and altar explained to Bainville's satisfaction why the "peasant masses had not participated in the traditional *chouannerie* that one anticipates during a revolution."[50]

From all of this evidence Bainville concluded that the March Revolution was primarily "national" rather than "social." The Provisional Government's willingness to honor the Tsarist alliances and resume the war effort was sufficient proof that the new regime intended to preserve historical continuity. In a striking exercise in wishful thinking that bordered on outright self-deception, he viewed the advent of parliamentary rule in Russia as merely the latest repetition of the numerous "palace revolutions" that had occurred in the history of the Russian Empire. The accession of the Provisional Government constituted a return to the tradition of popular sovereignty that had been established under the "republics" of medieval Russia. Once again, Bainville's readers encountered the doctrine of historical repetition, the notion that all historical events have precedents which can help the observer to forecast their outcome. But the March Revolution did display one novel characteristic that represented a possible cause for concern. Unlike its precursors, "the palace revolution of 1917 has ended in the

---

50. *Ibid.*, 31, 73, 77, 45, 53. The *chouannerie* was an uprising of Breton peasants who supported the cause of the monarchy during the French Revolution. Bainville's reference to that episode in a study of the Russian Revolution once again reflected both his propensity for viewing reality from a narrow French perspective and his belief in the tendency of historical processes to repeat themselves.

streets." Since no one seemed to have planned or foreseen the revolution, it was difficult to ascertain its future course. "The old recipes are gone," he lamented, and no one could predict with confidence what lay in store for the troubled eastern ally.[51]

A year before his Russian expedition Bainville had traveled to neutral Italy to strengthen the ties between the Action Française and the boisterous group of nationalist-interventionist militants associated with Enrico Corradini's *Idea Nazionale*.[52] In the spring of 1915 he attended the public demonstrations in favor of intervention on the side of the Triple Entente that helped to persuade the Italian government to abandon its policy of neutrality; returning to France, he reported his impressions of this vibrant flame of interventionism to his delighted compatriots.[53] Then at the beginning of 1916 he published *La Guerre et l'Italie*, an analysis which explained the Italian intervention as a logical outgrowth of the historical evolution of national feeling since the *Risorgimento*. Together with his study of Russia in the same year, this work signified an important shift in his evaluation of the role of liberal nationalism in modern European history. It also represented a major modification of his earlier critical estimate of Italian unification, a view he was forced to reassess once Italy had joined the war on the side of the Triple Entente.

At the beginning of the war Bainville had displayed little interest in the prospect of France's wooing the renegade member of the Triple Alliance. On the contrary, he regarded Italy's neutrality as a blessing for the Entente, since it freed France and her allies from the obligation to reward Italy with postwar territorial compensations at the expense of the Austrian Empire, whose territorial integrity he considered important for French security.[54] Furthermore, as we have seen, he thoroughly disapproved of Italy's parliamentary

51. *Ibid.*, 70, 93.
52. Charles Maurras, *Quand les Français ne s'aimaient pas*, 129; Linville, "Jacques Bainville," 243.
53. Bainville, "Le Mois historique de l'Italie: mai 1915," *Revue des deux mondes* (October 1, 1915), 559–87.
54. Bainville, *Journal inédit: 1914*, September 13, 1914.

system on ideological grounds and regarded the achievement of Italian unification at the expense of Austria and the Papacy as a contributing factor in the trend toward international anarchy in Europe after 1870.

But Italy's timely intervention in 1915 forced Bainville to revise his earlier evaluation of France's new ally, and he proved to be quite dexterous in executing a doctrinal about-face. His wartime study of Italian politics began with a caustic attack on the German Emperor for slandering the Italian kingdom with the label "jailer of the Papacy" in order to curry domestic Catholic support after the cessation of Bismarck's anticlerical campaign. Bainville conveniently forgot that he had himself dedicated his prewar book on Bismarck to "the glorious memory of the Pontifical Zouaves who fell on the field of battle while defending the French cause against Italian unity at Rome." He now discovered reasons to justify the Holy Father's expulsion from the Papal lands: though deprived of its temporal sovereignty, the Papacy had retained its independence and remained the supreme spiritual authority in the nation. He praised the satisfactory relationship that now existed between Pope and King on the Italian peninsula, and predicted a full reconciliation. His kind words for the valiant Italian patriots who succeeded in "shattering the rule of Austria" while Northern Italy was "in chains" must have startled those readers who recalled his earlier defense of the Habsburg Empire as the indispensable gendarme of European equilibrium. But in the spirit of wartime unity this lapse in consistency passed unnoticed and unchallenged by his critics.[55]

Nevertheless, this belated endorsement of Italian unity by a former opponent of the Italian national cause required some justification. This Bainville provided by emphasizing the decisive role played by the House of Savoy in the movement of national unification. He conceded that the instigators of the *Risorgimento* were "Liberals, Democrats, Jacobins even, who represented the tradi-

---

55. Jacques Bainville, *Italy and the War*, trans. Bernard Miall (London: Hodder & Stoughton, 1916), 31, 170–71, 82, 84. See also Bainville, *Bismarck et la France*, dedication.

tions of the French Revolution," and that the renegade monarchy that supported their cause had betrayed Catholic, conservative Europe. But he suggested that the recent turn of events in Italy should cause French royalists to reconsider their negative evaluation of the Italian royal house as a traitor to the principles of legitimacy and religion, "the scandal of the whole party of European conservatism." In fact, the Piedmontese monarchy, with a "sure eye for realities," had perceived that it "might well be overpowered and overthrown by the Italian nationalist movement—unless it were to place itself at the head of that movement." Its shrewd decision "to plunge itself into the *Risorgimento*" instead of resisting the nationalist tide qualified the House of Savoy as one of those "monarchies which have succeeded in evolving and becoming pliant, instead of resisting and breaking." And this pragmatic policy was to pay lavish dividends in the future. The likes of Mazzini, Garibaldi, and Manin were hoodwinked into exchanging their republican sympathies for loyalty to the monarchy, "the champion of the people's cause." Even such revolutionaries as these had come to understand that "their nationalism, in order to succeed, must become royalist."[56]

The Italian monarchy's success in co-opting the revolutionary fervor of the *Risorgimento* was seen by Bainville as a consequence of its flexibility and pragmatism. Rather than clinging to the outmoded traditions of the past, rather than linking his dynasty to the declining feudal and clerical order after the fashion of the unfortunate Louis XVI of France, Victor Emmanuel had steered a middle course between reaction and revolution. The results were what one might have expected from this triumph of royal realism over royal sentimentality. The king was able to engineer a "masterly synthesis" of the forces of the past and the forces of the future because he was the first to recognize that "the red of a Garibaldian shirt might . . . blend very well with the purple of a cardinal's mantle."[57]

Bainville observed the continuation of this pragmatic policy in the behavior of the present occupant of the Italian throne, Victor

56. Bainville, *Italy and the War*, 44, 46–47, 49, 57.
57. *Ibid.*, 47–49, 69.

Emmanuel III. By supporting Giolitti's broadening of the franchise in 1912, the Italian king resumed his predecessors' attempts to harness the forces of democracy. Learning from the example of Napoleon III and Bismarck, he realized that universal suffrage represented not a dangerous impediment to royal authority, but rather an effective instrument with which the chief executive could achieve popular ratification of his policies over the heads of haggling legislators. Bainville only regretted that the French monarchy had failed to recognize this fact. Had Charles X introduced a plebiscitary system based on universal suffrage, his descendant would today occupy the throne of France.[58]

It was this royal declaration of solidarity with the popular cause, Bainville believed, which enabled the Italian monarchy to shape and direct the sentiment of irredentism that lay at the heart of the interventionist movement in 1915. Like the *Risorgimento* spirit, interventionism began as a popular phenomenon, inspired by the frenetic appeals of poets and publicists impatient with the timidity of the politicians. But once popular emotion had attained the highest pitch of excitement, it was ripe for exploitation by the supreme arbiter of Italian affairs, the monarch. The House of Savoy, like the House of Capet, had presided over the formation of national unity, and the nation understandably turned to it for leadership in its hour of glory. By summoning an interventionist ministry to power at the crucial moment in 1915, the king had succeeded in steering the nationalist-irredentist sentiment in the proper direction, ensuring that it would not follow a revolutionary path.[59]

But Bainville stopped short of an unqualified endorsement of Italian irredentist claims against Austria. It troubled him that while neither France, England, nor Russia entered the war with territorial ambitions—certainly a dubious claim—Italy regarded the conflict as "a war of expansion and conquest." The taste for intervention

58. *Ibid.*, 146.
59. *Ibid.*, 226–32. Upon meeting Gabriele D'Annunzio, the illustrious poet-politician who helped to incite Italian public opinion in favor of intervention, Bainville exclaimed: "In 1848 you would have been Lamartine. But you were more fortunate than he. There was no need for you to start a revolution." *Ibid.*, 34.

had arisen from the well-springs of popular passion rather than from the realistic calculations of *raison d'état*. The French devotée of the principle of European equilibrium looked askance at the idealistic appeals to "sacred egoism" that emanated from Italian nationalist circles. Such centers of popular agitation portrayed Italy as a young nation seeking its rightful place in the sun at the expense not only of the Austrian oppressor to the north, but also of England and France, two established powers whose long tradition of national unity tied them to the defense of the European status quo. This type of aggressive nationalism was uncomfortably similar to the German brand that Bainville continually denounced as a serious threat to European stability. Like Germany, Italy had only recently undergone her national revolution. She still retained the poisonous influence of the principle of nationalities, which had prompted Germany to undo the Vienna settlement between 1864 and 1870. She remained impetuous, in need of action. The revolutionary and nationalist energy of the Italian people was bound inevitably to lead to foreign adventurism that could complicate the postwar territorial settlement.[60]

This lingering reservation motivated Bainville to alert Frenchmen to the possibility of future difficulties with their new ally across the Alps. He predicted the emergence of future territorial conflicts between Italy and the Yugoslav state that was likely to be carved out of the Habsburg Empire at the end of the war. He warned that the Franco-Italian entente could easily be replaced by a future rapprochement between Germany and Italy were the former to endorse the latter's designs along the Adriatic. Once again, the prospects for European stability would depend in part upon the monarchy's ability to purge Italian nationalism of its idealistic, revolutionary elements, to temper the heritage of Mazzini and Garibaldi with the realistic, traditionalist spirit of royal legitimacy.[61]

60. See James Joll's vivid portrait of F. T. Marinetti, one of the sources of inspiration for this belligerent brand of Italian nationalism, in his *Three Intellectuals in Politics* (New York: Harper & Row, 1960), pt. III. See also Bainville, *Italy and the War*, 116–18, 237ff.
61. Bainville, *Italy and the War*, 252–58, 237–40.

The publication of Bainville's *La Guerre et l'Italie* signified a radical break with French royalist tradition. For one thing, his decision to publish the work at the Librairie Fayard suggested that he had begun to seek a wider audience than that reached by the movement's own unofficial publishing house, the Nouvelle Librairie Nationale. It also implied a tacit recognition on the author's part that the heretical conclusions of the book might not sit well with his royalist associates. His endorsement of the constitutional method by which the Italian king had become a wartime leader, together with his advocacy of universal suffrage as a mechanism for preserving royal authority, established a certain distance between his own political doctrines and the antiparliamentary, antidemocratic dogmas of the Maurrassian creed.

This tolerant attitude toward liberalism and popular sovereignty increased with the likelihood of military assistance to France from the United States. In July 1915 Bainville predicted America's entry into the war, declaring that Frenchmen were wrong to regard the United States as a "vast democracy governed by radicals with pacifist tendencies," just as many had misjudged the tenacity of liberal England and republican France in 1914. The departure from Wilson's cabinet of the pacifist Secretary of State William Jennings Bryan appeared to Bainville as the perfect counterpart of John Morley's exit from the wartime government of Great Britain. Both events led Bainville to the conclusion that the pacifist idealism of the Protestant Anglo-Saxon countries had been superseded by a realistic assessment of the threat to world order posed by the German Empire. Democracy, he seemed to suggest, could be counted on to repudiate its pernicious principles at critical turning points in history.[62]

Other episodes during the war supported that conclusion. In March 1915 he claimed to have detected further evidence of a parliamentary regime acknowledging and profiting from its mistakes. The British government had discovered the inadequacies of the discredited platitudes of isolationist liberalism, and was busy re-

---

62. Bainville, *Journal*, I, July 27, 1915.

habilitating the policies of traditional diplomacy. The "radical-liberal" government of Asquith had avoided repeating the mistakes of its predecessors. Later, when Lloyd George, a Protestant *bête-noire* of the royalists, came to power across the channel, Bainville hailed him as a modern Cromwell who would restore authority and order. English liberalism had systematically renounced its formative principles because those principles proved ill-suited to the requirements of a nation at war.[63]

Bainville's newly acquired confidence in the reliability of popular sentiment proved to be something of a departure from orthodox royalist doctrine. Maurras had nothing but contempt for public opinion, never ceasing his quest for a military leader capable of engineering a monarchical restoration by force. This tactical disagreement between Bainville and Maurras harked back to the original difference between the two friends that had surfaced in the *Enquête sur la monarchie*. Bainville constantly emphasized the need to coax the masses into recognizing the superiority of royalism by means of proposals for practical reforms. It was only through such persuasion that Frenchmen could be made to realize that by restoring a strong executive authority in the person of the king, they would thereby enhance the safety of their savings and their soil. The salvation of France was much more likely to result from the prompting of a group of intellectuals armed with irresistible ideas than from the brutal intervention of a military camarilla.[64]

This emphasis on persuasion rather than insurrection, which even Maurras came to accept during the war, helped to reduce the bitterness that had characterized the relationship between the movement and the regime in previous years. The Action Française, as we have seen, had become a staunch supporter of the republican government's war policy, moderating its political criticism in the interests of national unity and offering up the cream of royalist youth to the slaughter on the Western front. Maurras and Bainville had both maintained regular social contact with prominent

63. *AF*, March 27, 1915; December 7, 1916.
64. See, for example, Maurras, *Mademoiselle Monk* (Paris: Stock, 1923); see also *Polybiblion*, 83 (April, 1916), 222.

republican politicians and continued to urge public support for the war effort. Their increasing coziness with certain elements of the republican leadership, together with their reluctance to resume their prewar indictment of the regime, alienated a few diehards among their following. Some went so far as to accuse the Action Française leaders of becoming puppets of the Republic and to threaten to cancel their subscriptions unless they returned to an undiluted royalism.[65]

This policy of collaboration resumed unabated, reaching a crescendo when Clemenceau came to power at the end of 1917. Bainville, who had long distrusted the fiery old Jacobin, gradually modified his opinion as Clemenceau demonstrated his determination to wage a war to the finish. Indeed, Clemenceau was so successful in satisfying the desire of Bainville, Maurras, and Daudet for strong leadership during the last stages of the war that, as Edward Tannenbaum has observed, they "virtually ceased to behave like royalists" during his tenure in office.[66] What such behavior demonstrated, above all, was that nationalism rather than royalism was the first priority for the leaders of the movement. The accession of a Radical politician who proved capable of conducting an effective war policy caught the royalists by surprise. Daudet later recalled that none of the movement's leaders had imagined that the old man would succeed in avenging the humiliation of 1870 by employing the very methods the Action Française had been advocating.[67]

While giving the new French premier the credit he deserved, Bainville could not resist remarking that the same result could have been obtained at much less cost to France had the Republic taken the steps that would have made it unnecessary to summon an im-

65. Comtesse Murat, *Souvenirs sur Jacques Bainville* (Paris: Editions d'Histoire et d'Art, 1938), not paginated; AN, F⁷12863, "Notes sur Action Française," no. 5.

66. Tannenbaum, *Action Française*, 149; see also AN, F⁷13950, no. 2, fol. 174, November 18, 1917, and Emmanuel Beau de Loménie, *Maurras et son système* (Paris: Centre d'Etudes Nationales, 1965), 120.

67. Léon Daudet, *Souvenirs*, 236–37. Daudet had been an admirer of Clemenceau long before the war, to the consternation of Maurras. For an analysis of the Action Française's relationship with Clemenceau during his wartime ministry, see Weber, *Action Française*, 108–10.

provisator like Clemenceau to save a war-torn nation. It was a tragic misfortune that it required a million and a half fatalities to persuade the "old anarchist" of the need to restore discipline and order. He could have learned that lesson merely by interrogating the past in the scientific manner proposed by the royalist advocates of political realism. "Such are the horrible, needless sacrifices," Bainville complained, "of a century that celebrated the experimental method in the sciences, which discovered many vaccines, but which has disdained the experimental method in politics."[68]

During the last months of the Great War, Bainville recognized that his countrymen were approaching a major turning point in the long history of their beloved nation. How absolutely crucial it was that they be prepared for the burdensome responsibilities that lay ahead in the period of peacemaking and postwar recovery! He was acutely aware of the important function exercised by public opinion in the formulation of national policy in a modern democratic state; the force of popular sentiment was certain to reassert its influence on French policymakers once the artificial consensus that sustained the "wartime dictatorship" had dissolved. In the age of mass democracy, no longer could foreign policy be conducted by diplomats insulated from popular pressures, except perhaps in the heat of battle. The actions of statesmen are constrained and shaped by "the ideas and sentiments" that prevail in a particular society at a given moment, he remarked. "Men think first. Then [their actions] are determined by their manner of thinking. That is why it is important to think correctly. The errors of governments and of peoples are those of the mind."[69]

The most important influence upon the thinking of men, Bainville believed, was the lingering force of historical memory. The images of past glory or past degradation that had been bequeathed to them by previous generations decisively influenced the way that people perceived the present and, hence, planned for the future. In an effort to alert Frenchmen to the subtle effects of this historical

68. Bainville, *Esquisses et portraits*, 38–40.
69. Bainville, *Histoire de trois générations*, 9.

consciousness on their present thought and behavior as they prepared to participate in the reconstruction of the European order, he
published on the eve of the German capitulation a striking essay
entitled *Histoire de trois générations*.

In this work Bainville sketched the progress of what he regarded
as the two dominant modes of historical thinking that characterized the three generations that inhabited France between the fall of
Napoleon I and the outbreak of the First World War. One such
approach to the past appealed to the imagination, the other to the
lessons of experience. One conceived of historical reality as a series
of universal truths and speculative abstractions disembodied from
a political or national setting, while the other concentrated on the
concrete existential realities of a particular time and place. One persisted in viewing human history as a perpetual Manichean conflict
between universal forces of good and evil, while the other confined
itself to the observable circumstances in the here and now. Bainville left no doubt regarding which method of historical understanding he believed the French people should adopt in the crucial
years that lay ahead. He hoped that the chastening experiences of
the present war would have cured them of the urge to interpret the
past from the standpoint of the eternal struggle between light and
darkness in some ideal realm and would have taught them that
both history and politics must be understood from the perspective
of concrete national interest.[70]

The source of the imaginary, abstract type of historical thinking
was the First Napoleon. Bainville painted a memorable literary
portrait of the exiled ruler rewriting the history of his reign to ensure the survival of the Napoleonic legend by implanting it in the
minds of future generations of Frenchmen. Anticipating the emergence of democratic political thought and literary romanticism, the
defeated emperor attached his name to those two incipient movements in order to associate his memory with eternal, universal
forces that were destined to triumph in the future. His audacious
program for "the reconstruction of Europe according to the princi-

70. *Ibid.*, 7.

ples of liberty, equality, fraternity, and justice" was carefully designed to stir visions of a future terrestrial paradise that were to
afflict succeeding generations of Europeans in general and Frenchmen in particular. "The cause of France was [henceforth to be]
that of universal enfranchisement," Bainville lamented. "For the
Holy Alliance of kings it would substitute the Holy Alliance of
Peoples." The history of Bonapartist policy was thus rewritten so
as to portray France's fifteen-year war as a campaign of national
liberation whose goals remained to be realized. "Germany, Italy,
Poland are our sisters," went the new refrain. "They must be en-
franchised and unified like ourselves." The cult of national honor
and military glory in the service of those revolutionary ideals represented a perpetual reminder to Frenchmen of their past grandeur
under the Napoleonic aegis.[71]

The romantic poets (principally Béranger and Hugo) appeared in
Bainville's historical scenario as esthetic accomplices of Napoleon's
ambitious project for immortality. They succeeded in stimulating
popular sympathy for the Imperial cause through their paeans to
the Napoleonic legend, thereby achieving for it the prestige that its
embodiment had so desperately sought from his island retreat. The
effect of this "Testament of Saint Helena" was the alienation of
future generations from the unexciting but realistic policies by
which Talleyrand preserved France from dismemberment and financial ruin at Vienna and the "experimental diplomacy by which
the Restoration and the July monarchies were to assure thirty-three
years of peace and prosperity" for France.[72]

The foundation of the Second Empire signified for Bainville the
ultimate realization of the Napoleonic dream. Blending the pursuit
of military grandeur for France with support for the principles of
national liberation, resistance to oppression, and universal democracy in regard to the rest of Europe, the nephew conducted a foreign policy which intoxicated the popular imagination while betraying the real interests of the nation. The Second Empire stood
for the principle of "national self-determination" when it was a

71. *Ibid.*, 23–27.
72. *Ibid.*, 29ff., 22–24.

question of maintaining benevolent neutrality while Bismarck created a Prussian-dominated Germany at the expense of Denmark, Austria, and the independent German states. It achieved a short-lived reputation for military grandeur through costly, diversionary expeditions to Northern Italy and the Crimea to liberate oppressed nationalities from the imperial domination of Austria and Russia. But the consequence for France was the alienation of two potential allies that might have been helpful in 1870.[73]

But, unhappily for the true national interests of France, the Napoleonic legend did not die with the Second Empire. It continued to exercise its baneful influence on a succession of French statesmen, producing a series of flawed foreign policies under the Third Republic. Just as after the humiliation of 1815, the parties of the left took up the cry of military revenge after 1871 at precisely the moment that a new Talleyrand was required to inaugurate a period of national consolidation with a moderate policy that would avoid antagonizing the European powers. The monarchist right offered just such an alternative, Bainville recalled, and received the overwhelming support of the French electorate in the first postwar elections of 1871. The French people had once again placed their trust in statesmen who, like Talleyrand, Louis XVIII, and Louis Philippe, recognized the folly of "adventures" at inopportune moments. Just as the two royal houses "had saved France from Waterloos and Sedans between 1815 and 1848," the old Orleanist Thiers made the best of a disastrous situation in 1871 by pursuing a cautious, realistic course. He wisely accepted the "fait accompli" of the loss of Alsace-Lorraine despite unrelenting pressure from the diehard supporters of *la guerre à outrance* on the left.[74]

The gradual dissipation of monarchist political power in France between 1871 and 1877 demanded an explanation from the modern defender of the royal cause. Why had the successful "monarchist" policy of Thiers failed to persuade the French people of the necessity of a restoration? To Bainville the answer to this critical question lay in the behavior of the monarchists themselves. The partisans of

73. *Ibid.*, 131ff., 150–51.
74. *Ibid.*, 201, 206–207.

restoration had irreparably damaged their own cause by the very success of their postwar policies: "The peace treaty was signed. The Commune was conquered. The Monarchy no longer seemed to have anything to offer, anything to do, and in the eyes of the voters, its supporters had lost their true raison d'être."[75]

But the monarchists also contributed to their own demise by succumbing to a form of political nostalgia that proved wholly incomprehensible to the modern mind (and distasteful to Bainville's own "realistic" brand of royalism). Instead of alerting Frenchmen to the difficulties in store for an elective democracy faced with the threat of an authoritarian monarchy to the east, the Bourbon and Orleanist militants prated about ancient principles of legitimacy and "moral order." These were expressions of a "dead language" that was foreign to the majority of the electorate, which had been born after 1789. Such behavior, coupled with the political romanticism of the Comte de Chambord, who "threw his crown out of the window" by refusing to accept the tricolor as the banner of his own restoration, was reason enough for French voters to repudiate these sentimental prisoners of the past.[76]

The appearance of the Boulangist movement in the late 1880s represented to Bainville a regression to the impractical longing for revenge that had plagued France in the early postwar years. The flamboyant general's popularity signified a widespread reaction against the moderate, realistic policies of Thiers and his successors. This movement, which united a motley crew of malcontents from all shades of the political spectrum under the banner of "wounded patriotism," constituted a revival of both the quixotic bravado of

75. *Ibid.*, 215.
76. *Ibid.*, 216–18. It is instructive to compare Bainville's criticism of the Comte de Chambord's refusal to compromise his legitimist principles in 1875 with his praise of the House of Savoy's marriage of convenience with the forces of liberal nationalism in Italy during the Risorgimento (See above, 109). Even more than Maurras, Bainville considered himself a hardheaded pragmatist who disdained sentimental royalism and its nostalgic yearning for the good old days. "When Frenchmen were in good health, when their intelligence was sound and vigorous," he once remarked, "the idea of tradition was no less foreign to them than was the idea of revolution. The notion of returning to the *chansons de geste* and Saint Louis's oak tree would have seemed as ridiculous to them as wearing their fathers' breeches and hats out of filial piety." Bainville, *Jaco et Lori* (Paris: Grasset, 1927), 200–201.

1871 and the thirst for national grandeur associated with the Napoleonic legend.[77] Then, with the rapid demise of the insurgent general and the rise to power of the Radicals after the turn of the century, the French left reverted to the pacifist idealism that represented the reverse side of the revolutionary coin. The leadership of the Republic thereafter sought to reduce military expenditures at a time when more were needed to counter the mounting German menace. The nationalist revival that engulfed France in the decade before World War I, in which Bainville and the Action Française played a major role, constituted therefore a defensive reaction against the excesses of idealistic, internationalist pacifism, rather than a rebirth of the Gambettist-Boulangist spirit of *revanche*. "How the times had changed!" Bainville exclaimed. That earlier, premature outburst of "mass frenzy" that had characterized Boulangism had given way to "a serious and anxious feeling of a people confronted with a [real] threat to its existence." The consequence of this "renaissance of national feeling" was an appropriate response to the menace of German aggression: the election of the patriotic but pragmatic Poincaré to the presidency in 1913.[78] Thus was Bainville able, by this deft sleight of hand, to maintain his distinction between the realistic nationalism of the new right after the turn of the century and the intemperate, inopportune nationalism of the "Jacobin" left in the 1870s and 1880s.

With the Great War rapidly approaching its end, Bainville counselled France to renounce the "pack of slogans" contained in the political creed of liberal democracy in favor of the realistic policy that had been conducted by the conservative forces throughout her history. In the early stages of the conflict he had begun to complain that many Frenchmen were once again succumbing to the eternal temptation represented by the "Testament of Saint Helena," the illusions that "earlier had done such a cruel disservice to the people of France." He urged his compatriots to renounce once and for all

77. Bainville's criticism of Boulanger represented another disagreement with his friend Barrès, who had been an early supporter of the general. It also expressed Bainville's distaste for the Caesarist-Bonapartist tradition of right-wing thought associated with Barrès and Paul Déroulède.
78. Bainville, *Histoire de trois générations*, 243, 266–67.

their "sentimental attraction" to the confused and iniquitous slogans of nineteenth-century liberalism—"The Principle of Nations, League of Nations, war against autocracies and reactionary powers"—that had dominated the thinking of successive generations of Frenchmen. He warned that a durable peace treaty was more likely to result from the calm deliberations of seasoned professional diplomats schooled in the "axioms of good sense" than from democratically elected politicians who lacked the foresight nurtured by experience and historical understanding. While the petty politicians would be immersed in the transitory concerns of the present, the true statesmen would be much more capable of profiting from the lessons of the past and applying them in such a way as to shape a more secure future. The iron laws of international politics, like those of social politics, had not ceased to operate in the modern world. They were waiting to be discovered and adapted to present circumstances by qualified leaders. "There is no old policy. There is no new policy," declared this theorist of the classical conception of historical repetition. "There is only *the eternal policy.*"[79]

The fleeting love affair between the unreconstructed monarchist and the wartime governments of the Republic did not survive the announcement of the armistice. Bainville had frequently voiced the premonition that the Republic would revert to the ineffectiveness and shortsightedness that had marked its foreign policy before the war as soon as the external threat of invasion would be removed. He maintained that this somber inevitability derived from the very nature of the regime. Since democratic policymakers were the prisoners of unexpected and uncontrollable shifts in public sentiment, they tended to react precipitously to contemporary crises instead of fashioning rational policies designed to accomplish durable objectives. At a critical stage of the war, French democracy managed to produce a Clemenceau in the nick of time. But now that victory had been achieved, Bainville feared that the citizenry would rapidly tire of the burdens of preparedness and vigilance. Before long they would begin to harbor illusory hopes of establishing instant

79. *Ibid.*, 277–79.

peace that would force French diplomats to ignore the successful principles that had helped to secure the military victory.

It has been noted how Bainville had learned to appreciate the critical contribution of popular-based patriotism in Italy, France, England, and even Tsarist Russia to the maintenance of national morale in the heat of combat. Indeed, he himself had occasionally lapsed into the poisonous brand of cultural chauvinism that pervaded the intellectual atmosphere of wartime Europe. He was among the first of the French intellectuals to answer with the appropriate dose of Gallic ethnocentrism the German intelligentsia's manifesto describing the war as a defense of German *Kultur*. He did not hesitate to brand the conflict as a cultural struggle between the forces of Western Civilization and those of Germanic "barbarism."[80] Such rhetorical excesses continued sporadically throughout the long war of attrition.

In October 1914 Bainville went so far as to advocate the suppression of German language instruction in French schools, arguing that the only justification for teaching Frenchmen the "treacherous" language was to train prospective spies. He later announced that the pagan cult of Odin was replacing Christianity so rapidly in Germany that France now found herself in mortal combat with "a conception of the world which has nothing in common with the foundations of French ideas." When the United States joined Spain in protesting Germany's inhumane treatment of Belgium, Bainville viewed this joint intervention of Anglo-Saxon Protestant and Latin-Catholic nations as an indication that "it is civilization in its entirety that is revolting against . . . the German *Weltanschauung*." Germany's behavior in the war had demonstrated that she occupies "an intellectual world separate from the rest of the universe" akin to the planet Mars. Her citizens were no more capable than Martians of comprehending Western values.[81]

But in spite of such occasional outbursts, Bainville was careful to avoid leaving the impression that he viewed the present conflict

---

80. Bainville, *Journal inédit: 1914*, September 28, 1914.
81. *AF*, October 10, 1914, cited in Bainville, *L'Allemagne*, I, 124; *AF*, October 23, 1915; November 26, 1916.

from an ideological perspective. He considered himself too firm a devotee of the balance-of-power principle to permit such irrational sentiments to affect his analysis. He conceded that ideological over-simplification was a necessary "accompaniment of war" which served to inspire popular sacrifices, but quickly added that wars are won and peace is secured by "realism" alone. He was particularly sensitive to the possibility that the Allied governments might come to view the conflict as a contest of irreconcilable political ideologies, a development which he feared would cause them to lose sight of the proven principles of diplomacy that alone could ensure European stability. In September 1914 he reproached Winston Churchill for characterizing the war as one of "democracy against autocracy," noting caustically that such idealistic rhetoric was inappropriate at a time when "French and English liberal democracy is expiating its blindness and its errors in the blood flowing on the plains of Flanders and Picardy." In January 1917, following one of President Wilson's moralistic speeches to the Senate about the sins of the Central Powers, Bainville complained that the American chief executive was "transposing political questions into the domain of morality." The French writer counseled the adolescent democracy to defer to the more hardened statesmen of old Europe, who had centuries of experience behind them.[82]

The conception of the war as a crusade of democracy against autocracy was personally repugnant to Bainville not only because of his own political orientation, but also because it replaced considerations of European stability with vague, ideological platitudes that could be exploited by any belligerent nation to justify its aggressive policy. He reminded his readers that the German left had explained its support of the Kaiser's war policy as a campaign to hasten the end of "Tsarist oppression," while the French Socialists saw the war as a means of crushing the monarchy of William II, the symbol of European "reaction." Frenchmen had to be taught to eschew such ideological slogans and to appreciate the geopolitical significance of the war. The past four years of bloodshed represented the effort

82. Bainville, *Journal*, I, November 9, 1918; January 26, 1917. See also Bainville, *Journal inédit: 1914*, September 1, 1914.

of an expansionist land power to establish hegemony over the continent of Europe. The impending victory of the Allies would mark the restoration of international equilibrium by a coalition of powers ranged against the "brigand state." As for the "ideas" underlying the war effort, they appeared only in the form of "shrapnel in the flesh of our soldiers." They are nothing more than "dum-dum ideas."[83]

The liberal governments of France and England, to Bainville's delight, appeared to have discarded their prewar ideals of pacifism, internationalism, and the principle of national self-determination in favor of the *"ancien régime* policy" of the balance-of-power formulated by Richelieu and Louis XIV. But the Russian Revolution and the American intervention had injected two novel elements into the war effort that appeared to justify Bainville's earlier apprehension about the likelihood of the conflict's taking an ideological direction. Though the American forces arrived in time to restore the strategic balance that had been upset by the removal of the Russian army from the eastern front, their presence filled Bainville with apprehension. They appeared to be directed by political leaders who were not only abysmally ignorant of the requirements of European equilibrium but also suffered from the very tendency to regard the war as an ideological crusade that he had been cautioning against in his columns. Instead of recognizing the necessity of reestablishing the continental balance that had been disturbed by the German drive for hegemony, Wilson began to portray the war as an epic confrontation between the Western concept of democracy and the authoritarian traditions of Eastern Europe; it was this formulation whose credibility had been temporarily enhanced by the collapse of the Romanov dynasty and its replacement by a liberal parliamentary regime.

Bainville's foreboding about the American President's intentions reached its peak in the months after the armistice. He began to despair over the extent to which fanatical hatred of both Bolshevism and Imperial autocracy had begun to influence American and British

83. *AF*, November 17, 1914, quoted in Bainville, *L'Allemagne*, I, 128; *AF*, September 4, 1914; Bainville, *Journal inédit: 1914*, September 29, 1914.

attitudes toward the postwar political settlement in Europe. He worried that Wilson would permit his messianic desire to make the world safe for democracy—at the expense both of the authoritarian regimes of the Central Powers and of the equally authoritarian regime of the Bolsheviks—to blind him to the harsh realities that faced the victors as they embarked on the difficult task of peacemaking and postwar reconstruction. The idea of combatting dictatorship with democracy struck Bainville as one of the most ridiculous ideas he ever had encountered.[84]

As the Allied diplomats met in preliminary discussions before the opening of the peace conference, Bainville entreated them to substitute hardheaded realistic thinking for the ideological posturing that had become increasingly popular among the Americans. Demagogic rhetoric, whether of the anti-Communist or liberal variety, was repellent to the French royalist thinker because it threatened to arouse the baser human instincts which were likely to produce bad policy. In a convenient lapse of memory he described the Allied effort in the Great War, with its unprecedented use of chauvinist propaganda, as "an abstract victory, a sort of mathematical demonstration" which had avoided stirring up the enthusiasm of the masses.[85] He entreated the diplomats gathering in Paris to apply to the establishment of a durable peace the same rigorous principles that Marshal Foch had employed to win the war. He sensed that the months ahead would produce decisions that not only would redesign the map of Europe but would also determine whether European civilization would retain its leadership in the world. The authority to make such momentous decisions, he believed, should be entrusted to statesmen well versed in the strategic requirements of the international system, rather than to shortsighted, sloganeering idealists and demagogues obsessed with currying public support for their ambitious schemes for the salvation of mankind.

---

84. Bainville, *Journal*, II (Paris: Plon, 1949), March 29, 1919.
85. Bainville, *Esquisses et portraits*, 43.

CHAPTER FIVE

The Reconstruction of the European Order
Bainville and the Versailles Settlement

*There are moments when certain governing ideas, certain decisions taken
under the influence of those ideas, certain words incorporated in diplomatic acts as a result of those decisions, produce incalculable long-range
consequences.*

Bainville (1920)

*Unique in its crystalline irrefutability, Bainville's luminous column guides
me unerringly across the desert of foreign policy.*

Marcel Proust (1920)

The enthusiastic public reception accorded Woodrow Wilson in
December 1918, during which the American statesman violated
diplomatic protocol by addressing the European people over the
heads of their leaders, caused Bainville grave concern about the
outcome of the forthcoming peace negotiations. What alarmed him
most of all was the possibility that the new ideological conception
of the war would affect the peace settlement in the same way that
it had begun to influence the war aims of the Allies in the final
year of hostilities. "The time has come to conclude a serious peace
based on realities," he forcefully declared after the opening of the
conference, "and to forget all these false 'principles,' if the Allies
want to prevent new bloodshed and general disaster. . . . A poorly
constructed peace carries within it [the seeds of] new wars."[1] The
peacemakers must resist the temptation to conduct the negotiations in the spirit of a democratic crusade against the twin evils
of monarchical autocracy and Bolshevik tyranny. Their aim should
be the fashioning of a carefully planned policy to destroy once and
for all the offensive capabilities of Germany.

1. Bainville, *Journal*, II, March 29, 1919.

Since the very beginning of the war, Bainville had publicly enunciated what he believed to be the only realistic means whereby this overriding objective could be achieved. The keystone of his recommendations was the resuscitation of the crumbling Habsburg Empire. Throughout the war he had repeatedly opposed the idea of including the total dismemberment of Austria-Hungary in the allied objectives.[2] His concern for the future of the Empire was based not upon a French royalist's sentimental attachment to an ancient Catholic monarchy, but rather upon what he considered the most rigorous canons of realistic statecraft. Less than two weeks before the armistice, he hailed Austria as a center around which anti-German sentiment in Central Europe could crystallize. "We do not like the Habsburgs any more than they like us," he announced, "and we would do with their crown what we would do with that of the Hohenzollerns, were it not for its utility" in a postwar diplomatic constellation directed against Germany.[3]

The valuable service that the old empire could render to France, in Bainville's view, was that of a federator of the bickering nationalities of Central Europe that had unilaterally declared their independence at the end of the war and were presenting their territorial claims to the victorious Allies at the peace conference. He regarded a resurrected Austrian Empire as a necessary evil that would deter Germany from exploiting for her own profit the national antagonisms that had already begun to surface in the successor states. Casting a suspicious glance at the German minorities in Bohemia and Western Poland, not to mention the German-speaking inhabitants of Austria itself, all of whom he suspected of clinging to the old *grossdeutsch* ideal of a vast Teutonic state extending from the Balkans to the Baltic and from the Rhine to the Vistula, he worried lest a regenerated Germany exercise an irresistible attraction upon these volatile populations. Central Europe is in a state of chaos that cannot help but produce future convulsions, he later observed. "Its present state is temporary. One day or another it will be refash-

2. See *Ibid.*, I, September 23, 1914, April 10, 1915, and January 18, 1918.
3. *AF*, October 31, 1918.

ioned. . . . It remains to be seen who will be the dominator or the
federator. What is essential is that it not be Germany."[4]

Bainville was most sanguine about the future of Poland, whose
tradition of nationhood he regarded as an important source of
solidity that would contribute to the preservation of her independence between Germany to the west and Russia to the east. Furthermore, Poland's Catholic heritage qualified her as a probable
friend of France. But he argued that the nationalist aspirations of
the other fledgling successor states should be rebuffed in favor of
Austrian hegemony if the stability of the region was to be maintained. He had remarked at the beginning of the war that the Habsburg Empire no longer represented a threat to European stability
and French security. Ever since the Peace of Westphalia the triumphant French monarchy had wisely chosen to preserve the Empire as the "gendarme of European order and peace" in Central
Europe. A powerful Austria was particularly necessary at the present moment now that Russia, the traditional barrier to German
eastward expansion, was no longer capable of fulfilling her traditional role of maintaining the balance of power in Central Europe
on account of her internal disarray.[5]

While advocating the creation of a Greater Austria to hem in
Germany in the south and east, Bainville, a descendant of transplanted Lorrainers, was understandably insistent upon similar
guarantees in the west. Fortunately, this area appeared to him
to present even more attractive opportunities, since it contained
historically centrifugal forces that could be manipulated by the
western powers at Germany's expense. Separatist movements had
spontaneously arisen in Hanover and Bavaria during the last stages
of the war; to Bainville these indigenous opponents of German unity represented ideal partners in an Allied-sponsored Balkanization
of the German Reich. Recalling how Richelieu and Mazarin had
effectively exploited German particularism in the interests of Euro-

4. *AF*, October 5, 1919.
5. Bainville, *Journal*, I, September 23, 1914. For a collection of Bainville's articles
dealing with Russia's role as a barrier to Germany's expansion to the east, see his
La Russie et la barrière de l'est (Paris: Plon, 1947).

pean stability, Bainville urged the French negotiators at the peace conference to seize the initiative and revive the "Westphalian policy." His recommendations on this issue were colored by a brand of wishful thinking that reflected his characteristic confidence in man's capacity for reversing long-established historical trends, the reverse of his deterministic tendency: the Hanoverians had never resigned themselves to the annexation of 1866 and therefore qualified as potential citizens of an independent monarchy. The establishment of an autonomist movement in Bavaria provided an excellent opportunity to restore the Wittelsbach pretender to the throne of Ludwig II.[6]

But Bainville claimed to perceive the most promising opportunity for chipping away at the western flank of the Reich in the traditionally Francophile Rhineland. Unlike the newly created nations to the south and east, this area was contiguous with a status quo power to which it could turn for protection against Prussian intimidation. As Allied troops entered the area in December 1918, Bainville was ecstatic about the opportunity to turn back the clock. In his enthusiasm he permitted his obsession with French national interests to peek through his carefully cultivated image of disinterested concern for continental equilibrium. "Having erased Sedan, we now must erase Waterloo," he observed. "France cannot be a great continental power unless she is a Rhenish power." As a monarchist, he favored the indirect method of the Bourbons rather than the direct method of Bonaparte. "French political wisdom has never consisted in immoderate acquisitions," he recalled. "In the days of France's European hegemony, she always preferred influence and infiltration to indigestion," a preference which required "time, prestige, and the utilization of circumstances."[7]

Though Bainville's hopes for a revival of Habsburg Austria were dashed by immediate postwar realities, a decentralized Germany continued to appear to him as a practical possibility. The separatist

6. *AF*, March 13, 1918.
7. *AF*, December 1, 1918. See F. Roy Willis, *France, Germany, and the New Europe, 1945–1967* (London: Oxford University Press, 1968), 16, for similar sentiments expressed by Charles de Gaulle after the Second World War.

movement that had sprouted in the Rhineland had been soliciting French support for the creation of a Rhenish-Westphalian Republic ever since the armistice, and Bainville became one of the most outspoken champions of such a policy. He frequently dined with General Mangin, commander of the Tenth French Army in the Rhineland,[8] who was actively encouraging separatist agitation (to the consternation of the Americans and the British, who, for reasons presently to be discussed, were intent on preserving the territorial integrity of the Reich). In his newspaper column Bainville promoted the cause of the Comité de la Rive Gauche du Rhin, a hastily formed French pressure group that spearheaded the campaign for Rhenish separatism.[9] Though, as Edward Tannenbaum has observed, few Germans would have looked forward to becoming citizens of a resurrected Baden, Hesse, or Lower Saxony,[10] the indigenous proponents of an independent Rhineland hatched separatist schemes, and Clemenceau included a proposal for the separation of the left bank of the Rhine in the French negotiating package at the peace conference.[11]

As the opportunities for French advantages in Western Germany continued to arise, Bainville viewed with similar enthusiasm the disintegrating political situation in Berlin. That the instigators of the unrest there drew their inspiration from the Bolshevik Revolution in Russia caused him little anxiety. He again displayed his willingness to place balance-of-power considerations above ideological preference.[12] As usual, history was his guide. He counseled the Allies to sit back and permit Prussia to be infected and consumed by the Sparticist-Bolshevik bacillus, just as Bismarck had bided his time while the Communards plunged Paris into a

8. Massis, Le Souvenir, 44; Lucien Corpechot, "Hommages à Jacques Bainville," 544–45.
9. Friedrich Grimm, Du Testament de Richelieu à Jacques Bainville (Le Mois Suisse: February, 1941), 8.
10. Tannenbaum, Action Française, 150.
11. Jere C. King treats the Rhenish separatist movement and its connections to the French army in his Foch Versus Clemenceau (Cambridge, Mass.: Harvard University Press, 1960), 28–43, 73ff.
12. Arno J. Mayer, Politics and Diplomacy of Peacemaking: Containment and Counterrevolution at Versailles, 1918–1919 (New York: Vintage Books, 1969), 87–88.

debilitating civil war in 1871. "If Germany were to become Bolshevik we would be absolutely delighted," he announced on the eve of the armistice. "We wish it with all our heart. France has never been secure except when anarchy ruled in Germany. . . . From a Bolshevized Germany, we would no longer have to fear what we underwent in 1870 and 1914."[13]

This pragmatic attitude toward the German revolution was consistent with Bainville's coldly realistic approach to the strategic dilemmas posed by the advent of the Bolshevik regime in Russia. A few months after the signing of the Treaty of Brest-Litovsk, he had added his voice to the chorus of criticism that was being directed at the assassins of France's former ally in the east. But his attacks on the Bolshevik government were inspired more by a feeling of betrayal at Russia's withdrawal from the war than by ideological distaste for the form of government she had adopted. History again armed him with a useful analogy. Just as the French Revolution had dismantled the Westphalian system, so the Russian Revolution had destroyed the strategic balance that had been established by the diplomats of the Triple Entente. Moreover, the events in Russia abruptly soured him on the liberal nationalism that he had cautiously endorsed after the March Revolution. "In losing Tsarism we have lost everything," he exclaimed, eating his words of a few months earlier, "and this proves that the only true alliances are those of [legitimate] governments." Brest-Litovsk represented the bitter fruit of the antiwar sentiment in Russian public opinion and revealed the Bolsheviks' abysmal ignorance of their fatherland's true national interests.[14]

Throughout 1918 and early 1919 French publicists of the right and center competed with each other to issue the loudest cry for Allied intervention on the side of the Whites in the Russian Civil War in order to smash the incipient revolution in Eastern Europe before it could spread to the west. But Bainville consistently op-

13. *AF*, November 1 and 11, 1918.
14. *Ibid.*, May 24, 1918. Compare this hostile attitude toward Russian public opinion to his earlier praise for the Russian people's loyal support of the Tsar and vigorous resistance to German influences. See above, 102–103.

posed intervention on the pragmatic grounds that it would represent little more than a diversionary expedition of dubious strategic
value, would overextend Allied military forces, and would deflect
attention from the pressing necessity to drive the definitive nail
into the Teutonic coffin. Even after Germany had been brought
to her knees, he continued to campaign against the Allied expedition in Russia. When Allied leaders injected the principle of anti-
Bolshevism into the peace negotiations, Bainville viewed this ideologically motivated attempt to quarantine contagious ideas as a
disastrous error.[15] He was particularly alarmed by the German
diplomats' tendency to view this ideological insecurity as a trump
card which could be played at critical moments to extract concessions from the victors:

> Our vision of European affairs has been warped by our obsession with
> Bolshevism. Under cover of this *grande peur*, Germany has reorganized
> herself. She has used the specter of Bolshevism to divert attention from
> her own affairs while at the same time ridding herself of this poison.[16]

Bainville was to repeat this warning over and over again throughout the twenties. "We cannot do anything about Russia," he declared at the beginning of 1920. "We can do a great deal about
Germany. It is she that we must render incapable, by preventive
measures, of one day destroying the peace with the cooperation of
Russia." Two years later, upon learning about the Rapallo Treaty,
Bainville observed that Russia was in an advanced state of decomposition and therefore posed no immediate military (as opposed to
ideological) threat to the west. "What must not be done is to fear
the Russian menace excessively," he warned. "To neglect or even
to favor Germany for the purpose of deflecting the Russian threat
would be the greatest of follies."[17]

Developments within Germany itself during the peace negotiations were also beginning to alarm the vigilant Bainville. Even
before the cessation of hostilities, he was predicting that the ide-

15. Mayer, *Politics and Diplomacy of Peacemaking*, 87ff., 303, 440. See also *AF*,
November, 1918, January, 1919.
16. *AF*, January 31, 1919.
17. *AF*, January 31, 1920 and May 18, 1922.

ological principles enunciated in Wilson's Fourteen Points would be used by the postwar German government as camouflage for perpetuating the strength and unity of the Reich. He warned that once Germany learned that it could satisfy its conquerors' mystical attachment to democratic political forms by cashiering the Hohenzollerns, it would jump at this opportunity to curry Allied favor. By choosing a socialist chancellor, it "will don the red cap, but it will still be Germany," he warned. When the German left confirmed Bainville's prediction a few weeks later by toppling the Imperial regime, he implored Frenchmen not to be deceived. "You will understand and know the German Republic better when it elects Hindenburg president," he announced on the 25th of November.[18] Once again, Bainville used a historical precedent analogically. He accused the German Social Democrats of plotting a return to the Pan-German policy of the revolutionary assembly in 1848.[19] The wily new socialist leaders would strive to reconstruct a vast militaristic empire on the basis of the Wilsonian principles of national self-determination just as Bismarck and his National Liberal supporters had cleverly exploited the principles of liberal nationalism hailed by the nineteenth-century Wilson, Napoleon III.

The evidence that Bainville adduced to support this view of contemporary German politics posited a conspiracy composed of unlikely bedfellows. The socialist leaders had deposed the Kaiser for purely "opportunistic" reasons," that is, in order to demonstrate their "democratic" intentions to the American president in the hope of gaining favorable treatment for Germany at the peace conference. He pointed to the continuity of personnel, institutions, and foreign policy that underlay the superficial constitutional and parliamentary transformation. The conspicuous presence of former Imperial servants, such as Hindenburg and Groener, in the new ruling set moved him to complain that the Hohenzollern civil service, diplomatic corps, and military command had been retained virtually intact by the German Republic. He cautioned that the Allies were unwittingly planting the seeds for a renewal of the Great-

---

18. Bainville, *Journal*, I, October 15, 1918; Joseph, *Qui est Jacques Bainville?*, 44.
19. Bainville, *Journal*, I, November 20, 1918; *AF*, November 14, 1918.

er German policy by favoring the creation of "a vast Socialist state organized, like the trade unions, on the Prussian model, and a republican Germany where the nationalist spirit would promptly be revived," and this without dismantling the Imperial administrative structure and the Bismarckian territorial system.[20]

Bainville's advice to the peacemakers, in sum, was to impose a Carthaginian settlement on Germany by shattering her into dozens of pieces after the fashion of Mazarin and Oxenstierna in 1648. He entreated the Allies to let Prussia dissolve into Bolshevik anarchy, to revive a greater Poland to balance Germany in the east, to retain a federated Austria to ride herd over the German minorities in the south, and to resuscitate the formerly independent Germanic states in the west. By exploiting these disintegrative tendencies, the Allies (and particularly France) would be taking the necessary steps to guarantee European stability, for "the reconstitution of Europe is neither possible nor even conceivable" if German unity is maintained. Here was the perfect opportunity to turn back the clock, to rectify the errors of the two Napoleons, to revive "the wise and prudent policy constantly followed by the French monarchy, which consisted in putting the German colossus to sleep, dividing it, enfeebling it, profiting from its religious quarrels, its territorial divisions, the rivalry among its princes, its lack of money, its backward civilization."[21]

For all his talk about European order and the preservation of Western civilization, the parochial interests of France remained foremost in Bainville's mind during the peace negotiations. It was this attitude that caused Edward Tannenbaum to observe that Bainville and his royalist associates exhibited "the widespread lack of understanding among many twentieth-century French nationalists for any nationalism other than their own." But the evidence suggests that Bainville never recognized this as a contradiction, for he regarded European order and French security as synonymous. "France is an ancient country which has legacies of her past al-

20. *AF*, November 1, 15 and 20, 1918.
21. Bainville, *Journal*, I, November 5, 1918; *Journal*, II, March 17, 1919.

most everywhere outside her borders," he observed. "That is what makes our interests conservative. We acquired a privileged position in the Europe of yesteryear; the more that Europe comes apart and is obliterated, the more we have to lose."[22]

But this preoccupation with the past did not lose Bainville readers and admirers in the present. By the end of the peace conference, he had firmly established his reputation as what one observer has called the most influential and most widely known expert on foreign affairs in France outside government circles.[23] He was a frequent guest at embassy dinners during the peace talks, where French and foreign dignitaries sought his counsel as the Allied diplomats prepared to announce their projects for the future of Europe. Two French diplomats of the old school, the Comte de Saint-Aulaire (a future ambassador to London) and Maurice Paléologue (a former ambassador to Saint Petersburg and future secretary-general of the Quai d'Orsay) became devoted admirers and loyal friends of the royalist writer.[24] Léon Bérard, Poincaré's former secretary who was soon to join the conservative government of the *Bloc national*, dined with Bainville several times weekly.[25] The American journalist W. Morton Fullerton recalled that during the peace conference he had introduced Théophile Delcassé to his old friend Bainville as "the Richelieu of the Third Republic." Some twenty "secret conversations" among the three men took place in Parisian restaurants in the winter and spring of 1919. Soon the republican statesman had formed a warm friendship with the royalist writer whose articles on foreign policy he had assiduously read each morning. Bainville had by then come to appreciate Delcassé's prewar labors on behalf of the Anglo-French entente, a diplomatic connection which, despite its weaknesses, Bainville regarded as a major factor in the Allied

22. Tannenbaum, *Action Française*, 150; Bainville, *Journal*, I, January 30, 1918.
23. Dubech, *Les Chefs de File*, 25. See also Grimm, *Du Testament de Richelieu*, 3, for a discussion of Bainville's influence on France's professional diplomats.
24. Interview with Hervé Bainville; Interview with Madame Jacques Bainville. Paléologue later sponsored Bainville's candidacy for a seat in the Académie Française; Saint-Aulaire was to contribute an introduction to a posthumous collection of Bainville's articles on French policy toward Eastern Europe.
25. Linville, "Jacques Bainville," 241.

victory. For his part, Delcassé wrote Fullerton praising the "good sense, discernment, and intellectual probity" of his royalist interlocutor.[26]

But it was not the Delcassés (nor the Poincarés, nor even the Clemenceaus) who were calling the shots at the American-dominated conference, and Bainville quickly began to sense that his specific recommendations for the reestablishment of the balance of power in Europe were falling on deaf ears. The victors' unwillingness to preserve the Austro-Hungarian state as a strategic counterweight to German power in Central Europe continually caused him concern. As early as the summer of 1918 he had noted with consternation that the Allied leaders were apparently preparing to proclaim the right of self-determination for the subject nationalities of the Habsburg Empire.[27] Half a year later, after the establishment of the new successor states in Central Europe, he warned that only viable political entities would be capable of attenuating the incipient ethnic conflicts in that unstable area. And Czechoslovakia, Yugoslavia, and Poland were hardly viable nations. Furthermore, he complained that the Allies had passively permitted the Sparticist uprising in Berlin to "perish" and the hopes for an independent Rhineland to "go up in smoke," thereby enabling the unified German state to reconstitute itself.[28] He recognized that the French government could not be held responsible for this shortsighted Central European policy. Clemenceau's original negotiating position at the conference had been realistic in that it was "the only one that [took] account of the future while England and America [remained] immersed in the present." But the French premier had been forced to yield by Wilson, whom Bainville was

26. Jacques Bainville, *L'Angleterre et l'empire britannique* (Paris: Plon, 1938), preface by W. Morton Fullerton, iv. See also Linville, "Jacques Bainville," 258–59. Delcassé's attitude toward Germany in the postwar period closely paralleled Bainville's. He refused to vote for the ratification of the Versailles Treaty because it gave France "neither reparations nor security" and publicly advocated permanent French military occupation of an independent Rhineland as a means of providing France with "natural frontiers." Porter, *The Career of Théophile Delcassé*, 334, 336.

27. Bainville, *Journal*, 1, June 2, 1918.

28. *AF*, January 24, February 14, 1919, in Jacques Bainville, *L'Allemagne*, 2 vols., (Paris: Plon, 1939), II, 14–15, 18.

by now reviling as the "American incarnation of Napoleon III."[29]

The day after the Versailles Treaty was submitted to the German delegation, Bainville bitterly denounced the settlement in an article entitled "A Peace Treaty too Lenient for the Harshness it Contains" ["Une Paix trop douce pour ce qu'elle a de dur"]. This oft-quoted phrase expressed his conviction that the treaty contained the worst possible combination of the carrot and the stick. The territorial amputations, reparations requirements, and disarmament clauses were so "harsh" that they would reduce the German state to a condition of "servitude" and would represent a perpetual pretext for revision. Yet the Allies had failed to adopt adequate sanctions with which to enforce adherence to these severe provisions of the treaty.[30]

In the following day's article, ominously entitled "German Unity Consecrated at Versailles," Bainville voiced his second and most serious reservation about the treaty. By their failure to dismember the Bismarckian state, the peacemakers had preserved a political organism that was capable of rebuilding the war machine that had plunged Europe into four years of agony. To those Frenchmen who claimed that the presence of the German left in the seat of power constituted a solid guarantee of German good behavior, he again invoked the lessons of the past in reply:

> How did Prussia after Jena recover from its disaster? By the exploitation and adaptation of the ideas of the French Revolution. The old Prussian conservatives were less dangerous for the world than the innovating patriots. Who can say that other innovators will not regenerate the Germany of the Hohenzollerns in the future as Prussia had been regenerated by the reformers of the past century?

French democracy had once again failed to profit from the mistakes of the past. "May 7, 1919 has not erased the date of January

---

29. *AF*, February 14 and April 21, 1919. He later compared the diplomatic achievements of Richelieu, who had "obtained the most results at the least cost," with those of Wilson, who Bainville believed was coming perilously close to presenting the Allies with a "pyrrhic victory." Jacques Bainville, *Richelieu* (Paris: Beytout, n.d.), not paginated.

30. *AF*, May 8, 1919. See also Tannenbaum, *Action Française*, 150–51.

18, 1871." The German unity that had been forged in the Franco-
Prussian War was reaffirmed in the very palace from which the
French monarchy had once maintained surveillance over a frag-
mented Germany.[31]

The severe treatment that the rump state of Austria had received
at the hands of the victors seemed to Bainville an open invitation to
German domination of the area, spelling doom for the unrecogniz-
able remnant of the old empire. "We will have to give an independent Austria the means to survive," he warned, "if we do not want
her independence to be a brief fiction." Moreover, he chided the
Allies for being so foolish as to dismember Germany in the east
and still expect to enforce the settlement on the Rhine. The German state, left unified and strong at its core, had been provided
with an irresistible temptation to "fish in the troubled waters" of
Poland, Czechoslovakia, and Austria, fledgling states with German-speaking populations whose independence could not easily
be defended by the Western powers. Meanwhile, he was convinced that the failure to support the Rhenish separatist movement was erasing the last possible hope of "westernizing" the
German giant. "If Germany is not federalized by its western region," he warned, "it will remain subjugated by its evil part, its
eastern and Prussian part." Upon returning from a visit to the
Rhenish city of Mainz in September 1919, he summarized what he
regarded as France's options with uncompromising clarity: "The
Rhineland liberated from Prussia or eternal war. The choice is
ours."[32]

There was no question in Bainville's mind that the anarchical
state of affairs in Central Europe virtually guaranteed that the treaty
would be put to the ultimate test by the midthirties. Confronted
with the superior power of the Allies in the west, he announced,
Germany will behave like a lamb in that area while preparing to
play the wolf in the east. Fifteen years or so after the peace conference, with the Allied occupation forces withdrawn from the

31. *AF*, May 9, 1919.
32. Bainville, *Journal*, II, May 10, 1919; June 20, 1919; *AF*, September 4, 1919.

Rhineland, she would begin to move against the successor states of the Habsburg Empire, which collectively constituted "a vast powder keg between the Danube and the Niemen." He cast the scenario for German recovery in blunt language. The realities of history and geography dictated that "it is in the east that she [Germany] will begin her liberation and her revenge," he warned. "If we do not intervene the day she tries to reconstruct her eastern frontier, if we repeat the terrible abstention of Sadowa, then . . . the danger will be ours."[33]

To Bainville's consternation, critics within the victorious nations were already calling for even greater concessions to Germany before the ink on the treaty was dry. The British economist John Maynard Keynes argued in his *Economic Consequences of the Peace* that the stringent reparations requirement imposed on the defeated power would produce an economic upheaval in Central Europe that would plunge the industrialized world into a prolonged economic crisis. Influential public servants in England and America were beginning to regard German economic recovery as a major policy objective and were urging that the harshness of the settlement be mitigated.[34]

On the first anniversary of the signing of the treaty Bainville publicly responded to these new attitudes in a lengthy essay entitled *Les Conséquences politiques de la paix.* Notwithstanding his disclaimer in the introduction that it was "not a reply to Keynes," the shadow of the British economist hovered over the entire work.[35] Applying Maurras's dictum *politique d'abord* to the terms of the peace settle-

33. Bainville, *Journal*, II, June 20, 1919; Jacques Bainville, *Les Conséquences politiques de la paix* (Paris: Nouvelle Librairie Nationale, 1920), 179.
34. See John Maynard Keynes, *The Economic Consequences of the Peace* (London: Macmillan, 1920). See also Arnold Wolfers, *Britain and France Between Two World Wars* (New York: Norton, 1966), 201–211.
35. Bainville, *Les Conséquences politiques*, viii. At least one observer has pointed out that Bainville's critique of the Versailles treaty was a natural outgrowth of his two wartime works, *Histoire de deux peuples* and *Histoire de trois générations*, and "would have been written even without Keynes' book." See Vidal, *La Pensée de Jacques Bainville*, 80. For its part, the *Action française* delighted in announcing that Bainville's book corroborated Marshal Foch's stern judgment of the peace treaty. See *AF*, November 17, 1920.

ment, Bainville ridiculed the popular misconception that socioeconomic processes are the principal agents of historical change. "Economic chaos is serious," he conceded, "but political chaos is even worse." Since the seat of political power in a nation is decisive in matters of war and peace, he reasoned, the political consequences of the Versailles treaty were much more important than its economic consequences.[36]

It was not Keynes's denunciation of the harsh financial obligations imposed on Germany that provoked Bainville's counterattack. Indeed, he had himself recognized how onerous a burden these obligations represented if enforced to the letter. Bainville's reasons for criticizing the reparations settlement were thoroughly political, rather than economic. Instead of regarding the German war debt as a moral repayment for recent sins, the victors ought to utilize the reparations clause as a *political* instrument to achieve precise objectives. Specifically, they should distinguish between the potentially prowestern interests in Germany and the antiwestern, "Prussianized" sector, reducing the burden on the former and increasing it on the latter. Under present circumstances the effect of the imposition of "a common obligation" on all Germans was to supply them with a "common interest" in resisting the treaty.[37] A more discriminating policy would have served to weaken Prussia while winning the confidence of those Germans who had traditionally resisted its hegemony.

In any case Bainville regarded it as a foregone conclusion that Germany would eventually renege on her financial obligations (with the acquiescence of the British) and that France would find it difficult to compel payment by itself. The unilateral French occupation of the Ruhr appeared to him as the only available method of enforcement.[38] With regard to the problem of German rearmament, the only solution was to allocate small defensive armies to each of the federal states; instead, the peacemakers at Versailles had "given a single army to Greater Germany, that is, to Prussia"

36. Bainville, *Les Conséquences politiques*, 7–8.
37. *Ibid.*, 30.
38. *Ibid.*, 78. *AF*, February 14, 1919, in Bainville, *L'Allemagne*, II, 18.

(a policy which he believed would inevitably result in violations of the disarmament clauses).[39]

Sustained British opposition to such divide-and-conquer policies appeared to confirm Bainville's prejudices regarding the curious alliance of moral and economic motives that, he believed, had long typified the "Puritan" mentality. He persisted in suspecting that financial and commercial interests dictated Britain's increasingly lenient German policy: London bankers and Manchester exporters conspired to revive the Central European market for British capital and industrial products without regard to the threat that an economically prosperous Germany might later pose to European security. That this economic greed was clothed in the discredited moral principle of national self-determination merely increased his sense of outrage. By constantly reiterating the old refrain that German nationalism deserved the same rights as any other, the British remained ignorant of the political consequences that would inevitably flow from a policy predicated upon the alleged rights of the German people. "Other treaties have been political treaties," he observed. "This one was a moral treaty." And the British continued to prefer moralistic platitudes to sober political reasoning.[40]

But even assuming the wisdom of basing a diplomatic settlement upon such a principle as the right of nationhood, Bainville argued, the dismemberment of Germany remained the policy that fitted the objective. For the young nations that had been formed from the Habsburg Empire deserved to have their national independence protected as well. "The policy of nationalities, even more than the policy of the balance-of-power, requires the dissociation of Germany," he declared. "Small states are not secure [if they are] in the vicinity of a single state that remains large." Thus, for these new nations in Central Europe, the gigantic German state in their midst "can only be either a menace or an attraction. Between submission and struggle, there is no middle road."[41]

The assumption that the western powers could depend upon the

39. Bainville, *Les Conséquences politiques*, 58.
40. *Ibid.*, 15, 23.
41. *Ibid.*, 33.

Habsburg successor states to withstand the fatal menace or attraction of their formidable neighbor never fully satisfied Bainville.
Czechoslovakia, with its three million German citizens representing
a dangerous temptation to German interference in Czech affairs,
could scarcely be expected to survive without outside support. He
noted "the extreme prudence" that characterized Prague's postwar
attitude toward the German state. "And prudence rapidly becomes
neutrality. And unconditional, absolute neutrality soon becomes
subjection." Similarly, he detected an overriding temptation for
Germany to absorb the German-speaking state of Austria. Recalling the historical precedent that frequently returned to haunt him,
he asserted that the future of Central Europe "rests at the mercy of
a new battle of Sadowa, or of its political or moral equivalent."[42]

Nor was he convinced that the constitution of a Greater Poland
provided a surer guarantee against a future German *Drang nach
Osten*. "What is Poland's greatest weakness?" he asked. "It is that
it is not a state." It is instead a geographical monstrosity without
natural frontiers straddling "the vast plains of Eastern Europe."
Moreover, its ethnographic borders are "mobile and constantly
contested because of the mixture and conflict of races, languages,
and religions." The peacemakers, in short, had supported Poland's
demand for independence "without giving her the means to maintain it" between two powerful neighbors.[43] Once again he reminded his readers that this untenable situation could have been avoided had the Allies been willing to overcome their mystical faith in
national self-determination and chosen to incorporate Poland in a
revived Habsburg Empire.

What most alarmed Bainville about the creation of a large but
vulnerable Polish state was that it virtually precluded the revival of
the Franco-Russian alliance that had saved France from disaster in
1914. As a self-proclaimed realist he did not hesitate to weigh the
costs and benefits of such an alliance in the postarmistice period,
in spite of his ideological distaste for the new Russian regime. He

42. *Ibid.*, 34, 170.
43. *Ibid.*, 130, 133.

noted with approval that the Tsarist officer corps had been preserved virtually intact by the organizers of the Red Army and predicted that the Bolsheviks would eventually pursue a foreign policy not unlike that of the old regime. The Red Army's counterattack against the Polish forces in the summer of 1920 seemed to bear out his suspicions, both about the continuity of Russian foreign policy and the difficulties that lay ahead for the Polish state in its efforts to survive. The Russians had marched on Warsaw as though a Romanov rather than a Lenin were in the Kremlin, he observed. Even Bolshevism obeys the iron law of national continuity.[44]

Over and over again Bainville reiterated his fear that a weak Poland would eventually serve as the basis for a Russo-German understanding. Shortly after the opening of the peace conference he had accurately summarized Poland's predicament: she could rest secure only so long as her gigantic neighbor to the east continued to suffer the debilitating effects of political chaos, military weakness, and diplomatic isolation. "From the day that a Russian state is reborn and is capable of conducting a foreign policy," he predicted, "its alliance will automatically be forged with Germany against the countries formed at their common expense. Poland, as in her time of sorrows, will be caught in the crossfire." This preoccupation with the probable role of Poland as the catalyst of Russo-German cooperation resurfaced in his reply to Keynes. "From the moment that Poland was reconstituted at the expense of both countries," he noted, "the community of interests and sentiments was established. . . . Poland seems to have been invented to hasten the rapprochement [of Germany and Russia]." He was certain that France and England would some day be confronted by an alliance between the Slavic hordes and the German barbarians. He reminded those Frenchmen who recalled the long tradition of Franco-Russian friendship of the events of 1813 and 1917. Each time that their government had made common cause with the eastern em-

---

44. See E. H. Carr, *The Bolshevik Revolution*, III (New York: Macmillan, 1953), 65–67, 273–74; Bainville, *Les Conséquences politiques*, 97–99, 123.

pire against the Germanic powers, "that alliance had been terminated by the defection of Russia."[45]

Most important of all, Bainville never wavered in his conviction, first expressed during the peace conference and repeatedly reasserted throughout the twenties, that the maintenance of German unity had doomed the peace settlement from the beginning. "Concentrated in the interior, Germany has been dissociated on her periphery," he noted sadly. The existence of a powerful, centralized state surrounded by islands of strategically vulnerable territory that swarmed with German minorities aching to be reunited with the fatherland was a perpetual encouragement to German irredentism. "The surgeons of Versailles," as he put it in one of his arresting metaphors, "have sewn up the stomach of Europe without having drained the abscess."[46]

While Bainville entertained no illusions about the invulnerability of the new states of Eastern Europe, nor about their value in helping France to contain Germany, he was much more optimistic about the utility and solidity of an alliance with Italy. But he despaired over the humiliation that country had suffered at the peace conference, where the newly created state of Yugoslavia had received preferential treatment at Italy's expense in the redistribution of Habsburg territory along the Adriatic. He complained that this high-handed application of the principle of nationalities in the interests of the new and untested Yugoslav state had transformed Italy, a former ally, into a revisionist power; the probable consequence of this failure to satisfy her territorial demands was obvious: she would eventually be driven into the arms of her fellow revisionist power, Germany.[47]

But it was the deterioration of France's relations with her other traditional friends that alarmed Bainville most of all. After having dozens of allies and supporters during the war, he observed, France

---

45. Bainville, *Les Conséquences politiques*, 97ff., 126–27; Bainville, *Journal*, II, February 8, 1919.

46. Bainville, *Les Conséquences politiques*, 61, 92.

47. *Ibid.*, 145–48.

could regard only Belgium as a reliable friend within a year after Versailles. Britain's growing hostility to French interference in the Rhineland, not to speak of her recent repudiation of the defense treaty with France, convinced him that his country could expect little help from its former ally. Situated "on the margin of the European world," Britain had once again elected to "disengage herself from the affairs of the continent." She was proving to be less concerned about maintaining the balance of power in Europe than in looking after her commercial and maritime interests in her far-flung empire. Bainville bitterly recalled that the war had demonstrated the "mediocrity of the military force that the United Kingdom can muster to resist a first strike," conveniently forgetting the critical role played by the British expeditionary force in halting the German advance in the autumn of 1914. Nor could France count on the United States for active assistance, since it too had lost interest in "European complications" and reneged on its commitment to France.[48]

France's frantic quest for allies at the beginning of the postwar decade would have been unnecessary, Bainville noted, had the German Republic begun to evolve along the peaceful, democratic lines that the Big Four had envisioned. But the centralized structure of the new regime precluded such an evolution, for it was rapidly liquidating the federalist tendencies that had been tolerated under the Hohenzollerns. Was it not significant that the Weimar constitution retained the term "*Reich*" to describe the new regime and mentioned the word "republic" only once? Had not recent events in Germany confirmed his suspicions that the new democratic leadership was capable of perpetuating the repressive, authoritarian system of the Imperial past behind a smokescreen of democratic rhetoric? He took note of the bloody counterrevolution that was sweeping Germany in the name of anti-Bolshevism, the "extraordinary terrorist repression" inaugurated by the Socialist

---

48. After the Anglo-American failure to ratify the security treaty with France, the French government signed a mutual defense pact with Belgium in 1920. See Bainville, *Les Conséquences politiques*, 94ff.

Noske and executed by military vigilantes, which had permitted
the centralized German Republic to "resist the contagion of Bolshevism" and consolidate its power.[49]

Anglo-American blindness to the threat of a resurgent Germany
left France alone as the superintendent of continental stability. She
was consequently saddled with a burdensome military budget that
was sapping her economic resources while leading to what Bainville saw as a revival of the prewar "armed peace." He considered
the possibility of a military intervention to assist the separatist
movements that continued to limp along in western Germany
throughout the early twenties, but eventually rejected it on the
grounds that history had demonstrated that "German particularism has never been imposed from without. Napoleon's experiences decisively demonstrated that." Since the days of Louis XIV
France's traditional role had been to "favor the movements of se-
cession that spontaneously emerged in the interior" rather than to
interfere directly in Germany's affairs. Though he believed that the
treaty had virtually assured "an eternal war" between the two
nations, he denied that history revealed any "temperamental incompatibility" between Frenchmen and Germans. What it did
demonstrate was that certain political preconditions were required
before Franco-German cordiality could be reestablished on a firm
footing. Unfortunately, the principal *sine qua non* for such friendship was German disunity, which by the beginning of the twenties
was rapidly becoming a practical impossibility.[50]

Having reluctantly recognized the preservation of German unity
as a *fait accompli* by the beginning of the 1920s, Bainville hastened
to develop and promote contingency plans for the preservation of
peace and stability in the postwar world. Though he remained an
advocate of the realistic strategy of the balance-of-power, he appreciated the increasingly important role played by modern political ideologies in the formulation of foreign policies. As we have
seen, he himself had invoked the Metternichean principle of monarchical and aristocratic solidarity for purely realistic reasons in his

49. *Ibid.*, 76, 48ff., 156.
50. *Ibid.*, 55, 65, 37, 84.

earliest writings.[51] France, even with the albatross of a republican regime after 1871, had enjoyed the friendship of foreign courts because of her monarchical past and because of the "traditions inherited from the era when the prestige of our civilization and our language was unrivaled."[52] But his prewar diagnosis of the popularity of the monarchical form of government required revision in light of the disappearance of the royal houses of Eastern Europe and the proliferation of parliamentary republics. Perceiving the obsolescence of the monarchical principle as a basis for the postwar restoration of a European continent swarming with infant democracies, Bainville flirted with two alternative principles, but developed serious misgivings about both.

The first alternative principle Bainville considered was liberal nationalism. Given the proliferation of nation-states in postwar Europe, he wondered whether a new international system based on the principle of national self-interest could replace the doctrine of the solidarity of thrones that had served to protect the continent from the ravages of a general war for a century after the Congress of Vienna. He was willing to concede the possibility, but insisted on reminding his readers that a sense of nationhood was a complex phenomenon that could not be generated overnight. "There are many nationalities but few nations," he observed. "What makes a nation is the habit of living together. A border has a precise meaning when citizens realize that beyond it the mores, customs, and memories to which they are attached cease to exist." He continually reminded his readers that the new political units carved out of the carcass of the Austrian Empire lacked the requisite attributes of genuine nations, such as an ingrained sense of national identity and natural frontiers. Hence they hardly represented solid guarantees against the instability of Central Europe from which Germany was bound to profit.[53]

This concern about the future of the Habsburg successor states reappeared in Bainville's writings after the conclusion of the mili-

---

51. See above, 56, 66.
52. Bainville, *Les Conséquences politiques*, 107.
53. *Ibid.*, 102, 101–103.

tary alliance between France and Poland in 1921. This alliance, he believed, was rational and beneficial for both sides, and therefore worthy of French support. But history had demonstrated that a weak, vulnerable Poland was incapable of maintaining its independence in the unstable regions of Eastern Europe. And, as he had lamented in earlier columns, the democratic republic of Poland (with its attendant political disabilities) was hardly better suited to defend the national interest in the twentieth century than was the aristocratic republic in the eighteenth.[54]

Bainville was convinced that the young nations that had come into existence in the nineteenth century, such as Greece, Belgium, Rumania, Bulgaria, Italy, and Germany, had succeeded in establishing their viability and maintaining their territorial integrity because they were given monarchs to tutor them, foster their economic prosperity, and protect them from external interference. But no such qualities of leadership were discernible among the leaders of the new nations to the east. He considered it a grave error to have established "pure democracy" in countries which "have everything to create, everything to establish, frontiers to defend, and heterogeneous populations to hold together."[55] What was even more threatening to the future peace of Europe was the introduction of party politics in the newly established nations. This, he feared, would encourage subversive intrigues with foreign powers and exert a debilitating influence on foreign policy.[56]

For confirmation of his belief that national independence depended on the benevolent authority of a legitimate ruler, Bainville cited the words of the republican historian Ernest Lavisse: "The only nations which have been great in modern times are those which had established dynasties in the Middle Ages: Bohemia, Poland, and Hungary lost their independence because their fortunes were entrusted to the hazards of the election of a king."[57] Would not the same result follow, Bainville asked, from the elec-

54. *AF*, July 29, 1920, February 22, 1921.
55. Bainville, *Les Conséquences politiques*, 106.
56. *Ibid.*, 107.
57. *Ibid.*, 131–32.

tion of parliamentary leaders? His affirmative answer precluded his endorsement of liberal nationalism as the underpinning of the new European order.

Having discarded the alternative of liberal nationalism, Bainville momentarily toyed with the idea of proposing that the French government exploit the incipient racial and ethnic antagonisms in Central Europe in order to check German strength. He confessed to a passing daydream of a vast continental alliance of Slavism, which would unite the Central European nations and Russia to form an insuperable barrier to the spread of Pan-Germanism. But the potential dangers and uncertainties of such a policy quickly brought the daydream of Pan-Slavism to an end. "From the day that the idea of race has been thrown into Western civilization," he observed, "date the most atrocious convulsions of humanity." Recalling that Bulgaria, a prewar hotbed of Slavism in the Balkans, had joined the Central Powers against its ethnic brethren in 1915, he remarked that history has shown the mythology of race to be as capricious as that of nationalities.[58]

This skepticism about the principles of throne, nation, or race as solid foundations of a new European equilibrium under French auspices caused him eventually (and one suspects, reluctantly, in view of his previous pronouncements[59]) to adopt the principle of counterrevolution instead. A prescription for such a policy coming from a Frenchman would have been a curiosity in the years before the First World War, when France was still viewed with suspicion by monarchical Europe because of its revolutionary heritage and its democratic political institutions. But the replacement of the Habsburg, Hohenzollern, and Romanov Empires by liberal-, socialist-, or communist-dominated successor states had caused a rightward shift of France's position along the European political spectrum: since the old monarchical governments had fallen and had been replaced by disorder and chaos, the intellectual, moral, and political position of the French people had totally changed. By the single

58. *Ibid.*, 118–19.
59. See above, 131–32.

fact that she had remained what she was and that she continued to exist in the same conditions, France had become reactionary. Through a paradoxical historical development, the historic fountainhead of revolution in the modern world had become "the country of counterrevolution . . . the country of order *par excellence*, the antithesis of Bolshevism and anarchy." To his readers Bainville posed the crucial question: once the nations of Europe begin to recover from the present political and economic difficulties, is it not likely that they will forgive France her revolutionary past and turn to her, the one nation that represented the most solid bulwark against the anarchic tendencies of the present, for guidance? "What was our revolution of 1789," he asked, "compared to the one in Moscow?"[60]

These sentiments also reflected Bainville's increasingly favorable attitude toward the succession of right-wing governments that ruled France between 1920 and 1924. Clemenceau's wartime coalition had split into a conservative *Bloc National* (dominated by Clemenceau, Millerand, and Poincaré) and a *Cartel des Gauches* (led by the Radical Edouard Herriot and the Socialist Léon Blum). The November 1919 elections had returned a solid majority in the Chamber for the rightist group and the senatorial elections of January 1920 had produced a similar majority for the conservative republicans in the upper house. Many of the policies pursued by these conservative postwar governments satisfied the proponents of integral nationalism beyond their wildest expectations. The educational reforms of Léon Bérard (which temporarily restored the classical curriculum to secondary education), the occupation of the Ruhr to exact reparations payments from Germany, and the resumption of diplomatic relations with the Vatican, for example, had all been proposed in the pages of the *Action française* before becoming official policy. In the face of such satisfactions, which seemed to imply a change of direction in republican thinking, the royalists briefly revived the ideological cease fire that they had declared at the outbreak of the war. Symbolic of this new attitude

60. Bainville, *Les Conséquences politiques*, 195–96.

was the election of Léon Daudet to the Chamber in 1919. For the next five years this bitter enemy of the parliamentary game participated in the very political process that his movement had been belittling since the turn of the century.[61]

What cheered Bainville most about the rightward drift of the Republic was the "national and counterrevolutionary" foreign policy of the regime. Prime Minister Alexandre Millerand's decision to dispatch a military mission headed by General Weygand to advise the Polish army during its successful defense of Warsaw in the Russo-Polish war struck him as proof that devout republicans (and former socialists) were capable of rehabilitation. France's support of Poland was "national" because it enhanced French security by preserving the most valuable counterweight to German eastward expansion. It was "counterrevolutionary" because it helped to protect war-torn Eastern Europe from the infection of Bolshevism. More significantly, it served to establish France as the spearhead of the forces of European reaction, thereby providing Bainville's nation with an ideology which, for a change, it could export to other countries without having to fear the consequences. It now had the means to ingratiate itself with the conservative ruling circles of Europe that were attempting to shore up their defenses against the domestic political threat from the left or, as in the case of Poland, the external military challenge from Bolshevik Russia.

It thus began to appear that the French royalist writer was beginning to moderate his distaste for the political system of France. The republican regime had apparently detached itself from the revolutionary tradition that had alienated conservative opinion in the past; consequently, a reevaluation of French democracy was in order. As was his custom, Bainville searched for and discovered a historical precedent to illumine the recent turn of events:

Very slowly, after half a century, the Third Republic has undergone the evolution that the Second had undergone in a few months. Nothing

---

61. For a discussion of the royalist movement's attitude toward the succession of right-wing governments in France during the 1920–1924 period, see Osgood, *French Royalism since 1870*, 101–102, Weber, *Action Française*, 127–47, and Tannenbaum, *Action Française*, 152–53.

resembled the Republic of 1848 less than that of 1849. The same difference can be found between the Republic such as we see it in 1920 and such as we knew it in 1914 and even during the war.[62]

The republican regime had (at least temporarily) been domesticated, rehabilitated, purged of its evil spirits. Accordingly, Bainville was prepared to bury the ideological hatchet to make common cause with the French government in the forthcoming task of national reconstruction.

The Republic, for its part, hastened to return the compliment. Despite his caustic criticism of the peace treaty to which the French representatives signed their names in 1919, Bainville's support of the government's war policy did not go unrecognized and unrewarded. During the parliamentary debates over the ratification of the Versailles Treaty, the editorial board of *Le Temps* (the leading newspaper of the moderate republicans) offered him a frontpage column. Though he declined this offer because it was tendered on the condition that he cease his collaboration with the *Action française*—a break with his old comrades which he was by now apparently psychologically unprepared to make—he did begin to contribute articles on a regular basis to other republican journals that made no such demands, such as *La Liberté* and *Le Petit Parisien*, and later, *Le Petit Journal*, *Le Capital*, and *L'Eclair du Midi*. A year later the government itself expressed its appreciation for his wartime efforts by naming him to the Legion of Honor. It was beginning to seem as though Bainville had finally liberated himself from the sectarian straitjacket that had bound him since the beginning of his career.[63]

62. Bainville, *Les Conséquences politiques*, 195–96.
63. Linville, "Jacques Bainville," 219, 368; *Dictionnaire national des contemporains* (Paris: Lajeunesse, 1936), 40. Elie Bois and Robert Kemp, in "Hommages à Jacques Bainville," 522, 582–83.

PART TWO

The Road to
Respectability

CHAPTER SIX

The Defense of
The West

Oh, how fragile civilization is! . . . It is like a delicate flower.

Bainville

In the early years of the postwar decade, a number of develop-ments helped to secure for Jacques Bainville that wider audience to which he had gained access through his major wartime works, *L'Histoire de deux peuples*, *La Guerre et l'Italie*, *Comment est née la révolution russe*, and *L'Histoire de trois générations*. Furthermore, during this period his writings underwent a subtle shift of empha-sis that indicated continued broadening of his intellectual horizons. By the mid-twenties, he had completed the transformation from a relatively ethnocentric advocate of French national interests to a defender of the bourgeois social order of the Western world which he feared was imperiled by the forces of barbarism emerging from the East.

The first of these developments was set in motion by an episode of the last months of the war. On August 24, 1918 the Catholic philosopher Jacques Maritain received a letter from a provincial notary informing him that a recently killed French infantryman named Pierre Villard had bequeathed a million francs to him and to Charles Maurras. Maritain vaguely recalled having received sev-eral impassioned letters from Villard during the previous year in-forming him that the young soldier had derived great inspiration from the philosopher's teachings. Villard had declared that he also owed his intellectual formation to Maurras, Georges Sorel, and Pascal. Maurras subsequently suggested that he and Maritain pool their unexpected legacy to found a new periodical devoted

to propagating royalist political doctrine and Thomist theology.[1]
Maritain's response to this proposal was ambivalent at first. The
lingering antidemocratic influence of his two spiritual godfathers
Léon Bloy and Father Charles Clérissac had predisposed him to
view with sympathy the political principles of the Action Française.
Indeed, he himself echoed the royalist movement's shrill slogans
of integral nationalism, announcing at the time of his inheritance a
desire to "combat without respite the ideas and men who came to
power by means of the defeat of the fatherland and with the intention of betraying the soul of France."[2] Yet for all his contempt for
the Republic, Maritain's own intellectual preoccupations rested
principally in the spiritual realm. He hesitated to make common
cause with a political movement whose declared policy toward the
Catholic church was unabashedly agnostic. But this original hesi-
tation was rapidly overcome. Meanwhile, Léon Daudet had by
chance encountered a young man named Henri Massis in a railroad car, and soon discovered that he was one half of the pseud-
onymous "Agathon," whose prewar diatribes against the French
university system had made him something of a hero in rightist
youth circles.[3] Since Massis had subsequently achieved some noto-
riety as a Catholic writer, and was an acquaintance of Maritain's,
the royalists eagerly enlisted him to serve as the mediator between
their movement and the philosopher of the Thomist renaissance.[4]

Massis assured Maritain that while the proposed new review
"would need the clientele of the Action Française in order to get
off the ground," it would nevertheless be an "independent organ,
with no express connection" to the royalist movement. As a gesture
of good faith, Maurras suggested that the less controversial Bainville and the certified Catholic Massis be entrusted with the joint
editorial control of the periodical and that Maritain edit the philos-

1. Jacques Maritain, *Carnet de notes* (Paris: Desclée de Brouwer, 1965), 139–40,
177–79. It was later discovered that Villard had been a member of the Etudiants
d'Action Française before the war. Albert Marty, *L'Action Française racontée par elle-
même* (Paris: Nouvelles Editions Latines, 1968), 172.
2. Raïssa Maritain, *Les Grandes Amitiés* (Paris: Desclée de Brouwer, 1949), 343.
3. See above, 97.
4. Henri Massis, *Maurras et notre temps*, I, 146.

ophy section. After Maritain accepted these conditions, *La Revue universelle* was born. But the major participants in this joint venture had conflicting views of its implications. Maritain's wife noted in her diary that the foundation of the periodical marked "the first time that the Thomist philosophy had such a large entrée into the world of culture." Pierre Gaxotte, Maurras's private secretary during the war, later claimed that Bainville had assumed control of the review in order to propagate Maurrassian ideas in higher echelons of French intellectual life. Georges Valois, the director of the publication board, later insisted that the periodical was nothing but a disguised annex of the Action Française through which Maurras and his colleagues acquired various social advantages. Maurras himself described it as the royalist movement's "philosophical, literary, and social organ of propaganda and of national and international penetration."[5]

Massis later revealed what can only be described as a measure of bad faith in his earlier promise to Maritain regarding the review's independence from the Action Française. He claimed that the royalists had decided to found the new periodical as part of a concerted effort to renew the old prewar spirit of nationalism. They had originally considered reviving the fortnightly *Revue de l'Action française* as their principal propaganda machine. But the loss of key members of its editorial staff in the war had depleted its ranks, and the remainder of the royalist leadership was preoccupied with putting out the daily newspaper. They therefore decided to set up a semiautonomous publication under independent management to communicate the general principles of integral nationalism to a wider audience.[6]

Regardless of which version of the circumstances surrounding its birth one accepts, the *Revue universelle* was to assume an im-

5. Jacques Maritain, *Carnet de notes*, 179; Jacques Maritain, *Journal de Raïssa* (Paris: Desclée de Brouwer, 1963), January 16, 1920; Pierre Gaxotte, ed., *Charles Maurras, 1868–1952* (Paris, Plon, 1953), 35; Georges Valois, in *La Volonté*, January 4, 1929 (see also AN, F⁷13207, "Notes sur L'Action Française." Valois had by this time severed his ties with the royalists and had launched his career as the founder of one of France's first fascist movements); Charles Maurras, *Tombeaux* (Paris: Nouvelle Librairie Nationale, 1921), 305.

6. Massis, *Maurras et notre temps*, I, 145–46.

portant place in Parisian journalism during the interwar period. It proved sufficiently resilient to survive the resignation of Maritain in 1927, a defection that had been in the cards for some time but was precipitated by the Papal condemnation of the Action Française in the preceding year. Though the departure of France's leading Catholic theologian led to a dramatic decline in the number of religious articles, Bainville and Massis continued to attract a distinguished group of contributors on literary and political subjects from the royalist and republican right.[7]

Faithful to its title, the *Revue universelle* became much more eclectic than might have been expected of an organ controlled by the prophets of such a narrow brand of French nationalism as that of the Maurrassians. Bainville's programmatic statement in the first issue was conspicuously lacking in the type of ideological polemic that typically filled the pages of the *Action française*. The new periodical, he explained, was not even aimed primarily at the French public, but rather was intended for all those citizens of the Western world who were fortunate enough to possess a reading knowledge of that supreme vehicle of universal culture, the French language.[8]

Bainville's introductory essay spelled out his ambitious design for the regeneration of a European civilization ravaged by war and revolution. Pondering this design since the armistice, Bainville progressively shifted his attention from the problem of safeguarding

7. *Ibid.*, 157. According to Massis, Maritain declared his independence from the Action Française because he wanted to "reserve for nonroyalists the possibility of being nationalists in the sense of integral fidelity to the fatherland, and of being conducted to the monarchy" through nationalism rather than vice versa. One gets a different story from Maritain himself in his *Primauté du spirituel*, which was a rejoinder to Maurras's "Politique d'abord." Maritain later confessed that his "entente cordiale" with the royalists was a terrible mistake, attributable to his "political naïveté." Jacques Maritain, *Carnet de notes*, 180. His wife later referred to the "illusions" and "negligence" that led her husband to make common cause with the Action Française, though she insisted that he had always maintained his "philosophical independence" from the movement. Raïssa Maritain, *Les Grandes Amitiés*, 343–44. In addition to old Action Française stalwarts such as Maurras, Daudet, and Marie de Roux, and sympathizers such as Eugène Cavaignac, René Benjamin, Edmond Pilon, and Louis Bertrand, the *Revue universelle* received contributions from such eminent members of the French literary set as Paul Valéry, Francis Jammes, Henry de Montherlant, and André Maurois.

8. *Revue universelle* (hereinafter cited as *RU*), (April, 1920), 1.

French security along the Rhine to a more universal concern for the future of Western civilization itself in the face of the simultaneous growth of Bolshevism in Russia and anti-imperialist nationalism in Africa and Asia. Whereas before the war, he had dismissed imperialism as a profligate diversion of wealth and manpower, he had gradually come to appreciate the valuable function of the colonial empires in extending European influence to the non-European world. Bainville believed that the most serious long-term consequence of the war was that Europe's weakness and vulnerability were revealed to colonial subjects.[9] By squandering its precious resources in an orgy of internecine bloodshed, the Old World had inadvertently strengthened the dark forces of barbarism that were struggling to cast off the shackles of their civilizing masters. The German Empire's attempt to achieve undisputed hegemony in Europe had thereby jeopardized the future of European civilization itself. The old custom of resolving intra-European conflicts through mutually respectful diplomacy had rested upon a common fund of shared values that was rapidly disappearing in the postwar world:

> It is not only the European system that has been burst by revolutions. It is the European spirit. In a large section of Europe the monarchies, the courts, and the aristocracies conserved a certain community of ideas, language, and manners, a memento of a time when French was the language of Frederick II. In their place have come nationalist democracies, conscious only of themselves, which are turning Europe into a Tower of Babel.[10]

Apocalyptic predictions of the approaching decline of the West were not uncommon amid the spiritual confusion of postwar Europe.[11] In order to lend an air of urgency to his own somber premonition, Bainville did not hesitate to trot out the familiar analogy of third- and fourth-century Rome capitulating to the barbarians. He recounted to his readers the story of the Roman patrician Sym-

9. Bainville, *Journal*, II, June 24, 1925.
10. Jacques Bainville, *Heur et malheur des Français* (Paris: Nouvelle Librairie Nationale, 1924), 6, 14.
11. See below, 163–64.

machus, who died shortly before Alaric's invasion comforted by
the conviction that his civilization was eternal. "How many Sym-
machuses we have today!", Bainville exclaimed, sadly observing
that most Europeans were basking in the Indian summer of European civilization while anti-Western rebellions brewed throughout
the world, "From North Africa to China."[12]

Nor did he share the optimism of those who trusted the Euro-
pean-trained native elites to perpetuate the traditions and protect
the patrimony of the Old World in the colonial lands. "One of the
greatest mistakes that the Western world has committed," he
noted, "is to imagine that the colored peoples, in acceding to its
type of civilization, would be drawing nearer to it." To justify their
demands for independence from the colonial powers, the Western-
educated, indigenous elites of Africa and Asia had shrewdly appropriated the principles of human liberty and equality that the
European left had been trumpeting since 1789. Following the Chinese Revolution of 1911, Bainville had predicted that such outbreaks of anti-Western violence would become more numerous as
long as the ideology of national liberation continued to receive
such publicity.[13] "When one has millions and millions of yellow
and black subjects," he repeated after the war, "what a strange
idea it is to proclaim the principle of popular self-determination."[14]

But how to stem the tide of anti-imperialism that threatened to
terminate the era of European world supremacy? Recognizing that
the world war had spawned resistance to European colonial domination, Bainville regarded the prevention of another debilitating
intra-European conflict as the Old World's only hope. And that in
turn required some form of European federation. Either a single
power would have to establish and maintain continental stability
through unilateral force of arms, or several powers would have to
agree upon a multilateral federating principle that would unite the

12. *RU*, I (April, 1920), 1. See also Jacques Bainville, *Couleurs du temps* (Versailles: Bibliothèque des Oeuvres Politiques, 1928), 55, 16–17; Bainville, *Journal*, II,
June 24, 1925.
13. Bainville, *Couleurs du Temps*, 57; *Journal*, I, July 15, 1913, II, September 30,
1926.
14. Bainville, *L'Angleterre*, 127.

nations of Europe in a common purpose. He recognized that France was no longer capable of reimposing a "French peace" on the continent and that Britain's imperial interests dictated a return to her traditional policy of isolation. This left a revived Germany as the prime candidate to preside over the forcible confederation of Europe, a cure which Bainville understandably regarded as worse than the disease. The absence of an effective federating *power* impelled him to advocate the adoption of a federating *ideology* that could unite the nations of Europe in defense of their common civilization. His belief in the paramount role of ideas as determinants of historical change enabled him to envisage the possibility of European salvation. "The solution of social problems is subordinate to the restoration of intellectual order," he announced. "The correct ideas will triumph only if they have the means of expressing themselves, if all those who think similarly meet and collaborate."[15]

In attempting to delineate the structure of this proposed pan-European ideology, Bainville once again permitted his parochial French nationalism to emerge. He persistently maintained that the only suitable cornerstone for such intellectual collaboration was the cultural heritage of France, the one European nation that had demonstrated throughout history a unique capacity for exercising dominance over European civilization without stifling the creativity and encroaching upon the independence of other nations. He recalled that in her years of greatness France was "not only tolerant, hospitable, affable, and curious about the genius of others, but also sought out the foreigner, incorporating [foreign] men, ideas, and things into her patrimony."[16]

This universalistic conception of French civilization had earlier been reasserted by a group of French writers of diverse political persuasions who had issued in the pages of the *Revue universelle* a manifesto calling for the creation of "an intellectual federation of the world based on French thought." Bainville believed that French traditions were admirably suited to such a purpose, since they had historically succeeded in "obtaining the adherence of and produc-

15. *RU*, I (April, 1920), 3.
16. Jacques Bainville, *Maximes et réflexions* (Paris: A la Cité des Livres, 1931), 17.

ing harmony in minds that are entirely different by origin." Indeed, he sensed that the entire world was once again turning to France during the postwar period of cultural confusion in the hope that "she might again place herself at the head of a civilizing movement."[17]

But France was a land of diverse traditions and ideals, including many that were mutually incompatible. Which of these did Bainville believe should be selected for exportation to other European nations as a basis for a new Europe-wide consensus? He noted that the aging defenders of the Republic continued to insist that "the France of the Revolution, the country of the Rights of Man, the land of emancipation, will discover friendship and support among foreign revolutionaries and liberals." But he claimed that the new republican elite in France had itself lost faith in democratic principles and was therefore incapable of resurrecting them as the ideological underpinning of a new European order.[18] The obsolete doctrines of liberal democracy were hardly suited to the task of reconstituting the material and moral resources of war-torn Europe. Of what value was the principle of human liberty to the citizens of a devastated continent hungering for the more essential benefits of personal and national security?

Having dismissed the French revolutionary tradition as a unifying principle of European order, Bainville turned his attention to an alternative tradition that possessed the advantage of being both indigenous to France and potentially useful to Europe in her present agony. The hallowed tradition of classical French rationalism, whose virtues were recognized throughout the Western world, could form the basis for a European ideology that would unite all those who desire the salvation of Western civilization.[19] While seeking to achieve her own national renaissance, not on the basis of the obsolete doctrine of liberal nationalism but according to the rationalist principles of her classical heritage, France could discover allies among those Europeans who recognized in the clas-

17. *RU*, I (April, 1920), 1.
18. Bainville, *Réflexions sur la politique*, 96.
19. *Ibid.*, 93 and *RU*, I (April, 1920), 2.

sical spirit the foundation of a new European synthesis. Bainville discovered in postwar France at least one reason for believing that the time was ripe for a reaffirmation of seventeenth-century traditions for the purpose of rescuing Western culture from its plight in the twentieth: his good friend Léon Bérard, the French Minister of Public Instruction between 1921 and 1924, succeeded in temporarily reestablishing the Latin requirement in the lycées in what was universally viewed as the beginning of a campaign to restore the classical curriculum.[20]

Bainville thus viewed France as the linchpin of the intellectual and the political counterrevolution that he regarded as the only solution to the malaise of postwar Europe. Just as French military expertise had helped to save Poland from the assault of the Red Army in 1920,[21] French classical culture could serve to inoculate the Western world against the contagious ideas of Bolshevism in Europe and its iniquitous offshoot, anti-imperialism in the colonial world. Bainville's own *Revue universelle* was to play a major role in this campaign to fortify the intellectual defenses of the West against the new threat from the modern "barbarians." "The Revolutionary International is organizing; it has newspapers and periodicals that are spreading its doctrine and supporting its cause," he warned at the end of his programmatic statement in the *Revue's* first number, "The attack being international, the defense must also extend to [other] nations." The purpose of the new organ must be to "assemble the forces of the intellect against the powers of dissolution . . . that are threatening the reason and order of the universe."[22]

These dire warnings about the impending threat to Western civilization represented by the triple evil of Bolshevism, German-

20. Bérard became the godfather of Bainville's only son Hervé. Interview with Hervé Bainville. See Talbott, *The Politics of Educational Reform in France*, 78, 80, 84–86.

21. Like most French observers during the interwar period, Bainville vastly overrated the role played by General Weygand's military mission in the defense of Warsaw in 1920. For a definitive exposé of the falsity of these French claims, see Norman Davies, *White Eagle, Red Star: The Polish-Soviet War, 1919–1920* (New York: St. Martin's, 1972), 221–25.

22. *RU*, I (April, 1920), 1–2. Maurras later hailed the *Revue universelle* for promoting "the necessary expansion of the French idea that we had proposed twenty years earlier." Maurras, *Tombeaux*, 305.

ism, and Asiatic "barbarism" were repeated in 1927 by Bainville's collaborator Henri Massis in an essay entitled *Défense de l'Occident*. The book was widely regarded—and touted by its author—as a Gallic reply to Spengler's *Der Untergang des Abendlandes*. That is to say, it represented another salvo in the continuing polemic between French and German intellectuals over the true meaning of Western civilization.

Yet despite the Spenglerian backdrop, Massis's work was more directly influenced by a more recent contribution to the same debate by the German scholar Ernst Robert Curtius. In a work entitled *Französischer Geist im neuen Europa*, Curtius had tried his hand at the intellectual game that German and French writers had been playing for decades: the attempt by each competitor in the Franco-German cultural conflict to detect sympathy for its cause in the enemy's own backyard. Just as Bainville had earlier sought to expose Francophile elements within German culture in the writings of Heine, Goethe, and Neitzsche,[23] Curtius set out to identify Germanic trends in modern French culture. He interpreted the recent victory of the *Cartel des Gauches* in France as a nationwide repudiation of education minister Bérard's attempt to restore the classical curriculum to secondary education. This reversal, the German professor argued, was an indication that the Latin spirit in French culture had finally been definitively submerged by the Gothic spirit of Celtic France.[24]

Like his co-editor at the *Revue universelle*, Massis was convinced that the classical and rationalist tradition of France represented the most reliable and universally acceptable weapon for the defense of Western values. But whereas the agnostic Bainville had emphasized the cultural conflict between classical civilization and the various manifestations of "eastern barbarism," the devoutly Catholic Massis predictably stressed the religious origins of the chasm that separated the two worlds. He blamed the present crisis of Western

23. See above, 15, and below, 276n.
24. See Ernst Robert Curtius, *Französischer Geist im neuen Europa* (Stuttgart: Deutsche Verlags-Anstalt, 1925), 264ff. See also Henri Massis, *Défense de l'Occident* (Paris: Plon, 1927), 20–21n.

civilization on the progressive encroachments on the universality of Catholicism that had shattered the unity of Christian Europe during the past four centuries. Bolshevik Russia, intent on launching a "spiritual war" against the civilized world of Europe, had discovered in German Protestantism "a sort of preordained complicity, a secret connivance, a foundation of permanent hostility to the principles of Roman-Christian culture." In short, the secular heirs to the Orthodox and Protestant schismatics shared a common hatred of unitary Catholicism, and this potent combination of Germanism and Slavism threatened to replace classical civilization as the dominant intellectual force of the Western world.[25]

The faint rumblings of nationalist discontent in the Far East furnished Massis with additional evidence of this barbarian conspiracy against the civilizing tradition of Roman Catholicism. He traced the spiritual doctrines of Gandhi, the universal symbol of the colonial world's struggle against European domination, to the romantic irrationalism that had afflicted the European continent itself in the previous century. Roman-Christian culture was thus confronted with the interrelated challenge of Eastern mysticism, German idealism, and Bolshevism. Indeed, Massis managed to blame the appearance of anti-Western nationalism in the nonwestern world on the historical influence of religious thought in Europe, seeing it as completing the disintegration of Roman Christianity that had begun with the division of the Empire in the fourth century.[26]

The agnostic Bainville was fully in accord with his Catholic colleague regarding the necessity of transmitting the classical values of Western civilization from generation to generation as a perpetual guarantee of its survival, though he placed less emphasis upon its roots in premedieval Christianity. "In order to avoid being unsettled by Bolshevism and its substitutes," he warned, "one must be conscious of the superiority of Western civilization." If Europe were to succumb to the corrosive ideas emanating from the East, it would be imitating past civilizations which declined because they had lost faith in the legitimacy of their governing principles. Such

25. Massis, *Défense de l'Occident*, 113–15.
26. *Ibid.*, 180–81, 199–200, 239–40.

had been the case with the aristocratic system of France in 1789. The bourgeois French society of the postwar period was due to suffer the same fate "if it begins to believe, as it already has too strong a tendency to do, that the future is always on the left and that the success of the socialist ideology is inevitable."[27]

As usual, Bainville hailed the two great Channel powers as the only nations capable of providing the cultural and material resources that could salvage what remained of the European idea. "Europe is no longer governed by men who had an English nurse and a French preceptor," he later lamented. "We are therefore not surprised to see the sense of Europe disappear and barriers erected between similar peoples." But he was not so naïve as to believe that the vigorous reassertion of the traditional verities to revive the concept of a common European patrimony would alone suffice to save Western civilization from ruin. Since the barbarians at the gate were arming themselves with weapons as well as ideas, the guardians of the civilized world were obliged to rely on military force as well as spiritual unity to defend their precious heritage. The French army could perhaps be trusted to protect the continent from the dual threat of an awakened Russia and a revived Germany. But the British navy would have to take the lead in maintaining order in the extensive area of the colonial world under European domination. The exhaustion of European civilization after four years of self-destructiveness had produced a tenuous international situation in which all that was required to precipitate the universal retreat of the white nations was the loss of that domination of the seas which had enabled them to penetrate Africa and Asia during the past century.[28]

As the international dimensions of the "barbarian" menace became apparent to Bainville during the twenties, he became more and more willing to look across the Channel to the notoriously unreliable Britain for support in the campaign to defend the West. "France and England," he had observed at the end of the war, "are

27. Bainville, *Couleurs du temps*, 44.
28. Bainville, *Heur et malheur des Français*, 14; *La Liberté*, June 19, 1923; *AF*, February 16, 1927, in Bainville, *L'Angleterre*, 106.

united by all the forces of nature and history to join in the common defense of their liberty, their possessions, and their wealth."
Though he continued to distrust anti-Bolshevism as the basis for
French global strategy (since it diverted attention from what he
viewed as the more immediate threat of a revived Germany), he
became increasingly alarmed at the Soviet-inspired unrest in the
Far East, which posed a potential threat to French Indochina and
the British East Asian Empire. He suspected that an Anglo-French
alliance against Bolshevik-supported challenges to colonial rule in
Asia would one day become a practical necessity for both nations.
"The Soviets do not invade," he observed. "They send to the
Asiatics the carefully prepared poison of their doctrine and propaganda," a potent dose that was "more dangerous than the Red
Army." He also foresaw the necessity for common action in Africa,
where he detected similar signs of unrest that threatened to undermine Anglo-French dominance of that continent. In the last analysis, it was French military superiority in Europe and British naval
predominance on the high seas that guaranteed the preservation
of European supremacy in the world. The fates of the British and
French empires were inextricably linked. They would "endure or
perish together."[29]

Taking heart from Britain's fervently anti-Bolshevik policy after
the end of the war, Bainville was hopeful that she would not waver
in her commitment, if not to stamp out the disease at its source, at
least to quarantine it at the frontiers of its mother country. Indeed,
he believed the Soviet goal of universal revolution doomed to failure as long as the British Empire continued to function as the "cita-
del of order" in the world. And he remained convinced that the
island kingdom's dependence on her African and Asian possessions for markets and raw materials guaranteed her perpetual commitment to the maintenance of "equilibrium and general stability"
as a condition of her very existence as a great power.[30]

29. *AF*, March 29, 1918, April 9, June 4, 1927, August 2, 1928; February 5, 1930;
Bainville, *L'Angleterre*, 116; Bainville, *Couleur du temps*, 48.
30. Bainville, *Couleurs du temps*, 47, 59. Yet he continued to fear that Britain's
preoccupation with imperial interests would divert her from more important obliga-

But Bainville's confidence in Britain's willingness and ability to suppress the revolutionary unrest that had begun to brew in her empire did not remain unimpaired. He interpreted the Labour Party's mounting sympathy for Indian self-government as the first step in a more generalized repudiation of imperial responsibilities that might characterize some future Socialist government. He feared that a Britain stripped of her colonial possessions was doomed to disappear from the international stage, where her presence was so desperately needed by her codefender of Western civilization on the European continent. He frequently referred to British agriculture's inability to accommodate the demands of domestic consumption. He predicted that the granting of independence to India would set off a chain reaction of national liberation movements throughout the colonial world that would eventually leave the mother country bereft of adequate sources of food and fiber, not to speak of protected markets for industrial products and capital.[31] Such a transformation would destroy the international order, with the former guarantor of world stability reduced to the status of an economically depressed, militarily impotent island incapable of sustaining and defending its own inhabitants.

An additional aspect of British behavior in the first half of the twenties increasingly alarmed Bainville. He had long believed that British foreign policy was dictated not by the necessity of preserving European stability and world dominance but by the fluctuating requirements of the Anglo-American financial community. His antipathy for this social group dates from the prewar years and often rivaled in intensity his disdain for Germany itself. He frequently observed that the financiers of Wall Street and the City of London invariably pursued the dual objective of free trade and world peace because the international capitalist system depended on unimpeded access to markets and the sources of raw materials. According

---

tions in Europe. "If the policing of the continent is not undertaken in a serious manner, Egypt and India will be in danger," he warned. "If we do not keep a careful watch on the Rhine and the Danube, the Straits and the Suez Canal will require a renewed effort of defense." *AF*, February 19, 1920.
    31. *La Liberté*, July 27, 1928; *AF*, November 8, 1929.

to Bainville, this obsession had driven the potentates of international finance capitalism and their political allies to subordinate the security interests of the West to their own narrow economic interests, as, for example, when they had pressed for economic concessions to Germany that yielded material benefits but were demonstrably unsound from a strategic point of view.[32]

So mordant was his criticism of this economic underpinning of foreign policy that Bainville's analysis of the causes of the Great War occasionally resembled the neo-Marxist interpretation of that phenomenon as a consequence of the internal contradictions of capitalism: Germany's lack of economically valuable colonies, coupled with the crises of overproduction that accompanied the advanced stage of her industrialization, had transformed her into a restless industrial giant "stifled within her borders" and desperately in need of "trade outlets and markets." Her loss of foreign markets due to the trend toward economic nationalism at the end of the nineteenth century drove her to covet new territory in the hope of transforming its inhabitants into "obligatory customers for her exports." He asserted that the post-Bismarckian German leaders were "businessmen" (he invariably used the English word) who think "à l'américaine" and pursue a policy of merchants. Fortunately for France, and for the world, the war had dispelled the Anglo-Saxon illusion of basing world peace on the principle of free trade and international economic interdependence. But he complained that this illusory conception had reappeared in British thinking during the twenties in spite of the terrible lessons of the war. Indeed, Britain's policy at the Peace Conference was already directed toward laying the groundwork for "the salvation of German finance and [future British] collaboration with it."[33]

Equally alarming in the eyes of Bainville the French nationalist was the undisputed primacy of the dollar and the pound sterling as the two principal vehicles of international monetary exchange. In the heyday of international capitalism during the twenties, many

32. *AF*, December 23, 1912, March 9, 1917.
33. *AF*, May 19, 1924, January 2, 1913, March 9, 1917 (in Bainville, *L'Angleterre*, 40–41), April 16, 1919.

Europeans had come to place inordinate faith in the Anglo-American financial community, the managers of the world's reserve currencies, to restore international stability by financial manipulation rather than by the traditional political means. Indeed, Bainville argued that the practitioners of financial diplomacy had moved in to fill the vacuum caused by the inability of the political elites of the Western world to stem the inevitable degeneration of democratic government into instability and impotence. The bankers of New York and London had assumed the management of world affairs now that the "socialist, socializing, or socialistically inclined democracies have demonstrated their incapacity."[34] The Anglo-Saxon powers may have fought to make the world safe for democracy, but their postwar diplomatic policies were aimed at making it safe for investment and commerce.

Even the leftist coalition that came to power in France in the spring of 1924 was willing, to Bainville's surprise, to support these policies of financial stabilization. Herriot, Briand, and the other architects of the Cartel des Gauches failed to recognize that the leadership of the Western world was passing into the hands of plutocrats across the Channel and across the Atlantic whose stewardship of world affairs represented no improvement over the discredited policies of European statesmen.[35] British and later American efforts to coax Germany back into the fraternity of civilized nations with generous economic concessions were based on the error "of believing that commerce, like music, sweetens [national] customs." Bainville feared that this attempt to enshrine the principles of finance and commerce as the basis for international stability was beginning to lull the citizens of Western Europe into a false sense of security. "People today think that the key to the immense difficulties in Europe is in the hands of New York businessmen," he complained, "as if the habit of handling money and of lending it at interest prepares one to direct the [affairs of the] world. We

34. *AF*, October 17, 1925.
35. *Ibid.*, For a recent interpretation of this development, see Stephen A. Schuker, *The End of French Predominance in Europe: The Financial Crisis of 1924 and the Adoption of the Dawes Plan* (Chapel Hill: University of North Carolina Press, 1976).

attribute to plutocracy an intelligence and an ability that it does not have."[36]

Bainville's antipathy for financial diplomacy reached its height in the spring of 1924 during the deliberations of the Dawes Committee, which was drawing up a plan for the resolution of the reparations dispute that had prompted the French military occupation of the Ruhr a year earlier. As the bankers and economists deliberated, he lashed out at what he sensed to be "a vast conspiracy to rehabilitate Germany" masterminded by the Anglo-American financial community. France's unilateral military intervention had accomplished its objective: German industries in the Ruhr had resumed reparations deliveries under French pressure in spite of their government's obstructionist policy, thereby exploding the myth of Germany's inability to pay. But the collapse of the mark, precipitated by the German government's inflationary method of subsidizing passive resistance in the Ruhr, had frightened the international financial community into believing that the continued prosperity of the industrialized world was gravely threatened by imminent economic catastrophe in Germany.[37]

The official report of the Dawes Committee gave Bainville even greater cause for alarm than he had originally anticipated. Not only would the Anglo-Saxon banking community grant loans and credits to the Weimar Republic in an effort to shore up the faltering German economy, but France herself would be asked to contribute to the financial salvation of her erstwhile enemy. For the French government to commit the hard-earned savings of its citizens to the purchase of "securities more risky than Russian ones" was folly on purely economic grounds. More important, it was disastrous from the standpoint of national security. The Dawes proposal reminded Bainville of the Turkish bond issue that was floated in France in early 1914 "which was used to pay for the cannons and munitions of Gallipoli and whose dividends were paid in tombs."[38]

While Prime Minister Edouard Herriot was in London voting to

---

36. Bainville, *Réflexions sur la politique*, 83.
37. Bainville, *Journal*, II, March 9 and 15, April 3, 1924.
38. *Ibid.*, May 1, 1924.

ratify the Dawes Plan, Bainville revived once again the specter of "a world government ruled by bankers."[39] This new oligarchy remained totally ignorant of the long range political consequences of the policies it conducted, preferring to concentrate on the short term economic benefits.[40] Who was prepared to guarantee that the restoration of German prosperity would not at some future date serve as the material basis for the renascence of German military power? The essence of the dispute between Germany and the victors of 1918 was not the reparations issue; it was the territorial settlement which deprived the vanquished nation of population and resources that it continued to covet. Financial concessions alone were insufficient to ensure Germany's voluntary compliance with the territorial provisions of the treaty. They merely strengthened the hand and whetted the appetite of a country whose principal objective was political: the revision of the 1919 frontiers. And such a revision would destroy the European balance and render France vulnerable to a new invasion. The ratification of the Dawes Plan therefore represented a first step in the dissolution of the Versailles system, the termination of the solid guarantees represented by the occupation of the Ruhr, and the beginning of Germany's economic and eventual military recovery. Momentous matters such as these, Bainville complained bitterly, "do not enter into the calculations of bankers."[41]

Bainville's writings on foreign policy during the early twenties portrayed France as an increasingly vulnerable, isolated nation confronted with potential enemies and competitors eager to encroach upon her economic, political, and cultural sovereignty. The doctrines that the great powers adopted in pursuit of their national goals—the international capitalism of Britain and America, the Communist ideology of Russia, the incipient pan-Germanism that he detected beneath the pacific facade of the Weimar Republic—represented direct challenges to France's national interest.

This image of French isolation and vulnerability in Bainville's

---

39. *Ibid.*, July 17 and 23, 1924.
40. *AF*, October 17, 1925, in Bainville, *L'Allemagne*, II, 123.
41. Bainville, *Journal*, II, July 28, August 9 and 29, 1924.

writings was conveyed by frequent references to the singularity of French institutions. In a period when France's democratic *political* system no longer represented an oddity, as in the prewar years, but was being emulated in variant forms by many of the newly established nations to the east, he chose to concentrate on the peculiarities of her *economic* institutions in order to emphasize the uniqueness of her position in postwar Europe. He frequently called attention to France's anomalous status as a developed industrial nation whose economic system had preserved numerous vestiges of the precapitalist era. As such, she occupied an intermediate position between the highly industrialized systems of England, Germany and the United States, and the agricultural societies of the rest of the world. Bainville concluded that France's unique economic system isolated her in the international community by reducing the number of points at which her interests and those of her potential allies might coincide. The predominance of small and medium sized property owners rendered France inherently conservative. Industrial and commercial England, on the other hand, was dominated by plutocrats and proletarians, both of whose economic interests were in direct conflict with those of the French. He feared that the contrasting economic systems of the two countries, notwithstanding their similarities in other spheres, constituted a perpetual obstacle to the fashioning of a coordinated foreign policy that would prevent a resurgence of German aggression and would contain Bolshevism. "Such contrary situations in every area, so few needs in common," he lamented, "have made it difficult for Frenchmen and Englishmen to speak the same language."[42]

Recognizing the increasingly important role that industrial capitalism was playing in the reconstruction of Europe in the twenties, Bainville began to devote more and more attention to financial affairs. In 1920 he published a work with the enticing title *After the War: How to Invest Your Wealth*. It offered financial advice to those French *rentiers* who had managed to protect their savings from the

42. *AF*, February 19, 1920.

ravages of war, inflation, and the revolutions in Eastern Europe. This book, together with the occasional articles on finance that he had contributed to the *Action française*, attracted the attention of the Parisian financial world, and in 1924 he was awarded a weekly column in *Le Capital*, its unofficial organ. Within a few years the amateur journalist who had earlier become an instant expert on the problems confronting the Quai d'Orsay was to become, with scarcely more intellectual preparation, a leading commentator on the affairs of the *Bourse*.[43] The advocate of French national security thenceforth became a vigorous proponent of France's capitalist economic system as well.

The spirited defense of French capitalism that appeared in Bainville's postwar writings was based less on economic than on political arguments. As a good Maurrassian, he judged all economic systems according to the effectiveness of their contribution to the security and stability of the state. A great civilization "does not exist in a vacuum," he declared. "It does not exist in ideal regions. It assumes above all security and facility of life, which in turn assumes . . . sound and abundant finances." The term "capital" recurs throughout Bainville's works, but always in its broadest connotation. It referred not only to machinery, property, raw materials, precious metals, etc., but also in a more general sense to the totality of the efforts and accomplishments of past generations, without which French civilization could never have attained its advanced state of political and cultural development.[44] Indeed, he regarded economic prosperity as a precondition not only of political, diplomatic, and military power, but also of cultural superiority. Great civilizations emerged in history only after their elites had succeeded

43. Bainville's most important articles on economic and financial affairs were collected and published posthumously as *La Fortune de la France* (Paris: Plon, 1937). Interestingly, Bainville does not appear to have profited personally from speculation on the stock exchange. "How rich I would have been," he once remarked, "if I had made the investments that I advised." Joseph, *Qui est Jacques Bainville?*, 52.

44. He accepted Maurras's special definition of "capital": "Civilization is the social state in which the individual who enters the world discovers there incomparably more than he brings with him. In other words, civilization is first and foremost a capital. It is in the last analysis a transmitted capital." Bainville, *Heur et malheur des Français*, 11, 19.

in freeing themselves from the burden of providing their material comforts.

Thus, the ultimate source of French national security and cultural leadership was the accumulated savings of the frugal middle class. The depletion of that vast reserve of capital, Bainville believed, would produce devastating consequences in every area of French life. In this regard the heavy losses of French foreign investment during the revolutions in 1917–1919 in Central and Eastern Europe left an indelible mark on his economic thinking during the twenties. He denounced the Bolshevik government's refusal to resume the interest payments on French loans and investments that had been negotiated under the Tsarist regime. He fretted over the possibility that France's *rentier* class would in turn become the "milking cow" of the fragile new nation states on the European continent that were eagerly soliciting foreign investment in their fledgling economies. These economic developments alarmed him not because of his empathy for the dispossessed or vulnerable bondholders, but because he regarded excessive capital exports as a drain on France's accumulated national wealth, hence a threat to the vitality of French civilization itself.[45]

This overriding fear that the French bourgeoisie risked being economically enervated to the profit of others led Bainville to adopt an economic philosophy that bordered on autarchy. "Money is a weapon," he had once declared. "French money, born of the French earth, engendered by the labor of all [Frenchmen], should fecundate French enterprises before being spent on the foreigner." France would never have become a world power without the patient efforts at capital accumulation of her middle classes. The construction of the Suez Canal, for example, was made possible not only by the engineering genius of a de Lesseps but also by the willingness of thousands of small investors to underwrite an enterprise that they

45. For two slightly divergent views on the effects of capital exports on the domestic economy of France, see Rondo Cameron, *France and the Economic Development of Europe: 1800–1914* (Princeton: Princeton University Press, 1961), 71–88, 485–501, and Charles Kindleberger, *Economic Growth in France and Britain: 1851–1950* (Cambridge, Mass.: Harvard University Press, 1964), 40–41, 58–59.

felt would yield both financial benefits to themselves and strategic benefit to the nation. He was fond of citing J. P. Morgan's advice, "Always be bullish on your own country," and cautioned against investment in economic ventures controlled, either directly or indirectly, by potential enemies of France. Hence, Bainville's principal reason for championing the cause of the French bourgeoisie was his conception of it as the economic class chiefly responsible for "the ceaseless formation of the material as well as the spiritual capital of the nation." To those socialist critics who denounced the possessor of capital as a parasite, he replied with the familiar argument of the classical liberal economists that the entire society automatically benefited from the financial activities of each enterprising investor.[46]

But capitalism possessed other virtues in addition to serving as the material basis of civilization, the engine of national prosperity, and the guarantor of national security. These valuable services that it rendered to the nation were equalled by the benign psychological effect that it exercised upon the individual French citizen. Bainville's frequent paeans to the French middle class dwelled on the "moral" function of capital accumulation. "Our bourgeoisie represents less an economic formation than an intellectual formation," he observed. "The status of bourgeois comprises a way of life and a manner of thinking." The middle-class families that have promoted the accumulation of French capital "had more consideration for ideas than for wealth, which they regarded as a means rather than an end." Capitalism, in short, had a moral as well as a practical justification.[47]

What were the moral characteristics that Bainville associated with the middle classes? First and foremost were the virtues of thrift, austerity, and self-denial, which were conducive not only to a prosperous economic system, but also to a stable and vigorous polity. At the outbreak of the war he had permitted himself a momentary

46. Vidal, *La Pensée de Jacques Bainville*, 25, 37; *AF*, February 26, 1914; Bainville, *Au Seuil du siècle*, 117–18; Jacques Bainville, *Après la Guerre: Comment placer sa fortune* (Paris: Nouvelle Librairie Nationale, 1919), 64–65, 191.

47. Vidal, *La Pensée de Jacques Bainville*, 12, 23; Jacques Bainville, *Lectures* (Paris: Fayard, 1937), 93, 357; *Le Fauteuil de Raymond Poincaré*, 14–15; Bainville, *Couleurs du temps*, 74.

expression of amusement at the sudden disruption of the epicurean life-style of the Montmartre cabarets.[48] In the early twenties he resumed his criticism of the "douceur de vivre" of the prewar years, when Paris was replete with "idlers" of all sorts. He beseeched his countrymen to avoid the temptation to revive the discredited ethic of *la belle époque.* "The future is for the humble virtues of work, discipline, and patience," he warned. "Humility: that is what the European catastrophe teaches us." The life of luxurious self-indulgence and conspicuous consumption must give way to a commitment to saving and self-denial, for "France has its fortune to recover."[49] The heavy demands that capitalism imposed on the individual citizen constituted its own *raison d'être.* Capital is accumulated through prudence, privation, and sacrifice. The apex of human accomplishment was the ability to create a fortune and to transmit it intact to one's heirs.

Bainville considered the small businessman or investor much more likely to exhibit these admirable tendencies than the industrial magnate or the plutocrat. Indeed, he frequently bemoaned the gradual replacement of the small tradesman by the promoters of commercial and industrial concentration and the circumspect *rentier* by the greedy speculator. Since the possessors of large fortunes were insulated from the menace of economic ruin by the very size and diversity of their wealth, they were less inclined to cultivate the virtues of alertness, thrift, and caution. But the owners of small and medium-sized fortunes were obligated continually to inform themselves about the state of their nation's economy.

What impressed Bainville above all about capitalism was the invaluable political function that it performed, namely, the replenishment of France's ruling classes. The bourgeois dynasties that had replaced the old aristocratic families during the nineteenth century as the source of the political, diplomatic, military, and ecclesiastical elites of France were responsible for perpetuating the policies of the *ancien régime* within the framework of the democratic republic. The genius of France lay in its ability perpetually to recreate a vigorous

48. Bainville, *Journal inédit: 1914,* August 13, 1914.
49. *Ibid.,* and Bainville, *Heur et malheur des Français,* 19.

middle class, which itself engendered an aristocracy of achievement. For the past several centuries the French *petite bourgeoisie* had
been an inexhaustible seedbed of talents. It had produced men like
Raymond Poincaré, who represented for Bainville the archetype
of the noble bourgeois, whose perseverance and self-abnegation
had enabled him to acquire both personal wealth and political
power.

Had he not been so self-effacing, Bainville might have used his
own career as an instructive example of the Calvinistic work ethic
and its rewards. His work in journalism and history-writing kept
him almost perpetually at his desk, either at his office or at home, a
regimen that was rarely interrupted by vacations or leaves of absence. He received ample recompense for his efforts. In the process
of acquiring a powerful influence on his contemporaries he amassed
a personal fortune from the royalties of his books and published
collections of his articles.[50]

The type of elite that was produced by the gradual accumulation
of wealth struck Bainville as infinitely preferable either to an elite of
birth or to an elite of intelligence. He dismissed the old belief in
a hereditary aristocracy in favor of a dynamic elite of talent and
achievement. He was equally hostile to an aristocracy of *licenciés*
and *littérateurs*. As one historian has observed, Bainville "abhorred
esthetes and intellectuals vaticinating in the shelter of their ivory
tower . . . who express ideas without caring about their repercussions." The Poincarés of France could ill afford such irresponsibility,
for their personal well-being was inextricably tied to the prosperity
of the nation itself. Bainville took enormous comfort from the fact
that the vast majority of French students, the intellectuals of tomorrow, hailed from the ranks of the bourgeoisie whose sober good
sense he admired.[51]

Even that large mass of petit bourgeois citizens who had never
achieved more than a modest standard of living played an important political role in Bainville's rather anachronistic conception of
the ideal social order. The small property owner who had acquired

50. Massis, *Le Souvenir*, 33. Interview with Madame Jacques Bainville.
51. Vidal, *La Pensée de Jacques Bainville*, 27ff.

even the minutest stake in the economic system automatically became a vigilant, stalwart guardian of the political stability and social
order of France, "the quintessential nation of the *petit propriétaire*,
the possessor of moderate wealth."[52] In short, the virtues of caution, moderation, and patience that such a system of ownership
encouraged and rewarded were precisely the attributes of the conservative political order that Bainville advocated for France.

But such panegyrics to the French middle class as the agent of economic progress (and hence national greatness) were balanced in
Bainville's writings by a critical evaluation of the *political* behavior
of that social class since the French Revolution. He could not ignore the historical truth that the numerous political crises that had
plagued France since 1789 were largely the work of the bourgeoisie
itself. If political stability and economic prosperity go hand in hand,
how could one explain the peculiar fact that the very social class
which had produced the economic wealth of the nation had also
periodically succumbed to the temptations of revolutionary idealism and "called forth the evils from which it is suffering and given
rise to the ideas that are ruining it." Early in his career Bainville
had expressed bewilderment at the propensity of the middle classes
for "sacrificing one by one their [economic] principles to revolutionary oratory." "Once they were liberals," he exclaimed, "then democrats; now here they are Christian socialists."[53] Concern about this
anomaly colored his economic thinking throughout his life and contributed to the formation of his ambivalent attitude toward the
French bourgeoisie.

This dual conception of the economic industriousness and the
political naïveté of the middle class was expressed by Bainville in
a fictional sketch of what he regarded as a typical French bourgeois
family. Over the years the Gobemouches[54] had amassed a fortune
in textiles after Colbert had awarded them a government subsidy to

52. Bainville, *Après la Guerre*, 66.
53. Massis, *Le Souvenir*, 70. See also Bainville, *Les Moments décisifs de l'histoire de France*, 33. Bainville, *Journal*, I, February 22, 1902.
54. Vidal, *La Pensée de Jacques Bainville*, 24. The term *gobe-mouche* in French means "simpleton."

encourage the creation of national industries. But the fortune was progressively depleted by a succession of heirs whose diligence was unfortunately surpassed by their fascination with revolutionary ideas after 1789. One became an admirer of Rousseau and assumed the title of Citoyen Gobemouche in the Constituent Assembly, only to be guillotined during the Terror. Subsequent descendants became soldiers of fortune in Napoleon's armies, romantic poets, and liberal deputies intoxicated with visions of military glory in the name of the eternal principle of the rights of man. The last in the long line of Gobemouches died penniless in an East Prussian internment camp during the First World War. He had been sent there by a German officer, who, in his prewar capacity as an international banker-spy residing in France, had converted Gobemouche to the cause of Franco-German friendship by introducing him to the utopian designs of Kant and Schiller for international peace.[55]

What perplexed Bainville most of all about the contradictory historical role of the bourgeoisie was the tendency of the middle class to revert to a conservative position once its material interests began to be threatened by the very movements of social radicalism that it had helped to set in motion. The very same bourgeois who revered the mystique of the French Revolution would leap to the defense of his possessions when the propertyless masses began to take that mystique seriously. Bainville was at a loss to account for the social group personified by "the arch-bourgeois [Adolphe] Thiers," who, as a historian, was capable of "glorifying the revolution of 1789" and then, as a statesman, of "crushing the revolution of 1871, of excusing Danton for the September massacres and then of executing the Communards for the massacre of hostages." Like that of most Frenchmen, Bainville's own familial heritage was marked by such apparent inconsistencies. His father had played hooky from the lycée to participate in the protest demonstrations following Louis Bonaparte's suspension of the constitution in 1851. But his grandfather, after rounding up the wayward son, stopped off on the way home to purchase some shares of railroad stock in the expectation

55. Jacques Bainville, *Filiations* (Paris: A la Cité des Livres, 1923), 19ff.

that the advent of an authoritarian regime would bring prosperity and the prospect of profit. From such perplexing behavior, Bainville learned that "the bourgeois love revolution at a distance, at the fireside, when order reigns in the streets, when there is no danger that the mob will open the prison doors and assassinate the president of the Chamber of Commerce."[56]

The political immaturity of the French middle class represented for Bainville not merely a foible to be satirized but also a source of profound pessimism. It led him to reject the widely held belief in the inevitability of economic progress in favor of a cyclical theory of perpetual rise-and-fall. Numerous fortunes that had been centuries in the making were destroyed in a few turbulent months of war or revolution, catastrophes which he identified as the consequences of political decisions. The modern world had discovered, at great cost, that civilization requires not only a prosperous economic system but also "a stable political order."[57] And there was little that he had observed in the past behavior of the French middle class in this regard to give him confidence in an inevitably bright future.

Such skepticism about the ability of the bourgeoisie to recognize and protect its own vital interests prevented Bainville from uncritically endorsing the economic theory of laissez-faire. Indeed, it led him very close to the doctrine of corporatism. He implicitly distrusted the theory of economic liberalism because of its historical connection with democracy, the political system least conducive to capitalistic accumulation because it encourages consumption at the expense of production and therefore "squanders [national] wealth without replacing it." The economy should be controlled and directed by the political authorities, since capitalism's principal *raison d'être* was to be found in the services that it performed for the nation as a whole. "We must replace [economic] liberalism with the or-

---

56. Vidal, *La Pensée de Jacques Bainville*, 25; *AF*, February 27, 1913; Jacques Bainville, *Le Jardin des lettres* (2 vols.; Paris: Editions du Capitole, 1929), I, 181–83; Bainville, *Histoire de trois générations*, 124–25.

57. Bainville, *Heur et malheur des Français*, 8, 14. "Capital is condemned to be destroyed a large number of times" in each century. He also observed that "the wisdom of the French bourgeoisie says that it is often more difficult to preserve a fortune than to make one." . . . [T]he value of things has an incessant ebb and flow." Bainville, *Journal*, I, June 7, 1914.

ganization of production," he declared. "It is a singular aberration to believe that neither man's intelligence nor his will should intervene to regulate that daughter of our intelligence and will: industry." Bainville urged the Anglophile apologists of laissez-faire in France to read Carlyle's diatribes against unregulated capitalism. Even more to the royalist writer's liking was the semicorporative system of the Austrian Empire, which had rejected the principles of economic liberalism because they endanger the prosperity and grandeur of the state. What postwar France required was a government capable of managing and directing the course of economic recovery. The future of French industry, Bainville believed, depended not solely on the effort of individual entrepreneurs and investors, but also on proper guidance from the public authorities.[58]

An equally important reason for Bainville's distrust of an unregulated economy was his recognition that classical liberalism tended to ignore the problem of class conflict, a phenomenon which threatened the political stability of modern states in the postwar era. His conception of the inevitability of conflict between capital and labor constituted a reactionary variant of the Marxian dialectic, with the roles of heroes and villains reversed. "Human history," he announced, "is a record of struggles between those who save and those who spend, between producers and consumers. These struggles have sometimes assumed the character of civil wars. It is the case of one tribe wanting to appropriate the more fertile soil and wealth of another tribe, or else within the same tribe, the have-nots wanting to expropriate the haves."[59]

As a consequence of this historical development, modern capitalism was doomed to perpetual instability, Bainville believed, unless the power of the state were brought to bear on the economy to establish greater rapport between capital and labor. The role of the

58. Vidal, *La Pensée Jacques Bainville*, 38, 43; Bainville, *Couleurs du temps*, 162; Bainville, *Le Vieil Utopiste*, 13, 14; Bainville, *Le Coup d'Agadir*, 244–45; Bainville, *Après la Guerre*, 198. Vidal admirably summarizes Bainville's hesitant endorsement of liberal individualism: "He is an individualist, but not a liberal. Liberty for him is not a value in itself; it is valuable only through the use that is made of it."

59. Jacques Bainville, *Paraboles hyperboliques* (Paris: Editions du Capitole, 1931), 95.

government should be that of a disinterested arbiter rather than that of an ally of one of the disputants in this historic struggle. Excessive wage demands on the part of labor "would end up killing the goose that laid the golden egg" and should therefore be resisted. "But it is in no one's interest that there be plutocrats on the one hand and proletarians on the other who have no attachment to the industry that requires their labor."[60]

This latter concern often made Bainville appear as alarmed as any Marxist at the social alienation caused by the development of unregulated capitalism in France. As early as 1901 he had contributed to a fund-raising campaign launched by Socialist militants on behalf of striking miners in the north. Accompanying his monetary pledge was the slogan "Against the freedom to work," an expression of solidarity with those miners who resisted the efforts of the owners to organize opposition to the concept of compulsory unionization. That his name appeared alongside the names of men who attached to their contributions such declarations as "My only hope is revolution" caused him no perceptible concern. On the contrary, a year later he was calling for a reconciliation of the royalist and socialist movements in France on the basis of a common sympathy for the plight of the industrial working class and a shared hatred of republican individualism. He praised Socialists such as Jules Guesde and Hubert Lagardelle for recognizing the necessity of replacing the anarchical social order of the Third Republic with a more integrated form of social organization.[61]

This anxiety about the poisonous quality of social relations in industrial society appears to have been deeply felt. "There is at present no contact between the classes of society, no rapport, that establishes intimacy and confidence," he complained. "The large business concerns, the big stores, the universal bureaucracy all

---

60. Bainville, *Après la guerre*, 20.
61. Renauld, *L'Action Française contre l'Eglise*, 418–19; *La Petite République*, March 10, 1901; Jacques Bainville, "Anti-démocrates d'extrême-gauche," *RAF*, VII (July 15, 1902), 121–28; Linville, "Jacques Bainville," 119. The Action Française actually formed a brief alliance with a number of syndicalist followers of Georges Sorel in December 1911 on the basis of a common hatred of the bourgeois republic. See Curtis, *Three Against the Republic*, 47–48, and Tannenbaum, *Action Française*, 191–93.

tend to make the relations between men more impersonal every day."[62] His sensitivity to the social costs of industrial capitalism led him to criticize the Le Chapelier law, the measure enacted during the French Revolution which outlawed guilds and labor unions. He even went so far as to justify the insurrections of the Lyon silk weavers in 1831 and 1834 on the grounds that the economic misery produced by the early stages of the industrial revolution was unbearable and the government had done nothing to mitigate it.

Finally, government regulation appeared to Bainville as a prerequisite of French industry's ability to compete on the world market. In the prewar years he had frequently complained that the timid economic diplomacy of the Third Republic had placed French businessmen at a disadvantage vis-à-vis their counterparts in the other industrial nations.[63] Political intervention in the economy was a necessary fact of life in modern industrial states that could not be obfuscated by the obsolete platitudes of laissez-faire. The relationship between the government and the industrial and commercial classes must constitute an association of mutual advantage. Those who hold political power were well advised to implement foreign and domestic policies which favor the accumulation of wealth, and the middle class in turn had an obligation to remain loyal to the nation within which it prospered.

While Bainville regarded the *petite bourgeoisie* as the ultimate guarantor of social peace (despite its unfortunate propensity for occasional indulgence in revolutionary political posturing), he was for the same reason enamored of the agricultural population, the bulwark of that other declining sector that suffered economic dislocation and status anxiety during the period of economic modernization. "In countries where, as in France, there is still an agricultural population and a majority of *propriétaires*," he observed, "one need not fear social subversion." A firm believer in what he called the universal instinct of self-preservation, he was convinced that

62. Bainville, *Journal*, I, May 22, 1905. In spite of his concern about the gap between the plutocracy and the proletariat in France, he believed that that chasm was much narrower than it was in industrialized England.
63. Bainville, *Journal*, I, December 24, 1905.

France could continually count on the *paysan* to support the reestablishment of social order in the wake of social unrest. The counterrevolutions in the Vendée and Brittany during the French Revolution, as well as the rural based electoral backlash against urban revolutions in 1848 and 1871, were instances of a counterrevolutionary majority of small landowners rising up to defend their property when they felt it threatened by revolutionary movements formed by the propertyless urban mob. He attributed this inherently conservative outlook of the agricultural proprietors to "the redistribution of rural property" that had provided large numbers of the peasantry with something of their own to defend.[64] For obvious ideological reasons he declined to credit the nationalization and sale of Church lands during the Revolution with having produced the system of small land holdings which had transformed the French peasantry into such a counterrevolutionary force.

This idealized conception of the peasantry as a bulwark of social order was entirely consistent with Bainville's general economic philosophy. An advocate of the physiocratic doctrine that "all wealth comes from the land, since the land furnishes what is indispensable to nourishment, that is to say, to the very existence of man," he frequently reminded his readers that the great fortunes amassed by the middle classes during the nineteenth century depended on the labor of their peasant forebears.[65] Without her firm agricultural base, he believed, France could never hope to remain a great power in the world. Twenty million peasants, whose two preoccupations were thrift and social order, formed the bedrock upon which France's economic prosperity and social stability ultimately rested.

From this view of the land as the permanent basis of national prosperity and power followed a suspicion of industrialization and urbanization that Bainville was never able entirely to overcome. He remained convinced that these processes of economic modernization, by forcing down the value of rural property and depopulating the countryside, threatened to deprive France of the sources of her

64. *La Liberté*, December 17, 1926; Bainville, *Heur et malheur des Français*, 18; Bainville, *Après la Guerre*, 38.
65. Bainville, *Le Jardin des lettres*, I, 18; Bainville, *Heur et malheur des Français*, 18.

wealth and stability. He also clung to the questionable conviction that a society blessed with a large agricultural population was less likely to support costly expeditions of foreign conquest: "No one loves peace more than the farmer. No one loves war less; he has nothing to gain from it, except the right to furnish cannon fodder." But while France's peasant class abhorred war, the bellicose spirit was a natural accompaniment to "an industrial giant, a country with [problems of] overproduction and overpopulation, such as Germany."[66]

Despite his frequent pleas for state intervention in the national economy, Bainville was far from an indiscriminate advocate of *étatisme*. He did believe that the government should play an active role in attenuating the conflict between capital and labor and could enhance the prosperity of a nation by promoting national security, ensuring domestic order, and maintaining a stable currency. But he also recognized that political intervention in economic matters could have destructive repercussions. The three dangers that he foresaw resulting from state interference in the economy were inflation, confiscatory taxation, and ultimately, nationalization of industry.

Inflation was an economic problem that plagued every industrial nation in Europe after the Great War and Bainville regarded it as the principal threat to the accumulation and preservation of capital. The inflationary spiral of the early twenties appeared to him as merely the latest in a long series of economic crises that were caused by defective monetary policies. The inflationary practices urged upon the French government in 1718 by the Scottish monetary reformer John Law had prevented the Bourbon monarchy from reestablishing a sound financial system. The printing of paper currency had precipitated a flurry of speculation that resulted in instant profits for a select few. But this inflationary system was nothing more than "the production of paper, the creation of fictitious wealth that produced the illusion of prosperity" and eventu-

66. Bainville, *Après la Guerre*, 32, 39; *AF*, May 19, 1924.

ally spelled disaster for the French government. Subsequent statesmen failed to learn the lessons of the past: the printing of *assignats*
during the Revolution produced the same disastrous consequences.
To Bainville the collapse of the *assignat* in the 1790s was analogous
to the depreciation of the franc and especially the mark in the 1920s,
both of which currencies were the victims of ravaging inflation.
French statesmen of the twenties had again failed to profit from the
experience of their predecessors.[67]

But the seductive appeal of an inflationary monetary policy had
proved virtually irresistible to all classes, as Bainville knew well. The
farmer and the merchant both tolerated inflation because their products gave the illusion of fetching a better price in paper money. The
worker accepted it because his wages appeared to increase. "Like
many intoxicants," Bainville remarked, "inflation begins by producing agreeable sensations" whose destructive aftereffects are not
felt for some time in the form of lower purchasing power. The only
solution to this pervasive illusion that he could envisage was to
"make the masses understand" that inflationary progress is not real
progress. But he was scarcely optimistic on that score, convinced
as he was that "financial reform in an elective democracy is impossible" because the public clamor for cheap money, like the democratic politicians' acquiescence in it, was virtually an inevitability.[68]

Currency revaluation represented for Bainville merely a temporary palliative rather than a lasting remedy. When the Poincaré
government sought to reverse the inflationary policies of the Cartel
des Gauches after 1926, Bainville scorned the general air of confidence that followed, acidly commenting that "after the euphoria of
inflation we have the euphoria of revaluation. These two opiums
resemble each other in that they induce boundless dreams." The
stopgap measures such as those proposed by Poincaré did little
more than produce a provisional stability which was incapable of
resisting for long the upward trend of prices and wages. Moreover,

---

67. Bainville, *Nouveau dialogue dans le salon d'Aliénor*, 39ff.
68. Quoted in Vidal, *La Pensée de Jacques Bainville*, 53–54; Bainville, *Nouveau
Dialogue*, 40; *AF*, September 12, 1926.

Bainville insisted that a stable currency constituted a precondition for national vitality and that a weak currency represented "the most serious symptom of national disintegration" and an invitation to despotism.[69]

When Bainville confronted the issue of government paternalism and taxation, the libertarian, antistatist side of his political instinct became unmistakably apparent. Nothing outraged him more than the highly centralized bureaucratic system of France, which he saw delving into every corner of the citizen's life in order to direct his activities and siphon off revenue from his earnings. He frequently insisted on differentiating "administrative centralization," which he condemned for inhibiting the free exercise of the citizen's economic talents, and "political centralization," which he deemed necessary to the prosperity and security of the state.[70] The central government should confine itself to interventionist policies favorable to the accumulation of wealth, the maintenance of a stable currency, and the provision for the common defense. What alarmed him about the increasingly interventionist practices of European governments was the immense power that was being amassed by the centralized state and the numerous functions that it had begun to exercise. Such paternalism, he pointed out, was virtually irresistible to the parties concerned:

> Today it is to the State that each person applies. . . . Commerce and agriculture are competing with each other to claim its protection. . . . The result is that the State comes to regulate and direct everything

69. Bainville, *Couleurs du temps*, 177–79; Bainville, *Nouveau Dialogue*, 40; *AF*, September 12, 1926, January 2, 1927; Jacques Bainville, *Dictators*, trans. J. Lewis May (London: Jonathan Cape, 1937), 10. Such monetary views were similar to those espoused later by de Gaulle. See Edward Morse. *Foreign Policy and Interdependence in Gaullist France* (Princeton: Princeton University Press, 1973), 204–51.

70. Vidal, *La Pensée de Jacques Bainville*, 46–47. Bainville defended the widespread practice of tax evasion, claiming that it is legitimate when the government fails to provide the nation with adequate security or protection for private property. He did, however, concede that the citizen had a "fiscal duty" during wartime, when "the sacrifice of money is nothing compared to the sacrifice of blood." Bainville, *Après la Guerre*, 241–42. He was especially hard on inheritance taxes, for the obvious reason that they prevented the transmission of accumulated capital across the generations, a process which he believed to be essential to the maintenance of civilization. See Vidal, *La Pensée de Jacques Bainville*, 46–47, 62.

The Defense of the West 189

at the request of the interested parties themselves. The citizens of the past could no longer bear to be subjects. Those of today have become slaves.[71]

The inevitable accompaniment of political direction of the economy that Bainville deplored most of all was taxation. He took comfort from the fact that tax evasion was a time honored French tradition dating from the last years of the *ancien régime*: "The liberalism and individualism of the French Revolution were forged in the struggle that the possessing bourgeoisie of the eighteenth century had waged against a fiscal policy very similar to the one that we know today." He placed such emphasis on the evils of taxation because he regarded fiscal autonomy not only as a prerequisite to economic prosperity, but also as the ultimate guarantee of personal liberty. He attributed the unrivalled success of the American economy in the early twenties to the absence of what he viewed as the confiscatory tax systems that were being instituted by European governments. Furthermore, he pointed out, "from the individualist point of view, wealth is the condition of independence. The man who depends on others for his existence is not free. His thought itself is in bondage."[72]

While inflation and confiscatory taxation in the capitalist nations represented the most immediate economic evils in Bainville's view, the more fundamental threat of socialism posed the principal long-range peril to the economic viability of Europe. The internal challenge of democratic socialism threatened to undermine the very precondition of European domination in the world. That supremacy had nothing to do with racial superiority, Bainville recognized: "What makes the white men superior in modern times, what preserves their advantage, is their capitalist organization and their reserves of capital." Were the socialist ethic of consumption to replace the capitalist ethic of capital accumulation and production in Europe, that continent would rapidly lose its position of domi-

71. As quoted in Vidal, *Le Pensée de Jacques Bainville*, 35.
72. Bainville, *Le Jardin des lettres*, I, 73–74. *Ibid.*, 78; Bainville, *Après la Guerre*, 74–75; Bainville, *Le Jardin des Lettres*, I, 75–77.

nance vis-à-vis the non-European peoples of the globe. Bainville saw socialism as the ultimate destroyer of wealth and therefore the foremost enemy of civilization because he was convinced that "in a society where effort is not recompensed and rewarded, no one will make an effort any longer." He regretfully predicted the nationalization of the railroads and the mines in France, claiming that the result would be a disastrous decrease in efficiency.[73]

Early warning signs of the nefarious influence of socialist doctrine were detected by Bainville in the various social welfare measures enacted by the British government since the 1890s. He sensed that the British ruling elite recognized the threat that socialism posed to the economic restoration of Europe, and even credited the Bank of England with having played a major role in preventing the accession of a socialist government in postwar France through its financial policies. But by permitting the gradual introduction of socialism at home, England was defeating its national purpose. Her preeminent international position in the nineteenth century was based on her production of superior industrial machinery, such as the steam engine, and her possession of industrial raw materials, such as coal. Any policy that would lead to the depletion of these resources, such as government sponsorship of excessive consumption, would eventually spell economic disaster:[74]

> The government of England has ceased to be oligarchic. The system of alms has become legalized. Its name is relief funds, social insurance, pensions. England is becoming a vast charitable institution. Let things continue thus and, rich as she is, she will end up devouring her accumulated reserves, especially if an imprudent foreign policy causes her to lose her position and her markets in India, China, Egypt, etc.[75]

Viewed in its entirety the economic doctrine that Bainville developed in the financial pages of *Le Capital* and the *Action française* and in various published works during the 1920s constituted an eclectic mélange of nineteenth century classical liberalism spiced with

---

73. Bainville, *Couleurs du temps*, 58; Bainville, *Journal*, II, October 19, 1926; Vidal, *La Pensée de Jacques Bainville*, 34; Bainville, *Après la Guerre*, 108–45, 198.
74. Bainville, *Couleurs du temps*, I, 142; *La Liberté*, November 16, 1929.
75. *La Liberté*, November 16, 1929.

generous doses of modern corporatism and eighteenth-century mercantilism. Nowhere in his writings can one discover an unconditional endorsement of modern industrial capitalism as a perfect or even superior economic system. He became an ardent defender of capitalism not so much because of his admiration for the theoretical doctrines of economic liberalism, but more because he became convinced that the implementation of those doctrines, modified by correctives drawn from corporatism and mercantilism, were conducive to the political stability and economic prosperity of the nation. One observer characterized Bainville's socioeconomic thought as "nonsystematic individualism," arguing that his liberalism was not a theoretical principle (as it was for Adam Smith, or the early John Stuart Mill), but rather was "experimental" in the sense that it was adapted to the practical requirements of a stable social order.[76] The criteria that Bainville consistently applied to proposals for economic reform were Francocentric and pragmatic: were the proposals suited to the particular requirements of the French economic system and would they contribute to the preservation of France's economic prosperity?

The keystone of Bainville's economic philosophy was his emphasis on France's unique position as an industrial and agricultural nation of medium size and strength relative to her gigantic and puny neighbors in the world. In the final analysis, his economic pronouncements in the twenties constituted an articulate protest against advanced industrial capitalism on behalf of the marginal social groups that were being rendered obsolete in the modern world by that system. These groups felt threatened both by the socialist menace from below and the concentration of financial, industrial, and agricultural power at the top of the economic pyramid, all of which endangered the preeminently French tradition of small- and medium-scale production.[77] It was to the *rentier*, the *petit commerçant*, and the small farmer, social groups that had been transformed into potent political forces since 1789, that Bainville

76. Vidal, *La Pensée de Jacques Bainville*, 95.
77. As noted above, he recognized both the advantages and disadvantages of this economic *via media*. See Marcel Chaminade, in Massis, *Le Souvenir*, 36–37.

directed his appeals. For it was these groups that were most likely
to benefit from the advantages of the social stability and economic
prosperity that he regarded as the principal consequences of his
royalist political program.

Hence, Bainville's defense of French capitalism represented an
attempt to reach the objective that he had first enunciated in his
contribution to Maurras's *Enquête sur la monarchie*: identifying the
cause of monarchical restoration with the practical aspirations of
the French people. His overriding purpose was to drive a permanent wedge between two systems that had developed interdepen-
dently in France: political democracy and economic capitalism. He
sought to convince the bourgeois devotées of the republican tradition—the descendants of Flaubert's Homais or of his own Gobemouche—that an authoritarian monarchy could most effectively
defend their material interests by providing the security and stability that enabled commerce and industry to prosper. By demonstrating through historical arguments that democracy inevitably
resulted in socialism and that it destroyed accumulated wealth by
engendering inflation, excessive taxation, and conspicious consumption, he hoped to disrupt the French bourgeoisie's historical
love affair with the democratic ideal.

In place of this ideal Bainville proposed the anachronistic alternative of a France comprising a thrifty, industrious middle class
and a yeoman peasantry, protected, encouraged, and guided by a
hereditary ruler whose foremost concern was the interests of his
subjects. In reality France was isolated and threatened by a postwar world that seemed to be falling under the domination of the
Anglo-American magnates of high finance and heavy industry.
With the threat of a Russian-inspired revolution in Europe as well
as in the Third World forever in the background, Bainville's vision
must have been a comforting one to the little man—the shop-
keeper, the small investor, the farmer. The typical French bourgeois, the perennial booster of the Radical Party, was politically
progressive but socially and economically conservative. It was to
that inner core of instinctual socioeconomic conservatism that Bainville addressed his royalist appeal.

In his effort to discredit the popular belief that political democracy and economic progress were natural allies, Bainville characteristically relied on history for support. He was particularly fond of reciting the numerous technological achievements of monarchical societies. The pharaohs had constructed the pyramids, Louis Philippe had launched France's railroad boom, the Hohenzollern dynasty had presided over the scientific and technological progress of nineteenth-century Germany, and Marconi had invented the wireless under the auspices of the House of Savoy. The lesson to be learned from these historical examples was that the type of political stability and social order which an authoritarian system alone was capable of maintaining represented the environment most conducive to national prosperity. Material progress depended on international peace and domestic order. Such requirements could scarcely be met, he never tired of reminding his readers, by the undependable institutions of democratic rule and parliamentary sovereignty; what was needed was a strong executive authority based on the hereditary principle of legitimacy.[78]

78. Bainville, *Le Jardin des lettres*, I, 172–73; Bainville, *Réflexions sur la politique*, 110.

CHAPTER SEVEN

Royalist History in Respectable Garb

Bainville transformed history from a conjectural science into an exact science.

François Mauriac

The more I got to know [Bainville] . . . the more I felt myself conquered. That perfect and sober courtesy, the remarkable freedom of his thought, the elegant way in which he concealed the enormity of the labor that he accomplished each day, the charming absence of illusions and the taste for the true value of works and men, rendered him ever more desirable to see and converse with.

Paul Valéry

Bainville's defense of Western culture in *La Revue universelle* and his apologia for French capitalism in *Le Capital* and other organs of opinion definitively established his nationwide reputation as a skillful and persuasive advocate of Western civilization during a period when its vitality and permanence were being brought into question. These forays into journalism outside the Action Française movement brought him a wider audience for his historical writing. This exposure was soon to transform him from the royalist movement's resident expert on the French past into one of the most widely read and highly respected historians of the interwar period.

His newly acquired popularity and respectability was the consequence of a deepening friendship with a man who was ideally suited to expose him to a wider world. Shortly before the war, Bainville had been introduced to the eminent Parisian publisher Arthème Fayard by Léon Daudet, who had been Fayard's classmate at the Lycée Louis-le-grand. Bainville and Fayard developed an intimacy that was nourished by frequent visits by the royalist writer to the Fayard family property in Normandy. While in Paris, the two men dined together weekly, discussing matters of mutual interest in literature, journalism, and politics. Though Fayard lacked previous royalist attachments and had once been an outspoken Dreyfusard, his deepening friendship with Daudet, Bainville, and, eventually, Maurras himself converted him to sympathy with the nationalist (as opposed to the royalist) doctrines of the Action Française. The publisher's friendship with the royalist triumvirate rapidly began to mature into an ideological alliance, a meeting of minds that was actively promoted by Fayard's old family friend and protégé, Pierre Gaxotte, who had become Maurras's private secretary during the war while completing his studies at the Ecole Normale.[1]

The earliest consequence of this friendship was the publication of Bainville's wartime work *La Guerre et l'Italie* by the Librairie Fayard. Later, at the theater once in 1922, Fayard asked Bainville if he would be willing to contribute a one-volume history of France to a new series entitled *Les Grandes Etudes Historiques*, which the publishing house was about to launch under the editorial direction of Gaxotte (who had become a full-time employee at Fayard). The purpose of the new series was to make general historical works available to the French reading public. Such an undertaking obviously required the services not of highly specialized technicians of historical research, but rather of "historical scholars who were also artists" and who could write in an idiom that had a broader appeal.[2]

This ambitious endeavor was the most recent in a long succession of campaigns to bridge the gap between the specialist and the general public that Fayard had waged at the end of the last century. In the 1890s he had persuaded the novelist Alphonse Daudet (Léon's father) to permit the publishing house to republish his complete works in cheap editions, remarking that many people admired but could not afford them. The only means of making a

1. Interview with Marcel Wiriath (1970). Interview with Madame Jacques Bainville. Interview with Hervé Bainville. Interview with Pierre Gaxotte.
2. Interview with Pierre Gaxotte. Interview with Marcel Wiriath. *Histoire de la Librairie Arthème Fayard* (Paris: Fayard, n.d.), not paginated.

profit from books in such inexpensive editions was to increase drastically the volume of sales at a time when few writers entertained the hope of selling more than a few thousand copies of their works. The phenomenal commercial success of Daudet's *Oeuvres complètes* helped to bring about a revolution in the French publishing industry. After succeeding his father as head of the firm in 1894, Fayard brought out inexpensive editions of the works of Barrès, Bourget, and others in a new series entitled *La Bibliothèque Moderne.* The reading public to whom the expensive editions were inaccessible flocked to the bookstores to buy up these new offerings at 96 centimes.

Similar series on a variety of topics were soon to follow. After observing a young schoolboy laboriously recopying passages from expensive editions of the classics that his parents understandably forbade him to bring to class, Fayard launched just before the war the *Meilleurs Livres* series, which presented the Greco-Latin and French classics at prices all could afford. In 1921 he founded *Les Oeuvres Libres*, a forum for contemporary writing aimed at the reader of average means to which Léon Daudet and Bainville frequently contributed essays.[3]

When Fayard punctuated his request that Bainville consider writing a one-volume history of France with the observation that "all those that now exist are boring, yet the subject is excellent," he struck a responsive chord. Bainville had long believed that such a work written from a royalist viewpoint was both ideologically desirable and commercially promising. He had frequently remarked that French historians failed to pay sufficient attention to the lessons to be learned from the succession of past events in their antiquarian quest for the colorful anecdote or the illustrative detail. "The historians of yesterday," he once observed, "strove to render history striking to the imagination by depicting the men of the past as differing as much as possible from the men of today." He hoped that in the future historians would strive to assist their readers in

3. *Histoire de la Librairie Arthème Fayard; Dictionnaire National des contemporains,* 255.

comprehending the long-range consequences of historical events by emphasizing the continuity and interconnection of successive generations.[4]

One of Bainville's principal objections to professional historical writing in France was its failure to provide an adequate explanation of the brilliant policies of the *ancien régime*. How then could modern Frenchmen be expected to profit from the successes and failures of their forebears? Soon after Fayard's request, Bainville told a friend that his compatriots required a history of France that emphasized the central importance of the perennial Franco-German conflict. Such a book should explain to Frenchmen how their ancestors dealt with the military threat from the east that he was convinced would reappear within a generation.[5]

But Bainville was not at all convinced that he was the man to do it. "I do not know the history of France. Not enough to write about it," he replied when Fayard first broached the subject. The response of the great editor perfectly captured the spirit of amateurism that pervaded French letters: "Well, this will be an excellent opportunity for you to learn it."[6] Fayard informed him that he was not interested in sponsoring another specialized monograph, but wanted instead "a synthesis, an overview," which would identify the important trends and developments of the past. Bainville balked at Fayard's first offer, but finally succumbed to the publisher's blandishments, which were accompanied by the promise of a generous advance together with the guarantee of a front page column in a new weekly newspaper which Fayard, at Bainville's urging, planned to publish in the near future.[7]

Thus, Bainville embarked on the project that was to bring him fame and fortune as a historian with the same degree of reluctance with which he had launched his career as a foreign affairs commen-

---

4. *Histoire de la Librairie Arthème Fayard*; Interview with Madame Jacques Bainville; Bainville, *Journal*, I, October 12, 1913.
5. Bainville, *Journal*, I, July 3, 1914; Interview with René Wittmann.
6. Interview with Marcel Wiriath. Wiriath was the son-in-law of Arthème Fayard. *Histoire de la Librairie Arthème Fayard*.
7. Interview with Marcel Wiriath; Interview with Pierre Gaxotte.

tator fifteen years earlier.[8] Fortunately, both Maurras and Fayard
had proved to be persuasive patrons. Bainville spent most of 1923
researching and writing the book, and began his weekly column in
Candide (which was also edited by Gaxotte) in 1924, the same year
that his *Histoire de France* reached the public.[9]

The royalist historian's magnum opus did not break any new
ground in the political history of France. Indeed, it offered few interpretations that had not already appeared in his own *Histoire de
deux peuples* and *Histoire de trois générations*. But it was a tour de
force of concision, distilling the essence of the royalist version of
the French past in a brisk narrative form. The underlying theme of
the work, skillfully interwoven with the historical events described,
was the heroic effort of the French monarchy to preserve and protect its existence in the face of perpetual threats from within and
without. The Roman conquest had prevented the "Germanization"
of France and bequeathed to the conquered province the rich cultural heritage of classical antiquity. The Capetians ensured the survival and security of that precious legacy by inaugurating the process of national unification and securing popular acceptance of the
principle of hereditary rule. As a consequence, France emerged
from the Middle Ages as a strong, secure country blessed with in-
comparable advantages of national unity and political continuity.

The religious wars of the sixteenth century threatened to destroy
the splendid political accomplishment of the Capetian kings. Catholic leaguers and Protestant conspirators chipped away at the increasingly fragile edifice of the French state while foreign powers
profited from the decadence into which France had been plunged
by divisive religious fanaticism. The accession of Henri IV and the
Bourbons responded to the French people's craving for a regime of
authority after a century of civil and religious discord. The Bourbon
monarchy succeeded in restoring order and beating back such "revolutionary" insurrections as those of Cinq-Mars and the Fronde.
Cardinal Richelieu centralized political power in the hands of the

8. See above, 51.
9. Interview with Hervé Bainville. Interview with Pierre Gaxotte. See also Weber, *Action Française*, 504.

monarch at the expense of the fractious nobility and restored French predominance in Italy, Germany, and the Netherlands. Building upon this enviable achievement, Louis XIV proceeded to usher in a prolonged period of social peace at home and French hegemony, both cultural and military, on the continent. This period of power, prosperity, and peace endured until the last quarter of the eighteenth century, when the subversive combination of aristocratic envy and mass demagoguery shattered the political mechanism that had transformed France into the preeminent nation-state of the Western world.

As the Bainvillian interpretation of the post-Revolutionary period in France added nothing to his earlier analysis of that epoch in *L'Histoire de trois générations*, it need not detain us here. Suffice it to say that the themes of monarchical strength and republican weakness recurred throughout. The three republics and two illegitimate dictatorships that France had endured since 1789 were responsible for the multitude of problems that had beset her since the collapse of the absolute monarchy. Revolutions and foreign invasions had sapped the strength and vitality of this accursed nation that had once been the envy of the Western world. Yet the book ended on an uncharacteristic note of optimism. The Great War had depleted France's intellectual and material reserves. A Herculean effort of national recovery was the order of the day. But the nation's industrious population, which had recovered from so many convulsions in the past, was still capable of such a renewal in the twentieth century. Already Bainville detected signs of that thirst for a return to order and authority which alone could rescue France from her present plight. "If one did not have this confidence," he concluded, "it would not be worth while to have children."[10] His only son had been born three years before.

The enthusiasm with which the book was received surpassed all expectations. The reading public expressed its approval by gobbling up the entire first edition in a few weeks, and the arbiters of literary excellence in the editorial offices of the periodical and daily

---

10. Bainville, *History of France*, 473.

press contributed eulogistic endorsements. Even a handful of academic historians grudgingly joined in the cheering. Most of the reviewers focused their attention on three aspects of the work—its style, its methodology, and its ideological implications.

Paul Souday, the literary critic of the staunchly republican *Le Temps*, enthusiastically greeted the book as a "lucid, impartial exposé" of past errors and successes. Contrary to what one might have expected of a devout royalist, he observed, Bainville had avoided the slightest hint of political partisanship. What it proved above all was that "the natural turn of his mind is objectivity." In his capacity as "a realist, a positivist, a practical man who detests and despises illusions, chimeras, and fancy words," the royalist historian had attained a degree of impartiality and comprehensiveness unequalled by any textbook writer. Moreover, he had accomplished a feat of historical synthesis by covering the history of France from Caesar to the occupation of the Ruhr in 500 pages.[11]

Similar words of praise flowed from the pen of Jean Prévost at the *Nouvelle Revue française*. Noting the indispensability of general histories as instructive guides to the French public, this young defender of classical taste hailed Bainville's as "the clearest and liveliest" product of that genre he had ever read. Praising the author's dignified tone, effort at impartiality, and ability to subsume a wealth of factual details under a general conception, he described it as "the only textbook of French history that can be read for pleasure." He then turned his critical lance on the professional historians of the university. Bainville's work was particularly successful because it avoided the evil of oversimplification without lapsing into such spurious affectations of erudition as elaborate footnotes, references, and citations. It made no claim to originality and relied entirely on secondary sources. It was the work of a well-informed amateur who knew the history of his country and was concerned about its future and the happiness and prosperity of its citizens.[12]

In an even more sympathetic review, Bainville's former lycée

11. Paul Souday, in *Le Temps* (May 15, 1924).
12. Jean Prévost, "Histoire de France," *Nouvelle Revue française* (October 1, 1924), 478–79.

classmate Amadée Britsch of *Le Correspondant* took the occasion to pull out all the stops in the conservative literary intelligentsia's campaign against the academic historical profession. The royalist historian, he argued, had produced a persuasive rejoinder to the specious, didactic works of the republican *universitaires*:

> There exists an official version of our history, written from half-baked or agreed-upon formulas for the use of the triumphant regime. Despite the grand words Science and Truth, history is largely written for the convenience of the living, and the present continually tends to color the past, according to its needs. If our savants can revise accepted formulas in light of recent scholarship or to fit the requirements of their ideology, a simple *littérateur* has the right to play their game, from the present point of view, in the name of common sense. [13]

Britsch took pains to protect Bainville from the allegation of ideological bias that was bound to come from the academic historical profession. He cited the royalist historian's uncompromising condemnation of the aristocratic émigrés who had abandoned the fatherland during the Revolution as one of the many examples of Bainville's spirit of impartiality.

Britsch also strove to preempt the expected criticism on methodological grounds. It was true that Bainville had not immersed himself in original sources after the fashion of "the severe method of those *érudits*" at the university who refused to admit amateurs into the garden of Clio. But the author's intention was not to dredge up obscure facts about the past; it was rather to "orient his compatriots" who were floundering in "the confusion and disquiet of postwar Europe." In order to drum up popular support for a prudent policy for the future, Britsch observed, Bainville had sought to familiarize Frenchmen with the lessons of the past. Enough time and energy had been expended in uncovering the complex mosaic of French history to permit one capable writer to summarize the results of monographic research and communicate it to the public in readable form. [14]

---

13. Amadée Britsch, "Une Nouvelle Histoire de France," *Le Correspondant* (October 10, 1924), 92; "Hommages à Jacques Bainville," 527.
14. Britsch, "Une Nouvelle Histoire de France," 92, 95, 89.

Most reviewers were quick to notice that Bainville had not addressed his work to the traditional royalist following. Prévost described the book as "a eulogy for the French bourgeoisie." Another
critic observed long afterward that Bainville's *Histoire de France*,
together with the other volumes in the *Grandes Etudes Historiques*
collection, had "transcended the royalist public to reach much more
extensive social strata," especially the conservative middle classes
which felt threatened by the leftward drift of French republicanism.
Another observed that Bainville's cosmopolitan outlook, which he
had acquired through familiarity with other societies, was tempered
by a devout nationalism which reflected the parochial, bourgeois
instincts of a "good *père de famille.*" [15]
    But the astonishing commercial success of Bainville's history of
France signified for Britsch more than just a personal triumph for
the author. It represented nothing less than a turning point in modern French literary history. Britsch observed that since the First
World War Fayard's propensity for publishing novels was gradually giving way to a preference for popular history. The entertaining,
impressionistic *Louis XIV* of the royalist sympathizer Louis Bertrand, the first work to appear in the *Grandes Etudes Historiques*
series, had set in motion this transition from the novel to history.
But Bainville's work, eschewing the picturesque, sentimental qualities that adorned Bertrand's portrait of the Sun King, concluded
the publishing revolution that had helped to bring about the revival
of public interest in history. Britsch believed that Fayard was on
the verge of transforming itself into a generator of historical syntheses, an enterprise that promised to be both financially reward-
ing and socially beneficial. [16]
    The contagious effect of Bainville's successful attempt to resur-
rect the old genre of historical vulgarization was later recalled by
Philippe Ariès, a young royalist militant who was to become one of
France's most distinguished free-lance historians after the Second
World War. Serious works of history had seldom reached a wide
audience before the appearance of Bertrand's and Bainville's best

---

15. Prévost, "Histoire de France," 479; Ariès, *Le Temps de l'histoire*, 50.
16. Britsch, "Une Nouvelle Histoire de France," 88–89.

sellers, Ariès observed. Thereafter, the royalist works at Fayard sold as well as many of the most popular novels. Even the "pedantic hauteur" of the academic historical profession, with its restricted clientele of scholarly specialists, was incapable of immunizing its own members against the temptation of commercial success and public renown. Without mentioning names, Ariès accused many professional historians who had previously written nothing but erudite monographs of having quickly "surrendered to the current of opinion and humbly aligned themselves behind Bainville and Gaxotte" and their fellow popularizers at Fayard, adopting the rules of the new genre "with the awkwardness of debutantes."[17]

The onslaught against the university historians occasioned by the publication of Bainville's book in the spring of 1924 continued unabated for the rest of the year. Chiding the eminent gentlemen at the Sorbonne for using their academic credentials as a substitute for imagination and originality, Marcel Azaïs of *Les Essais critiques* hailed Bainville as a historian whose mind "presides at the synthesis" of historical facts and whose literary talents enable him to present them in an intelligible form. He predicted that the accusations of political partisanship that were certain to be raised against Bainville would emanate principally from the "pontiffs" of republican orthodoxy in the university, whose own historical writings were "incomprehensible" to all but their fellow pedants. The political principle that underlay Bainville's work was less a tenderness for monarchy than a distaste for regimes that govern according to the whim of public opinion. The royalist historian applauded the monarchy only when it pursued correct policies in the face of a hostile and ignorant populace. The indispensable value of his analysis was its relentless search for the historical sources of erroneous policies and its effort to demonstrate how successive French governments had failed to profit from past errors.[18]

The rightist press predictably chimed in with spirited paeans to the achievement of its ideological compatriot. Edmond Pilon, writing in *La Revue universelle*, praised his editor for avoiding the ex-

17. Ariès, *Le Temps de l'histoire*, 29–30, 31, 274–75.
18. Marcel Azaïs, in *Essais critiques* (May 1, 1924), 637–39, 133, 135.

cessive historical dramatization typical of the old romantic school
of historiography while refusing to adopt the "irritating and unbearable pedantry" of the university historians. Pilon also reminded his readers that any effort to rewrite the history of France in a
concise, entertaining form necessarily ran the risk of receiving the
disapprobation of the professional historians. Bainville's willingness to employ the past as a source for present edification opened
vast new perspectives for the genre of historical writing. His *Histoire de France* surpassed the narrow conception of history popularized by "the textbook writers, enclosed in their dates, limited by
their chronologies," who produced little more than "barely coherent collections of disparate materials" with little instructive value.
By seeking to elucidate the linkages between apparently unrelated
historical events, Bainville had performed the dual service of identifying for the Frenchmen of today their historical origins and inspiring confidence in the future of their fatherland.[19]

Léon Daudet celebrated his colleague as the elucidator of the
hitherto "invisible concatenations" of historical change, as the
French writer who had definitively identified the principal causal
agents of France's historical development. He predicted that Bainville's emphasis on the political determinants of historical evolution would effectively counteract the economic interpretations of
history which had begun to appear in the works of professional
historians in France.[20] A number of reviewers railed against the
ideological prejudices that had distorted much of French history
writing since 1789 and attributed the popularity of Bainville's work
to the author's skill at exposing that distortion and isolating from
the mass of historical facts the scientific laws that regulate human
behavior.

The new work received similar acclaim from conservative critics
across the Channel, where it was soon translated into English. A
typical response from right-wing observers in Great Britain was
that of Charles Whibley of *The English Review*, who echoed many
French reviewers' claims that the commercial success of the book

19. *RU* (June 1, 1924), 637–39, 641–42.
20. *AF*, March 31, 1924.

was proof of popular dissatisfaction with professional history. He noted that the province of historical writing had been "annexed in England by the Whigs, [and] in France by Radical rhetoricians" who used it to bolster their own political preferences. The popularity of Bainville's book signified the revival of interest in the writings of traditionalist historians. For Whibley the question of scholarly objectivity, which was to trouble certain French readers of Bainville, was a dead issue. While crediting Bainville with having purged the last drop of rhetoric and sentimentality from his work, he defended the absence of the perfect impartiality demanded by the professional historians. History is not a "dry-as-dust science" as the university historians persisted in proclaiming, and "if the historian is anything better than a gatherer of unrelated facts, he cannot exclude himself and his thought from his narrative." Faith in such objectivity was, in any case, a chimera, since all historical writing is inevitably colored by the author's own temperament. Bainville had legitimately selected from the mass of available facts those which served his overriding purpose, that of reawakening national pride in his readers.[21]

This reference to the patriotic function of historical writing reappeared in a favorable review of Bainville's *Histoire de France* by an eminent authority on French historical scholarship: Gustave Fagniez, a university-trained paleographer and cofounder, with Gabriel Monod, of the *Revue Historique* who had defected to the nationalist cause at the turn of the century. As with the Englishman Whibley, what was most appealing to Fagniez in Bainville's book was the benign influence that it was likely to exercise on French self-esteem. By providing a valuable synthesis of the historical developments underlying the creation of the modern French nation, it would encourage Frenchmen to "discover in the evidence of the past the courage and hope that they will perhaps need on the eve of new trials." Fagniez noted with approval that Bainville's principal aim in writing it had been to emphasize the essential unity of his nation's history by "reducing it to the permanent psy-

21. Charles Whibley, "A History of France," *English Review* (November, 1924), 626–27.

chology of the French people as it is manifested in analogous circumstances" in the present.[22]

Recalling Bainville's harsh words about his own historical training in the preface to his *Histoire de France*, Fagniez noted that the author belonged to a generation that had developed a distaste for traditional history because of its tendency to eschew "the art of explaining the interconnection of events, of identifying their origin, their evolution, . . . and their consequences." That Bainville had relied exclusively upon secondary sources for his historical data with no discernible attempt at verification did not trouble the eminent paleographer from the Ecole des Chartes. The explanatory brilliance and synthetic perfection of the work more than compensated for its lack of erudition.[23]

The reviewer for the *Revue de synthèse historique* (which had been founded at the turn of the century as a forum for critics of scholarly specialization) attributed the popularity of Bainville's work to the clarity of its style, the sobriety of its tone, and most important, its admirable concision. The author had wisely avoided the temptation to conceive of historical periods as nothing but agglomerations of meaningless facts, and his "meritorious effort at impartiality" enabled him to select and emphasize certain preeminent historical developments in a narrative relatively untarnished by his own political prejudices.[24]

But interspersed among such plaudits was occasional criticism that tended to follow a consistent pattern. What had appeared as praiseworthy virtues to friendly critics elicited denunciations from detractors. Bainville's reputed originality became a grave violation of the canons of historical scholarship in the eyes of professional historians. His skill at synthetic reductionism was assailed as oversimplification by those who appreciated the complexity of histori-

22. Weber, *Action Française*, 36; *Séances et travaux de l'Académie des sciences morales et politiques: compte rendu* (November–December, 1924), 336–38.

23. See above, 9; *Séances et travaux*, 315–16. Fagniez correctly identified the works of Antoine Cleophas Dareste and Emile Bourgeois as the most important secondary sources upon which Bainville relied.

24. A. Roubaud, "Une Synthèse de l'histoire de France," in *Revue de synthèse historique*, XXXVIII (December 1924), 163–64.

cal change. Ironically, the allegation that appeared least often in the handful of hostile reviews of the royalist theoretician's magnum opus was the one that might have been expected to predominate: the charge of ideological bias.

The most frequent criticism of the book centered on Bainville's penchant for emphasizing political and diplomatic events at the expense of the underlying socioeconomic processes.[25] This was the principal objection of Roubaud of the *Revue de synthèse historique*, who blamed Bainville's "simplistic, exclusively political" conception of history as a perpetual Manichean confrontation between the "*esprit révolutionnaire*" and the "*esprit conservateur*" for ignoring the broader social determinants of historical change. Britsch tempered his otherwise highly favorable review in *Le Correspondant* with the observation that the excessive attention devoted to the intricacies of cabinet diplomacy and high finance caused Bainville to underestimate the influence of public opinion. He might have added that both preoccupations derived from Bainville's journalistic assignments at the Quai d'Orsay and the Bourse, and reflected his restrictive conception that the proper role of the state was as guarantor of national security and financial stability. Fagniez likewise observed that Bainville emphasized affairs of state to the exclusion of the broader and deeper concerns of the society at large.[26]

Several commentators also took issue with what one critic called Bainville's propensity for reducing the intricate unfolding of historical events to "a strict mechanism." Paul Feyel of the *Revue bleue*, again returning to the mordant passages of Bainville's preface, sought to explain this mechanistic conception of history as a reaction against the historical instruction that the latter had received in his youth, which had devoted insufficient attention to the interconnectedness of historical facts. The author's attempt to compen-

---

25. Prévost ("Histoire de France," 479) observed that the greatest lacuna in the work was its sketchy treatment of economic history. It is perhaps worth noting that, aside from a handful of pioneers such as Emile Levasseur, Henri Hauser, and Jean Jaurès, professional historians themselves had devoted little attention to economic history before the end of the First World War. See Rondo Cameron, ed., *Essays in French Economic History* (Homewood, Illinois: Richard D. Irwin, Inc., 1970), 1–4.

26. Roubaud, "Une Synthèse de l'histoire de France," 167–68; Britsch, "Une Nouvelle Histoire de France," 93–94; Fagniez, in *Séances et travaux*, 315.

sate for this defect of his early training had resulted in the opposite
error of regarding the history of the French nation as the tale of a
machine that "had functioned well for a long time" under the benign supervision of monarchs until it was irremediably "thrown
out of gear" by a gang of ignorant and malicious men in 1789. Surely the evolution of France from a barbaric province of Rome to a
powerful modern state, the reviewer caustically observed, was a
much more complex development than that. Britsch of *Le Correspondant* attributed Bainville's narrowly mechanistic conception of
history to his positivist world view, which reduced all the metaphysical aspects of human behavior to a monistic "political physics." It was this very tendency toward a sort of rationalist reductionism, he contended, that accounted for the popularity of the
work. Precisely because he had omitted sophisticated ideas, elu-
sive arguments, and other imponderables from his account, Bainville's historical generalizations made sense to the average reader.[27]

Surprisingly, the severest attack on the political bias of Bainville's
history did not emanate from the liberal historians of the university.
It came instead in the form of a polemical work by a self-professed
republican nationalist of the Michelet tradition named Jacques Reboul, who sought to discredit the royalism of the Action Française
in the name of the very cause of nationalism that it espoused. While
acknowledging the valuable service that Bainville had performed
by delivering his readers from "the hodge-podge and puerilities
of the textbooks," Reboul berated Bainville for perpetuating the
erroneous identification of French nationalism with the royalist-
Catholic tradition. The Maurrassian writer had skillfully sought to
resurrect the moribund cause of royalism by arbitrarily and selec-
tively interpreting historical data in such a way as to establish a
number of dubious propositions about the services performed by
the monarchy. Saint Louis, who appears in Bainville's work as the
archetype of the hereditary ruler dedicated to the interests of the
nation, was in reality "the elected official of a clerical-Germanic

27. Paul Feyel, in *Nouvelles littéraires* (April 11, 1925); Paul Feyel, "Les Livres
nouveaux," *Revue bleue* (November 15, 1924), 789–90; Britsch, "Une Nouvelle Histoire de France," 96–97.

clique." The royalist historian conveniently forgot to mention that Charles VII had abandoned Joan of Arc, the true symbol of national unity, in her hour of need. By portraying Richelieu as the organizer of French prosperity and security, Bainville neglected to mention that the renowned minister's persecution of the Huguenots jeopardized France's economic prosperity and national unity by depriving it of Protestant business expertise and sowing religious dissension. Bainville's selectivity enabled him to brand the proto-revolutionary Etienne Marcel as an opportunistic traitor for changing sides in 1358 while praising the converted royalist Talleyrand's good judgment in abandoning Bonaparte for the Allies in 1814.[28]

But Bainville's principal shortcoming, in the eyes of this republican patriot, was his inability to perceive the continuity of policy that underlay the change of political regimes in France since 1789. The royalist historian was wrong to characterize the Bourbon Restoration as a return to the policies of the *ancien régime*, since it had retained many of the institutions established during the Revolution. The First Republic and the First Empire were not responsible for squandering the bulk of France's old colonial possessions, as Bainville implied. "England simply succeeded in depriving us in 1814 of the colonies that she had begun to take at the Treaty of Paris" during the reign of Louis XV. The most egregious manifestation of this political continuity, which Bainville recognized but refused to let modify his antipathy to republicanism, was that "the French republic is resuming . . . the ambitions of royalty" with the same dedication exhibited by royal councillors under the *ancien régime*.[29]

The expected barrage of criticism from the academic historical profession never materialized, probably because the professional historians considered the work unworthy of comment. But the few *universitaires* who did take notice felt obliged to direct a few pot shots at its obvious methodological deficiencies. Louis Halphen, writing in the *Revue historique*, greeted the book as "one of the most intelligent—and most irritating—books that have been written on

---

28. Jacques Reboul, *M. Bainville contre l'histoire de France* (Paris: Editions du Siècle, 1925), 11–12, 53, 66–67, 75–79, 97–98.
29. *Ibid.*, 19, 95–96.

our history." Professional historians could accept the book for what it was: a well-written, entertaining synopsis which was predictably replete with factual inaccuracies and ideological bias, defects to be expected from a nonspecialist with an axe to grind.[30]

In a similar vein Roubaud of the *Revue de synthèse historique* called attention to several passages that revealed a serious absence of documentation and numerous errors of fact. "The author is correctly seeking to show the relations between events, unlike the professors who had so poorly instructed him in history," he charitably observed. "But these relations can be established only after a thorough and objective study of the facts." The goal of historical objectivity, though unattainable, can and must be approached through a process of discipline, patience, and scrupulosity, yet this was precisely what was lacking in Bainville's method. He attributed this failure to the royalist historian's eagerness to assign degrees of praise or blame to each historical actor and to interpret events according to *a priori* standards of judgment instead of striving, in a professional manner, to understand the past on its own terms.[31]

But the reviewer of the *Revue de synthèse historique* acknowledged the necessity for general historical syntheses and recognized the appeal that such works held for the average reader. He conceded that Bainville's book responded to an important need, and noted that its very defects—the oversimplifications, the excessive systematization, the absence of documentation—had been a major element in the book's success.

> It is doubtless true that insofar as scientific methods have been imposed on the historians, their works have become less accessible to the general public. Even apart from the works of [monographic] scholarship, most of the syntheses are still too imposing in their dimension and too specialized in their subject to reach a large number of readers. . . . Busy people who are seeking to revive the vague historical memories that they have retained from their studies or to learn what they never knew are naturally looking for short and easily read books.

30. Louis Halphen, "Jacques Bainville: Histoire de France," *Revue historique*, CXLVII (September–October, 1924), 99–100.
31. Roubaud, "Une Synthèse de l'histoire de France," 163–66.

He therefore concluded that the general design of Bainville's book was justified and deserved the serious attention of scholars in spite of its faulty execution.[32]

What the commercial success of Bainville's *Histoire de France* had proved to professional historians, Roubaud observed, was that they should "no longer restrict themselves to writing for a tiny elite" of specialists, but should attempt instead to contribute to the "edification of the public." He wondered whether it might not be possible in the future for technically trained professional historians to present to the masses a continuous exposition of the history of France by means of a series of very general syntheses, conceived according to the rigorous methods of historical scholarship.[33] Such a belated proposal must have caused no little irritation to the disciples of those professional historians who had compiled a veritable library of just such general works since the turn of the century in an effort to bridge the gap between the *érudit* and the public.[34]

The other major criticism of Bainville's scholarly methods did not appear until shortly after his death in early 1936. Ernest Roussel, a protégé of the aging university historian Charles Seignobos (who contributed a preface to Roussel's work), boldly reformulated the standards of historical scholarship that had been established in the French university system and found Bainville's work totally deficient on those grounds. The writing of history was no longer simply a question of reading a few letters and memoirs and summarizing their contents in "a few supple phrases"; it required a willingness to examine the complete documentary record of the past as well as a capacity for self-discipline and methodological rigor. One cannot even begin to address historical subjects without possessing a familiarity with "at least everything included in the curriculum of the Ecole des Chartes," he announced, in a less than subtle slap at the

32. *Ibid.*, 169.

33. *Ibid.*, 169–70. Roubaud was reviving a criticism of the monographic proclivities of professional history in France that had originated with Henri Berr. See Keylor, *Academy and Community*, Chap. VIII.

34. The best known among these was Lavisse's *Histoire de France depuis les origines jusqu'à la Révolution*, which had appeared in nine installments between 1900 and 1909.

amateur historians in France who had not benefited from academic training in the discipline. He compared Seignobos's recently published *Histoire sincère de la nation française* to Bainville's *Histoire de France*, concluding that "a mind that is only artistic cannot really write history" because of its propensity for relying on unverified legends and secondary sources instead of the contemporary documents.[35]

Several reviewers focused on Bainville's celebrated present-mindedness, his fondness for discovering historical analogies of contemporary events. Most hailed this practice as an admirable means of introducing a sense of unity to French history and of eliciting lessons for future conduct. "History sometimes profits from not having been written by historians," declared Paul Ballaguy in *L'Eclair*. The discipline is actually enriched when a politically conscious writer with a keen sense of realism that is "fortified by experience in the present" applies himself to the study of the past. Historical events frequently possess a significance for modern man which escapes the professional historian's antiquarian gaze and therefore must be discovered by untrained eyes. For other critics this conception of the dialectical interplay of past and present operated in the inverse sense. Gilbert Charles asserted in *Le Divan* that Bainville's ability to write lucid commentaries on contemporary problems derived from his practice of drawing upon his knowledge of the past to furnish heuristic analogies to experiences in the here-and-now.[36]

The present-minded approach to historical study represented for Bainville the principal *raison d'être* of the discipline. He had frequently expressed the conviction that historical writing is a worthless enterprise unless it is guided by the concerns of the historian's own time. It was a natural sentiment coming from a politically committed journalist who grappled daily with problems of immediate concern. He once described history as "a sort of cone whose base is in the present and which becomes more slender as it approaches

35. Ernest Roussel, *Les Nuées maurrassiennes* (Paris: Flory, 1936), 12–15.
36. Paul Ballaguy, in *L'Eclair*, April 12, 1924, cited in *AF*, April 15, 1924; Gilbert Charles, in *Divan*, 105 (January, 1925), 51.

the past."[37] In his pursuit of the past for the sake of the present, he often committed the sin that professional historians had cautioned against since the days of Ranke: the tendency to twist historical events into a distorted analogical relationship to the present. One reviewer warned that Bainville's preoccupation with contemporary problems and his perpetual quest for heuristic analogies in the past caused him to "lose sight of the differences between historical periods." He regretted that this lack of appreciation for historical particularities had caused Bainville to neglect the important influence that time and place exercised on human behavior.[38]

The members of the academic historical profession, who had long endured allegations of pro-Germanism from French rightist circles,[39] were particularly sensitive to Bainville's conception of the perpetual conflict between France and Germany, a principal theme of his *Histoire de France*. Reviewing a passage in which Bainville has Clovis fending off the threat of Germania, Roussel could not contain his disgust at this attempt to reduce centuries of parallel national development to such a simplistic confrontation. "Already!!! At the end of the fifth century, the 'Germans' have become the 'hereditary enemies' of the French! When there did not yet exist either Germans or Frenchmen." Lucien Febvre reacted in similar fashion to the type of historical reductionism practiced by those historians who were "always speaking to us of France as a constant reality, perfectly defined, identical to itself throughout the ages." His future collaborator Marc Bloch had observed somewhat earlier that the great virtue of history was its capacity for acquainting students with the variability of human institutions and for encouraging them to understand past societies on their own terms and to accept the reality of historical change.[40] Yet change was precisely the aspect of history that Bainville continually denigrated in his

---

37. Cited in *Almanach des lettres françaises* (April 14, 1924), 257ff.
38. Roubaud, "Une Synthèse de l'histoire de France," 165–66.
39. See above, 34–35, 37, 39n.
40. Roussel, *Les Nuées maurrassiennes*, 14; Lucien Febvre, "Politique royale ou civilisation française," *Revue de synthèse historique*, XXXVIII (December, 1924), 37; *Bulletin de la Société des professeurs d'histoire et de géographie* (November, 1921), 16. Febvre's later work, *Le Problème de l'incroyance au XVIe siècle*, perfectly exemplified

writings, and particularly in his *Histoire de France*. He preferred to dwell on the constants of human behavior, the timeless verities that permitted the man of the twentieth century to identify with and learn from the experience of the man of the sixteenth.

But the complaints of the scholarly specialists could not erase the undeniable appeal that Bainville's unified conception of the French past had exercised among many impressionable Frenchmen of the interwar generation. A year after its publication, an opinion poll conducted by the nationalist journal *L'Eclair* revealed that 150 writers had designated Bainville's *Histoire de France* as one of three books they would like to see representing the cause of French civilization throughout the world. The commercial success of the book suggests that it had reached an audience much larger than either the academic or the literary elite.[41]

The personal testimony of Philippe Ariès is suggestive in this regard. Describing Bainville's *Histoire de France* as the "breviary of my first adolescence," Ariès noted that his copy was "covered with annotations and markings" beside passages he considered incisive and penetrating. What most appealed to this young student of history was Bainville's conception of the objective reality of the past as an "arsenal of arguments for the present." Bainville's doctrine of historical repetition enchanted Ariès because it implied "the possibility of avoiding the effects of dangerous causes by rediscovering in history cycles that are analogous to causality."[42] The historian no longer needed to be content with his role as a passive recorder of past events (as the scrupulous canons of historical scholarship seemed to demand), but was permitted to take an active role in shaping the future by eliciting and disseminating the lessons of the past.

Ariès proceeded to explain why Bainville's brand of history proved so appealing to Frenchmen of the interwar period. He was

---

the conviction of the two editors of the *Annales* that historical periods are discontinuous and that conceptions drawn from present experience cannot be applied to the distant past. See H. Stuart Hughes, *The Obstructed Path: French Social Thought in the Years of Desperation* (New York: Harper & Row, 1968), 45–47.

41. *L'Eclair*, September 5, 1925; see the Appendix.

42. Ariès, *Le Temps de l'histoire*, 26–29.

certain that style played an important part. The average French reader was a practical, sober-minded model of common sense to whom Bainville's dry, clear, and concise style represented a welcome alternative to the florid prose of romantic history writing and the pedantic obscurity of academic scholarship. The typical French bourgeois was in search of "a history of political facts"—not the unique, isolated, nonrepeatable facts recorded by the professional historians, but rather those facts which yield generalizations comprehensible to the common man and applicable to his contemporary experience. Both the romantic historians of the nineteenth century and the academic *érudits* of the twentieth were guilty of overemphasizing particular elements of the past at the expense of a broader understanding of successive periods of historical development. The romantics, such as Thierry and Michelet, strove to recapture history in its pristine, picturesque form, revelling in the "singularity and exoticism" that gave past civilizations and eras their esthetic appeal. Professional academic historians also sought to reconstruct the experience of the past for its own sake, in the name of scholarly accuracy rather than art, establishing the principle that history proves nothing and contains no lessons of use in the present.[43]

Both romantic and academic historical writing, in Ariès view, therefore deprived modern man of the type of intellectual solace that he desperately sought in the past. Modern man's mounting curiosity about his past differed markedly from the romantics' nostalgia for the rustic simplicity of medieval life. It represented a curiosity about the entire sweep of historical development, not a particularistic passion for the more colorful periods. He felt himself to be a link in the chain of time, the culmination of a vast historical continuum, which cannot be isolated from past ages no matter how unique or exotic they may appear to scholar or poet. He had come to view history "as a prolongation of himself, as a part of his being."[44] It was precisely this image of history that Bainville conveyed in his writings.

43. *Ibid.*, 51–52, 263, 267.
44. *Ibid.*, 32–33.

This quest for the lost historical connection was particularly evident in French society during the interwar period. Ariès attributed this widespread nostalgia for ancient France to the prompting of what he called "the Capetian school" of twentieth-century French history writing, of which Bainville was the master. The trauma of wars, revolutions, economic crises, and the other upheavals that taxed the resilience of France on the eve of the era that H. Stuart Hughes has called the "years of desperation" led many Frenchmen to seek solace in the comforting memories of past grandeur. Revolutionary societies such as France had become increasingly conservative and intensely conscious of their historical roots in reaction to the turbulent forces of a modernity which had passed them by. Such societies, faced with an increasingly threatening international environment, strove to insulate themselves from the present by reassuring their historical claim to superiority. Bainville's conception of history incorporated both a nostalgic reminder of France's past grandeur and a reputedly "positivist" attempt to discover those historical laws of human behavior which could yield comforting explanations of France's present plight.[45]

It was this second aspect of the Bainvillian historical doctrine which, according to Ariès, had the greatest appeal for the French bourgeoisie in particular. By establishing the principle of the universality and permanence of human nature throughout history, Bainville had succeeded in reaffirming the classical conception of man which had been expelled from literature during the nineteenth century by the romantic novelists. Ariès savored the irony of this achievement. The classical ideal of "eternal man," which had "retarded the birth of historical consciousness for several centuries," was paradoxically re-emerging as the central theme of a new historical school:

> In the nineteenth century, the novel assured the triumph of social types differentiated according to time, place, and condition. On the contrary, history . . . now maintains the fiction of the classical man. It poses as a principle the permanence of human nature, unaltered by the transitory

45. *Ibid.*, 49–51, 57–59.

modifications of historical development [le devenir]. The idea of the permanence of man thereby becomes a commonplace in the manner of thinking and of conversing in bourgeois society.[46]

Ariès asserted that Bainville's work had conferred a new respectability on the notion "that the differences between historical periods are illusory, that men have not changed, that their actions are repeatable, [and] that the study of these repetitions enables one to grasp the laws of politics." The nineteenth-century romantic conception of the unique, nonrepeatable character of each successive historical period was gradually giving way to a revival of the classical belief in the immutability of human nature and in the uninterrupted operation of universal laws of behavior over time. Such a doctrine, which emphasized the stable, static, continuous nature of human existence, comforted the French middle-class reader who was perplexed by the turbulent events of the twentieth century. No such assurance had been forthcoming from the conception emphasizing the discontinuity of historical periods and the perpetual dynamism of historical change. More important, this classical philosophy of history furnished the bourgeoisie with a moral justification for its preeminent social position. If human nature appeared as a fixed, permanent entity "exposed to the same dangers, ready to succumb to the same temptations," society required the tutelage of "an enlightened class" that appreciated the complexities of human existence.[47]

Ironically, Ariès claimed to perceive a filiation between Bainville's conception of history, which he labelled "conservative historicism," and the Marxist theory of history that had recently begun to infiltrate French academic circles in the 1920s.[48] Both schools

46. *Ibid.*, 55, 323. Ariès curiously failed to recognize the important role played by Durkheimian sociology in the repudiation of the classical conception of human nature. For a brief discussion of this development, see Keylor, *Academy and Community*, 192–93.

47. Ariès, *Le Temps de l'histoire*, 29, 323, 269–70.

48. See David Caute, *Communism and the French Intellectuals: 1914–1960* (New York: Macmillan, 1964), 276ff. for a treatment of the origins and development of Marxist historiography in France. See also Paul Farmer, *France Reviews its Revolutionary Origins: Social Politics and Historical Opinion in the Third Republic* (New York: Octagon Books, 1963), 89ff.

of history forsook questions of individual psychology in order to concentrate on the interplay of "institutions." Both viewed institutions not as products of specific conditions generated in a particular historical period and geographical milieu, but rather as entities governed by general laws of development "that are deduced from their repetition in the course of history." An institution that emerged in a past society rapidly transcended "the singularity of the customs that produced it," thereby acquiring a general characteristic which "links it to all the other institutions that have preceded and will succeed it."[49] Conservative historicism's nostalgia for a past golden age and Marxism's optimistic faith in a future Utopia both tended to reduce the diversity of human experience in history to accommodate their respective *a priori* formulations. Confronted with the confusion and unpredictability of events in the modern world, Ariès declared, historians of both left and right have consoled themselves with the conviction that history is an "abstract mechanism." The principal difference between the two historical schools was that political institutions exercised the determinative function in Bainville's mechanistic scheme that were exercised by economic institutions in the Marxist system.

Bainville's indictment of the reigning traditions of professional historical writing in the preface to his *Histoire de France* came as something of a surprise. He had occasionally grumbled about the failure of the university historians to acquaint French students with the extraordinary accomplishments of the monarchy and often complained about the meaningless recitation of military events and sentimental references to past epochs that had passed for historical education during his youth.[50] But he had never been party to the public campaign against the French university and its historical tradition that had been waged since the turn of the century by such academic renegades as Charles Péguy, Pierre Lasserre, Henri Massis, Louis Dimier, and René Benjamin. Yet Bainville's simmering

49. Ariès, *Le Temps de l'histoire*, 56.
50. Bainville, *History of France*, v; Bainville, *Journal*, I, July 3, 1914.

resentment at the Mandarins of official history at the Sorbonne and their disciples in the lycées had come to a boil by the mid-twenties. He began to hold them responsible for helping to hasten the decline of French civilization with their erroneous historical teaching.

On the eve of the armistice, Bainville had declared that France could no longer afford works of history written from an international or revolutionary point of view. What was now required was history designed to reawaken French national pride and self-confidence.[51] The publication of his *Histoire de France*, with its narrowly nationalistic tone and its thinly veiled apologia for the royalist tradition of French history, represented an unmistakable provocation to the university historians who were striving to reassert the values of cosmopolitan humanism and liberalism that had been so severely tarnished during the war. The professional historians' conspiracy of silence in the face of his popular work, interrupted by the occasional outbursts of criticism mentioned above, provoked an uncharacteristic flurry of defensive rage in the man who had prided himself on his moderation and *sang-froid*.

The Bainvillean critique of the university historians and their defenders in the world of letters was multifaceted, but it centered upon what he regarded as professional history's spurious claim to scientific objectivity and its hypocritical refusal to recognize that quality in its ideological enemies. This dispute became more pronounced after the publication of Julien Benda's *Treason of the Intellectuals* three years after the appearance of Bainville's *Histoire de France*. In his celebrated book Benda denounced Bainville's work as a modern version of the didactic nationalist tracts of nineteenth-century German historians. Its author was nothing more than a propagandist who interpreted the past "from the point of view of the passions of his own time."[52] Benda's charge hit home, having emanated not from a professional historian in the university but

51. Bainville, *Histoire de trois générations*, 7.
52. Julien Benda, *The Treason of the Intellectuals*, trans. Richard Aldington (New York: Norton, 1969), 72–73n.

from a literary intellectual with impeccable credentials as a defender of classical taste in literature and an objective observer of French
politics, two virtues which Bainville claimed for himself.[53]

Since Benda's influential critique was aimed principally at the intellectual betrayal by the *"clercs"* of conservative nationalism and
made only cursory mention of the intellectuals of the left, Bainville
seized the opportunity to correct the mistaken impression that intellectual prostitution was the special prerogative of the right. He
strove to expose the numerous instances in which the republican
historians of the university had descended from the ivory tower to
do battle in the arena of partisan politics. Bainville accused the Sorbonne historians in particular of having time and time again surrendered to the temptations of power and fame presented by the
call of politics. Since the turn of the century the university had
scarcely been a training ground for the objective scholarship that
Benda adored, but rather had succeeded in forming "apostles of
Dreyfusard spiritualism," fanatical ideologues striving to "Calvin-
ize the schoolchildren of France."[54] The convergence of the secular
faith of Dreyfusism and the religious creed of Calvinism in the republican university[55] had conspired to squeeze out the last vestige
of objectivity from its members. What better indication of this
"trahison" could be cited than the united front formed by the scholarly community in support of the campaign in favor of Dreyfus
and against the Catholic church?

What irritated Bainville even more than the professional historians' participation in political affairs of the present was what he
viewed as their politically biased interpretations of the past. "A
wise historian has said that one could trace at will either a sinister
or an enchanting tableau of France under the *ancien régime*," ob-

53. It was perhaps for this reason that Bainville frequently remarked to his
friends that Benda was one of the few French writers for whom he felt nothing
but contempt. Interview with Madame Jacques Bainville.
54. Bainville, *Le Vieil Utopiste*, 82, 89.
55. The conception of the French academic historical profession as a hotbed of
Protestant conspirators was strengthened by the fact that two preeminent professors were Protestant—Gabriel Monod and Charles Seignobos.

served a character in one of Bainville's fictional pieces. "We know that the sinister tableau has generally prevailed."[56] Bainville remarked that Taine's optimistic faith in science as the appropriate vehicle for redressing the balance that had been tipped by French historians against prerevolutionary France had proved to be a dangerous illusion. Taine of all people should have realized that the adoption of the methods of scientific history did not ensure the triumph of scholarly integrity. His masterly demonstration in *Les Origines de la France contemporaine* of the evils of the revolutionary mentality had not resulted in a revised estimate of the significance of 1789. Instead, the academic historical profession had simply abandoned scientific objectivity for ideological polemic. The professional historians

> immediately arose to combat Taine and the counterrevolutionary movement that might have emerged from his books. Even at the Sorbonne there were professors destined to struggle against his influence, to denigrate his word. For Science is an object of disinterested passion for only a few individuals. Most of the "savants" live at the expense of the State, are servants of the State; that is why they must teach the doctrine of the State.[57]

By redefining the term "science" to accommodate their own particular ideological and methodological preferences, Bainville argued, the Sorbonne historians enjoyed the prerogative of disqualifying those works that take issue with their historical interpretations as "unscientific."[58] In a Voltairian *conte* entitled *Nouveau Dialogue dans le salon d'Aliénor*, Bainville employed the classic device of an imaginary dialogue to dramatize this allegation. Madame Simonin, a society lady displaying a copy of Bainville's *Histoire de France* on her drawing room table, is rebuked by her friend Monsieur Giradot, a university professor, for possessing a history book that had

---

56. Bainville, *Nouveau dialogue*, 65.
57. Bainville, *Le Vieil Utopiste*, 117.
58. He might have mentioned, in support of this allegation, Alphonse Aulard's warning that any doctoral candidate caught citing Taine as an authority on a fact of history would be disqualified. Alphonse Aulard, *Taine: historien de la Révolution française* (Paris: Colin, 1901), viii.

not been officially designated as a serious work. What claim does the author have to the name of historian? he asks. "He has graduated neither from the Ecole Normale nor the Ecole des Chartes. He is a rather clever journalist, that's all. Has he ever conducted original research? Presented a thesis at the Sorbonne? Never."[59]

After declaring his unwillingness to read such a work which, owing to its author's lack of professional training, was bound to be replete with unscientific judgments, the professor affirms that the only truly scientific method of writing history was not to write it at all, for "the narration deforms it." Seignobos, the dean of Sorbonne historians, was correct in observing that "history is not written, it is photographed." Doctor Huguet, another visitor to the lady's drawing room who served as the archetypal representative of Bainville's *bien pensant* clientele, ridicules his academic friend's gullible acquiescence in the scientific pretensions of professional history. Seignobos's works present an infinity of detail, he concedes, but neither the sense nor the character of historical events is conveyed. The next assignment for Professor Seignobos, the doctor declares, must be "to invent colored historical photography."[60]

The doctor then proceeds to outline the familiar Bainvillean canon of historical interpretation. The official historians err in believing that historical facts are objective, timeless entities passively recorded by the scholar. On the contrary, man's view of the past must be perpetually revised to fit his experience in the present. The liberal historians of the early nineteenth century had celebrated the French Revolution as a unique historical event, a glorious turning point in the history of mankind's progress toward freedom. They did not foresee that the defeat of 1870 and its bloody domestic aftermath would produce a revised interpretation of the revolutionary epoch that reflected the terrible lessons produced by contemporary developments. Taine, Albert Sorel, and others who witnessed the disaster of 1870–1871 constituted a new historical school which rewrote the history of the revolutionary past in a form rad-

59. Bainville, *Nouveau dialogue*, 5–6.
60. *Ibid.*, 9–10, 11.

ically different from that of liberal historiography.[61] These revisionist historians discovered reasons in their own contemporary experience to distrust the revolutionary movement in France and its logical outcome, the Republic. What better proof that history is a subjective science? Our conjectures about the past "depend on us, on our dispositions, on our state of mind," Huguet remarked. "We perpetually reconstruct the past from the viewpoint of the present."[62]

Such present-mindedness required that the historian probe the historical archives for evidence that is most germane to problems of the present and the future, instead of respecting the integrity of the past. Historical writing, therefore, was for Bainville above all the art of abbreviation. The historian must perpetually abridge the evidence he encounters, for without such abridgment he would be forced to devote as much time to writing history as had been devoted to making it. Since Bainville believed that the exigencies of the present dictated a nationalist, monarchist basis for such an abridgment (just as other historians felt the need to use internationalism and republicanism as the prism through which they viewed the past), he unabashedly defended the tradition of didactic, present-minded history that Benda and other defenders of scrupulous detachment condemned.

The popularity of Bainville's *Histoire de France* represented an impressive testimony to the appetite of the French public for historical writing that isolated from the infinite factual details of the past a finite collection of heuristic generalizations applicable to the reader's present experience and served them up in concise, luminous prose. For such services, tens of thousands of dyed-in-the-wool republican readers were apparently willing to forgive him the royalist tinge of his historical writing and embrace the lessons that it contained.

61. See Farmer, *France Reviews its Revolutionary Origins*, 28–37, 45–50, for a discussion of the revisionist interpretations of the Revolution after 1870.
62. Bainville, *Nouveau dialogue*, 21, 25–29, 46.

CHAPTER 8

Cassandra in the Era of Pollyanna
The Domestic Situation, 1925–1932

*That fine spirit, that sad and dear Cassandra, did not have to consult the
gods to see clearly but depended solely on his knowledge of history.*
François Mauriac

The publication of Bainville's *Histoire de France* in the spring of
1924 coincided with the advent of a pervasive mood of optimism in
France regarding the prospects of a durable European peace. Germany was soon to give the impression of having reassumed her
place as a legitimate member of the new international order by
acknowledging her territorial losses to France and endorsing the
principle of collective security on entering the League of Nations.
The postwar traumas of inflation, social dislocation, and financial
chaos in Europe seemed to be giving way to a period of prosperity.
The apparent viability of the new successor states of the Habsburg
Empire appeared to vindicate the Wilsonian ideal of national self-
determination based on the principle of popular sovereignty. The
League of Nations, though weakened by the absence of the United
States and Soviet Russia, represented the first serious attempt to
institutionalize a system of multilateral arbitration since the collapse of the Concert of Europe. It was an age of unbridled faith
in the future. With a stroke of the pen, statesmen could solemnly
renounce the recourse to military force as a means of resolving
international disputes. Bankers could believe themselves capable
of inducing German economic prosperity (and therefore political
moderation) with strategically placed loans and investments.

The last half of the postwar decade was also an era of good feeling within France. Paris had reestablished its pre-eminence as a
cultural and artistic haven in the eyes of lost generations from the

four corners of the earth who flocked to its cafés and galleries and classrooms. The French economy partook of the wave of prosperity that swept Western Europe after the reconstruction of the devastated territory, the influx of American capital, the resumption of German reparations deliveries, and the stabilization of the franc and the mark.

Most important of all, the atmosphere of perpetual crisis that had characterized the political system of the Third Republic in the prewar years seemed to have dissipated. The haunting memories of MacMahon, Boulanger, Dreyfus, Combes, and the political disruptions associated with their names began to fade in minds entranced by the jazz band, the cinema, the automobile, and other diversions associated with that epicurean era. The political, religious, and socioeconomic controversies that had plagued the Third Republic in its early years seemed relics of a bygone age to those optimists who wished to believe in the permanence of the new economic prosperity and political consensus.

The Action Française, as we have seen, had itself helped to lay the groundwork for this spirit of political harmony in the immediate postwar years, lending its tacit support to the rightist governments in that period and even offering one of its own leaders, Léon Daudet, as a successful candidate for parliament. But this uneasy truce between the Republic and the royalist movement came to an abrupt end with the electoral victory of the Cartel des Gauches in the spring of 1924. The conservative republican leaders of the postwar governing coalitions who had enjoyed the tacit support of the royalist movement, Millerand, Poincaré, Bérard, and others, were replaced by an alliance of left-wing republicans which received the endorsement of the Socialist Party.[1] In the same election Daudet was swept out of office, thereby terminating the royalists' brief experiment with parliamentarianism.

The new leftist government proceeded to undo much of the work that had been accomplished by its predecessors. It forced Millerand

1. François Goguel, *La Politique des partis sous la Troisième République* (Paris: Seuil, 1946), quoted in Fabrègues, *Charles Maurras*, 280.

out of the presidency, repealed Bérard's educational innovations, reintroduced a number of anticlerical reforms, and almost succeeded in severing diplomatic relations with the Vatican. Joseph Caillaux and Louis Malvy, victims of the wartime purges who had been branded as traitors by the royalists, were rehabilitated and accorded positions of power. Most significantly, the new leftist cartel abandoned the aggressive foreign policy of Poincaré in favor of détente with Germany, symbolized by the evacuation of the Ruhr, the Rhineland mutual guaranty pact, and the Locarno treaties.

In this period of international harmony and domestic tranquility and prosperity, it would have been entirely understandable if Jacques Bainville had settled down to enjoy the fruits of literary success represented by the substantial royalties from the _Histoire de France_ and other books, the income from articles contributed to half a dozen newspapers, and the numerous honors that a grateful reading public had bestowed upon him. His purchase of a sumptuous apartment at 31 rue de Bellechasse shortly after the war, together with the birth of his son, Hervé, in 1921, represented more personal reasons for him to forsake the daily rigors of polemical journalism and the time-consuming regimen of didactic history writing for the material and psychological comforts of the prosperity and prestige he had recently acquired.[2]

Still another reason for a retreat from the forefront of the Maurrassian crusade may have been the publication in December 1926 of the Papal decree placing the _Action française_ and books of Maurras on the Index. Though Bainville himself was an agnostic who brushed off the Papal condemnation as a matter of little consequence,[3] it soon became apparent that the Holy Father's momen-

2. Tannenbaum's assertions (_Action française_, 58–59) that Bainville was "the only leader of the Action Française who made enough money from his books to live comfortably" and that the others "would probably have starved without the income from their movement" may or may not be true. But Bainville indisputably enjoyed much more financial independence than did his fellows.

3. "Despite the Pope, the Cardinal, the Nuncio, and the rest, everybody here is in excellent form," he wrote to friends during the condemnation crisis. "The Action Française is like the Church itself. Persecutions do it good." Quoted in Weber, _Action française_, 232. For a discussion of Bainville's religious views, see Renauld, _L'Action Française_, 122–23, 132–33, 150–52.

tous action had driven a permanent wedge between the royalist movement and that respectably conservative, Catholic constituency that Bainville had so assiduously and so successfully courted. If he ever hoped to reduce his role in the faltering crusade of the Action Française and cultivate his own garden, the appropriate moment for a declaration of political independence was at hand.

Yet it was precisely at this high point in his career (and the low point in the fortunes of the movement) that Bainville released a torrent of polemical writing unequalled in intensity even in the early years. Updated versions of the old pronouncements about the illusions of internationalism and the certainty of a future Franco-German conflict helped to revive his prewar reputation as the Cassandra of French journalism.[4] He cultivated the image of the unheeded prophet of doom, but without relish or self-congratulation. To a questionnaire inquiring how his books were conceived, and whether they brought him personal satisfaction, he replied: "Always in sadness. . . . I cannot bear to read a single one of them." When asked for whom they were intended, he answered that "he who does not write for everyone is lost."[5] He expressed the hope that his commentary on German affairs would both alert the public to the threat that that nation posed to French security and encourage Frenchmen to consider the long-range consequences of the policies currently pursued.

But Bainville's congenital skepticism about human nature impaired his confidence in the public's capacity for learning the lessons of the past. "The masses are no more reasonable than they are imaginative," he noted in his column. "It is requiring too much of them to ask that they push the application of a principle of causality beyond that which explains why water moistens and fire burns. In any case, they are not even curious about the causes."[6] But he wrote on. The decade of the twenties was his most prolific period,

---

4. The Catholic novelists François Mauriac and Henry Bordeaux were especially fond of comparing their friend Bainville to the unfortunate Greek prophetess. See, for example, Mauriac in Massis, *Le Souvenir*, 102, and Henry Bordeaux, *De Baudelaire à Soeur Marguerite* (Paris: Flammarion, 1936), 227.

5. Gaston Picard, *Nos Ecrivains définis par eux-mêmes* (Paris: Goulet, 1925), 18.

6. Bainville, *Journal*, III, May 8, 1932.

both as a journalist and as a historian. He flooded the literary
market with somber omens of impending political unrest, financial
chaos, and war, hoping against his best judgment that the somnolent French public would awaken in time to read his handwriting
on the wall.

His weekly column in Fayard's and Gaxotte's *Candide*, to which
he began contributing in 1924, invariably expressed, in the tradition of the journal's title, his increasing pessimism about the future
of France and mankind.[7] In one such article he railed with uncharacteristic bitterness at the stupidity of the common man. He
sarcastically announced his intention to found a newspaper entitled *The Enemy of the People* (after Ibsen's play). "For too long the
populace has been told that it represents perfect goodness, justice,
and light, and that a hidden God resides within it," he exclaimed.
"At the risk of receiving stones through my window panes, I would
begin my editorial in these terms: 'Poor imbeciles' or 'unfortunate
dopes.'" It is surprising that "things are not even worse," he concluded, "when one considers the hopeless asses who vote and the
poor souls who are elected."[8]

In addition to his pessimistic prognostications in the columns of
Candide, Bainville published two books in 1927 that further revealed
his increasingly negative view of human nature. Both works en-
deavored to trace what he viewed as the disastrous political policies of the republican regime to their intellectual origins in the nineteenth century. The first was an extended essay entitled *Le Vieil
Utopiste* (The Old Utopian), a term he had first used in his *Histoire
de trois générations* as a personification of the past century. He conceived of this work as an attempt to expose the surviving remnants
of nineteenth-century utopian thought in the present, particularly
in the realm of politics. It contained the familiar indictment of the
illusions that the Maurrassians held responsible for the decline of
French grandeur: romantic idealism, revolutionary political theory,

7. These articles were collected and published posthumously in Jacques Bainville, *Doit-on le dire?* (Paris: Fayard, 1939).
8. *Candide*, 1928, in *ibid.*, 181.

and Protestant spiritualism. But it restated the case more forcefully, reflecting the greater sense of cultural despair prompted by the
terrible destruction of the war.

To be sure, the past century received much less harsh treatment
from Bainville than it had from his colleague Daudet, who, with his
characteristic flair for dramatic exaggeration, had denounced the
period from the rise of Napoleon to the Dreyfus Affair as *Le Stupide
Dix-Neuvième Siècle*. Indeed, Bainville regarded the century in
which he had reached maturity with mixed emotions. He admitted
to a certain "tenderness" for that bygone epoch and to an inability
to shake himself free from its influence. But he could never bring
himself to forgive its intellectual elite for having forsaken the institutions, customs, and traditions that had produced the unity of
the French nation during the *ancien régime*. These zealous advocates of abstract political and philosophical theories had succeeded
in sowing the disunity that currently plagued the modern world.[9]

Bainville argued that the most damaging nineteenth-century
doctrine that was reappearing in postwar France was the mystique
of the French revolutionary tradition. Once again a new generation was demonstrating its inability to learn from the tragic mistakes of the past. As in earlier days, the memories of '89 and '48
were beginning to fire the imagination of the intelligent but woe-
fully naïve youth of the middle class, which insisted on embracing
the very doctrines that promised to bring about its own destruction. Nor was this naïveté confined to the uninitiated. Bainville
could not contain his disbelief when his old literary hero Anatole
France, the author of the antirevolutionary novel *Les Dieux ont
soif*, announced his support of the Bolshevik Revolution. "It appears that Anatole France has become the Saint of Bolshevism,"
Bainville incredulously observed. "If all the Bolsheviks were like
him, we would see amazing things in the future paradise." Would
the old classicist writer advocate the study of Latin in the workers'
utopia, in light of his oft-repeated observation that anyone lack-

9. See Léon Daudet, *Le stupide dix-neuvième siècle* (Paris: Nouvelle Librairie Nationale, 1922); Bainville, *Le Vieil Utopiste*, 5–7.

ing a knowledge of the classics was doomed to ignorance and imbecility?[10]

He was similarly annoyed by the spectacle of the thoroughly bourgeois attorney and littérateur Léon Blum dispensing revolutionary rhetoric on the hustings and in the Chamber while spending his spare time frequenting fashionable literary salons and defending wealthy clients in the courts. He snickered at the bourgeois socialists' excuses for the patent contradiction between their political and personal lives. To their retort that "one has to make a living while waiting for the social revolution," he countered with the observation that it was an ideal situation indeed to be able to combat bourgeois society while profiting from the social and financial rewards it conferred. The ease with which so many middle-class revolutionaries clung to this hypocritical position explained to Bainville's satisfaction "why there were so many millionaire socialists and so many anticlericals who sent their daughters to Sacré Coeur."[11]

Bainville viewed bourgeois "revolutionaries" such as France and Blum as both naïve idealists and self-conscious poseurs playing at revolution in the tradition of their nineteenth-century predecessors. But this fact did not exempt them from responsibility for the consequences of their political posturing. As the events of 1789–1793 demonstrated, revolutions have a way of developing a momentum that leaves their original supporters in the lurch. There was no doubt in his mind that "the first executioner's cart will be reserved for citizen Léon Blum and his comrades" after a Communist coup and that the rest of his bourgeois socialist colleagues would soon follow him to the grave in a modern reenactment of the Terror. The same fate was in store for the spiritual successors of Lamennais, the self-deluded band of social Catholics who "bless the medallions of San Lenino, the saint who divides up the land."[12]

10. *Candide*, 1924, in Bainville, *Doit-on le dire?*, 11.
11. *Candide*, 1926, in *ibid.*, 102; 1927, pp. 162, 165–66.
12. *Ibid.*, 151; *Candide*, 1927, *ibid.*; 1925 and 1928, pp. 67, 171; 1930, p. 252. For the official attitude of the Action Française toward Christian Socialism in France, see Charles Maurras, *Le Dilemme de Marc Sangnier* (Paris: Nouvelle Librairie Nationale, 1921).

It was this tradition of revolutionary idealism which served as the whipping boy in Bainville's second work of 1927, entitled *Jaco et Lori*, a Voltairian *conte* which represented the fictional counterpart to his *Vieil Utopiste*.[13] As in his earlier satire on the Gobemouche clan (which addressed the same problem),[14] Bainville reduced the experiences of several successive generations to a concise narrative woven together with a single theme. The story traced the tribulations of two parakeets caught up in the turbulent social and political events in France from 1848 to the end of the world war. It centered on the progressive disillusionment of Jaco, the male bird, with the various revolutionary doctrines and movements that emerged in nineteenth-century France.[15]

Starved for love and nourishment—the social unrest of the February days of 1848 had separated him from his beloved and from his daily meal—Jaco is rejuvenated by the emotion of the barricades and adopts one of the revolutionary leaders as his master. He soon recognizes the excessive zeal of his master as misplaced idealism, and predicts that its costs will far outweigh its benefits. "Ca finira mal" he announces pessimistically, and this anguished warning reverberates throughout the work as the same revolutionary mystique mechanically repeats itself.[16]

The bird is then sold to Victor Hugo, who helps engineer the return of Napoleon III with passionate evocations of the exploits of his great uncle, the Soldier of the Revolution. Jaco is once again momentarily seduced by reveries of glory. But his new master is exiled, democratic ideals degenerate into Bonapartist realities, and a new war eventually leaves the French nation prostrate before a united Germany and in the clutches of another republican regime. By now Jaco is too suspicious of democratic slogans to join the rev-

---

13. In the same year Bainville described the philosophical *conte* as "the superior form of writing." Quoted in *La Revue hebdomadaire* (April 2, 1927), 101.

14. See above, 179–80.

15. One observer characterized this work as "the *Histoire de trois générations* told by a parakeet." Massis, *Le Souvenir*, 110. As the pessimistic qualities of the avian hero's personality emerge in the work, it becomes obvious that "Jaco" is in many respects the fictional counterpart of Jacques.

16. Bainville, *Jaco et Lori*, 62–69.

olutionary campaign. Recalling the enthusiastic chanting of the Marseillaise as the troops marched to battle in 1870, he notes that "the day of glory that the hymn promised to the children of the fatherland did not arrive." Instead, the future held in store military humiliation, political instability, and economic chaos. When he confronts the "confused, bloody, and puerile ideas" of the Paris Commune, he wonders why Frenchmen tend to "repeat the same follies every twenty years." He hazards the prediction, based upon his experience, that "the cause of order will have its turn."[17]

When the smoke of the counterrevolutionary fusillades clears, the France of small shopkeepers and peasant proprietors reasserts its primacy. But soon this tranquil, mundane existence is interrupted by new claims upon his fertile imagination, and little Jaco, like his human masters, is swept up in the excitement engendered by various causes. He later attempts to explain the reasons for his perennial *volte face*:

> After the emotions of the siege, after the convulsions that had followed it, peace and tranquility, the assurance of the availability of food, the relief at no longer having to jump at each cannon shot, were making me appreciate the material comfort of bourgeois life. But the nature of parakeets resembles in this way the nature of men: we promptly forget privations and anxiety and feel only the boredom of days that never vary. This is why the ills of the world are never cured by adventures. . . . The assured supply of bread no longer prevented me from feeling the indigence of my spiritual life.[18]

Jaco is next sold to an Alsatian aristocrat, who disturbs the bird's tranquility by introducing him to another cause that has repeatedly fired the imagination of Frenchmen: the cult of the past. His new master explains to him that "the idea of tradition is, in essence, not conservative, but democratic and revolutionary," a product of 1789. Before that date the French aristocracy was quite the reverse of traditionalist, for it "thought of the present and the future much more than about the past."[19] But the events of the Revolutionary

17. *Ibid.*, 88, 151ff.
18. *Ibid.*, 184–85.
19. *Ibid.*, 198ff.

era inspired a new nostalgia for the past golden age among the displaced elite, transforming it from an innovative into a conservative force.

This obsession Jaco considers quite as despicable as the revolutionary's mania for the golden age of the future. He detects striking similarities between the nostalgic sentimentality of the Restoration romantics such as Chateaubriand and the utopian sentimentality of the romantic revolutionaries of 1848, such as Lamartine. He contrasts the attitude of unreality that pervaded this romantic cult of the past to the rational sobriety of the classical French mind, exemplified by the classical writers of the seventeenth century (and, by implication, their royalist heirs in the twentieth). Faced with the future prospect of a nation inhabited by men eternally dissatisfied with their lot and vulnerable to the seductive call of an irretrievable past or an unattainable future, the despondent parakeet greets every promise of earthly happiness during the remainder of his life with the recitation of his Cassandra-like refrain: "Cą finira mal."

The underlying theme of *Jaco et Lori* was one that, throughout his career, Bainville could not let go: the incurable propensity of the French bourgeoisie to undermine its own material interests (which depend on social stability and international peace) by succumbing to revolutionary idealism. An ancillary theme was the ineluctable tendency of a revolution to progress further and further to the left, turning upon its instigators to repay their support with ingratitude. "Just like Saturn devouring his children," Bainville observed, referring to a fictional character modelled on Adolphe Thiers, the progressive of 1830 who was passed over in 1848, "the Revolution forgot the services that that incorruptible liberal had rendered it." After a conservative republican votes to adopt the democratic constitution of 1875, he is defeated in the following election by "a true but Opportunist Republican who was succeeded by a Radical, who had to give up his seat to a Socialist, who began to worry about the progress of Communism in his district."[20]

20. *Ibid.*, 12, 10.

The message that Bainville continually sought to convey to his middle-class readers was that their instinctive sympathy for revolutionary agitation ran the risk of unleashing social forces that were inimical to their own survival. He was again seeking to sever the French bourgeoisie's sentimental attachment to revolutionary republicanism and convert it to the twentieth-century school of counterrevolutionary royalism. In conjunction with this campaign, his assault on the nostalgic sentimentality of romantic royalism constituted an attempt to disassociate the Action Française from the anachronistic doctrines of the past, with which it had been identified for so long in the mind of the French public.[21]

In *Jaco et Lori* the familiar device of satire served to punctuate Bainville's mordant view of the human condition. When the pessimistic parakeet overhears a discussion of the workers' rebellion of June 1848, he deflates the mystique of revolution with a touch of realism couched in a façade of naïve ignorance. "Without ever having seen a revolution, I began to become frightened," he recalls. "I wondered if I would still have grain in my feeding trough and I prudently made some provisions."[22] When his temporary master, an active participant in the revolution of 1848, declares his devotion to beloved Poland, Jaco naturally infers that *la Pologne* is the man's mistress. Such touches of what a contemporary critic called Bainville's "subtle and corrosive irony"[23] established his reputation in the eyes of many observers as the modern heir to the tradition of Voltairian skepticism about human nature that had been abandoned by Anatole France in his old age. As his friend Pierre Varillon observed, "The *meilleur des mondes possibles* of Pangloss and the *Ça finira mal* of Jaco are only complementary forms of the same state of mind that refused to become indignant in the face of universal stupidity, knowing that it is incurable and that the severest lessons will not correct it."[24]

As a consequence of his belief in the primacy of politics, it was

21. *Ibid.*, 198ff.
22. Bainville, *Jaco et Lori*, 65.
23. Jean Heritier, in *La Revue du siècle*, 22, tome VI (December 15, 1927), 318.
24. *Revue hebdomadaire* (April 20, 1927), 104.

in the realm of domestic statecraft and foreign policy that Bainville perceived the most dangerous manifestations of human imbecility. The subject of French political stability during the twenties began to preoccupy Bainville after the collapse of the wartime *union sacrée*, the failure of Clemenceau's presidential candidacy, and the return to the French tradition of impotent chief executives and shifting parliamentary coalitions. Though the possibility of a domestic revolution caused him some anxiety, the structural weaknesses of the French political system represented the greatest source of concern.

Foremost among these disabilities was the problem of ministerial instability. In a stinging parody of France's six-month cabinets entitled "Les Anciens Ministres," Bainville has one of the soon-to-be-deposed politicians dejectedly observe that "the principles that vivify democracies are fatal to ministers" while he ruefully awaits the arrival of his successor. Bainville was particularly depressed by the lack of continuity between successive governments and by the common practice of rotating portfolios among deputies on the basis of political influence rather than expertise in matters within the purview of their ministries. "What would you say," he asked rhetorically, "about a newspaper in which the editor of the financial page would suddenly be called to the theatre section and end up writing the medical column?"[25] (An appropriate response might have been that it sounded like a description of Jacques Bainville's career at the *Action française*).

But an even more serious defect in the French republican tradition, in Bainville's eyes, was its debilitating hostility to executive authority. The scuttling of Clemenceau's presidential candidacy in 1920 and Millerand's resignation in the face of parliamentary pressure four years later appeared to confirm Bainville's suspicion that the lessons of the war had not allayed the Third Republic's traditional fear of a strong leader.

He metaphorically expressed his disdain for this age-old prejudice in a typically Bainvillian *conte* about an ancient Arabian king-

25. *Candide*, 1924, in Bainville, *Doit-on le dire?* 9–10; 1932, p. 303.

dom that decides to replace its hereditary monarch with an elective ruler who would reign for a seven-year term. The first such monarch is overthrown in twenty months because "he was found to be too intelligent." Succeeding rulers are chosen on the basis either of their stupidity[26] or of their willingness to leave the business of politics to others, and all are in turn ousted for a variety of trivial reasons. When domestic disorder breaks out and a recently defeated enemy refuses to pay tribute, a newly-elected Sultan named Mihl-er-Rhan (an obvious reference to Millerand) tries to restore order and exact the tribute (read: reparations from Germany) but is betrayed and overthrown by his former colleagues (Herriot *et al.*). He is succeeded by Sultan Al-Gastouni (Gaston Doumergue), who surrounds himself with his predecessor's betrayers, including a magician named Joseph (Caillaux), who miraculously "fabricates false money" by "creating gold out of mere paper" (a reference to Caillaux's financial schemes to resolve the problem of inter-Allied debts). When the fortunes of the country change for the worse, the Sultan's nurse asks him if things were not better when the kingship was hereditary. He punishes her for such a blasphemous utterance, declaring that no one, or rather everyone, is to blame for the country's woes since in a democracy the people rule and take responsibility for their actions.[27]

The leadership of the Action Française, as we have seen, had hailed Clemenceau's acquisition of virtually dictatorial power in 1917. But this suspension of the tradition of parliamentary supremacy proved to be but a temporary aberration in the heat of national crisis which did not survive the end of the war. Bainville refused to harbor the slightest illusion that Clemenceau's momentary triumph over republican orthodoxy represented a cause for optimism on that score. Once again, history was his guide: "We need disasters in order to bring about the appearance of a savior who runs the risk of arriving too late and of no longer being capable of saving anything at all, like Vercingetorix, whom the Gauls made their

26. This was a reference to Clemenceau's oft-quoted remark that stupidity was the quality he valued the highest in presidential candidates.
27. Jacques Bainville, *Polioute* (Paris: A la Lampe d'Aladdin, 1926), 48–62.

leader when the independence of Gaul was already lost. There is nothing to guarantee that next time a Clemenceau will arrive at the right moment to expel the invader or a Poincaré to stop the fall of the franc."[28]

Several years after Clemenceau's abortive bid for the presidency, Bainville concluded that the Republic had actually rendered the aging leader a service by refusing him an office so hemmed in by constitutional limitations as to virtually assure the failure of any attempt to strengthen it from within: "Imagine Clemenceau at the Elysée, the Tiger in a cage, spending his days visiting expositions, watching the Grand Prix, resolving ministerial crises. . . . What a blessing for his memory that our sliding back into the parliamentary swamp did not cause us to forget the savior of the country."[29]

The source of this republican distrust of a strong executive, Bainville believed, was a fatal combination of public apathy and parliamentary jealousy. The average voter was likely to know more about the rules of soccer or poker than about the constitutional relationship between the executive and the parliament.[30] The legislative representatives, on the other hand, were for the most part aware of the need for a strong, independent presidency, but were unwilling to confer real power upon anyone who was likely to use it for fear of seeing their own influence decline.[31] "All the parties have their programs of dictatorship," he observed, but if a strong man were to appear, each special interest group would quickly exclaim: "Ah no, not that one" and greet his attempt to govern

---

28. Bainville, *Journal*, III, June 24, 1930.
29. *Candide*, 1929, in Bainville, *Doit-on le dire?*, 221–22.
30. *Candide*, 1924, in *ibid.*, 20.
31. Though Bainville considered factional jealousy an unavoidable aspect of the parliamentary system, he conceded that the two party system of postwar Britain was comparatively stable and efficient. "In order for the parliamentary system to work well," he insisted, "there must not be more than two large parties which succeed each other to power, fight each other, and hold each other in check." But he believed that such a system was feasible only in the special geographical situation of England. When a prerevolutionary Russian liberal mentioned to Bainville his proposal for transplanting the British parliamentary system to his native land, Bainville asked him if he had also thought "of surrounding Russia with water." The parliamentary regime that has been "transported from London to Paris and elsewhere," he noted, "has not yielded exactly the same fruits in our regions." Bainville, *Journal*, II, April 17, 1923.

with "Ah no, not like that." The truth was that "today people admire no one, respect no one, have confidence in no one." Whenever an attempt was made to amend the constitution in favor of a strong executive, the left needed only to raise the cry of "La République en danger," and the maintenance of parliamentary sovereignty was assured. For the principle of executive authority was viewed as a remnant of the monarchical system, and the specter of a king-like president caused devout democrats to shudder. "A personality necessarily pursues a personal policy," Bainville sadly observed. "None of that, Marianne. Beware of strong individuals."[32]

His contempt for the doctrine of legislative supremacy notwithstanding, Bainville was careful not to endorse without qualification the institution of an omnipotent president of the Republic as a surrogate monarch. This hesitancy on his part represented a reaction to the schemes of various republican politicians in the twenties that were designed to strengthen the power of the traditionally ceremonial presidency.[33] Such a proposal was launched during the mid-twenties by Louis Latzarus in a work entitled *La France veut-elle un roi*? Though hastening to answer that question in the negative, the author declared that the suspension of democratic liberties during the war had convinced even good democrats that authoritarian rule was not incompatible with republican principles. What France needed was strong, effective leadership, he concluded, a goal that could be achieved within the existing political framework: "Pas un roi, mais un chef."[34]

The prospect of increasing the power and autonomy of the republican head of government or head of state posed a serious dilemma to those royalists like Bainville who had long been endorsing the principle of autocracy. A Clemenceau had been acceptable to the royalists because he was just the man to inspire confidence and because he had proved himself to be an effective spokesman

32. *Candide*, 1926, in Bainville, *Doit-on le dire?*, 121, 124; 1931, pp. 282–83.
33. André Tardieu was perhaps the best known of these republican critics of legislative supremacy. See Rudolph Binion, *Defeated Leaders* (New York: Columbia University Press, 1960).
34. Louis Latzarus, *La France veut-elle un roi?* (Paris: Editions du Siècle, 1924), 120, 123, 145ff.

for the French national interest. But subsequent candidates for positions of power possessed no such credentials. When the leftist faction in the Chamber of Deputies attempted in vain to elect Briand to the presidency in 1931, Bainville denounced the illustrious French diplomat as a "sort of Napoleon of peace," declaring that he (Bainville) had "little taste for dictators, even pacific ones, who today are named Aristide, but tomorrow might be named Robespierre, Lenin, or Léon Blum." Five years earlier, when Marshal Pilsudski staged a successful coup in Poland with the support of the Socialists, Bainville took the occasion to warn that soldiers of the left represented a greater threat to elected governments than soldiers of the right. To a British diplomat who asked if the postwar popularity of the general staff foreshadowed a right-wing military coup in France, Bainville replied that the tradition of loyal obedience in the higher echelons of the officer corps would prevent it. The diplomat should advise his government, he continued, that instead of worrying about Marshal Foch it should keep its eye on some "minor Masonic artillery lieutenant who is unknown to all of us."[35]

Bainville's interpretation of Bonapartism as a manifestation of the historical trend toward the dictatorship of the left contributed to this distrust of authoritarian schemes within a republican context. It was also another instance of the revisionist historian's propensity for employing evaluations of the past to buttress the journalist's observations on the present. His portrayal of contemporary representatives of the revolutionary republican tradition as heirs to the Bonapartist legacy flew in the face of most historical scholarship, which portrayed the French emperor as the archetype of the modern counterrevolutionary dictator-soldier who smothers the flame of the revolution in the name of order and stability. In two subsequent historical works, Bainville sought to refute this interpretation of the Bonapartist phenomenon that had been popularized by the professional historians in the French university.[36]

---

35. *Candide*, 1931, in Bainville, *Doit-on le dire?*, 283; 1926, pp. 116–17.
36. For an analysis of the professional historians' evaluation of the Napoleonic dictatorship, see Pieter Geyl, *Napoleon, For and Against*, trans. Olive Renier (New Haven: Yale University Press, 1967), 356ff.

The first major attempt by Bainville to marshal the historical evidence to support a revision of the Napoleonic legend was *Le Dix-Huit Brumaire*, a monographic analysis of the causes of the coup d'état of 1799, which he published in 1925. Casting aside the conventional scholarly interpretation of the Napoleonic rise to power as a reactionary counterrevolution, Bainville asserted that it had been "provoked in the interest of the revolution in order to reaffirm the revolution," which had reached an impasse by 1799. The ruling elite of the First Republic recognized that the social disorder prompted by the newly acquired class consciousness of the lower orders, the financial chaos produced by the disastrous fiscal reforms of the Convention, the inability of successive revolutionary regimes to form a stable government, and, above all, the "endless war," had all combined to strengthen the hand of the reactionary peace party that had come to accept the prospect of a royalist restoration as a solution to these pressing problems. Faced with the possibility of a counterrevolution, the guardians of the revolutionary heritage—the politicians surrounding Siéyès and their intellectual apologists, the ideologues—chose to place their faith in a republican general who promised to "save the Republic, not to overthrow it," by stabilizing the revolutionary situation. This momentous decision came in the nick of time, Bainville insisted, for "the logic of the situation required either a dictator to continue the Revolution or the Bourbons to end it."[37]

This unconventional interpretation of the genesis of the Bonapartist dictatorship was not entirely novel. Though most professional historians of the First Empire continued, after the fashion of Alphonse Aulard, to view Napoleon as a counterrevolutionary despot who arrested the Revolution, a contrary interpretation had been introduced into French historiography by two maverick historians outside the academic historical profession, Albert Vandal and Albert Sorel.[38] In the best tradition of a Sorbonne *thèse*, Bain-

37. Jacques Bainville, *Le Dix-Huit Brumaire* (Paris: Hachette, 1925), 7ff, 69, 119, 122–23.
38. See Geyl, *Napoleon, For and Against*, pt. IV, chap. V; pt. V, chap. IV; and pt. VI, chap. I.

ville painstakingly recorded his intellectual debts to these precursors, frequently invoking their authority to challenge the conventional wisdom of professional history.[39] He relied on Vandal for the factual basis of his narrative. From Sorel he appropriated the judgment that the Revolution was inexorably driven by an iron law of historical development to pursue the unattainable objective of France's natural borders as well as the view that Bonaparte, as a spiritual son of the Revolution, merely resumed that policy after his accession to absolute power.

Though Bainville's work represented a direct challenge to the historical interpretations of most existing scholarship on Bonaparte, it went virtually unnoticed in the professional periodicals.[40] But this topic continued to occupy his attention. In 1931 he brought out a much more ambitious, far-reaching analysis of the subject, a vast biographical panorama that embraced the entirety of Bonaparte's career. Commissioned by the Académie Française, its publication helped to smooth the path for Bainville's entrance into that august fraternity four years later.[41] So broad was its perspective, so controversial were its conclusions, and so astonishing was its commercial success, that it could not be ignored.

When Bainville's *Napoléon* appeared in the spring of 1931 as a volume in Fayard's *Grandes Etudes Historiques* series, it was an instantaneous best seller in the tradition of his *Histoire de France*. It was to become what Pieter Geyl, the leading expert on Napoleonic historiography, called "probably the most read biography of Napoleon in our time." It added little factual information that could not be found in the works of Vandal and Sorel, upon which Bainville had relied totally and uncritically. But its stylistic merits more

39. See Bainville, *Le Dix-Huit Brumaire*, 40–41, 97, 125. Both Sorel and Vandal came from royalist families, were anti-Dreyfusards, and taught at the privately endowed Ecole Libre des Sciences Politiques, a haven for conservative scholars before 1914. See AN, F⁷12721, "Ligue de la Patrie Française"; André Bellesort, *Les Intellectuels et l'avènement de la Troisième République* (Paris: Grasset, 1931), 67–68; Geyl, *Napoleon, For and Against*, 254.

40. One university historian did contribute a belated but favorable review of the work in the *Bulletin de la Société des Professeurs d'Histoire et de Géographie* (January 1928), 113.

41. Linville, "Jacques Bainville," 344; Geyl, *Napoleon, For and Against*, 377.

than compensated for its lack of originality, at least so far as the reading public was concerned.[42]

The wide distribution of Bainville's *Napoléon* helped to popularize the revisionist interpretation of the Napoleonic phenomenon that he had employed in his earlier monograph on the 18th Brumaire. The book reaffirmed the author's conviction that Bonaparte was a soldier of the Revolution who seized power in order to rescue the Republican regime and preserve its accomplishments. It unveiled a striking portrait of a young officer fired by the ideas of the Enlightenment whose authoritarian instincts together with his burning ambition to become the "syndic of the discontented" attracted him first to Jacobinism and then to the principle of enlightened despotism. This blend of authoritarianism and populism perfectly suited the new leader to the task of imposing Apollonian form on the Dionysian excesses of the Revolution, and the shrewdest champions of the Republic were quick to recognize this opportunity to further the cause. The Abbé Siéyès saw in Bonaparte the ideal agent for restoring order and authority to a body politic plagued by anarchy. Other first generation revolutionaries understood that the Republic would perish on account of the weakness of its executive power unless a resolute commander-in-chief could arrive in time to preserve the territorial acquisitions of the Revolution and purify the decadent Directory.[43]

This conception of the young Bonaparte as a Jacobin on horseback did not transcend the bounds of credibility. Bainville spiced his narrative with quotations establishing the young officer's spiritual debt to Rousseau, Raynal, and other precursors of the Revolution in an effort to enhance the verisimilitude of this interpretation. But it required a veritable feat of prestidigitation to explain the

42. See the Appendix; see also Geyl, *Napoleon, For and Against*, 376. The response of the professional historians was predictably less enthusiastic, though one scholar, writing in the journal of the Aulard school, *La Révolution française*, was impressed with the "dazzling literary value of the book" and endorsed Bainville's description of Bonaparte as the "regenerator of the Revolution." See Albert Meynier, "A Propos du 'Napoléon' de M. Jacques Bainville," *La Révolution française; Revue de la Société de l'Histoire de la Révolution*, LXXXV, no. 4 (October–December 1932), 315–20.

43. Jacques Bainville, *Napoléon* (Paris: Fayard, 1931) 49, 93, 110ff.

subsequent policies of Napoleon the First Consul and Emperor in this light. What could possibly have impelled an ideological confrère of Robespierre to conclude a concordat with the Papacy, marry a Habsburg princess, and establish an ersatz nobility?

Bainville tackled this enormously challenging task of explanation with his customary talent for legerdemain. He detected a consistent pattern in Bonaparte's relations with the royalists both inside and outside France that could be summarized in the pithy observation: "He used them but never served them." The transformation of the soldier-statesman from a child of the Revolution into a proponent of monarchical absolutism had been prompted and sustained by the domestic plots and foreign intrigues that continually menaced the solidity of his regime. He became a legitimist by circumstance rather than by preference, learning to appreciate the royalist truism that political stability required the tradition of orderly succession and orderly succession presupposed the principle of hereditary legitimacy. After the final threat to his empire represented by the Malet plot, Bainville maintained, Bonaparte became the "founder of a fourth dynasty," and resolved to become "more legitimate than Louis XVI." What he failed to recognize was that the only effective cure for the perpetual problem of succession was beyond his grasp. For the sole remedy—to become a truly legitimate ruler, a king rather than a crowned soldier—was unavailable. This harsh reality the Emperor himself belatedly acknowledged after his defeat with the observation that "only a Bourbon can succeed me."[44]

But while Bainville's Napoleon had one foot in the legitimist camp, he was never quite able to extricate his other foot from the camp of revolution. He was to the end a man obsessed with two contradictory goals. He sought to reestablish domestic tranquility and European stability in order to placate conservative interests but remained wedded to the policy of achieving national grandeur by preserving "the conquests of the Revolution." It was his inability to renounce the latter objective that constituted his fatal flaw

44. *Ibid.*, 114, 156, 338, 398ff., 208, 364, 398, 298, 402–405, 430.

and foreordained the collapse of his regime. Following closely the conclusions of Sorel, Bainville argued that the deterministic law of historical development which compelled the Revolution to extend its putative benefits to the rest of Europe collided with a contrary determinism which obliged the allied coalition to resist it. Bonaparte would never sign a peace treaty which abandoned the territorial conquests of the Republic, because his very raison d'être was to conserve them. The Allies, and particularly Britain, which could not tolerate French mastery of Belgium, would not rest until France had been restored to her former boundaries. The consequence was a fated clash of wills and armies that was destined to result in the loss of French hegemony in Europe as a whole.[45]

Bainville's definitive judgment of his illustrious historical subject was negative. He did not fail to appreciate the valuable services—even from a royalist perspective—that Napoleon had rendered to the French nation. He credited the emperor with having restored everything that had been absent in republican France for a decade: social order, economic prosperity, financial stability, national security, religious faith. Nor was he able to conceal his grudging admiration for the tragic grandeur and the esthetic qualities of the man's life and career. But the immense suffering and humiliation to which his reign eventually condemned the nation, coupled with his failure to establish a lasting tradition of legitimacy, outweighed the benefits of his rule. "Except for glory, except for art," the historian concluded, "it would probably have been better if he had never existed."[46]

Bainville's two major studies of Napoleon thus constituted harbingers of the new royalist fear that the Wilsonian system of universal democracy in Europe, which was already in an advanced state of decomposition when he published his *Napoléon* in 1931, would give way to a twentieth-century equivalent of Bonapartism (in the Bainvillian definition of that phenomenon). Faced with the

45. *Ibid.*, 224, 128, 216, 405.
46. For a contrary interpretation of Bainville's judgment of Bonaparte, see Geyl, *Napoléon, For and Against*, pt. VI, chap. VI; Bainville, *Napoléon*, 136, 496.

prospect that military coups might produce demagogic dictatorships of the left throughout Europe, the royalists were forced to
reevaluate their tactical program. Maurras's faith in a military
Putsch as a catalyst for a royalist restoration in France was brought
into question. For the man on horseback might turn out to be not
the General Monck of Maurras's dreams, but rather a latter-day
Bonaparte who, instead of catalyzing a royalist counterrevolution,
would merely pursue with greater efficiency the nefarious policies
of the revolutionary republic. Though this apprehension was not
to gain full force until the advent of the Hitlerian dictatorship,
it was sufficient to give Bainville second thoughts about supporting
a "revolution from above" during the twenties.

As Bainville became increasingly pessimistic about the likelihood
of a monarchist restoration in France (a sentiment that was fueled
by the disastrous Papal condemnation of the Action Française in
1926) he began to devote more attention to the variety of authoritarian alternatives that had emerged in other European nations.
The curious dictatorship that had been installed across the Alps
continued to fascinate French observers of all political persuasions
throughout the twenties. Within a few years after Mussolini's
march on Rome, Fascism had begun to exercise a powerful attraction on those members of the French royalist movement who were
becoming increasingly disheartened by the failure of the Action
Française to mount a serious campaign to overthrow the Third
Republic. During this period the ranks of the movement were depleted by defections to a number of indigenous French Fascist
movements. The trail had been blazed by Georges Valois, the former director of the Maurrassian publishing house, the Nouvelle Librairie Nationale. In 1925 this royalist renegade founded the *Fais-
ceau* on the model of Mussolini's black shirts and began openly to
imitate the methods and style of his Italian idol.[47] Within a few
years a bevy of young militants who had once marched to the

---

47. For a discussion of these indigenous fascist organizations in France, as well
as of their relationship to the Action Française, see J. Plumyène and R. Lasierra,
Les Fascismes français (Paris: Editions du Seuil, 1963); Robert Soucy, "The Nature of
Fascism in France," in Walter Laqueur and George Mosse, eds., *International Fas-*

royalist tune—Marcel Bucard, Robert Brasillach, Pierre Drieu La Rochelle, Eugène Deloncle, and others—had been won over to the cause of French Fascism. It was inevitable that Bainville would feel obliged to address himself to the question that was causing increasing dissension within the Action Française itself: was the Italian example one that the French movement could follow without abandoning its royalist principles?

Bainville's evaluation of Italian fascism underwent a radical transformation as the true nature of the regime became more apparent to him (and, one might add, as the defection rate from the Action Française to various French fascist movements increased). Two days after the march on Rome he confessed to a profound lack of comprehension of the "mystery" that was unfolding in Italy, but this did not prevent him from attempting to situate it in its historical context. "We can now say that it is the classic coup d'état in the Roman style," he asserted with his characteristic air of certainty. "Mussolini has crossed his Rubicon." Pushing the historical analogy to its furthest limit, Bainville portrayed the Duce as a modern Caesar intent on rescuing the Italian peninsula from the ravages of parliamentary democracy, which had reached "the end of its men, its ideas, and its power."[48]

But after this early comparison to Caesar, Bainville took pains to distinguish the new movement from the precedents of illegitimate authoritarianism that Europe had witnessed in the past by calling attention to the tacit support that had been tendered to the Fascists by the two symbols of legitimacy in Italian society, the monarchy and the Papacy.[49] To Bainville, Mussolini's *Putsch* resembled neither the 18th Brumaire nor the 2nd of December. His victory was accomplished in a legal and legitimate fashion through the King's refusal to sign the decree of martial law that Prime Minister Facta had submitted on the eve of Mussolini's triumph. Bainville inter-

---

cism: 1920–1945 (New York: Harper & Row, 1966); 27–55; Raoul Girardet, "Notes sur l'esprit d'un fascisme français, 1934–1939," in *Revue française de science politique*, V (1955), 529–46; Nolte, *Three Faces of Fascism*, 95–96; and Weber, *Action Française*, 132–35, 208–209.

48. Bainville, *Journal*, II, October 30, 1922.
49. *Ibid*.

preted this signal fact as an unmistakable indication that the popular new movement in Italy had been harnessed by the traditional forces in Italian society. "Republican in origin," he concluded, Fascism "discovered the instrument of its success in the monarchy."[50]
But what had become of the traditional alliance between parliamentary liberalism and royalist nationalism that Bainville had praised on the occasion of Italy's entrance in the war? Why was it necessary to rescue the nation from the electoral regime which, in Bainville's earlier formulation, had served Italy so well?[51] He attributed this apparent contradiction in his thought to the historical transformation of Italian political affairs. Democracy is not without its seductions, he conceded. "When the task of governing was easy, when Europe was prosperous and lived on the reserves of a peaceful time, it seemed not only very agreeable, but the best form of government." But the parliamentary system had failed Italy in her time of crisis in the aftermath of the war. "Power abdicated, Bolshevism was spreading everywhere, and the authorities closed their eyes." The system of universal suffrage, which had previously channeled popular support for Italy's intervention in 1915, had recently produced a tumultuous, disorderly parliament. Therefore, Bainville concluded, "the two ideas of liberalism and nationality, formerly closely associated in Italy, are henceforth separate." A regime of authority was therefore required to redirect the energies of the Italian people in the interests of the nation. Mussolini's critique of the liberal parliamentary regime, he noted, "is not negative. It is constructive. He is replacing what he has destroyed."[52]
Moreover, Bainville identified a guiding principle of Italian Fascism which it shared with two other governments of national union that had assumed power in the autumn of 1922—the Cuno government in Germany and the Bonar Law ministry in England—namely, the defense of capitalism in the face of the socialist threat. The simultaneous victories of these three regimes of the right rep-

50. Jacques Bainville, preface to Pietro Gorgolini, *Le Fascisme*, trans. Eugène Marsan (Paris: Nouvelle Librairie Nationale, 1923), vii–ix.
51. See above, 109–10.
52. Bainville, *Couleurs du temps*, 29.

resented, along with the succession of conservative governments in France during the same period, a Europe-wide resistance to social disorder that demonstrated the capacity of bourgeois society to defend its endangered interests.[53]

Those middle-class liberals who shuddered at the violent methods employed by the Duce to shore up the bourgeois order Bainville accused of hypocrisy. When the Manchester *Guardian* took issue with an unabashedly pro-Mussolini speech by Winston Churchill and branded Fascism "un-British" because it relied on terrorism, assassination, and violence, Bainville reminded the editor that England's own history was steeped in blood. He compared Mussolini's extralegal activities to Cromwell's execution of Charles I, both of which having been dictated by cruel necessity, and the Fascist squadristi to the Jacobites, who were "not exactly bathed in rosewater." Politics, he reminded the queasy and squeamish, "consists not only in enunciating principles. One must also be prepared to impose them." The French republican regime, with its perpetual curse of weakness and instability, typified for him a government that was incapable of imposing its will, whereas "on the other side of the Alps, it is Mussolini who governs. There is no shadow of a doubt there."[54]

It is clear from these early favorable judgments of the Fascist regime that Bainville originally regarded it not as an ominous revolutionary threat to the international status quo, but rather as an Italian product of the same conservative, counterrevolutionary tradition from which the Action Française had emerged. "Fascism was born of the instinct of self-preservation," he announced at the beginning of 1923. "It was born of a natural requirement of men and societies: order." In an effort to reassure French conservatives that the former socialist militant had decisively broken with his past, Bainville contributed a favorable preface, conspicuously situated before an introduction written by Mussolini himself, to the French translation of Pietro Gorgolini's explanation of Fascist doctrine in 1923. While taking note of Mussolini's refusal to accept the desig-

53. Bainville, *Journal*, II, November 27, 1922.
54. *Ibid.*, December 8, 1922; *Candide*, 1926, in Bainville, *Doit-on le dire?*, 133.

nation of "reactionary," Bainville insisted that "Fascism is a reaction and nothing else"; it constituted a vigorous movement of "resistance to anarchy and dissolution."[55]

But if Fascism represented to Bainville a response to the decay of Italian political institutions, it also offered a solution to the economic chaos generated by the war and the threat of social revolution. The strains on Italy's financial and industrial system caused by the war required a massive effort at reconstruction, which in turn demanded discipline and self-sacrifice from the Italian people. But such discipline was continually undermined by the contagious doctrines of Communism and socialism that had driven postwar Italy to the brink of decomposition. It was only through the imposition of Fascist discipline that Italy was saved from economic ruin. Mussolini's austerity program, Bainville maintained, was precisely what Italy required for her to return to the road of prosperity and social cohesion. The Italian dictator had succeeded in eliminating the threat of socialism, restoring confidence in the business community, and satisfying the needs of the working class. But most important, he had begun to encourage thrift and self-sacrifice by reminding the Italian people that progress in the history of humanity had occurred only when man overcame his propensity for idleness, gluttony, and self-indulgence.[56]

As a proponent of monarchical legitimacy Bainville harbored a profound distrust of personal dictatorship that rivaled that of the most devout republican. But instead of railing against dictatorships after their appearance, he asserted that the urgent task of modern states was to make them unnecessary. "If men were wise and moderate," he declared, "there would be no need for dictators." But a nation governed by a parliamentary regime was so prone to anarchy and social disorder that the intervention of a dictator remained a virtual inevitability. Fortunately, a dictatorship is by its nature unable to maintain itself without reaching out for a durable basis of support in order to achieve a measure of legitimacy as well

55. Bainville, *Journal*, II, February 5, 1923; Bainville, preface to Gorgolini, *Le Fascisme*, v.
56. Bainville, *Journal*, II, February 5, 1923, February 5, March 20, 1923.

as to assure a peaceful transfer of power. It is a natural law of societies, he asserted, that a successful dictatorship eventually requires the services of a legitimate monarchy, the historical guarantor of "continuity, duration, and [orderly] succession." It cannot
endure on its own for long, since "dictatorship is only a resting
place between convulsions." The death of a king changes nothing,
but the death of a dictator invariably produces a struggle for succession that is the breeding ground of revolution.[57]

But it soon became evident to Bainville that Mussolini had no
intention of serving as a dutiful servant of the House of Savoy.
Instead of supporting the restoration of absolute monarchical authority in Italy, the Duce had proceeded to increase his own dictatorial powers at the expense not only of the Italian Parliament, but
of the royal house as well. As a latter-day Caesar (like Bonaparte),
he overthrew a democracy but failed to replace it with a regime
based on the principle of monarchical legitimacy. He relied instead
upon a form of charismatic authority with a popular base. Accordingly, as the true nature of the Fascist regime began to come to light
in the latter half of the 1920s, Bainville became less and less convinced that it was capable of providing the domestic stability that
had eluded Italy under the parliamentary system. By deriving his
authority from his personal ability to sway the masses, Mussolini
was treading on shaky ground. For a population that had bestowed
its favor upon an inspirational leader could just as easily withdraw
it, given the undependable and unpredictable nature of public opinion. And the recurrent problem of succession would haunt the
Italian despot as it had haunted the Roman Caesars and later
Bonaparte, preventing his regime from achieving the stability and
continuity that a hereditary monarchy alone could ensure.[58]

Bainville extended his analysis of the iniquitous domestic consequences of Fascism to the international arena as well. As we have
seen, his endorsement of monarchism was largely determined by
his Metternichian conviction that a Europe governed by intermar-
ried, hereditary, legitimate rulers was best suited to the task of pre-

57. *Ibid.*, January 5, 1925, June 1, 1926; Bainville, *Réflexions sur la politique*, 36–37.
58. Bainville, *Réflexions sur la politique*, 37.

serving international equilibrium and repressing the type of populist nationalism that he regarded as the foremost threat to European
stability. Just as the monarchical Concert of Europe had been necessary to repair the damage caused by Bonaparte's drive for European
hegemony and to enforce the provisions of the Vienna settlement,
such a royal alliance was now necessary to enable Europe to recover
from the Hohenzollern quest for domination as well as to protect her
from a repetition of German aggression by compelling adherence
to the treaty of 1919. Mussolini's behavior toward the Versailles
settlement soon became a cause for alarm in Bainville's eyes. When
the Duce joined the German call for revision in a speech delivered
in November 1930, Bainville expressed the fear that the Italian dictator would upset the European apple cart, particularly if he were to
conclude that Italy stood to reap territorial and other advantages
from an entente with Germany. When Mussolini promised that Italy
would never provoke war, Bainville reminded his readers that Ca-
vour and later Sonnino had issued similar assurances before plung-
ing their nation into battle to satisfy national territorial ambitions.
He worried that Corsica, Nice, and other French regions with large
Italian populations would become the object of "an expedition of
black shirts comparable to that of Garibaldi's red shirts."[59]

Hence, the royalist writer had gradually come to recognize in
Fascism not the long-awaited conservative response to anarchy and
disorder, as he had originally thought, but rather an antidemocratic
regime that had preserved the demagogic spirit of populist democracy while purging it of its destructive parliamentary institutions.
Mussolini's simultaneous assault on parliamentary government
and his public pose as the voice of the people reminded Bainville
more of Bolshevism than of the traditionalist conservatism of
the Action Française. In evaluating Fascism and Bolshevism, he
claimed, one can perceive several "points of resemblance amid
their violent contrasts." Both had abandoned the principle of popular government yet continued to rule in the name of the people.
To those members of the right who might object to this effort to

59. Bainville, *Journal*, III, November 4, 1930, October 29, 1930; Bainville, *Couleurs
du temps*, 19.

link the counterrevolutionary regime in Italy with the revolutionary regime of Russia, he replied that Mussolini's dictatorship had
forfeited its title to conservatism. "Dictatorship is in no way incompatible with the republican regime," he asserted. "When the safety of the republic requires a dictator, a man of the left will always
be there to present himself." A Mussolini will inevitably emerge as
the incarnation of the popular will who is willing to rescue the
nation from parliamentary impotence and corruption.[60]

Hence, what had first appeared to Bainville as a reactionary response to the decadence of liberal democracy revealed itself to be
the inevitable product of democracy. Just as the former Jacobin
Bonaparte had destroyed the Revolution in order to save it, the
former socialist Mussolini had dissolved parliamentary democracy
in order to implement its program with greater efficiency. As the
modern incarnation of the Caesarist-Bonapartist type of dictatorship, Fascism posed a threat not only to the conservative interests
in Italy, but also to the stability of the entire continent of Europe.
For a popular dictatorship was inevitably driven to undertake ambitious foreign adventures in order to tighten its grip on the public
imagination. And since the path to a second Roman Empire was
blocked by the modern heir of Roman Gaul, and since the Italian
despot enjoyed the adulation of numerous followers in France,
Bainville's attention remained riveted to the Italian dictatorship for
the remainder of his life. In many respects Italian Fascism represented the logical consequence of parliamentary mismanagement,
impotence, and corruption. What had happened in Italy could
happen in France, if the Third Republic continued its headlong
slide into decadence behind the smokescreen of optimism and
false hopes.

60. Bainville, *Maximes et réflexions*, 38; Bainville, *Journal*, II, January 5, 1926.

CHAPTER NINE

Cassandra in the Era of Pollyanna
The International Situation, 1925–1932

How tired I am of always having to repeat the same thing.

Bainville

Bainville's growing interest in the new regime across the Alps was motivated principally by domestic considerations, above all because of the appeal that Mussolini-style Fascism had begun to exercise on members of the Action Française. But in the course of the 1920s he understandably became increasingly preoccupied with the political developments across the Rhine, which were bound to produce more momentous consequences in his own nation. With the passage of time, Bainville's opinion of the Versailles treaty underwent several modifications. But he never wavered in his pessimistic certainty that the German government would attempt to revise the treaty within his lifetime. Most of his writings on foreign affairs throughout the twenties and early thirties emphasized the necessity of forestalling or at least postponing indefinitely the disastrous consequences for his beloved France that he knew would result from such revision.

These misgivings about the peace treaty continued until the mid-twenties and only gradually dissipated in the face of exigent realities. He persisted for quite some time in clinging to the belief that a decentralized, federated Germany furnished the only ironclad guarantee against a revival of the pan-German policy of the prewar years. As late as April 1924 he was still harboring the unrealistic expectation that the reappearance of a separatist movement in Hanover signified the first step in the progressive dismemberment of the Bismarckian Reich.[1]

1. Bainville, *Journal*, II, April 28, 1924.

But his greatest cause for hope were events in the Rhineland,
that strategically situated buffer zone between the two hereditary
enemies whose autonomy Clemenceau had failed to secure at the
Paris Peace Conference. Though the short-lived Rhenish Republic
had collapsed during the summer of 1919, Bainville continued to
champion the cause of Adam Dorten, a leader of the separatists
who made frequent but fruitless journeys to Paris in the early twenties to press for a renewal of French assistance. During the occupation of the Ruhr in 1923, a Rhineland Republic was proclaimed at
Aachen with French and Belgian support. In May of that year
Bainville reiterated his plea for the political as well as the military
neutralization of the Rhineland, claiming that an independent
Rhenish state represented the most effective deterrent to German
aggression against France. He continually reasserted his conviction
that a profound and pervasive sentiment for autonomy existed in
the Catholic, pro-French Rhineland. He recalled that no less a
Rhenish notable than the Mayor of Cologne, Konrad Adenauer,
had attended a separatist gathering in February 1919 that discussed
plans for the proclamation of a West German Republic in the Catholic Southwest, and Bainville suggested that greater French support for such efforts might have turned the tide in the immediate
postwar years.[2]

But Bainville's realism gradually compelled him to acknowledge
the futility of such schemes to revise the Versailles Treaty to
France's benefit. In the course of the twenties, he grudgingly
accepted the document, with all its imperfections, as the best available mechanism for the maintenance of French security. By the
middle of the decade the former critic of the peace was willing
to affirm that "France wants to maintain that state of things created

2. *Ibid.*, April 11, 1923; *AF*, May 19, 1923. (The abortive campaign for an independent Rhenish state is described briefly in Ernst Fraenkel, *Military Occupation and
the Rule of Law: Occupational Government in the Rhineland, 1918–1923* [London: Oxford University Press, 1944], 33–37.) A more extensive discussion of this movement
may be found in Walter A. McDougall, *France's Rhineland Diplomacy, 1914–1924*
(Princeton: Princeton University Press, 1978). *AF*, July 12, 1930; *AF*, May 15, 1930.
(For a discussion of Adenauer's role in the separatist movement, see King, *Foch vs.
Clemenceau*, 32–33, 36–37, 41.)

by the treaties of 1919. She does not want any change to be made in them." But in order for the treaty to succeed in its objective of preserving the strategic and territorial status quo, it would have to be applied to the letter, with or without the acquiescence of the defeated power. And the German governments of the early postwar years had displayed little inclination to abide by its provisions, preferring to drag their feet on reparations deliveries and issue periodic objections to the unjust nature of the territorial settlement. Bainville refused to recognize any justification for German resentment at the harsh clauses of the treaty, recalling that his own country had endured the Peace of Paris (1815) and the Treaty of Frankfurt (1871) despite similar provisions for reparations, military occupation, and the loss of national territory along its eastern frontier.[3]

European stability, Bainville frequently asserted, depended on the willingness of the great powers to honor the diplomatic settlements forged after the termination of wars. So long as existing treaties, no matter how imperfect they might be, were subject to criticism and demands for revision, no nation in Europe could feel secure. "Respect even for bad treaties is desirable for general peace and tranquility," he declared. Napoleon III's assaults on the treaties of 1815, military in Northern Italy and verbal in Belgium and Luxemburg, had helped to produce the calamity of 1870. William II's tampering with the post–1871 balance of power had led inexorably to the catastrophe of 1914–1918. It was a historical truism that "the revision of treaties, sooner or later, means war, because peace depends on the maintenance of borders and the status quo."[4] Barring a firm commitment (which was nowhere in evidence) by the German government to accept the fait accompli of 1919, the only solution to this impasse was a firm resolve on the part of France and England to compel adherence by diplomatic pressure and, if necessary, by military force. But to Bainville's dismay, it was precisely such a policy of firmness that the victorious Allies (including

3. Bainville, *Couleur du temps*, 4, 86, 16; *AF*, October 13, 1925.
4. *AF*, August 23, 1929; December 19, 1928.

France herself after the departure of Poincaré in 1924) were unwilling to conduct.

The Locarno Treaties of 1925, in which Germany freely accepted the territorial settlement in the west in return for various Allied concessions, struck Bainville as the triumph of German realism over Franco-German myopia. He did not oppose a genuine policy of Franco-German friendship. On the contrary, as late as 1928 he was announcing that Frenchmen "want only to live on good terms with Germany. We invite her to consider the war as a relic of the past." But he insisted that détente must include a solid guarantee that Germany would accept the entire territorial settlement of 1919. Such a quid pro quo would have helped the cause of world peace while gradually serving to reacclimate the vanquished nation to her reduced role in world affairs. But Britain and France had failed to extract from Stresemann at Locarno a renunciation of German territorial claims against the Habsburg successor states. They had received only "moral" instead of "material guarantees," and therefore "the act of faith that has been demanded of us [the French people] is becoming more and more difficult to consent to." He feared, in short, that the Locarno negotiators had striven to establish a durable structure of peace with a stroke of the pen, when the occasional brandishing of the sword was in order. He inveighed against the "pactomania" that dominated the diplomatic thinking of French foreign minister Briand and predicted that Locarno would serve as "chloroform to anesthetize the [very] people who have reason to tremble for their security." What worried him most about the attempts by Briand and Stresemann to lay the groundwork for Franco-German reconciliation was "the way that the affair has been presented to us, as if it were a question of promoting one of those pharmaceutical products that, the prospectuses tell us, can cure any illness."[5]

5. Bainville, *Journal*, II, September 29, 1926; January 29, 1926; Bainville, *Couleurs du temps*, 85–86, 133 (see also *AF*, October 13, 1925); *Candide*, 1926, in Bainville, *Doit-on le dire?*, 128.

The pharmaceutical metaphors soon gave way to others as Bainville strove to express his growing apprehension about the durability of the Locarno settlement. When the two architects of European détente shared the Nobel Peace Prize in 1926, he responded in the pages of *Candide* with a historical allegory that left no doubt about his opinion of the Norwegian committee's verdict. He recalled that Alfred Nobel had introduced his new invention, dynamite, to Napoleon III, but noted that the emperor had already possessed his own form of dynamite, the explosive principle of nationalities, which was ultimately responsible for France's defeat and the collapse of his dynasty. Now Briand and Stresemann had been awarded the prize endowed by the inventor of the explosive for forging the Locarno Pact, which Bainville regarded as "a stick of dynamite, perhaps a bit more inconspicuous, but just as dangerous." He did not have to range very widely to gather evidence supporting this ominous declaration. The day after the two foreign ministers had accepted their honor, the Allied Conference of Ambassadors announced that Germany was in violation of those disarmament clauses of the peace treaty relating to the export of war materials and to eastern fortifications.[6]

It was on the shoulders of the ubiquitous Briand that Bainville placed the major responsibility for the shortsighted, illusory policy of Franco-German reconciliation symbolized by the so-called spirit of Locarno. He characterized the French foreign minister as a juggler manipulating flaming torches above the heads of the French people, sadly observing that "if he does not succeed with his tour de force, it is on us that the fire will fall." Bainville attributed to Briand's self-image as a Christ-like savior of humanity his willingness to trifle with the security of France and her citizens by granting lavish concessions to her hereditary enemy. In his messianic quest for a perpetual European peace based on a mutual understanding between France and Germany, Briand was in danger of "losing sight of the real world in which other diplomats,

6. Bainville, *Journal*, II, December 14, 1926; *Candide*, 1926, in Bainville, *Doit-on le dire?*, 134.

who do not aspire to the role of messiah, are a bit less concerned about the redemption of humanity than about the *Anschluss*."[7]

What made this risky policy so dangerous in Bainville's view was that Briand's counterpart in Germany, Stresemann, was under no such illusions. It was the recognition of this fact that had led the royalist writer to denounce Locarno as chloroform for France and dynamite for Germany. During the Paris Peace Conference he had predicted that Germany would be restored to her former greatness only when she returned to the Bismarckian realism that had served her so well in the nineteenth century. As early as 1921 he had already designated Stresemann, the imperialist-turned-republican, as the man most likely to mastermind such a feat. The greatest threat to French security was represented not by the belligerent nationalists in the Reichswehr and the Freikorps, but rather by the shrewd practitioners of *Realpolitik* who, like their illustrious precursor, knew how to achieve the objectives of the nationalist party without resorting to its provocative (and self-defeating) methods. "The vigorous passions of the extreme right can be utilized by reflective men," he warned. "Something new is beginning in Germany."[8]

The confirmation of these early premonitions came in the summer of 1923, at the beginning of Stresemann's brief stint as Chancellor. Bainville saw behind the new German leader's efforts to cultivate French favor by unconditionally terminating passive resistance in the Ruhr and resuming reparation deliveries the same ulterior motive that had temporarily transformed Bismarck from the brutal chancellor of blood and iron into a paragon of moderation in the years before 1870. "Had Bismarck been immoderate, he would have been less dangerous," he declared. "What made his policy worse for us and for Europe was its realism." Stresemann was the familiar Bismarckian wolf in sheep's clothing, assuming a deceptively reasonable posture that was infinitely more menacing

7. *Candide*, 1926, in Bainville, *Doit-on le dire?*, 119; and 1931, pp. 264–65.
8. Bainville, *Journal*, II, September 23, 1921.

than a blatantly nationalistic one. "The more moderate he is, the more he is to be distrusted."[9]

Other historical analogies occurred to Bainville as Stresemann, in his subsequent post as German foreign minister, labored to transform the Locarno settlement into a peaceful, multilateral revision of the Versailles treaty. Bainville saw the German statesman as a reincarnation of the early nineteenth century Prussian military reformer Hardenberg, whose progressive rhetoric had served as a smokescreen for the growth of Prussian military strength after the defeat in 1806. He reasserted his conviction that the "calculators," the reputed moderates such as Stresemann and General von Seeckt, were contributing more to the reconstruction of the German war machine than "firebrands such as Hitler and Ludendorff." Stresemann's proposals in the Reichstag for a Rhineland security pact to allay French fears of German intentions in the west revived in Bainville's mind the haunting memory of the Iron Chancellor carefully preparing the way for France's defeat in 1870 with duplicity and false promises. "It is not through the menace of instant revenge that Germany will become dangerous again," he warned.

> It is by shrewd and patient preparation of the army and the conditions that will enable her to regain what she has lost. Bismarck was able to anesthetize and deceive France, even after Sadowa. He did not uselessly rattle his saber. He knew that patience and the passage of time accomplish more than force, and that rage and force should be employed only after deliberation. . . . If the rebirth of Bismarckism frightens us, it is because of the clever progression of its development and moderation of its beginnings; the amicable interview at Biarritz preceded the Treaty of Frankfurt.[10]

On the occasion of Stresemann's death in 1929, Bainville rendered him a tribute that must have perplexed those German nationalists who had vilified the architect of Franco-German reconciliation as the gravedigger of the fatherland. "Bismarck's greatest disciple," he announced, had left as his legacy "the finest diplo-

9. *Ibid.*, August 26, 1923.
10. *AF*, May 4, 1924; Bainville, *Journal*, II, March 25, 1925.

matic achievement that Europe has seen since the time that Bismarck led Prussia from the humiliation of Olmütz to Sadowa and Sedan." Biarritz, Sadowa, Sedan: those code words were intended to revive historical memories that had long lain dormant in the minds of modern Frenchmen. Once again, the doctrine of historical repetition furnished Bainville with an arsenal of arguments against the conciliatory foreign policy of the republican government.[11] Bismarck had gained French acquiescence in his eastward aggression in 1866 by implying respect for French security in the west. Then, having secured his eastern flank, he hurled the full force of his armies against France. Locarno, Bainville continually asserted, would eventually produce the same result.

The illusions fostered by the new policy of Franco-German rapprochement were not the only recent international developments that alarmed Bainville. The various schemes for disarmament and the mutilateral renunciation of war that periodically emanated from Geneva caused him no less consternation. For they represented symbols of the spirit of naïve idealism and blindness to harsh realities that he believed was leading France down the road to disaster. Since the beginning of recorded time, he announced in the pages of *Candide*, the world has been divided between "those who say that in order to have peace, one must be on one's guard, be strong, and be respected, and those who say that to prevent war one must have confidence and dissolve the regiments." Though hardly an enthusiast of the arms race—he had, it may be recalled, condemned the armed peace before the First World War as an unproductive drain on the French economy—he insisted that proposals for arms control or disarmament be based on a careful assessment of the probability of their success. "The limitation of

11. *AF*, October 4, 1929. The Battle of Sadowa assured Prussia's victory over Austria in 1866, which had been achieved with the benevolent neutrality of France. Biarritz was the site of the meeting between Bismarck and Napoleon III prior to the Austro-Prussian War in which Bismarck issued vague intimations of Prussian support for French territorial claims on Belgium and Luxemburg in order to secure French neutrality. Sedan was the site of the decisive engagement of the Franco-Prussian War.

armaments makes sense only if one examines it in relation to political realities," he observed. "What is important is to foresee the conditions in which a war could take place, the alliances that would form, and the combinations of resources that would result from it."[12]

The treaties of 1919 and 1925 seemed to Bainville defective bases for a substantial reduction in defense expenditures, because they had failed to resolve the multitude of national disputes which fueled the fires of militarism. The principal prerequisite of universal disarmament was the reconstruction of a Europe in which each nation accepted its existing frontiers and remained committed to the preservation of the territorial status quo. But the post-war pacts had simultaneously failed to satisfy the defeated powers while lulling the victors into a false sense of security that prompted them to relax their vigilance and entertain dangerous illusions about universal disarmament and collective security. Moreover, by redrawing the map of Europe "not according to the classical idea of the balance of power but rather according to the romantic idea of nationalities," the peacemakers had slid into a grave contradiction. For the presence of discontented minorities within weak states provided a source of perpetual instability that large states, such as Germany, could exploit for their own ends.[13] Such a fatal combination foredoomed the cause of European peace.

It was not the European people's frantic search for a structure of international cooperation that elicited such mordant criticism from Bainville; it was their refusal to recognize that historical developments in the modern world had rendered such cooperation impossible. He had long regretted the disappearance of that unified conception of European civilization that had represented perhaps the most durable legacy of the Roman Empire. The Protestant Reformation had set in motion the process of politico-religious dissociation that had reached its crescendo during the French Revolution. The revolutionary movements of cultural nationalism that

12. *Candide*, 1926, in Bainville, *Doit-on le dire?*, 134; Bainville, *Journal*, II, March 31, 1927.
13. Bainville, *Journal*, II, February 11, 1926; *Journal*, III, March 28, 1928.

had emerged since 1789 had shattered whatever hopes remained for the reconstitution of a supra-national, Christian Europe. It was the democratic proponents of liberal nationalism in the modern world who were responsible for destroying the closest approximation of a "United States of Europe," the Habsburg Empire, which had united under a single authority the diverse national groups of Central and Southern Europe. The people of Europe had decisively rejected international unity in favor of national identity.[14]

The triumph of this potentially unstable and disruptive doctrine of liberal nationalism had, in Bainville's view, predetermined the failure of the League of Nations. He had accordingly opposed French participation in the new world body from the very beginning. But his attacks on the organization in Geneva became more strident in the course of the twenties. The principal defect of the League, he reiterated time and again, was the patent inequality of its member states. He likened the doctrine of collective security to a mythical contract between a Frenchman of average means and the Baron de Rothschild. When the common citizen proposes that each signatory agree to bail out the other if he succumbs to economic ruin, the Baron wisely refuses, because he represents a billion francs while the other represents a few thousand. The idea of one nation committing itself to assist another which claims to be the victim of aggression moved Bainville to envision a farce in which Spain promises to help Estonia defend herself against a Russian attack and then immediately demands Estonian divisions to help Spain liquidate the menace of Moroccan insurgency.[15]

Bainville reserved his most potent venom for the alternative proposal launched by French statesmen such as André Tardieu for the creation of an international military force under the auspices of the League with the authority to intervene against nations branded as aggressors. "Where would the army of peace in retreat reassemble its forces?" he asked. "Within the walls of Geneva?" The last straw

14. Bainville, *Journal*, II, October 21, 1925.
15. *Candide*, 1924, in Bainville, *Doit-on le dire?*, 35–36. Spain and France were faced with a native rebellion in their Moroccan colonies during the twenties, while the Soviet Union continued to press its claims against Estonia, whose independence from Russia had been secured at Brest-Litovsk.

was the League's enthusiastic acceptance of German membership in 1926 as a consequence of the Locarno agreements, a policy which, to Bainville, was akin to "introducing the wolf into the sheep-fold."[16]

It would have been asking too much to expect the skeptical Bainville to believe in the possibility that the wolf could be domesticated and civilized. What precluded Franco-German cooperation was the singularly aggressive nature of the German mentality. Though he frequently revived the old economic and demographic arguments to account for what he regarded as the German people's irresistible urge to expand their nation's frontiers to embrace the entire German-speaking population of *Mitteleuropa*, he much preferred to explain it by citing the peculiarities of the German national character. In 1927 he republished three of his earlier works on Germany in a single volume entitled *L'Allemagne romantique et réaliste* as part of Fayard's new series "Les Ecrivains de la Renaissance Française." In the preface he implored his countrymen to resist the temptation to turn their backs on German literature, philosophy, and political theory, entreating them instead to devote themselves to a thorough analysis of German thought as a "public service." Only through familiarity with the twisted mentality of their traditional adversaries, he argued, would Frenchmen be capable of understanding why the history of France is "a model of continuity" while that of Germany is "a tissue of extravagances."[17]

In this new edition Bainville temporarily revised his earlier definition of Germanism. No longer did the "realist" aspect of the German mind represent the principal threat to French security, as in the days of Bismarck. The Bismarckian practice of submitting foreign policy to the criteria of raison d'état was now being superseded by a reversion to the spirit of the "idealistic, romantic" Germany of the pre-Bismarckian period. He trotted out all the old epithets about the transcendence of German thought and its inevitable tendency to foresake the real world for an imaginary concep-

16. *Ibid.*, 1932, p. 302; Bainville, *Journal*, II, March 13 and September 9, 1926.
17. Bainville, *L'Allemagne romantique et réaliste*, 3–10

tion of a universal, eternal *Deutschtum*, unbounded by limitations of time or space. A German Catholic leader's recent assertion that a revival of the "Holy Germanic Roman Empire" was the only reliable guarantee of European order demonstrated that aggressive instincts were not confined to the Protestant North. The "transcendental philosophy of Fichte" had implanted in the consciousness of all Germans the notion that their fatherland was a perpetually expanding entity.[18]

Bainville ridiculed those Frenchmen who attempted to deal with Germany without understanding how German philosophy contributed to this expansionist mentality, which was incapable of accepting territorial limitations imposed by mundane diplomatic arrangements. This transcendental philosophy of Pan-Germanism conceived of the German nation not as a product of concrete historical conditions, as was the case with French thought (which understood that France had achieved its national unity through a natural process of organic development over many centuries), but rather as an abstract idea which recognizes neither historical continuity nor geographical limits. "Germanism has [always] existed and continues to exist beyond frontiers," he remarked. "It is not a product of history. Germany is everywhere that a community of Germanic spirit, culture, and sentiment can be found." And since that ideal community can be found everywhere "from Strasbourg to Riga," the concept of *Deutschtum* constitutes "a permanent appeal" to "indefinite realizations." All the paper guarantees in existence, Bainville declared, echoing the earlier warning of his hero Heine, would not be able to contain this furious national ambition once it was loosed on the world.[19]

But who would precipitate the next outburst of Pan-Germanism? Would it be the surviving traditionalists who had served the Hohenzollerns, or the crafty neo-Bismarckians of "realist" Germany?

18. *AF*, July 27, 1932, in Bainville, *L'Allemagne*, II, 178–79. (He had earlier cautioned against French support for a Germany united under Catholic auspices. "We will not be any more disposed," he remarked, "to aggrandize an apostolic empire than a Protestant or Republican empire." Bainville, *Journal*, II, January 12, 1921.) Bainville, *Journal*, III, June 3, 1931.

19. *AF*, November 25, 1930.

Or would it be the German left, which Bainville regarded as the reincarnation of the idealist, romantic Germany of Fichte and the revolutionary Pan-Germans of 1848? The answer to this crucial question took on enormous importance for Bainville throughout the second half of the 1920s. He pored over every German newspaper and periodical he could get his hands on in an effort to keep abreast of political developments in the Weimar Republic. His objective was to discover indications of which factions were gaining the support of the German people.

As we have seen, Bainville's original reaction to the German revolution of 1918, the expulsion of the Kaiser, and the accession of the Social Democrats, was negative. He feared that the democratic left in Germany, to obtain acceptance of its territorial designs, would resurrect the expansionist program of the 1848 Frankfurt parliament while exploiting the Allies' dual fear of the rise of Bolshevism and the revival of militarism. But the rash of abortive *Putsches* and successful assassinations perpetrated by the resurgent German right between 1919 and 1923 had caused him to modify his scenario for the future of German politics. Shortly after the murder of Walther Rathenau by nationalist zealots in June 1922, he observed that, contrary to his previous expectations, the German left had been "decapitated" by the terrorism of the right. Far from wresting control of the German state from the parties of the past, German liberals and socialists were returning to the spirit of "docility" that had characterized their behavior toward the Kaiser before 1914. He attributed this rapid decline of German Social Democracy to its recognition that its objectives coincided with those of its putative domestic enemies. "In reality, the German Republic cannot help but be nationalist," he announced. "That is why it submits to all the intimidations of the right" and the guardians of the old order in the military.[20]

This apprehension about the growing power and influence of the German officers' corps reached its zenith in 1925 on the occasion of Hindenburg's election to the presidency. "Hindenburg is

20. Bainville, *Journal*, II, June 28, 1922.

elected to succeed Ebert who had succeeded William II," Bainville exclaimed. "A rapid reversal. In less than seven years, Germany has liquidated its revolution." He predicted that future generations would find it difficult to believe that France had "waged
war to destroy Prussian militarism" and then strived to "preserve
that result by signing a pact with Hindenburg" at Locarno.[21] Nothing in the behavior of the succession of Weimar governments during the remainder of the decade caused him to modify his skeptical
attitude toward German democracy.

In light of these ominous developments in Germany, Bainville
viewed with disbelief and dismay the French government's decision in the summer of 1929 to evacuate the Rhineland within a
year, five years ahead of schedule. From the time of the armistice
onward, as we have seen, he had admonished the French public
to demand that its government furnish more effective support to
the separatist movement that had sprouted in this strategically
situated buffer zone. Even after the definitive collapse of Rhenish
separatism in 1923, he continued to recommend a strong French
presence in the area. He again called upon history to convince his
readers of the significance to French security of the Rhenish city of
Mainz, "the most important place on the continent." The Roman
conquerors of Gaul had established a "surveillance post" in the
city, from which point they had been able to shield their client
state from the barbarian tribes of the eastern forests. The First
Republic, aware of its strategic value, had occupied Mainz at the
beginning of its campaign of conquest in 1793. Napoleon, who well
appreciated the value of symbolism, had received the homage of
the Germanic princes there, and later recognized that his cause
was lost when the Grand Army was forced to evacuate the city.[22]

Upon learning of the proposal for the French withdrawal in August 1929, Bainville warned of grave consequences after the
temporary aura of good will between the two Rhine powers had
worn off. But he expected these warnings to fall on deaf ears, as
had so many of his previous auguries. In the same year, upon re-

21. *AF*, April 28, 1925; Bainville, *Journal*, II, October 26, 1925.
22. *AF*, June 30, 1930, in Bainville, *L'Allemagne*, II, 152ff.

turning from the funeral of Marshal Foch (the most outspoken advocate of a Rhenish buffer state), he dejectedly observed that, while the funeral of an esteemed war hero might normally have been expected to evoke memories of the past conflict and its lessons for the present, "everyone had tacitly agreed no longer to speak of war" amid the euphoria of détente. The premature evacuation was bound to have two deleterious effects on France. It would whet the appetite of the German people for further concessions and it would inspire doubts in France's allies in the east about her willingness to deter German aggression. "Do people really think that everything will be finished when we evacuate the Rhineland?" he asked with exasperation. "On the contrary, it is certain that everything will begin, that the territorial demands will follow."[23]

To make matters worse, the Rhineland evacuation was being repesented in the French press as a gesture of good faith toward Germany that was justified by Stresemann's acceptance of the Young Plan for the definitive resolution of the reparations impasse. Bainville denounced the Young Plan (which reduced the total reparations bill while establishing a definite payment schedule) as a humiliating and costly capitulation to Anglo-Saxon intimidation and German recalcitrance. Throughout the twenties he had expressed great resentment at the American government's obdurate insistence on collecting the French war debt while urging upon Paris a conciliatory policy toward German reparations. With considerable bitterness he recalled that when Louis XVI had magnanimously declined to require advance payment for France's contribution to the fledgling American republic during its war of independence, George Washington had written in his diary, "Oh generous nation!" Such generosity was lacking in Washington's rapacious successors, now that the situation had been reversed. The American inspired Young Plan reduced Germany's obligation to France without insuring that she would honor even that scaled-down commitment. Despite its intricate schedules and deadlines, the repayment

---

23. *Candide*, 1929, in Bainville, *Doit-on le dire?*, 217, 204; *AF*, August 23, 1929.

program was hardly the last word on the subject of reparations. What France naïvely regarded as a definitive solution Germany recognized to be a provisional arrangement, no more permanent than the frontiers of 1919.[24]

In the following year, after the last French soldier had left the Rhineland, abandoning it to "the vengeance of the Prussians," Bainville blamed this disastrous retreat on the "Locarnian idylls."[25] By the end of 1931, after Brüning's and Hindenburg's assaults on parliamentary government, the stunning Nazi legislative victory of 1930, the French evacuation of the Saar, and the German proposal for a customs union with Austria, Bainville read in Stresemann's posthumous memoirs the message that appeared to confirm what he had suspected all along about the foreign minister's duplicity. The latter's famous letter to the Crown Prince in September 1925 seemed to imply that the Nobel laureate regarded the Locarno pact as a ruse designed to liquidate the reparations burden, the Allied occupation, and eventually the territorial settlement of Versailles. "The Locarno game was not difficult to understand," Bainville observed, with a hint of self-congratulation. "One did not have to be a Talleyrand or a Machiavelli to figure it out."[26]

After the disappearance from the scene of the modern practitioner of Bismarckian realism in 1929, it began to appear to Bainville that the spirit of "romantic" Germany was regaining its hold over the Teutonic masses. He viewed the Hitlerian party from the very beginning as a twentieth-century revival of the patriotic crusade that

24. Bainville, *Journal*, III, February 22, 1927 (see also *AF*, August 18, 1929); *AF*, July 1, August 23, 1929; Bainville, *Journal*, III, May 27, October 12, 1930.

25. *Candide*, 1930, in Bainville, *Doit-on le dire?*, 246–47. To protect France from the consequences of Briand's diplomacy, Bainville endorsed the defensive military strategy that was being proposed by Pétain, Painlevé, and Maginot (who was a personal friend of Bainville): "A system of defensive fortifications is particularly necessary to a country which has no reason to provoke war, but which has reasons to fear it, other nations having reasons to attack it." Interview with Hervé Bainville; Bainville, *Journal*, III, December 19, 1928.

26. *Candide*, 1932, in Bainville, *Doit-on le dire?*, 307. It may be noted that Stresemann's reputation as a convert to the cause of internationalism, a reputation that endured for decades after his death despite the efforts of Bainville and others to expose its falsity, has been seriously undermined by Hans Gatzke in his *Stresemann and the Rearmament of Germany* (Baltimore: The Johns Hopkins University Press, 1954).

had incited popular support for the movement of German unification in the 1860s. He refused to interpret the rising popularity
of the Nazi movement after the elections of 1930 as a sign of a
shift in German public opinion from left to right. "These two terms
no longer mean anything," he insisted. "[They] are no longer applicable to Germans who have been swept away by a violent and
primitive nationalist movement whose popular origin and character
cannot be denied." A mass-based phenomenon, Nazism transcended the old political definitions. The significance of the phenomenal
Nazi legislative gains in 1930 lay "neither in Hitler nor in his one-
hundred-seven deputies," but rather in "the facility with which the
German people follow those who recommend violence."[27]

"One must be completely ignorant of history to believe that democracy is necessarily pacific," Bainville declared in the spring of
1932. "The success of the Hitlerian party . . . is a phenomenon of
pure democracy." Frenchmen must be made to realize that the
Nazi quest for power is not a conservative, antidemocratic counterrevolution, but rather an expression of the profound desire of
the German people to risk everything in order to "shatter the
chains of Versailles."[28] It is possible that Bainville's effort to identify Nazism with the tradition of mass democracy was motivated
in part by his fear that the Action Française might be identified
with the German movement in the public mind. It was one thing
for the French royalists to be linked to Italian Fascism. But the
Maurrassians had based their program of monarchical restoration
upon a nationalistic antipathy for Germany. They could hardly
afford to allow their cause to be tainted by association with the
most recent mouthpiece of German nationalism and militarism.

In any case, the widespread expectation in France that the "democratic" forces in Weimar Germany would refuse to tolerate a return to domestic autocracy and foreign aggression elicited harsh
rejoinders from Bainville. Was it not the same German people who
had recently returned scores of Nazi agitators to the Reichstag?
The German left had had its opportunity to demonstrate its com-

27. *AF*, June 17, 1931; September 16, 1930.
28. *AF*, June 17, 1931; Bainville, *Journal*, III, April 27, 1932.

mitment to the Republic in the summer of 1930, when Hindenburg and Brüning suspended the constitutional provisions for legislative sovereignty. Instead, it had demonstrated either its impotence or its acquiescence. He could not help but compare the behavior of the German left to its equivalent in his own country. "When a Marshal-President attempted to intervene in politics in France [in 1877], the republicans told him to submit or resign. And Mac-Mahon promptly did both. In Germany, it is the republicans who submitted to the Marshal-President."[29]

Not only was the democratic and socialist left in Germany acquiescing in the gradual revival of German militarism, Bainville charged, but it actually retained a fond reverence for the deposed autocracy. The willingness to allow the Hohenzollern pretender to maintain a residence in Germany and the refusal to exile the remainder of the royal family struck him as curious expressions of republican sentiment, as did the printing of postage stamps adorned with portraits of past royalty, a practice that was unthinkable in republican France.[30] The prospect of a Hohenzollern restoration haunted Bainville throughout the twenties, for he had learned from history that the German left, unlike its French counterpart, had never succeeded in conquering its customary deference to authority.

But the true menace, he recognized, was represented by the forces of the future rather than of the past. Bainville was certain that Europe faced a calamitous repetition of the Great War if the Nazi agitator and his accomplices were ever permitted to take control of the German state. And he was certain that it would be a "war of peoples, of elemental forces unchained, of great popular onslaughts driven by passion and instinct." European civilization would look back with wistful longing to the traditional, calculated, political conflicts of the past, once it had had the opportunity to witness "another Armageddon, an apocalyptic free-for-all pitting

29. *AF*, March 31, May 31, 1931; *Candide*, 1927, in Bainville, *Doit-on le dire?*, 142–43. This contrast has more recently been emphasized by A. J. P. Taylor in his *The Course of German History* (New York: Capricorn Books, 1962), 202.
30. Bainville, *Couleurs du temps*, II, 188–89.

races and peoples against each other in blind fury, when the very notion of [national] interest has disappeared, when the reasons for risking or not risking armed conflict have been abolished." Instead of a limited war with precise objectives, the world would be treated to the spectacle of "a true war of democracies," a bitter conflict "for all or nothing, without an escape clause and without nuances."[31] And such a future European war, he had been warning since the conclusion of the last one, promised not only to plunge his beloved France into her most terrible agony, but also to spell the end of the era of European dominance in the world.

31. Bainville, *Journal*, III, October 31, 1930.

CHAPTER TEN

The Final Years: Intimations of the Approaching Catastrophe, 1933–1936

*Bainville predicted everything that has been happening. I wanted
to believe that he was having a nightmare, that he was wrong.
. . . But here we are.*

Robert Kemp (September 1939)

When President Hindenburg named Adolf Hitler to the chancellor-
ship of the German Reich on January 30, 1933, he merely confirmed the suspicions of Bainville, who for several years had been
predicting the Nazi accession to power. Nor did Bainville see in
this event the cataclysmic disruption of historical continuity that
was being announced by those observers who had believed in the
vitality and resilience of the Weimar Republic. His conception of
historical change as a continuous unfolding of developmental laws
left no room for such quantum leaps as the putative Nazi "revolution." Germany's fourteen-year experiment in democracy had
served its intended purpose, which was to lay the groundwork for
the renascence of the fatherland "without unduly alarming the victors" of 1918. Hitler planned to "continue and amplify the policy of
Stresemann"; the Nazi program in foreign affairs was the logical
consequence of the succession of policies pursued by the Weimar
governments from 1919 to 1933.[1]

To underscore this conception of historical continuity—and to
puncture the pervasive illusion that Hitler had single-handedly
assassinated German democracy—Bainville republished an updated edition of his *Histoire de deux peuples* in 1933, appropriately re-
naming it *Histoire de deux peuples continuée jusqu'à Hitler*. In the re-

1. Fabrègues, *Charles Maurras*, 339; Bainville, *Journal*, III, March 13, 1934; November 18, 1933. (See also Bainville, *Bismarck*, vii.)

vised version he emphatically reaffirmed his conviction, expressed many times before the recent Nazi victory, that the rise of Hitler was the logical consequence of the myopic foreign policy of Briand and other Western diplomats during the preceding fourteen years. As we ponder the unfolding of historical development, he declared, "we observe the chain of causes and responsibilities. How interconnected they all are! How true it is, as August Comte said, that the living are governed by the dead!"[2]

Indeed, Bainville traced the origins of the present German dictatorship further back into the nineteenth century, when Germany had begun to achieve the same successes and France had begun to commit the same mistakes as had produced the present crisis. It was another instance of the operation of that old historical law: "If a strong authoritarian regime exists in Berlin, there will be a weak, anarchical regime in Paris. And vice versa." The Second Empire in France began its evolution toward the debilitating ideology of liberalism in the early 1860s at the very moment that Prussian liberalism was exchanging its lofty ideals for the brutal realism of Bismarck. In the following decade France adopted a flaccid Republic soon after victorious Germany had become an authoritarian Empire. The French left became increasingly antimilitarist during the Dreyfus Affair while William II and his military advisers prepared to invade France. And now, while Hitler was busy consolidating his power, the French Chamber of Deputies voted to reduce military expenditures. "The balance sheet is tragic for the past," Bainville lamented. "What will it be for the future?"[3]

As we have seen, Bainville was almost unique among Western observers during the twenties in regarding the nascent movement of National Socialism as a product of the revolutionary tradition in Germany. His opinion did not change after the advent of Nazi rule. "Popular Forces Unchained," was the phrase he employed to describe the events that had recently unfolded in Berlin. The Hitleri-

2. Jacques Bainville, *Histoire de deux peuples continuée jusqu'à Hitler* (Paris: Fayard, 1933), 8.
3. *AF*, February 28, 1933. Bainville, *Histoire de deux peuples continuée jusqu'à Hitler*, 9.

an movement was "so democratic and so popular" that Hindenburg, "the old conservative" who had resisted it as long as he
could, submitted to the inevitable only after surrounding Hitler
with two representatives of the traditional right, Papen and Hu-
genberg. These two monarchist defenders of the "old right" represented the only hope of moderating the impulsive demagogue,
and their chances of success were problematical.[4]

The evidence of their failure was soon forthcoming. After the
Reichstag fire, Bainville correctly predicted that Hitler would use
the event as a pretext for suppressing the German Communist Party and repealing constitutional protections of civil liberties. "The
struggle against Marxism is his raison d'être," he observed. "Without Communism and social democracy, there would not have been
a Nazi movement." And now, Hitler will exploit popular fears of
social revolution to install a dictatorship that would cause Europe
"to regret the Hohenzollerns."[5]

After the March 5th elections in Germany, which gave the Nazis
and their Nationalist allies a majority in the Reichstag, Bainville
proclaimed that German democracy had been "murdered by majority vote, by the will of the German people." Eight months later,
when ninety-two percent of the German electorate voted for the
Nazi list of candidates, he interpreted this expression of popular
will as an unmistakable mandate for the new regime. He conceded
that the absence of opposition candidates and widespread intimidation had preordained the outcome; but "can one terrorize forty
million citizens?" he asked. Of course not. It was the Fuehrer's
ideas, not his secret police, that had secured his victory, and "the
German people will follow Hitler wherever he wants to lead
them."[6]

The Hitlerian manipulation of mass emotion was viewed by Bainville as the modern embodiment of the revolutionary nationalist
ideal first enunciated in 1789. "They are singing 'Germany, awak-
en,' just as they sang *Le Réveil du Peuple* at the end of the French

4. *AF*, February 2, 1933; Bainville, *Journal*, III, February 1, 1933.
5. *AF*, March 2, 1933.
6. *AF*, March 7, 1933; Bainville, *Journal*, III, November 14, 1933.

Revolution," he remarked. "These are appeals to youth and to the future."[7] Horrified by the popularity of the Nazi program among the German masses, he even went so far as to express the fear that it might discover a sympathetic audience among certain militants of the French left[8] who hungered for simplistic, revolutionary solutions to the problems of modern life: "After Karl Marx, why not the anti-Karl Marx?" He saw little difference between the revolutionary idealism of the left and the revolutionary idealism of the right, both of which impulses sprang from the doctrines of Rousseau and were sustained by demagogy.[9]

Hitler's anti-Semitism seemed to Bainville the quintessential expression of this demagogic spirit in Germany; from the beginning the French writer viewed the German leader's anti-Jewish campaign as a tactic to win the German masses to the cause of National Socialism. "It is excellent propaganda," he remarked, "to embody an enemy in a certain group of persons and to imagine the existence of an all-powerful secret society." The German Jews had clearly been earmarked as scapegoats by the new regime, and would accordingly bear the brunt of its repressive policies. "Under William II, anti-Semitism existed only in the form of insults," he observed. "Under Hitler, it is likely to become a pogrom." Choosing to overlook the anti-Semitic tirades of his two closest friends, Maurras and Daudet, he assailed the "distorted versions of the doctrines of Nietzsche and Gobineau" popularized by Germany's "chancellor of racism," and declared that Hitler's references to Jews betrayed "a complete absence of the critical spirit."[10]

7. *Ibid.*, February 3, 1933.

8. The subsequent conversion to a Hitlerian Fascism of such former French leftists as Marcel Déat, Jacques Doriot, and their accomplices confirmed Bainville's suspicion.

9. *Candide*, 1933, in Bainville, *Doit-on le dire?*, 342. This effort to link Nazism to the revolutionary tradition and to stress its popular character was highly unorthodox at the time, though this historical interpretation has experienced a revival since the advent of the Second World War. See Peter Viereck, *Metapolitics: From the Romantics to Hitler* (New York: Knopf, 1941), and A. J. P. Taylor, *The Course of German History* (New York: Capricorn Books, 1962).

10. Bainville, *Dictators*, 246–48; *AF*, February 2, March 2, 1933. For discussions of Maurras's anti-Semitism, see Curtis, *Three Against the Republic*, 214–18, and Buthman, *The Rise of Integral Nationalism*, 230–34. For Daudet's, see Weber, *Action Française*, 71–72, 199.

Such objections to Nazi Jew-baiting were hardly based on hu-
manistic or liberal principles. Bainville himself had occasionally
matched Maurras's vituperative epithets against Jews with more
moderate but no less hostile declarations.[11] What alarmed him
most about the anti-Semitic policy of the Third Reich was that it
had served to release the previously pent-up irrationalism of the
German masses; Bainville knew too well that that irrationalist fervor could easily be redirected against the French. Hitler shrewdly
employed Wagnerian musical extravaganzas and other stimulants
to incite his listeners to new heights of frenetic ecstasy, appreciat-
ing the powerful appeal of such mysticism to the German mind:

> Without the songs of the Storm Troops, where would Hitlerism be? One
> had to have heard what went on during the 1933 elections, the songs,
> the hymns, the dramatic performances, the experimentation with a ra-
> diophonic art in which noise and music were more important than the
> words, speeches punctuated by thumps on the big drum—one had to
> have heard all of this in order to realize the degree of frenzy which the
> German masses can attain.[12]

But this is not to say that Bainville considered the German people unique in their susceptibility to the appeal of a charismatic per-

---

11. Bainville's comparatively mild brand of anti-Semitism, unlike that of Maurras and Daudet, never became an integral part of his political ideology. The sporadic
uncomplimentary references to Jews that appear in his writings comprise an inchoate mélange of racial, religious, and nationalist prejudices that cannot be dignified with the label of doctrine. He once declared that the assimilation of Jews was
impossible in France because "Judaism is not a question of religion, nor a question
of race, but a question of nationality." Jacques Bainville, *Une Saison chez Thespis*
(Paris: Editions Prométhée, 1929), 131. Yet elsewhere he refers to the "millenarian-
ism" and "religious frenzy" that is peculiar to the Jews. Bainville, *Au Seuil du
siècle*, 182. Still later he declares that Heine, who, along with Goethe, he considered the most "agreeable" of German poets, was prevented from becoming a truly
great writer by the "impurity of his blood" and his "Jewish nervousness." Bainville, *Le Vieil Utopiste*, 72. These confused and contradictory prejudices represented
sentiments that were rather widespread in conservative circles in France at the
time. Curiously, they did not prevent him from remaining on good terms with
members of the French branch of the Rothschild family. Interview with Hervé
Bainville.
12. In order to appreciate the gulf that separated Bainville from the youthful
French admirers of Hitler, one might compare this sardonic attempt to deflate Nazi
demagogy with the French fascist Robert Brasillach's fascination with the Hitlerian
mystique. See Robert Brasillach, *Notre Avant-Guerre* (Paris: Plon, 1941), 264ff.

sonality who manipulated slogans and symbols to acquire and pre-serve his power. On the contrary, as he surveyed the political developments throughout Europe since the end of the war, he detected in the behavior of the interwar generation in every country abundant evidence of a trend whose advent he had heralded in the early twenties: the abandonment of the liberal principles enunciated at the peace conference by the erstwhile proponents of universal democracy. He marveled at the specter of such "repentant liberals" as Churchill and Lloyd George singing the praises of Mussolini and of Social Democrats in Germany meekly submitting to Hitler without a fight. The surrender of the German democrats and socialists to the forces of antirepublican militarism constituted "the second deception that they have inflicted on their French comrades. They were no more willing to defend the Republic in 1933 than they were willing to oppose war in 1914. Where are the barricades? Where are the defenders of liberty?" The misguided assumption of French liberals that postwar Europe was bound to embrace the irresistible principles of democracy after the fashion of France had been brutally discredited by developments in other lands:

> Unfortunately, democracy has been rejected by the nations that count. . . . Since Italy got Mussolini and Germany Hitler, one speaks much less of the penetration of ideas and great international currents [of opinion]. Indeed, there is no reason for us to believe that fascist doctrines will not pass across borders as the democratic doctrines once did. And we must recognize that the immortal principles [of democracy] have lost most of their seductive power. [13]

Practically every major nation in the Western world furnished evidence of the incipient triumph of authoritarian doctrines over the obsolete principles of democracy that Bainville had been predicting since the early twenties. He noted that Dollfuss had transformed the Austrian Republic into an authoritarian dictatorship at the expense of those Austrian democrats and their supporters among the Allies who had pinned their hopes for stability in Cen-

13. Candide, 1933 and 1934, in Bainville, *Doit-on le dire?*, 361, 333–34, 350–51.

tral Europe on democratic rule in the German-speaking remnant of the Habsburg Empire.[14]

A similar development was unfolding across the Pyrenees, where the Spanish left had taken to the streets following its poor showing in the November 1933 elections. "What are they on the verge of creating?" he wondered as he read reports of Socialist and Communist unrest there. "A fascism pure and simple." The Spanish left's increasingly militant opposition to the moderate Republic established in 1931 was weakening democratic institutions and activating the forces of authoritarianism. He predicted that a continuation of such revolutionary activities in Spain would "produce a dictatorship that would make the regime of Primo de Rivera seem benevolent in comparison." He ridiculed the founders of the Spanish Republic of 1931 for having introduced parliamentary institutions during the very period that democracy was everywhere in retreat, and forecast "uncertain and troubled days" for the Spanish people before they were to enjoy the benefits of a durable political system.[15]

It had also come to his attention that the dictatorial power acquired by Stalin during the past decade had transformed Soviet Russia from a bubbling cauldron of civil war, social disintegration, and economic chaos into a dynamic unitary state ruled by a charismatic dictator. He had earlier discovered many similarities between Russian Bolshevism and Italian Fascism. A few days after Hitler's accession, he extended the comparison to National Socialism as well. Once again, the common denominator was to be found in the rejection of the outworn dogmas of parliamentary democracy. "This is a new form of political society," he declared. "The God-State suffers no dissidence and is represented by a minority that possesses full power, while the rest of the nation consists of passive citizens."[16]

The recent electoral results in the homeland of Woodrow Wilson

14. *AF*, March 11, 1933.
15. Bainville, *Journal*, III, March 13, 1934; *Candide*, 1935, in Bainville, *Doit-on le dire?*, 382; Bainville, *Journal*, III, October 3, 1934.
16. Bainville, *Journal*, III, February 3, 1933; *AF*, July 1, 1933.

itself constituted for Bainville the most resounding repudiation of the democratic ideal. Bainville described Roosevelt after a year of the New Deal as a democratic dictator who had spared his nation the trauma of a social revolution by establishing an authoritarian regime of *"étatisme."* The new American leader was even more powerful than the European dictators because of the American tradition uniting the functions of chief of state and head of government in the same office. Roosevelt, Bainville maintained, "is above all the man in whom the masses believe." The American president and the German dictator who had come to power in 1933 were prime examples of demagogues who captured the popular imagination in times of crisis by fostering "the illusion that the doctor is doing something" to remedy the nation's social and economic ills.[17] The Democratic landslide in the congressional elections of 1934 supplied further confirmation of this judgment. "Roosevelt is the object of a plebiscite," Bainville dramatically announced. Even the democratic United States was "acclaiming a miracle-worker [*thaumaturge*]." By restoring the concept of personal power to the native land of democracy, the American leader was following in the footsteps of the European dictators. "O democracy, O liberty. Everything has been carried away in the convulsions of anxiety and distress." Roosevelt's emergency economic measures were little more than camouflaged imitations of Mussolini's corporatism adapted to American conditions.[18]

Having foreseen the universal collapse of democracy in the post-war world, Bainville the unreconstructed royalist welcomed its demise. But he could not bring himself to feel jubilation because of the unsettling fact that the one nation that was stubbornly resisting the antidemocratic current was his own. History appeared to him once again to be repeating itself to the detriment of his be-

---

17. Bainville, *Journal*, III, March 8, 1934; October 28, 1933.
18. Bainville, *Journal*, III, November 9, 1934; March 28, 1934. For a recent comparison of Roosevelt's and Hitler's efforts to restore economic prosperity in their respective countries (which concludes that "Nazi and New Deal antidepression policies displayed striking similarities"), see John A. Garraty, "The New Deal, National Socialism, and the Great Depression," *American Historical Review*, LXXVI, no. 4 (October, 1973), 907–44.

loved country, providing yet another pretext for his conception of historical repetition to come into play. Just as France was an isolated Republic on a continent of hereditary monarchies between 1871 and 1914, she was now an isolated Republic surrounded by virile dictatorships, "the only great European state that lacks discipline and a leader." Yet this disparity did not seem to alarm France's somnolent citizens and shortsighted political leaders, he complained. Frenchmen had long entertained the illusion that they could indulge in their incessant domestic squabbles without concern for the world beyond. He conceded that in many ways France's relaxed and unbridled way of life was "more agreeable than existence under a dictatorship." But the crucial question was how long these epicurean habits could be sustained in the face of creeping authoritarianism in the rest of Europe, a phenomenon which had arisen as a reaction against the very type of self-indulgence that France was currently practicing.[19]

When the Third Republic turned to the seasoned conservative politician Gaston Doumergue after the rightist riots of February 6, 1934 to restore domestic order and public confidence in democratic institutions, Bainville viewed this development as yet another instance of French democracy's penchant for relying on age and experience to bail it out of national crises caused by political mismanagement: "Thiers in 1871, Clemenceau in 1917, Poincaré in 1926, Doumergue in February, 1934."[20] He had previously voiced misgivings about the periodic suggestions from various republican politicians to increase the authority of the president.[21] Now, however, he was willing to entertain the possibility. The royalist writer expressed interest in Doumergue's program of constitutional reform, which was designed to strengthen the power of the executive to deal with domestic problems. But he correctly predicted that it would founder on the shoals of French Republicanism's traditional opposition to any diminution of legislative sovereignty. The French people persist in clinging to the outmoded traditions of their repub-

19. Bainville, *Journal*, III, June 6, 1935.
20. *Candide*, 1934, in Bainville, *Doit-on le dire?* 353.
21. See above, 238–39.

lican heritage because they are unhappy in the present and have no confidence in what lies in store for them. While the followers of Hitler and Mussolini boldly march toward the future to the strains of martial music and Fascist hymns, Frenchmen are content to sing, "with a nostalgic sigh, the refrains of yesteryear," whether the Marseillaise or the Internationale.[22]

Bainville's reflections on the progress of dictatorship throughout the world in the first half of the thirties left one important question unresolved: was he now prepared to endorse the cause of dictatorship for France as an alternative to what he regarded as the debilitating system of the Third Republic? Though Fascism did not receive widespread support in France until the late thirties, an increasing number of Frenchmen were already clamoring at the time of the 1934 riots for the replacement of the Republic by an authoritarian regime ruled by a *chef* modelled on either the Italian Duce or the German Fuehrer. Probably because he felt obliged to clarify once and for all his position vis-à-vis the growing popularity of Fascism both within and outside France, Bainville published in 1935 a study of the development of authoritarian dictatorships throughout history, entitled *Dictateurs*. In this work he strove to explain the historical causes of dictatorship, compare the various dictatorships of past and present, and outline his views regarding the various proposals for a French brand of Fascism.

The first casualty of Bainville's analysis was the widespread conception of Fascist or Fascistic dictatorship as a strikingly new system of government peculiar to the postwar world.[23] "We are deluding ourselves with the notion that things are new," he announced, "when, in truth, we are only repeating the experiences of former generations and treading the paths that they have long since trod." Dictatorships had existed since the dawn of history; hence the task of the modern observer was to study their historical development in order to identify their causes. His own analysis of this phenom-

---

22. *Candide*, 1934, in Bainville, *Doit-on le dire?*, 369, 362.
23. This interpretation of Fascism as a phenomenon peculiar to the post–1919 period has been reaffirmed by Nolte in his *Three Faces of Fascism*, 3–9.

enon had left him with a particular impression about the conditions that engender such regimes: all past dictatorships appear to
have arisen in societies plagued by financial disorder, social unrest,
and political instability.[24]

According to Bainville's typically Euro-centric analysis, the earliest form of dictatorship appeared in ancient Greece; that system
was subsequently adopted by the Romans and spread to the rest of
the Western world. Like many of their successors, the Hellenic
tyrants exploited the grievances of the propertyless masses against
the rich, while the landed oligarchy defended the principle of republicanism against the tradition of one-man rule. Gathering
around them an assortment of "malcontents, vagabonds, and ali-
ens," the Greek autocrats had directed their efforts toward "cur-
tailing the privileges of the upper classes for the benefit of the
lower." Peisistratus and Pericles in Athens, Marius and Caesar in
Rome, all shared one trait. They were rigidly opposed to the old
institutions and the patrician classes that profited from them. A
similar spirit animated the Puritan dictatorship of Cromwell. The
career of the great Lord Protector makes one wonder if "a dictator
is not a necessary concomitant of revolutions, of the rise of democracies, and of the establishment of the parliamentary system." His
program harked back to the populist policies of the ancient tyrants,
promising "liberty, equality, and fraternity" to the masses at the
expense of aristocratic and royal power.[25]

As he reviewed the history of dictatorships in France, Bainville
insisted on the necessity of distinguishing between legitimate and
illegitimate regimes. The ministerial autocracy of Richelieu and the
absolute monarchy of Louis XIV were examples of benign dictatorships because they were rooted in the tradition of royal legitimacy,
which imposed severe limitations on the ruler. The eighteenth-
century philosophes, on the other hand, preferred parvenu autocrats such as Frederick the Great of Prussia to the legitimate monarchs of their own nation. Like the Huguenots before them, the

24. Bainville, *Dictators*, 9, 10.
25. Bainville, *Réflexions sur la politique*, 39; Bainville, *Dictators*, 17–24, 27–39, 50,
57–65.

philosophes were intent on uprooting and destroying the hierarchical social institutions of the *ancien régime* and chose to perceive in enlightened despotism the ideal agency of progress. They recognized that enlightenment "had to be forcibly imposed on the crowd of imbeciles that would insist on clinging to their old prejudices, especially their religious ones." This tradition of revolutionary, illegitimate dictatorship was perpetuated by Robespierre, and later, "the little Corsican usurper," who established personal political authority on the basis of a direct link between Emperor and people.[26]

Yet it served Bainville's purposes to temper his disapproval of certain authoritarian regimes that lacked the stamp of legitimacy. He declined to criticize the illegitimate dictatorial tradition in Latin America on the grounds that indigenous, legitimate dynasties were lacking in every nation save Brazil, thereby requiring the appearance of the next best thing. He praised Simón Bolívar as the archetype of the Latin American strongman, a sage political realist who freed his people from foreign rule and established political stability and social order. Contrary to his popular image as a subversive revolutionary, the great liberator was "an uncompromising opponent of democracy" who was disgusted by "the delirious hallucinations of Robespierre and Marat." Bainville had similar words of praise for Kemal Ataturk, whose authoritarian paternalism had transformed Turkey from the impotent remnant of a decadent Asiatic empire into a modern nation-state established on the European model.[27]

His favorite modern dictator was Salazar of Portugal, whose austerity, honesty and patriotism prevented him from seeking personal power and wealth at the expense of his nation. He was particularly taken by the Portuguese dictator's economic policies, which combined a dedication to balanced budgets with a commitment to modernize his backward country. He vigorously defended Salazar

26. Bainville, *Dictators*, 69ff., 81–88, 91–96, 109. This harsh judgment of the eighteenth-century philosophes contradicted his earlier effort to claim them as intellectual precursors of modern French royalism. See above, 31–32.
27. *Ibid.*, 135–41, 164, 196ff.

against attacks from his critics on the extreme right, the ultranationalist intellectuals who denounced the government's modest ambitions and demanded a more active foreign policy to restore national prestige. In contrast to the totalitarian regimes in Italy and Germany, the Portuguese government had acquired such a measure of respect that it had no need to resort to totalitarian methods to preserve its power. It was therefore "the wisest and most moderate" dictatorship in Europe.[28]

Bainville refused in the name of political realism indiscriminately to condemn or support dictatorship as a system of government appropriate to France. "Dictatorships are like a good many other things in this world," he asserted. "They can be the best or the worst form of government. There are some excellent ones, and there are some hateful ones." Dictatorships were not the creation of a willful individual, but rather were the inevitable consequence of circumstances. To populations that wished to avoid the hardships caused by dictatorial regimes, he offered the simple admonition: "Never put yourself in the position of being unable to do without them."[29]

But though he never ceased to believe that his own nation had long ago adopted a political system so unsuitable to its needs as to render an authoritarian solution inevitable, Bainville could not bring himself to endorse such a solution as a second best alternative to a royalist restoration. Having divested himself of the albatross of pro-Nazism in earlier writings, he was now prepared to dispel once and for all the conviction expressed by certain young royalist firebrands that the doctrines of Mussolini were compatible with the program of the Action Française. Italian Fascism was first and foremost a movement of revolution, he declared, recanting his earlier definition of it as reactionary.[30] "Those who want France to follow suit will do well to think twice about it. . . . The Gallic cock is not designed by nature to suck the dugs of the Roman

28. *Ibid.*, 235–39. The Portuguese dictator frequently expressed his profound intellectual debt to the Action Française. Weber, *Action Française*, 485–86; Interview with Marcel Wiriath.
29. Bainville, *Dictators*, 7, 165.
30. See above, 248–49.

wolf."[31] One can only assume that such a forthright statement was intended to supersede his previous (and much more ambivalent) declarations on the subject.

As in the decade before the First World War, so during the first half of the thirties Bainville's concern about internal political developments in France was overshadowed by his persistent preoccupation with France's national security amid a deteriorating international situation. Most of the military and diplomatic safeguards that had been established in 1919 to prevent the revival of German aggression and ensure the peaceful resolution of international disputes had either disappeared or proved ineffective by the middle of the 1930s. The world depression and the consequent suspension of German reparation payments signified to Bainville the bankruptcy of the illusion that the international financial community was capable of preserving European stability through economic arrangements. The demonstration of the League of Nations' impotence following the Japanese occupation of Manchuria in 1931 had brought into question the principle of collective security. Germany's withdrawal from the world body in the fall of 1933 had damaged it beyond repair.

All of this, of course, came as no surprise to Bainville. He had never entertained the slightest illusion about collective security or the League's effectiveness as a peacekeeping instrument. Nor had he ever placed much credence in the capacity of the Western powers to enforce the financial and territorial settlement that had been imposed upon Germany. He consistently maintained the view that the only effective guarantee of European peace was the encirclement of Germany by pro-Western states in the east and a defensive alliance of France, England, and Italy in the west. Only by rigid adherence to such traditional balance-of-power principles, he believed, could France expect to provide herself with effective protection against a renewed menace of German aggression.

During the last days of the Paris Peace Conference, Bainville had

31. Bainville, *Dictators*, 225.

warned that the maintenance of an independent Austria—whether Habsburg or Republican—was the foremost requirement of a durable settlement. At each expression of German or Austrian sentiment in favor of Anschluss, from the first faint rumblings after the armistice to Brüning's ill-fated proposal for an Austro-German customs union in 1931, he renewed this admonition with equal fervor. On the occasion of Chancellor Dollfuss's assumption of emergency powers in March 1933 to deal with local Nazi agitation in Vienna, Bainville predicted that it was only a matter of time before Hitler would intervene in the affairs of Austria to support indigenous Pan-German elements there.[32]

On the sixth of February 1934, while most Parisians were preoccupied with the Stavisky scandal and the right-wing leagues' protest march on the Palais Bourbon, the royalist writer's attention was riveted on Vienna. "The last days of the Austrian Republic are approaching," he announced, referring to the upsurge of Nazi terrorism following Dollfuss's efforts to suppress the party. If France permits the Austrians to be trampled beneath the German juggernaut, he exclaimed, it will be "worse than when we abandoned them at Sadowa." A few days later he implored England and France to exhibit greater appreciation of "the services that Dollfuss has rendered to the cause of Europe" and urged the two governments to reaffirm their commitment to "the principle that Austrian independence is inalienable." The assassination of the Austrian chancellor by Nazi militants in the summer of 1934 elicited from Bainville yet a more strident exhortation for France and England to emulate Mussolini, who had concentrated military forces at the Brenner Pass during the crisis, in a collective demonstration of resistance to German expansion.[33]

This mounting obsession with Hitler's designs on Austria derived from Bainville's assumption that the Fuehrer, like Bismarck, would strive to establish German hegemony in Central Europe with the compliance of France. Hitler's *Drang nach Osten* in the 1930s would be executed along the lines of Bismarck's devious

32. *AF*, March 11, 1933.
33. Bainville, *Journal*, III, February 6 and 18, June 17, and July 27, 1934.

policy of the 1860s. The German dictator would renew the Iron Chancellor's trick of issuing retractable promises to France of non-belligerency on the Rhine in return for a free hand in the east. But French acquiescence in a German victory over Austria would represent nothing but a temporary stay of execution, as it had proved to be after 1866:

> When Bismarck had defeated and expelled Austria, when he had chained the South German states to Prussia, he still desired war to consolidate these results by a victory over France. The same idea will come to Hitler or his successors after the realization of the *Anschluss*, the dislocation of Czechoslovakia, the recovery of territories from the Poles, or whatever similar kinds of things one can imagine.

As an astute student of balance-of-power politics, Hitler understood that the realization of his Pan-German ideal required "the destruction or the consent of France." Bainville hoped that French statesmen would bear in mind this inflexible truism, particularly when Hitler began to resort to obfuscatory and diversionary tactics, such as the proposition of a Franco-German "common front against communism" as a means of buying time for his eastern ventures.[34]

But the French people gave no signs of such perspicacity, at least not to Bainville's satisfaction. He continued to remind his readers that the German chancellor would succeed in resurrecting and executing this historic policy of Pan-Germanism only if public opinion in the Western democracies were so blind to the lessons of the past as to permit him to do so unchallenged. He was particularly alarmed by the willingness, nay eagerness, of important sections of the French and British public, not to speak of the ruling elites, to gamble on disarmament negotiations as a vehicle for reducing international tensions. During the first month of Hitler's rule, Bainville assailed those French pacifists who were blaming the inflexibility of their own government for fanning the flames of German nationalism. The evacuation of the Ruhr and then the Rhineland, the acceptance of German membership in the League of Nations,

---

34. *AF*, October 17, 1933.

and the progressive reduction of reparations requirements were hardly indications of inflexibility! Yet these and other concessions had done nothing to arrest the growth of German aggressiveness. On the eve of the crucial session of the disarmament conference in February 1933, he denounced the "absurdity" of French diplomats negotiating an arms reduction agreement with representatives of the new German chancellor who had openly advertised his plans to rearm Germany and revise by force the territorial settlement of 1919.[35]

Similar expressions of outrage from Bainville were occasioned by the early efforts at appeasement by the Italian and British governments. The first of these was the attempt to tame the German monster by inducing him to join a consortium of the European powers, where he could be watched and presumably influenced in a pacific direction. The French royalist writer heaped scorn on Ramsay MacDonald, who appeared intent on "humiliating English liberalism before the leader of Fascism" by rushing to Rome in the spring of 1933 to discuss Mussolini's ill-conceived (and ultimately abortive) project for a four-power pact linking England, France, Germany, and Italy. He accused the British and Italian leaders of secretly preparing to offer concessions to the German dictator that would betray France's eastern allies and, by extension, France herself. The Western nations must either "refuse to budge" on the question of the eastern frontiers, he warned, or be prepared to "join the 'butchers' club.'"[36]

Having recorded his opposition to Mussolini's four-power pact, Bainville continued to denounce all proposals for a European security system that included both Germany and Italy as members. Given England's traditional preference for isolation from the affairs of the continent, such an arrangement would imprison France in an alliance with two revisionist powers committed to the destruction of the existing international order. As a preferable alternative, he proposed the revival of the wartime coalition of France, England, and Italy, together with a strengthening of Western ties

35. Bainville, *Journal*, III, February 1, 1933; *AF*, February 2, 1933.
36. Bainville, *Journal*, III, March 21 and 30, June 11, 1933.

with Poland and the three nations of the Little Entente (Czecho-slovakia, Yugoslavia, and Rumania) in order to "bar the door to German expansion" on all four corners of the continent. The for-mer diplomatic constellation would serve to deter German aggres-sion in the west, while the latter would constitute a formidable barrier to Nazi ventures in the south and east. He considered such a system of encirclement workable because it linked nations whose hatred of Germany furnished the requisite common ground.[37]

But Bainville realized that a revival of the old wartime western entente of France, Britain, and Italy would present serious prob-lems that would have to be resolved before its durability could be counted on. Such a coalition was the surest "guarantee of peace," he remarked at the end of 1934. "The difficulty is to make this union permanent and solid." What endangered its permanence and solidity was both Franco-British ideological hostility to Italian Fascism and the suspicion harbored by Western leaders that Italy was herself planning major revisions of the Versailles settlement at the expense of Yugoslavia, a member of both the Little Entente and the French alliance system forged by Briand. Bainville was careful to specify that his advocacy of a rapprochement with Mussolini was based not on any ideological kinship with Fascism, but rather on a realistic assessment of Italy's potential as a southern counter-weight to Germany. At the beginning of 1935 he recalled Musso-lini's decisive role in deterring German intervention in Austria after the assassination of Dollfuss, remarking that the "community of interests" shared by Italy and the two Western powers repre-sented a sufficient reason for French and British democracy to bury the ideological hatchet and accept a military alliance with the Duce.[38]

But the problem of Italian revisionism constituted a more formi-dable stumbling block to Bainville's scheme for European security. He recognized that Mussolini's ambitions along the Adriatic jeop-ardized the future both of the Little Entente and of the Franco-Yugoslav Treaty of 1927, not to speak of the implied threat to Nice,

37. *Ibid.*, March 21, 1933, March 6, 1934, January 5, 1934.
38. *Ibid.*, December 14, 1934, December 30, 1934, January 1, 1935.

Savoy, and Corsica in the Fascists' grand design. He accordingly urged the French and British governments to extract from the Italian leader "a firm and precise declaration of his willingness to respect the treaties" and the territorial status quo in return for a recognition of an Italian sphere of influence in Austria.[39]

Hitler's denunciation of the disarmament clauses of the Versailles Treaty in March 1935 added fuel to Bainville's argument in favor of a three-power accord directed against Germany. Taking note of the Anglo-French failure to respond with force to this violation of the treaty, he predicted that such timidity would encourage Hitler to take the next logical step: the remilitarization of the Rhineland. The long-range project for revision initiated by Stresemann in the twenties was about to bear fruit. "The financial obligations of Germany have disappeared. Her military obligations are disappearing. Her territorial obligations will [soon] disappear." The only remaining hope for averting a European catastrophe was for France, England, and Italy to present a solid front against any further violations of the 1919 settlement. At the close of the Stresa conference in April (which had been designed specifically to develop that solid front), Bainville praised the three governments for reaching an interim agreement, but despaired over the vagueness of the association. More concrete objectives could have been realized, he asserted, "if the three Western powers, which are the only ones that can really guarantee peace, had arrived at a formal alliance and coalition."[40]

The fragility of the Stresa front was confirmed two months later by the Anglo-German Naval Agreement, a separate understanding between London and Berlin (concluded without consultation with Paris) which enabled Hitler to circumvent the Versailles naval limitations. What Bainville had seen as a tenuous alliance *à trois* had instantaneously dwindled to an even shakier bilateral connection between France and Italy. He noted with great bitterness that June 18, the date of the naval agreement, was also the anniversary of Waterloo. Perfidious Albion had once again sacrificed the security

39. *Ibid.*, January 1, 1935.
40. *AF*, March 19, 1935; Bainville, *Journal*, III, April 14, 1935.

of her continental allies to her maritime interests, leaving France exposed to the wrath of a German nation in a full state of rearmament.[41]

The selfish behavior of the British government elicited from Bainville the familiar epithets about the perversity of the island kingdom's historical traditions. When the Liberal foreign secretary Sir John Simon visited Hitler in March 1935 to explore the possibilities of a mutual understanding, Bainville denounced him as "a spiritual son of Gladstone" who was possibly preparing to repeat the latter's treachery in 1870. But British Liberalism did not hold a patent on appeasement, and Bainville was equally harsh on its advocates among the Tory leadership. After the conclusion of the naval agreement in June, he accused the new Conservative foreign secretary, Sir Samuel Hoare, of reviving the Salisbury tradition of "splendid isolation," hardly an improvement on Simon's discredited Gladstonism.[42]

The forthcoming British proposal for joint opposition to Mussolini's Abyssinian expedition in the autumn of 1935 was the last straw. This invocation of the principle of collective security by a nation that had violated the spirit of the League covenant by signing a separate naval agreement with the Nazis struck Bainville as the height of hypocrisy. Nor did the appeals to the principles of justice and national sovereignty on behalf of the autocratic Emperor of Abyssinia from a nation that had forcibly acquired a third of the African continent during the past half century strike a responsive chord. "What Mussolini claims for his country is what England did in India and Egypt," he remarked. "It is what we ourselves are doing in Tunisia and Morocco."

This is not to say that Bainville approved of the Abyssinian adventure. "It is not without apprehension that we ourselves see the Italians engaging their forces in East Africa," he asserted. "But at least we are considering only the superior interests of Europe. England is thinking above all of Egypt and the Sudan." He worried that a prolonged colonial war in East Africa would have dire conse-

41. *Ibid.*, June 29, July 5, 1935.
42. March 28, 1935, June 20 and 29, July 7, 1935.

quences on the continent since it would divert Italian troops from the Upper Adige, where they were needed to deter Germany from meddling in Austrian affairs. He therefore urged England to abandon Abyssinia to a speedy Italian victory in the interests of the European balance of power.[43]

This realistic attitude toward Italy's Abyssinian invasion characterized his thinking on the subject to the very end. His last articles contained urgent pleas to the League to withdraw the sanctions that it had imposed on Italy in November and mordant attacks on the parties of the Popular Front for claiming to be pacifist while endorsing a belligerent policy toward Italy. His reasons for advising France to court Italian favor remained the same: the overriding necessity to prevent a rapprochement between the two Fascist dictators and to keep Mussolini in the only coalition capable of preserving the balance of power in Central Europe.[44]

But the projected alliance with Fascist Italy and Conservative Britain was not the only diplomatic strategy that was being discussed in French governmental and journalistic circles in the mid-thirties. Many observers who recalled the traditional friendship between France and Russia were proposing the resurrection of the alliance that had foiled the German war plan in the autumn of 1914. French foreign minister Louis Barthou, a politician of the old balance-of-power school, had taken the first steps toward a reestablishment of the Russian connection in the spring of 1934. But he was re-

43. *Ibid.*, July 5, 7, and 23, 1935.
44. *Ibid.*, October 11, 1935, and *Candide*, 1935, in Bainville, *Doit-on le dire?* 390. This pragmatic approach to the Abyssinian question was the second instance of Bainville's differing with the majority sentiment in the League over the imposition of sanctions on expansionist powers. After Japan was officially condemned by the world body for invading Manchuria, he opposed sanctions against Japan on the grounds that they might force her into the German camp. "Imagine if Japan were to have no ties with England and France and if she were to side with Germany," he remarked. "From Manila to Saigon, from Singapore to Ceylon, what a clean sweep she could make." Bainville, *Journal*, III, February 25, 1933. As these statements imply, his disagreement with those who wished to punish Italy and Japan for their transgressions was based not upon an ideological affinity for Japanese militarism or Italian fascism, but rather upon a pragmatic desire to do anything to maintain German isolation.

moved from the scene in October of that year by an assassin's bullet. Pierre Laval, his successor at the Quai d'Orsay, resumed Barthou's negotiations with the Soviets and a Franco-Russian alliance was finally signed in May 1935.[45] The following year the Comintern officially adopted the Popular Front program, instructing all Communist parties to abandon their opposition to military appropriations and to support the anti-German policies of their respective governments. This abrupt turnabout soon produced the unprecedented spectacle of French Communist deputies voting for increases in military spending and calling for a tough stance toward Germany.[46]

During the year-long interlude between the signing of the Franco-Soviet Pact in May 1935 and its ratification by the Chamber of Deputies, Bainville conducted a vigorous campaign against the alliance in the pages of *Action française* and *Candide*. He based his opposition upon the "experimental principles" of diplomacy that he had learned from his study of the past. Above all, he sought to discredit the wishful thinking that he detected behind the nostalgic calls for the revival of the old agreement of 1894. "For an alliance to be solid," he warned, "it must be based on a mutuality of interests, and that mutuality does not depend on ephemeral matters. It is permanent or it does not exist. The former Russian alliance . . . took seventeen years to develop and solidify. Anything that is firm requires the passage of time." Moreover, he complained that historical memories tended to be highly selective, and urged those Frenchmen who recalled the services that Russia had rendered to France in 1914 to remember the eastern ally's record of betrayal. "Three times in less than two and a half centuries we have been the ally of Russia," he declared, "and three times Russia has deserted us." Was there any reason to believe that the Russians would be more faithful this time?[47]

45. See William E. Scott, *Alliance against Hitler: The Origins of the Franco-Soviet Pact* (Durham, Duke University Press, 1962).
46. See Daniel R. Brower, *The New Jacobins: The French Communist Party and the Popular Front* (Ithaca: Cornell University Press, 1968).
47. *AF*, December 15, 1934 and February 12, 1935. The references are to the Treaty of Saint Petersburg (1762), by which Russia defected from the French alliance

French optimism on this score was precluded, Bainville believed, by concrete reasons favoring a Soviet accommodation with Germany at France's expense. Throughout the interwar period he had periodically reaffirmed his conviction, first expressed during the Paris Peace Conference, that the prospect of a new partition of Poland constituted an irresistible basis for cooperation between these two revisionist powers. While German Chancellor Brüning and Soviet Foreign Minister Litvinov met to celebrate the tenth anniversary of the Rapallo Pact in April 1932, Bainville repeated his warning that the two nations were destined to forge an alliance on the basis of their common opposition to "the existing order and the existing treaties."[48]

The triumph of National Socialism in Germany did not compel him to revise this judgment. When Edouard Herriot had first floated the idea of a Franco-Russian alliance on the basis of a common front of anti-Fascist powers against Germany in February 1933, Bainville denounced the illusion of relying on ideological principles as a durable structure of diplomacy. He recalled that William II had failed to detach Nicholas II from "the atheists and regicides of the French Republic" by appealing to the sentimental principles of monarchical legitimacy before 1914 because concrete Russian interests in Southern Europe dictated an alliance with France at that time. Similarly, the geographical realities in Eastern Europe in the 1930s favored a rapprochement between Germany and Russia that no appeal to ideological solidarity—in this case, resistance to Nazism—could avert. Consequently, the ratification of the Franco-Soviet Pact would either force Poland into the hands of Germany, whom she was likely to regard as the lesser of two evils, or eventually result in a Russo-German pact of nonaggression that would enable the two revisionist powers to divide the Polish spoils. In any case, the German policy-makers had "reflected a great deal since 1918" about the causes of their nation's defeat and could be ex-

---

against Prussia during the Seven Years War; the Russian repudiation of the Treaty of Tilsit and withdrawal from Napoleon's Continental System in 1812; and the Bolshevik government's separate peace with Imperial Germany in 1918.

48. Bainville, *Journal*, III, April 19, 1932.

pected to avoid making the same mistakes. Bainville deemed it a foregone conclusion that Germany would strive at all costs to "avoid a two-front war and reserve all her forces for her principal adversary. It is entirely natural that, having decided to strike the first blow against France, . . . she will doubtless be content to take a defensive stance against Russia," a precaution which in any case would be necessary only if "we could expect from Red Russia services equal to those that White Russia rendered us in 1914."[49]

Even when the collapse of the Stresa front had left France isolated from England with only an increasingly tenuous tie with Italy, Bainville continued to counsel the French people to resist the temptation of the Russian alliance as a means of deterring German aggression. "French policy is not obliged to choose between cholera and plague," he had declared in October 1934 during the preliminary negotiations leading to the pact. As the government prepared to submit the treaty for legislative ratification a year later, he repeated his warning that France should not bite the Soviet bait, even in her present lonely position. The wisest posture would be "to remain equidistant from these two restless meteors" in Eastern Europe. In any case the Russian alliance offered nothing to France in the way of solid guarantees against German expansion in the west. The Red Army was weak and undependable, the Soviet economy was in such disarray that efficiency of production and transportation was "problematical," and Poland and Rumania understandably refused to permit Russian access to the heart of the continent. All the pact would accomplish would be to give Hitler a "*casus belli*," a pretext for "branding France as the aggressor." And since Germany had no common borders with Russia, the Nazi dictator's first move would be on the Rhine.[50]

It becomes apparent, as one closely examines Bainville's denunciation of the Franco-Soviet Pact, that his realistic assessment of the diplomatic underpinning of the balance of power in Central Europe

49. *AF*, February 23, 1933; Bainville, *Journal*, III, May 3, 1935, and *Candide*, 1936, in Bainville, *Doit-on le dire?* 396; *AF*, October 24, 1934, February 23, 1935.

50. Bainville, *Journal*, III, October 28, 1934; *AF*, November 30, 1935, January 2, 1936; *AF*, November 30, December 11, 1935, in Bainville, *La Russie et la barrière de l'est*, 152–55.

was strongly influenced by his growing fear of the ideological threat
to France posed by the Soviet Union and its international apparatus.
Even the Comintern's recent shift in policy did not allay this suspicion. Bainville recognized that both Nazi Germany and Communist
Russia had the capacity to export propaganda to other nations. But
while Germany could direct its Pan-German appeal only to those
nations with large German-speaking minorities, Russia possessed a
world-wide network of agents capable of channeling its ideological
message through the local Communist parties in most of the major
European countries. In spite of the Stalinist policy of Socialism in
One Country, Bainville persisted in believing that the Soviet Union
was not a nation-state in the normal sense, but rather "an ideal
fatherland without frontiers" which boasted sympathizers in every
nation who were eager to promote its universalistic ideology. The
advent of leftist unity in France merely increased these fears. In his
last articles he reminded his readers that Stalin possessed a considerable advantage over Hitler, namely, "a direct influence on [inter-
nal French] politics through the Popular Front." For that reason
alone the hammer and sickle represented a greater internal threat
to France than did the swastika. He apparently was willing to de-
emphasize the possibility (which he had noted in earlier writings)
that the Nazis could also discover sympathizers and collaborators
to do their bidding in France.[51]

From hindsight, Bainville's tortured efforts to expose the diplomatic and strategic defects of the projected Russian alliance appear
to signify a retreat from his commitment to realism. What other
power to the east could have tipped the continental balance against
Germany, particularly after Poland's signing of a nonaggression
pact with Hitler in January 1934 brought into question its dependa-

51. Bainville, *Journal*, III, July 28, 1934; see also *AF*, January 26, 1936; *AF*, November 23, 1935; *Candide*, 1936, in Bainville, *Doit-on le dire?* 396. In fairness it must
be noted that the unabashedly pro-Nazi wing of French fascism, led by the former
leftists Jacques Doriot and Marcel Déat, did not gain much support until after Bainville's death. Most of the native French fascist movements that operated before 1936
tended to emphasize the nationalist rather than the internationalist aspects of fascism, and were the offspring of earlier conservative nationalist movements in France
rather than extensions of foreign governments. See Remond, *The Right Wing in
France*, 281 and Plumyène and Lasierra, *Les Fascismes français*, 15ff.

bility in this regard? His stubborn insistence that France still enjoyed the luxury of avoiding a choice between Soviet Russia and Nazi Germany reflected the patently anachronistic conviction that France was still capable of shaping her foreign policies independently of other great powers, as in the golden era of the seventeenth century when she was the arbiter of European affairs. Bainville even saw fit to invoke the authority of Richelieu to support this uncharacteristic lapse into wishful thinking. "If one wishes to interpret correctly the policy of Richelieu," he announced, in one of his many briefs against the Russian alliance, "one will recall that the cardinal was preoccupied with preserving for France the ability to intervene when and where she pleases."[52]

Did Bainville's balance-of-power realism fade, in this instance, in the face of the mounting ideological threat from the united left within France? Charles Micaud has conclusively demonstrated that the fear of Communism that gripped the French right—especially after the advent of the Popular Front government and the outbreak of the Spanish Civil War in the summer of 1936—prompted French conservatives to abandon their traditional anti-German nationalism in favor of a new willingness to tolerate Nazi hegemony in Europe as a preferable alternative to what they feared most of all: a Russian-inspired social revolution throughout Europe. This "subordination of national to class interests" is seen by Micaud as a "defensive reflex" of the French middle classes: "When it appeared to them that liberalism was doomed, many French bourgeois began to look for protection in an autocratic regime that would respect their acquired social and economic position." This new orientation, symbolized by the notorious slogan *"plutôt Hitler que Blum"* (better Hitler than Blum), transformed many nationalists of the right from advocates of military preparedness and diplomatic activism into pacifists and appeasers who helped pave the way for the debacle of 1940.[53]

---

52. *AF*, May 9, 1935, in Bainville, *La Russie et la barrière de l'est*, 166.
53. Micaud, *The French Right and Nazi Germany*, 223–28. This view is supported by Pertinax (pseud. André Géraud), *The Gravediggers of France: Gamelin, Daladier, Reynaud, Pétain, and Laval* (Garden City, N.Y.: Doubleday, 1944).

Micaud includes Bainville in the category of "resigned nationalists," that is, patriots-turned-appeasers who opposed the Russian
alliance on the grounds that it was in France's interest to avoid a
showdown with Germany by encouraging her to divert her energies
to the east. The implication of this analysis is that, like many other
members of the French right, Bainville had begun to take the ideological threat from the Comintern more seriously than the military
threat from Germany. This conclusion, it seems to me, is totally unwarranted. Bainville's frequent expressions of hostility to Germany
on nationalist grounds, together with his criticism of Nazism as a
political ideology, should dispel any suspicion that he had become
one of those lapsed patriots of the French right who were prepared
to opt for rapprochement with Hitler as a more desirable fate than
citizenship under Blum. The evidence suggests that his opposition
to a Franco-Soviet alliance was based primarily on his realistic evaluation of the military value of the Red Army to France (which he
regarded as minimal both because of its own internal weaknesses
and because of the absence of a common border between Germany
and Russia) and of the diplomatic objectives of the Kremlin (which
he saw as coincident with those of Germany, particularly in regard
to their common interest in the partition of Poland). Perhaps the
fairest evaluation of his judgment in this matter might be that he
was wrong in the long run but correct in the short run.[54]

It is an intriguing question whether Bainville's ideological fear of
international Communism would have triumphed over his nationalism, anti-Germanism, and commitment to *Realpolitik* had he lived
to witness the victory of the *Front Populaire* in France and the *Frente
Popolar* in Spain. For it was these two events that contributed more
than anything else to the evolution of the French right toward a de-
featist and, in some cases, a pro-Nazi posture. Less than a month
before his death, during the Spanish electoral campaign and the formation of the leftist coalition in France, he was still denouncing

54. Micaud, *The French Right and Nazi Germany*, 46, 72; see Hilah Thomas,
"The Thought of Jacques Bainville on Germany: A Study in the Loyalties of Integral
Nationalism," (Honors thesis, Smith College, 1962), 73.

Hitler's call for the revision of the peace settlement of 1919. Such a position scarcely reveals the beginning of a transformation toward an ideologically motivated willingness to come to terms with the Third Reich as the only effective bulwark against the European revolution. Indeed, one contemporary French observer detected a growing difference of opinion on this issue between Bainville and his colleagues in the royalist movement. While Bainville remained a "merciless critic of Hitlerism" to the end, Maurras and other leading members of the Action Française were adopting a very different stance. "While approving, generally, of Bainville's theories," noted this source, who interviewed several royalists in the late thirties, Maurras and his associates had come to believe that "France should go to war only if and when she is directly attacked."[55] Such a sentiment represented the ultimate expression of defeatism, and there is nothing in Bainville's writings that suggests that he would have agreed with it. But would the developments on both sides of the Pyrenees in the summer of 1936 have caused him to change his mind? Would he have followed his mentor Maurras and his friend Daudet in hailing the collapse of the French Republic and the advent of a collaborationist regime in 1940? Would he have joined the handful of conservative nationalists who placed patriotism above political ideology and either rallied to de Gaulle or worked discreetly against the German occupation within France? Unfortunately, the answer to this question belongs to the realm of retrospective hypothesis rather than ascertainable fact.

But a partial answer may be found in two events that occurred in 1935, the year before his death. The first was the publication of his major historical study of the Third Republic. In one of those curious coincidences of history, Bainville's own life paralleled almost exactly that of the most durable regime in modern French history. Born a few weeks after the definitive consolidation of the Republic with the election of Jules Grévy to the presidency, he died a few

---

55. *AF*, January 11, 1936; Pierre Lazareff, *Deadline*, trans. David Partridge (New York: Random House, 1942), 179–80.

weeks before Hitler's military occupation of the Rhineland began
the process which eventually destroyed the regime. He had spent
his entire adult life attempting to demonstrate the inherent weaknesses of the republican system, yet he had seen it recover again
and again from the shocks of social disorder, economic crisis, diplomatic isolation, and military invasion. The collapse of the republic
that the royalists had been predicting and promoting for a third of
a century was not to take place during his lifetime. The rightist
riots of February 6, 1934, which perhaps came closest to producing
that result, were sufficiently menacing to expel a ministry, but not
to overturn a regime.

In the aftermath of this last in a long line of abortive attempts to
destroy the Republic from within, Bainville began to record his final
reflections on the political system under which he had lived, with
the intention of identifying the secret of its long life. What perplexed
and astonished him most of all was the endurance of France's democratic institutions amid a prewar Europe of monarchies and empires
and a postwar Europe that was rapidly succumbing to authoritarian
dictatorships of a Fascist, military, or royalist type.[56] Almost alone
among European nations, the Third French Republic, despite its
inauspicious origin, had weathered all the storms of the past sixty
years and retained its original institutions intact. In his passion for
historical reductionism, Bainville strove to identify the law of historical continuity which had guided French democracy through the
turbulence it had encountered since its inception.

Trying to account for the unexpected resiliency of the regime,
Bainville emphasized the contradictory challenges with which it
was confronted in its early years. In order to establish a democratic
system, he observed, the advocates of a republic in 1870 had to rely
on the support of leftist revolutionaries against the dominant forces
of Bonapartists and monarchists. But this marriage of convenience
with Parisian radicalism had frightened the property-owning majority into electing a postwar National Assembly dominated by

---

56. Jacques Bainville, *La Troisième République* (Paris: Fayard, 1935), 10.

monarchists. As a consequence, the republicans were forced to adopt an increasingly conservative posture to allay the fears of a Red Republic that had gripped rural and petty bourgeois France. Once Thiers had prudently sued for peace against the wishes of the advocates of continued resistance and then suppressed the Paris Commune, the Republic "began to take on a decent, reasonable, in a word 'conservative' aspect," enabling the French leader to mount "a sort of bourgeois throne." No past monarch had reestablished order and secured peace with such energy and decisiveness as the little bespectacled politician on whom executive power had been conferred.[57] Here again was an instance of that instinct of self-preservation and social equilibrium which Bainville had elevated to the status of a historical law.

Further evidence of this conservative corrective was to be found in the parliamentary deliberations that produced the constitutional laws of 1875 upon which the Republic was based. In a chapter revealingly entitled "The Constitutional Monarchy Under Another Name," Bainville proposed the paradoxical theory that the parliament of 1875 was ideally suited to the task of creating a constitution that could enable the Republic to endure precisely because it possessed a monarchist majority. Fearful of the excesses of democracy, the National Assembly rejected proposals for a unicameral, omnipotent parliament "sans frein ni modérateur," preferring to curb the power of the people by establishing an upper house elected indirectly and an executive power independent of the legislative body. He was convinced that only men of the right, imbued with a healthy suspicion of popular sovereignty, could have conceived the framework of such a system. "A President, a Chamber, a Senate, that was the entire Constitution of 1875. This trinity was, under other names, that of the Restoration and the July Monarchy." The constitution of 1875 constituted the least undesirable structure under the circumstances, since its monarchist authors were careful to establish its respectability and acceptability "by

57. *Ibid.*, 19–23, 32–33.

despoiling it of its revolutionary aspects" and to guarantee its viability "by furnishing it with several almost balanced forces."[58]

So perspicacious and clairvoyant were Thiers and his Legitimist
and Orleanist colleagues, Bainville asserted, that the political regime they created was able to survive their own demise. After the
death of Thiers and the resignation of MacMahon, the conservative
republican Jules Grévy continued to represent moderation and social order at the Elysée Palace, while the National Assembly fell
into the hands of a new aristocracy of wealth which merely transferred the seat of power from the monarchistic Faubourg Saint-
Germain to the stylish bourgeois 16th arrondissement. "One
scarcely noticed that the Republic was in the hands of Republicans," declared the royalist writer, so dedicated was the new political elite to the principles of order, equilibrium, and stability. This
conservative disposition enabled the regime to survive the succession of challenges to its legitimacy during the remainder of the
nineteenth century. Marshal MacMahon's attempted coup, which
Bainville denounced as a naïve, poorly conceived gesture of Bonapartist inspiration, was rebuffed not just by Republicans, but also
by Orleanists, who abhorred Caesarian democracy as much as
Jacobinism.[59] The conservatives were afforded another opportunity to demonstrate their repugnance for dictatorship during the
Boulanger crisis, and they performed well. Bainville characterized
Boulanger as "the Jacobin general," an heir to Gambetta who symbolized "the original sin of the Republican party, its old bellicose
tradition and that of the 'appeal to the soldier'"; the conservative
coalition had again been responsible for rebuffing this latest democratically inspired threat to the balanced system of 1875.[60]

58. *Ibid.*, 39–54. See also D. W. Brogan, *French Personalities and Problems* (New
York: Knopf, 1947), 86.

59. Bainville, *La Troisième République*, 78, 83, 89ff.

60. *Ibid.*, 123, 127–28, 137ff. Confronted with the irrefutable evidence of Orleanist collusion with the Boulangist conspirators, Bainville explained this potentially
embarrassing fact by pointing out that the monarchists had attempted to join forces
with the moderate left and center, but were rebuffed. "Excluded from the defense
of liberalism," he declared, "they were driven into the hands of the general whom
they despised." *Ibid.*, 127–28.

With the collapse of the Boulangist movement and the restoration of order, Bainville noted, the groundwork had been laid for "a Republic moderate in everything, a Republic without doctrine, administering like the July Monarchy" behind the façade of democracy. The old revolutionary mystique of the First Republic had been thoroughly domesticated by the monarchist institutions of the Third. It was an instructive comment on the long road that republicanism had travelled in the past century that the grandson of Lazare Carnot, a member of the Committee of Public Safety, was assassinated in 1894 by a latter-day defender of the revolutionary tradition, and that the Republic summoned the grandson of a minister of Louis Philippe to replace Carnot as President. The dangers of pure democracy were by then universally appreciated by the third generation of republicans who had become staunch opponents of the principles that had inspired the first.[61]

But the Dreyfus Affair constituted the first serious threat to the delicate balance of social and political forces that had furnished the Third Republic with its power of endurance. The Affair had "destroyed the government of the moderates and the conservative Republic," installing a radical regime "which threatened to dissolve everything" that had been accomplished since 1870. Waldeck-Rousseau, though "a liberal of the Restoration, a Voltairian bourgeois of Louis Philippe," became a prisoner of the radical left, and was replaced by the despicable Emile Combes, the persecutor of the church. Moreover, the rising forces of socialism and antimilitarism represented new evils to be reckoned with. "Everything that had been done to temper democracy by containing its excesses and attenuating its dangers was abandoned."[62]

But the embattled Republic proved once again that it was capable of recovering from even the most painful of afflictions. And once again it owed its salvation to the services of its traditional, conser-

---

61. President Sadi Carnot was assassinated by an Italian anarchist in 1894 and was succeeded by Jean Casimir-Périer, whose grandfather had headed a ministry under the July Monarchy in 1831–32; *ibid.*, 179, 185–86.
62. *Ibid.*, 201, 226, 231, 235ff.

vative elements. While France's internal disorder of the early twentieth century threatened to weaken her international position, the
seasoned diplomatic corps that she had inherited from the monarchical period remained isolated from those domestic perturba-
tions and labored to protect her interests in the world. This explained why "the years of ignominious decline at home were those
in which France acquired allies and an Empire." Soon thereafter,
the mistakes of the Radical Republic were rectified by a succession
of resolute leaders, notably Briand, Clemenceau, and Poincaré,
whose successful efforts to restore order and tranquility proved
that it was still possible to curb the deleterious impulses of democracy.[63] The alliance system forged by Delcassé and his sub-
ordinates in the foreign service remained intact, the army was not
destroyed, and the state was not dissolved. The brake had been
applied to arrest France's headlong plunge toward domestic anarchy and foreign disaster. The Republic was now prepared to
face up to its supreme challenge.

The *union sacrée* in 1914 had constituted in Bainville's eyes a sort
of "wartime monarchy" which permitted the government to suspend civil liberties in order to avoid the risk of popular interference
in the war effort. Later, by entrusting Clemenceau with absolute
power, the Republic had placed its fate in the hands of a trusted
septuagenarian just as it had in the days of its birth and at several
points thereafter. The same process repeated itself continually in
the postwar era. Doumergue and later Poincaré were summoned
to the helm of state in times of financial distress, and each succeeded in restoring public confidence. In the aftermath of the February
6, 1934 riots, the former was called upon once again to repair the
damage, and the Republic was saved.[64]

As always, the historical law that Bainville discovered operating
to secure the Third Republic against its domestic and foreign enemies throughout its history was the famous instinct of self-preservation. Lacking a coherent doctrine or a set of guiding principles,

63. *Ibid.*, 252, 253ff.
64. *Ibid.*, 283–84, 288–89, 294ff.

he observed, the Republic seemed to have as its supreme ambition the preservation of its existence. "The risks of the popular regime were corrected by experience, democracy preserved through gerontocracy." Each time that the forces of pure democracy and the mystique of 1789 threatened to destroy it, the regime punctually produced a strong, seasoned leader capable of "pulling it from the abyss in the nick of time."[65]

Nor did Bainville hesitate to claim credit for himself and his associates in the conservative intelligentsia for playing an important role in this rescue operation that saved the republic from the consequences of its democratic principles. "The criticism of the regime by the intellectuals, the writers, the independent elites," he declared, "has been beneficial to the Republic which, triumphant through election and left to itself, was in danger of perishing from its own excesses." Could it be that this lifelong enemy of the regime was finally reconciling himself to the position of the loyal opposition? Was he, in effect, coming to regard the proper function of the Action Française as that of a moderating, corrective influence on a conservative republic that was ever in danger of degenerating into a radical democracy? Was the Third Republic no longer the hated "slut" that must be destroyed for the good of France, but rather a volatile, unpredictable child that had to be periodically rescued from the consequences of its infantile behavior? There were those who interpreted the publication of *La Troisième République* as the author's tardy effort to make his peace with the regime.[66]

A second indication of Bainville's putative reconciliation with the Republic came in the same year of the publication of his book, when he was elected to the French Academy to fill the seat of the recently deceased Poincaré. That this august body would bestow such an honor on a leading member of the Action Française was in itself a sign that the official guardians of the French cultural tradition had

---

65. *Ibid.*, 185, 300–309.
66. *Ibid.*, 284; Joseph Lecler, "L'Oeuvre historique de Jacques Bainville," *Etudes* (June 5, 1935), 633, 640; see also Wladimir d'Ormesson, in *Le Temps*, February 11, 1936.

chosen to place Bainville in a special category apart from his royalist colleagues. Maurras had presented himself as a candidate in 1922 only to be decisively defeated in April of the following year by one of those numerous nonentities who have sat under the cupola of the Academy. The motive for this repudiation was largely political in nature. Marshal Joffre and Anatole France both announced their unwillingness to support Maurras's candidacy on the grounds that he personified an extremist movement. The victorious candidate completed his acceptance speech to cries of "Long live the republican Academy," an outburst which added insult to injury in a sordid affair that was replete with ideological overtones. The *Camelots du roi* retaliated by stealing the ballots and publishing in the *Action française* the pictures of the eleven academicians who had voted for their master Maurras.[67]

Henry Bordeaux, the conservative Catholic novelist and academician who sponsored Maurras's candidacy, had warned the royalist leader that his election was unlikely because of republican hostility to the movement that he incarnated. But Bordeaux consoled him with the prediction that the profoundly conservative majority in the Academy would eventually be willing to accept the less controversial Bainville as a more palatable alternative. The death of Poincaré in 1934 struck Bordeaux as the perfect occasion to propose Bainville as the replacement; it was entirely fitting that "the funeral oration of a great statesman should be delivered by a great political journalist." He solicited the support of three intimate friends of Bainville: Léon Bérard, Poincaré's former secretary and Minister of Public Instruction in the second Poincaré cabinet; André Chaumeix, the editor of the influential *Revue des deux mondes*; and Maurice Paléologue, a career diplomat who had served as ambassador to Russia during the Bolshevik Revolution and secretary-general of the Ministry of Foreign Affairs after the war. Bordeaux and Chaumeix finally persuaded Bainville to present himself as a candidate, and Bordeaux, after

67. Henry Bordeaux, *Quarante Ans chez les quarante* (Paris: Fayard, 1959), 64–66. Bordeaux to Maurras, March 13, 1923; Bordeaux memorandum, April 18, 1923; Bordeaux memorandum, May 24, 1923; in Henry Bordeaux, "Charles Maurras et l'Académie Française," *Les Oeuvres libres* (January, 1953), 3–5, 24; "Revue de la Presse," *AF*, June–July, 1922.

weeks of tireless campaigning on his friend's behalf, succeeded in drumming up the requisite academic support with the assistance of Marshal Pétain.[68] In March 1935, at the age of fifty-six, Bainville was elected by a vote of twenty to seven.[69]

It came as no surprise that such an illustrious and eminently respectable group of sponsors—a celebrated Catholic novelist, the editor of a leading literary journal, a distinguished ambassador, a republican politician and former minister, and the military hero of Verdun—encountered none of the ideologically motivated resistance to Bainville's candidacy that had sabotaged Maurras's earlier application for admission to this exclusive club of the French elite.[70] The historian-journalist of the *Action française* had evidently established an image of independence from his more controversial associates, who proudly advertised their commitment to smash the hated Republic. On February 6 of the preceding year, when royalist partisans were in the streets alongside the Fascist leagues marching toward the Chamber of Deputies, Bainville rejected Daudet's suggestion that they join the mob. He had not yet finished his daily article—which, as we have seen, dealt with foreign affairs rather than domestic counterrevolution.[71] Henri Massis recalls that, as he and Bainville strolled toward the western end of the Tuileries from the editorial office of the *Revue universelle* at 6 p.m. to observe the street fighting on the Place de la Concorde, Bainville remarked in an offhand manner: "The least that one can say about it is that the affair was very poorly prepared."[72] One need only compare this air of detachment to the blood-curdling calls for action that were arising from the editorial office at the rue du Boccador to appreciate the distance that Bainville had travelled on the road to moderation.

---

68. Bordeaux to Maurras, March 13, 1923, in Bordeaux, "Charles Maurras," 6–7; interview with Madame de Coudkerque-Lambrecht (1970); Henry Bordeaux, *Histoire d'une vie*, Vol. V (Paris: Plon, 1964), 268.

69. René Pinon received 5 votes and Daniel Halévy 2. See Lecler, "L'Oeuvre historique," 623, and "Trois Nouveaux Académiciens," 347.

70. Maurras did finally gain election to the Academy in 1938 by a much narrower margin.

71. See above, 286.

72. Lazare de Gérin-Ricard and Louis Truc, *Histoire de l'Action Française* (Paris: Edition Fournier-Valdès, 1949), 182–85; Massis, *Maurras et notre temps*, II, 76–77.

Nor did he do much to discourage this impression of having arrived. After returning from his courtesy visit to the academician Henri Bergson, he shocked Massis by praising this royalist bête noire as an *"homme de l'esprit,"* a term that Bainville had used only once before, in reference to Maurras himself (who doubtless would have bristled at sharing the honor with a Jew who had spent his life attacking the very positivist tradition that Maurras had been defending).[73] At the ceremony organized by the Action Française to celebrate Bainville's election, the new academician reassured his royalist colleagues of his undiminished devotion to them. He recalled that he had once told Maurras that he owed him "everything except life itself," and made a point of repeating the tribute before the royalist partisans present. He praised Daudet's good humor and personal magnetism, observing that while they frequently differed on certain subjects, their mutual respect and affection ran deep. He mentioned his third-of-a-century-long friendship with Maurice Pujo, the leader of the *Camelots du roi.*[74] But by the mid-thirties Bainville had acquired other loyalties as well. After receiving the congratulations and tributes of his associates in the movement, he attended a reception organized by a more disparate group of admirers that might not have been welcome at the first gathering.[75]

The occasion of Bainville's official reception at the Academy on November 7, 1935 could not have been more different from the spiteful celebration of Maurras's defeat twelve years earlier. An aura of heartfelt cordiality toward the new member pervaded the ceremony as he walked down the aisle between his two official sponsors, Bordeaux and Paléologue. The usually dapper, elegant, seemingly ageless little man was already terribly emaciated by the cancer of the esophagus that had been detected earlier in the year and was to take his life within three months. His audience knew that his acceptance speech would constitute the swan song of a

73. Massis, *Maurras et notre temps*, II, 187.
74. This speech was later reproduced in Jacques Bainville, *Vertu de l'amitié* (Paris: Private Printing, 1935).
75. Interview with Hervé Bainville. Interview with Madame Jacques Bainville.

man whose entire career had been devoted to criticizing the republican regime. Those present waited expectantly for what one of them was to call "the eulogy for the most republican of statesmen delivered by the least republican of historians."[76]

Bainville's address was a perfect combination of measured praise for the vitality of the regime that produced a Poincaré to lead it in its times of troubles interspersed with gentle references to its shortcomings:

> Amid conditions that were among the most precarious of its history, [despite] a penchant for mediocrity and vulgarity which, more than fifty years ago, was already worrying the philosophers, amid a [situation of] weakness which Renan and Taine suspected could not be remedied, our country still discovered talents and personalities capable of protecting it from decadence.[77]

Poincaré hailed from one of those bourgeois elites which had periodically rescued France from the brink of disaster through their good sense, conscientiousness, and honesty. As a republican from Lorraine, Bainville observed, Poincaré had recognized the grave threat to France posed by a strong, united Germany. This awareness had prevented him from succumbing to the illusory faith in the possibility of Franco-German friendship that had afflicted so many of his fellow republicans.

For Bainville, Poincaré's career had closely paralleled that of Thiers: both had risen above the petty political squabbles that debilitate parliamentary democracies in order to defend the national interest at critical periods in the nation's history. Such statesmen who were able to inspire confidence among the masses were essential to the success of a Republic, he remarked, adding that they would not have succeeded in their task had they not been assisted and sustained by an elite that was devoted to the public weal. Without the services of this aristocracy of talent and achievement, the destructive elements inherent in a parliamentary republic would

76. Henry Bordeaux, *De Baudelaire à Soeur Marguerite*, 225; Maurice Bedel, "Réception de M. Jacques Bainville à l'Académie Française," *Revue des deux mondes* (December 1, 1935), 708–710.
77. *Le Fauteuil de Raymond Poincaré*, 14.

have dissipated the material reserves of the nation and hamstrung the statesman's efforts to ensure its prosperity, stability, and security. This tribute to the bourgeois elite of France received thunderous applause from the distinguished assemblage.[78]

The official response by his friend, the playwright Maurice Donnay, was replete with praise for the valuable services that Bainville had rendered to France in his journalistic and historical writings. While taking note of the royalist ideology that informed them, Donnay emphasized Bainville's intellectual independence, reciting the long list of distinguished nonmonarchist periodicals and newspapers that had requested and received his collaboration. He informed the new academician that his predecessor had frequently expressed the desire to see Bainville join the forty immortals and intimated that the republican statesman harbored a secret feeling of kinship with the doctrines of the royalist writer. "Perhaps Raymond Poincaré envied you your ability to convey to Frenchmen from your position," he concluded, "verities that he was never able to say from his own."[79]

After this laudatory tribute, Bainville returned home to await the death that he and those close to him knew to be imminent. He had confided to friends that he longed to write biographies of two historical personages that had always fascinated him: Joan of Arc and Jesus. After completing his biography of Napoleon in the fall of 1931, he had been hard at work preparing a study of Louis XVI, but had interrupted it twice, first in the summer of 1932 to honor a request from the King of Egypt to write a short history of Bonaparte's Egyptian expedition as part of a general history of his kingdom, and in the spring of 1934 to record his final evaluation of the Third Republic. He spent the balance of the following year in terrible pain, preparing his academic acceptance speech. He was

---

78. *Ibid.*, 15–16, 26–27, 35, 41ff; Henri Bidou, "M. Bainville à l'Académie," *Revue de Paris*, VI (November 15, 1935), 453.

79. *Le Fauteuil de Raymond Poincaré*, 89, 135–36. Wladimir d'Ormesson, writing in *Le Temps*, put it even more bluntly: "Poincaré, as republican as he was, was much more 'Orleanist' than he himself realized. Bainville, as royalist as he was, was much more republican than he thought." *Le Temps*, February 11, 1936.

never able to return to the Louis XVI project. But he continued to dictate newspaper articles from his bedside to his friend Pierre Varillon, and maintained his lucidity to the end as dozens of friends and admirers dropped by the Bainville apartment on the rue de Bellechasse to pay their last respects.[80]

On February 6, 1936, a mere shell of a man bundled himself up to attend a session of the Academy, ignoring the excruciating pain that he had been enduring for months. On the same day his friend, the novelist Paul Valéry, met him at the library of the Institute checking out books. Later that evening, when the novelist visited him at his home, he was astonished to find the dying man working at his desk. On the eighth, Bainville dictated what was to be his last article for *Candide*, a final brief against the ratification of the Franco-Soviet pact that was about to be taken up by the French Chamber of Deputies. He began the next day, his fifty-seventh birthday, by discussing Rimbaud with Robert Brasillach and La Bruyère with Maurras, lending credence to the suspicion that he was a frustrated poet at heart.[81] He then asked his wife to send for Varillon to take dictation for his next article. But his condition worsened, and Madame Bainville, a devout Catholic, summoned a fervently royalist priest who was willing to administer absolution to an unrepentant agnostic whose political movement had been condemned by the Vatican.[82] Though an unbeliever to the end, Bainville had used the word "faith" at the close of his acceptance speech at the Academy, thereby touching off a flurry of unwarranted speculation among his Catholic admirers that he had made his peace with the mother church. He died at 2:30 in the afternoon in the presence of his wife, his young son, Maurras, and his two doctors. His last comprehensible words, uttered in response to the reading of the daily newspapers, perfectly summarized his dark

80. *Le Fauteuil de Jacques Bainville*, 54–55; see Jacques Bainville, *Bonaparte en Egypte* (Paris: Flammarion, 1936); "Hommages à Jacques Bainville," 557–59. Frédéric Delebecque, in Massis, *Le Souvenir*, 59ff.

81. Valéry, in "Hommages à Jacques Bainville," 662; Brasillach, *Notre Avant-Guerre*, 176; Massis, *Le Souvenir*, 2; Joseph, *Qui est Jacques Bainville?* 65.

82. Interview with Marcel Wiriath; interview with René Wittmann; interview with Madame Jacques Bainville.

view of the prospects of humankind, and more specifically of his countrymen: "pauvres gens!"[83]

On the eighth of February, the day before his death, he had murmured hopefully to Madame Bainville: "Send some cards to our friends. . . . Thursday, I want to see lots of people"[84] Thursday, February 13, turned out to be the day of his funeral, and he got his wish. Over ten thousand friends and admirers gathered to view the procession from the Bainville home on the rue de Bellechasse, where his body had lain in state, to the Church of Saint-Pierre-du-Gros-Caillou, where it was to rest pending its transfer to the Bainville family property near Marigny in Normandy for burial. A youth organization that had been established for the study of his works, together with several *Camelots du Roi*, formed an unofficial honor guard.[85] The ecclesiastical authorities were conspicuously absent, the Paris diocese having denied the deceased the benefit of a religious burial and disavowed the actions of the priest who had defiantly administered the last rites. But Bainville had many admirers among those clergymen who had never accepted in their hearts the Papal condemnation of 1926. Black cassocks were much in evidence in the funeral cortège, mingling with the finery of diplomats, statesmen, and soldiers. The military contingent was headed by two Marshals of France whom Bainville had counted as friends: Franchet d'Esperey and Pétain.[86]

At 1:00 P.M. the hearse began its westward journey, carrying Bainville for the last time from the neighborhood of the Café de Flore, where he had met Maurras thirty-six years earlier, and the

83. Bordeaux, *Histoire d'une vie*, V, 280; Daniel Halévy, in "Hommages à Jacques Bainville," 580; Albert Thibaudet, in Massis, *Le Souvenir*, 83. Interview with Hervé Bainville; *Le Temps*, February 11, 1936.

84. Henry Bordeaux, "La Mort de Jacques Bainville," *RU*, LXIV (March 15, 1936), 706.

85. Interview with Madame Jacques Bainville; interview with Pierre Juhel. Bainville remained a favorite of conservative youth. After his election to the Academy, he was presented with his academician's sword by a group of students who had financed its purchase by means of a public subscription. Interview with François Leger. See also A. Cahuet, "La Réception de M. Jacques Bainville à l'Académie Française," *L'Illustration* (November 16, 1935), 343.

86. Renauld, *L'Action Française*, 426–27, 54–55; Massis, *Maurras et notre temps*, 272–73.

office of the *Revue universelle*, where he and Massis had written their bi-weekly columns in defense of the West. As the procession approached the vicinity of the Palais Bourbon, where the debate on the ratification of the Franco-Soviet Pact was about to begin, a fortuitous event occurred which not only disrupted the solemnity of the occasion but also produced far-reaching consequences that Bainville would surely have deplored. An automobile carrying Léon Blum, who was about to launch the electoral campaign that would bring his Popular Front coalition to power within a few months, was inadvertently steered across the Boulevard Saint-Germain through the funeral train. Construing this untimely interruption as an intentional gesture of disrespect from the living symbol of the revolutionary tradition, several youthful members of a renegade royalist sect set upon the Socialist politician and beat him severely with objects torn from the car. Blum was hospitalized with a scalp wound after being rescued by construction workers who were repairing the walls of the nearby Ministry of War.[87]

This spontaneous outbreak of right-wing violence prompted a massive protest march from the Pantheon to the Bastille by two-hundred thousand partisans of the Popular Front three days later. More important, it persuaded the government that the time had finally come to crack down once and for all on the royalist movement. The Sarraut ministry issued a series of decrees dissolving the Action Française League, the Fédération des Camelots du Roi, and the Fédération des Etudiants d'Action Française.[88] Maurras had been formally charged with incitement to murder for his personal attacks on the advocates of sanctions against Italy during the Abyssinian crisis. It seems likely that the court's sentence of four months in prison, which was handed down less than a month after the attack on Blum, was influenced by that most recent outburst of royalist violence. Bainville would have appreciated the irony of such momentous events accompanying the funeral of a man who had so assiduously (and successfully) avoided publicity during his life.

87. *Le Temps*, February 15, 1936; *Le Populaire*, February 14 and 15, 1936; Joel Colton, *Léon Blum, Humanist in Politics* (New York: Knopf, 1966), 115–16.
88. Beau de Loménie, *Les Responsabilités*, 283; Renauld, *Action Française*, 208–209.

The events surrounding Bainville's death and burial moved his longtime friend, the critic Albert Thibaudet, to remark that the funeral had united in a single dramatic occasion the "three forms of historic French wars." The imbroglio over the church's refusal to participate recalled the great religious struggles of the past; the Blum incident and its aftermath dramatized the political divisions that had plagued France since the Revolution; and the opening of the debate on the Franco-Soviet Pact revived the seemingly eternal question of how to protect France from her rapacious neighbor to the east.[89] It was unquestionably this last issue—the menace of foreign invasion—that had caused Bainville the greatest concern during his career. For he had always considered the damage wrought by domestic quarrels, whether religious or political, insignificant compared to the terrible carnage and destruction that would inevitably accompany the second world war that he had been predicting since the conclusion of the first.

Death spared him the anguish of witnessing the fulfillment of his ominous prophecies. During the lifetime of this confirmed pessimist, France had suffered no military defeat, lost no territory, and (save the departments in the northeast during the First World War) endured no foreign occupation. But the day after his death the newspapers that carried his obituary also contained reports of German military activity in the Rhineland, the first in a series of developments that were to confirm posthumously his worst fears. After his remains had been transferred to the family plot in Normandy, his former collaborator Massis remarked that the feeling that Bainville's death had prompted in his admirers was, above all, the feeling of "danger." Another friend claimed that the somber premonition of doom that oppressed Frenchmen would be less burdensome if the royalist writer were still present to demonstrate to his compatriots, in a period when his daily counsel was most needed, how to "escape from that prison of consequences in which our errors have enclosed us."[90]

89. Thibaudet, in Massis, *Le Souvenir*, 176.
90. "Hommages à Jacques Bainville," introduction; F. de Villermont, "Absence de Jacques Bainville pour l'anniversaire de sa mort," *Revue hebdomadaire*, XLVI, no. 7 (February 13, 1937), 177.

From these and dozens of similar expressions of admiration that could be cited, it is clear that Bainville's reputation for clairvoyance survived him. Indeed, it was enhanced by the subsequent unfolding of the events that he had predicted: the remilitarization of the Rhineland; the German annexation of Austria; the demolition of Czechoslovakia; the conclusion of the Russo-German nonaggression pact at Poland's expense; and the coming of World War II. The collapse of the European order and eventually of France itself constituted a grim tribute to Bainville's reputation as the soothsayer of his nation. In this instance, he would doubtless have preferred to be proved a false prophet.

Epilogue

One cannot practice Bainville's [foreign] policies and condemn Maurras to death.

Andre Malraux (1944)

The France of today is too heavily impregnated by the ideas for which Maurras and Bainville stood, . . . which modeled a whole generation of French nationalists, including those who never professed them, for them to die; if only because, as Bernanos wrote in 1932, Maurras and Bainville, even when they were still alive, became a part of the history of their country.

Eugen Weber (1962)

Jacques Bainville's influence did not die with him in February 1936, a month which in retrospect may be viewed as a lull before the storm of military and diplomatic setbacks suffered by France between the remilitarization of the Rhineland and the disaster of June 1940. In a number of ways he continued to advise his countrymen in their terrible time of troubles. A few years before his death a series of *Cercles Jacques Bainville* had been formed in the principal cities of France to ponder his teachings and disseminate their message, particularly to the young generation. The *Cercle* in Paris boasted Marshal Franchet d'Esperey as its honorary president and five other academicians, including Bainville's friends Henry Bordeaux and Paul Valéry, on its organizational committee. Banquets and public speeches sponsored by the *Cercles* of Bordeaux, Marseilles, Nancy, and Nantes enabled the royalist propagandists and their sympathizers in the respectable right to circumvent the restrictions imposed on the Action Française's public activities by the dissolution of the league and its youth groups.[1]

1. Interview with Pierre Juhel; interview with Madame Jacques Bainville; Ludovic Vaccon, in "Hommages à Jacques Bainville," 665–66; Weber, *Action Française*, 416.

Meanwhile, the deceased historian's friends in the publishing industry rushed to fill the void left by the cessation of his daily columns. Soon after his death, Plon undertook an ambitious project entitled *La Collection Bainvillienne*, which would assemble and republish in book form thousands of Bainville's newspaper articles. The first volume in this series, *La Fortune de la France*, which appeared in 1937, grouped his columns on economic topics. Their pleas for a return to financial orthodoxy and their vigorous defense of the bourgeois virtues of thrift, savings, and free enterprise posthumously mocked the efforts at socioeconomic reform undertaken by the government of the Popular Front. In the same year came *La Russie et la barrière de l'est*, a collection of his articles on Russian and Eastern European affairs which made topical reading as the future of Briand's alliance system and Barthou's and Laval's Russian pact began to become matters of grave concern to France. In 1938 *L'Angleterre et l'empire britannique* reminded the reading public of England's ambivalence toward continental affairs at a time when French subservience to London's vacillating policy toward Hitler had become an accomplished fact. And then, in 1939 and 1940 respectively, Frenchmen were treated to two volumes of his collected articles on Germany, as the fateful confrontation between the two Rhine powers unfolded.[2]

The appearance of these posthumously published articles afforded those readers who sorely missed Bainville's daily commentary on current events the opportunity to review his earlier warnings about the deteriorating international situation and its inexorable consequences. Here again was the perfect expression of his belief in the permanence of human nature and the social environment, those historical constants which, together with the constraints of geography, dictated what he called the "eternal policy" of French statecraft. Since circumstances and conditions did not change in any fundamental way, Frenchmen in 1939 or 1940 could profit from the lessons of "political physics" contained in his articles of a dec-

2. Interview with René Wittmann; see Jacques Bainville, *L'Allemagne* (2 vols.; Paris: Plon, 1939).

ade earlier, and statesmen could avert disaster by applying them.

Nor were his journalistic analyses of current events the only fruits of Bainville's thought that continued to instruct the citizens of France after his death. His historical works continued to sell well during the same period. What is most striking in this regard is the extraordinary increase in popularity of his most celebrated studies during the years 1941 and 1942. That 41,800 copies of his *Histoire de France* could be printed in 1941, seventeen years after its publication, can only mean that his publisher sensed that thousands of Frenchmen of the new generation were intent on discovering explanations for their nation's ignominious degradation by turning to a writer whom they regarded as a familiar and accurate oracle.[3]

The Germans, ironically, proceeded to employ Bainville's writings for quite a different purpose. Both his *Histoire de deux peuples* and *Les Conséquences politiques de la paix* were translated into German after the fall of France and widely disseminated during the remainder of the war. The first was used to remind the citizens of the Third Reich that French Germanophobia had a long history, the second to prove that even the *Diktat* of Versailles had not satisfied the vindictive nation to the west.[4] Dr. Friedrich Grimm, a Nazi propagandist attached to the German embassy in Paris, toured occupied France bearing the message that Bainville and his disciples both inside and outside the Action Française had been responsible for perpetuating in the twentieth century the notorious "testament of Richelieu," which demanded a Germany impotent and divided.[5] But while Grimm repeated his refrain to sympathetic audiences of collaborators, the mounting popularity of Bainville's writings among other Frenchmen caused the Germans grave concern. A disgruntled Control Officer reported that the *Chantiers de Jeunesse*

3. See the Appendix.
4. See Jacques Bainville, *Geschichte zweier Volker* (Hamburg: Hanseatische Verlaganstalt, 1940); see Jacques Bainville, *Frankreichs Kriegsziel* (Hamburg: Hanseatische Verlaganstalt, 1940).
5. Linville, "Jacques Bainville," 359–60; Massis, *Maurras et notre temps*, 330; Joseph, *Qui est Jacques Bainville?*, 46; Friedrich Grimm, *Du Testament de Richelieu à Jacques Bainville* (Geneva: Le Mois suisse, 1941). Grimm also contributed an explanatory introduction to Bainville's two works that were translated into German.

(Vichy youth camps formed to impart military values to French youngsters) were riddled with history instructors who used Bainville's books to glorify Richelieu's policy of French hegemony on the continent.[6] In the summer of 1942 the occupation forces in Belgium banned all of Bainville's books, denouncing them as obstacles to that nation's rapprochement with Germany.[7]

The liberation of France and the advent of the Fourth Republic scarcely caused a decline in the popularity of Bainville's writings. On the contrary, since problems similar to those that had confronted France after the First World War emerged at the conclusion of the Second, many Frenchmen renewed their interest in his political wisdom. Over 50,000 copies of his *Histoire de France* and his *Napoléon* were printed in 1946 alone, and thousands more continued to roll off the Fayard presses during the remainder of the Fourth Republic. A new edition of the *Napoléon* appeared in 1958 in a series comprising the "twelve finest works of history" that had been selected by a jury of academicians. It was introduced by André Maurois, who hailed it as one of the few classic biographies of the emperor that had "preserved its prestige and rediscovered its public." Plon's *Collection Bainvillienne*, by the time of its completion in 1949, comprised nine volumes of his collected articles from half-a-dozen newspapers, while other publishers brought out similar collections of his interwar writings.[8] As Frenchmen still traumatized by the events of 1940–1944 struggled with such questions as

6. Bainville's widow supplied an anecdotal confirmation of the popularity of his historical works during the occupation. While shopping at a shoe store in Vichy in August, 1941, she identified herself to the owner, who proceeded proudly to show her ten of her husband's books in his tiny library. Joseph, *Qui est Jacques Bainville?* 45. See also Robert Paxton, *Parades and Politics at Vichy* (Princeton: Princeton University Press, 1966), 211.

7. Weber, *Action Française*, 43n; Paul Delandsheere and Alphonse Ooms, *La Belgique sous les Nazis* (2 vols.; Brussels, n.p. n.d.), II, 303.

8. See the Appendix; see Jacques Bainville, *Napoléon* (Paris: Fayard, 1958), preface by André Maurois, 8; Jacques Bainville, *Esquisses et portraits* (Paris: J. and R. Wittmann, 1946); Jacques Bainville, *La France*, (2 vols.; Paris: Editions Self, 1947); Jacques Bainville, *Comment s'est faite la restauration de 1814* (Paris: Editions Self, 1948); Jacques Bainville, *Les Moments décisifs de l'histoire de France*, ed. Pierre Gaxotte, (Paris: Robert Cayla, 1949); and Jacques Bainville, *Vitalité du capitalisme* (Liège: Editions Dynamo, 1960).

the proper treatment of postwar Germany and the appropriate political system for post-Vichy France, Bainville continued to find a hearing.

The extent of Bainville's impact on the thinking of Charles de Gaulle remains a matter of conjecture. Nevertheless, educated guesses are permissible and many have been ventured. Jean La-couture has noted that de Gaulle was an admirer of Maurras and read the *Action française* regularly. It is unlikely that the young cadet who was receiving his intellectual formation at the Saint-Cyr military academy while Bainville was launching his daily column on foreign affairs could have escaped the influence of the royalist historian-journalist. The quotation from André Malraux at the head of this chapter reveals that one of the general's closest advisers deemed that influence profound. Alexander Werth supports that judgment in a subsequent biography of de Gaulle, and an American political scientist has recently added fuel to such speculation by calling attention to the "monarchic tradition of foreign policy" that typified the Fifth Republic.[9] Without postulating a rigid causal connection, it is possible to speculate about what Eugen Weber has called the impregnation of the French elite with the ideas of the Action Française by isolating points of similarity. De Gaulle's proposals during the time of Yalta and Potsdam for the separation of the left bank of the Rhine and the destruction of centralized power in Germany, for example, harked back to Bainville's similar suggestions at the time of Versailles.[10] In a more general sense it also seems possible to detect in the French leader's abortive attempt in 1944–1946 to establish an executive authority independent of popular and legislative influence the imprint of the royalist writer's teachings.

9. Jean Lacouture, *De Gaulle*, trans. Francis K. Price (London: Hutchinson & Co., 1965), 48, 52; Alexander Werth, *De Gaulle* (Middlesex, Eng.: Penguin, 1965), 69; Morse, *Foreign Policy and Independence*, 317. René Remond views de Gaulle's nationalism as more eclectic, in that it "repudiates no chapter of the French epic and stems as much from Michelet and Barrès as from Bainville." Remond, *The Right Wing in France*, 370.

10. Werth, *De Gaulle*, 179. For a description of de Gaulle's Carthaginian plans for Germany after the Second World War, see Willis, *France, Germany and the New Europe*, 15–17.

The reappearance of the parliamentary republic in 1946, with its institutions of the weak chief executive, the multiparty system, and ministerial instability, constituted a repudiation of the type of political regime that Bainville considered essential to French prosperity and security. In foreign affairs, the Fourth Republic's growing subservience to the United States and its acquiescence in the political, economic, and military recovery of Germany were circumstances which Bainville would certainly have deplored. It is also likely that he would have looked askance at the suicidal colonial policies of the regime, which sowed social unrest at home and sapped French power and influence on the continent and in the world. De Gaulle's triumphant return in 1958 amidst a situation of international humiliation and domestic strife can be viewed as a repetition of that periodic craving for a national savior which Bainville had identified as a historical law of French politics.

The subsequent domestic and foreign policy of the Fifth Republic represented in a number of respects the fulfillment of Bainville's prescription for the treatment of France's perpetual political ills. Here was a regime presided over by a military leader who reinstated firm executive authority at the expense of parliament, who reestablished a flexible, independent foreign policy for France, who succeeded in reducing his nation's dependency on the "Anglo-Saxon" powers, and who strove, however unsuccessfully, to reoranize a powerful, independent Europe under French auspices. Even the Gaullist entente with Adenauer in the early 1960s represented the logical extension of a policy proposed by Bainville during the interwar period: the establishment of ties to the Catholic, Francophile elements of Western Germany to counterbalance the "Prussian" elements in the east. In light of these and other affinities between the vision of the royalist historian and the policies of the Gaullist republic, the Paris Municipal Council's designation of a *Place Jacques Bainville* on July 7, 1960 comes as no surprise.[11]

---

11. Roger Joseph, "Le Poète Jacques Bainville," *Revue moderne des arts et de la vie* (March 1, 1961), 23. The Gaullists were not alone among those Frenchmen who recorded their admiration for Bainville once the threat of the Action Française had subsided after 1945. The last two prime ministers of the Third Republic, Edouard

Notwithstanding the numerous instances in which Bainville's conception of France's role in the world found expression in the subsequent policies of French statesmen in the postwar period, he must be judged in the last analysis to be a man of the past rather than of the future. This is so in regard both to the social groups whose interests he championed and to the observations on France that serve as his most memorable literary contribution.

Eugen Weber has accurately identified the followers of the Action Française as comprising those social groups in France that felt threatened by the marked decline in their economic position and social status caused by the advance of industrialization and modernization. Among these vulnerable groups were the surviving remnants of the preindustrial and prerevolutionary age: aristocrats, army officers, and antimodernist clerics who had progressively lost their former social status and political influence in the course of the nineteenth century. But they were later joined by a new stratum of disgruntled defenders of vested interests: *rentiers* ruined by inflation and foreign revolutions, landowners and holders of urban real estate squeezed by currency depreciation and rent control, and uncompetitive shopkeepers, artisans, and small businessmen outpaced by larger, more efficient enterprises.[12]

This latter group, ironically, had earlier supported the Revolution of 1789 and benefitted from it. This social stratum had also provided what Sanford Elwitt has called "massive auxiliary support" to the republican movement in France during the final victorious struggle against the old order in the 1870s. But this time the world of petty production was denied "the rewards of victory," which were reaped instead, at its expense, by the forces of heavy industry and high finance.[13] Bainville himself had emerged from the ranks of this social milieu and, though he repudiated his father's political views,

---

Daladier and Paul Reynaud, admitted that they had always distinguished between the royalist historian, whom they respected, and his less admirable colleagues in the Action Française. See Linville, "Jacques Bainville," 357.

12. Weber, *Action Française*, 525. See also Tannenbaum, *Action Française*, 118–21, 129.

13. See Sanford Elwitt, *The Making of the Third Republic: Class and Politics in France, 1868–1884* (Baton Rouge: Louisiana State University Press, 1975), especially 306.

he retained the socioeconomic conservatism that was then the hall-
mark of Radical Republicanism. As a consequence, he was linked
by familial origin and sentiment to a group whose preeminent position in French society and politics had come to an end at the time of
his death. The program of economic modernization launched in
France after 1945 completed the process begun in the 1920s and interrupted by the depression and the war.[14] It swept away the static
sector of French society and ushered into power a new elite of tech-
nocrats and entrepreneurs imbued with an unshakable faith in the
values and techniques of economic growth, government planning,
and Europeanism.[15] This trend is perhaps best exemplified by Gis-
card d'Estaing, the heir to the de Gaulle-Pompidou legacy. Though
he sports an ancestral château and a name with the particle of
nobility, he is a man of the future whose vision of France (which is
shared by the postwar technocratic elite from which he emerged)
would have been entirely foreign to Bainville.[16]

The treatment of Bainville's socioeconomic views in this study
should leave no doubt that he was above all a relentless enemy of
modernity. This obstinate resistance to the socioeconomic trends
of his time continued to the very end. In 1934 he published a charming children's book in which he gave vent to his uneasiness about
the technological innovations that he had witnessed during his own
lifetime, magical and unfathomable genies such as the automobile
and the airplane which he contemplated with a mixture of awe and
suspicion.[17] He had frequently complained that innovations in
transportation and communication had impaired the process of
political decision-making. By erasing the distances of space and

14. See Martin Wolfe, "French Interwar Stagnation Revisited," in Charles K.
Warner, ed., *From the Ancien Régime to the Popular Front* (New York: Columbia
University Press, 1969), 159–80.

15. See Charles Kindleberger, "The Postwar Resurgence of the French Economy," in Stanley Hoffmann, *et al., In Search of France* (New York: Harper & Row,
1965), 118–58. See also John Ardagh, *The New French Revolution* (New York: Harper
& Row, 1968).

16. It is ironic that Bainville's own son has become a successful participant in the
new economic system of postwar France and Bainville's grandson (and namesake)
was educated at an American business school. Interviews with Hervé Bainville.

17. Jacques Bainville, *Les Etonnements de Michou* (Paris: Calmann-Lévy, 1934).

time that permitted reflection and calm deliberation, they encouraged precipitate action. His distaste for technological inventions that disrupt ingrained habits extended to his personal life. This avid smoker and prolific writer did not learn how to use a cigarette lighter and a fountain pen properly until shortly before his death.[18]

The eclipse of Bainville's socioeconomic world view by the forces of modern technology after 1945 was accompanied by the disappearance of many of those geographical conditions of foreign policy that he mistakenly regarded as eternal. The advent of the nuclear age, with its atomic-powered submarines, intercontinental ballistic missiles, and longrange strategic bombers, has rendered irrelevant many of the geographical considerations that served as the underpinning of Bainville's conception of European equilibrium. No longer do rivers, mountains, channels, even oceans constitute the natural impediments to military aggression that they did in the days when statesmen could hope to enhance the prospects of international security by adjusting frontiers in a calculated manner. No longer does the peace of the world depend solely on the maintenance of the balance of power in Europe and, more specifically, on the ability of the other continental powers to contain Germany. The conception of the European balance, developed in the seventeenth century during the rise of the European state system, had been superseded in the postwar era by the reality of the global balance and the prospect of universal annihilation. It is difficult to imagine Bainville adapting to, or even comprehending, such a world in which the meticulously calibrated calculations of his "eternal policy" have lost much of their significance.

This is not to say that these two trends—the collapse of the petit bourgeois social order in France and the Eurocentric world order—had not already begun during his lifetime. Warning signals of these developments were omnipresent in the interwar period, and there are more than enough indications that he noticed them. That he failed to draw the appropriate conclusions from this disturbing evidence was due not to any naïve optimism on his part—no one could

18. Dr. Albert Liacre, in "Hommages à Jacques Bainville," 595.

justifiably accuse of him that shortcoming—but rather to the very nature of his political creed and the people to whom it appealed. The Action Française failed to achieve its political objectives because its royalist ideology was, in the last analysis, an anachronism. But it succeeded in acquiring its considerable intellectual prestige and influence by supplying those Frenchmen whose social position and sense of national grandeur were endangered with powerful arguments in support of their lost cause and psychological comfort for their belief in its righteousness. It was the royalist vision of the French past, particularly the one popularized by Bainville in his dozens of books and thousands of articles, that proved most effective of all in this regard. That his interpretation of the past also yielded an enviably accurate forecast of the immediate future was an additional benefit. For it helped to extend his influence beyond the limited audience of his sectarian movement to touch thousands of Frenchmen who despaired about the social and international order that was coming to an end.

Appendix

NUMBER OF PRINTED COPIES OF SELECTED PUBLICATIONS
OF *LES GRANDES ETUDES HISTORIQUES* SERIES

Source: Librairie Arthème Fayard, as of May 5, 1970. These figures do not
include printings of other editions or foreign translations.

Jacques Bainville, *Histoire de France*

Year	Copies Printed
1924	70,000
1925	13,200
1926	6,600
1927	5,500
1928	6,600
1930	7,700
1931	6,600
1933	11,000
1935	5,500
1936	5,500
1937	5,500
1938	5,500
1939	11,000
1940	5,500
1941	41,800
1942	22,000
1946	30,800
1948	4,400
1949	4,400
1951	4,400
1953	4,400
1959	5,500
1961	3,300
1969	6,600
Total	293,300

Jacques Bainville, *Napoléon*

Year	Copies Printed
1931	57,750
1932	28,600
1933	6,600
1935	6,600
1937	6,600
1939	4,400
1940	8,800
1941	16,500
1942	11,500
1946	20,600
1948	4,400
1951	3,300
1954	3,300
1957	3,300
1962	5,500
1968	5,500
Total	193,250

Jacques Bainville, *Histoire de la Troisième République*

Year	Copies Printed
1935	41,800
1936	5,500
1940	9,900
1941	5,500
1942	11,000
1945	5,500
1949	3,300
1960	8,800
Total	91,300

Pierre Gaxotte claims that by the beginning of 1961, the total sales figures for two other books by Bainville were: *Histoire de deux peuples*, 88,000; *Histoire de trois générations*, 60,000. See Weber, *Action Française*, 276–77n.

Sources Cited

INTERVIEWS

Hervé Bainville
Madame Jacques Bainville
Madame de Coudekerque-Lambrecht
Pierre Gaxotte
Pierre Juhel
François Leger
Charles Popin
Marcel Wiriath
René Wittmann

ARCHIVES AND PRIVATE PAPERS

Archives Nationales. Sûreté. (Sous-série F⁷).
Archives de la Préfecture de Police, Département de la Seine.
Letters of Jacques Bainville. In the possession of M. Hervé Bainville.
Publication Records, Grandes Etudes Historiques series, Librairie Ar-
thème Fayard.

NEWSPAPERS AND PERIODICALS

L'Action française
L'Action française mensuelle
Almanach des lettres françaises
Annales
Bulletin de la Société des professeurs d'histoire et de géographie
Candide
Le Correspondant
La Critique
Le Divan
L'Eclair
Ecrits de Paris
Essais critiques
Le Figaro

La Grande Revue
L'Humanité
La Liberté
Mercure de France
Les Nouvelles Littéraires
La Plume
Polybiblion
Le Populaire
Revue Bleue
Revue de l'Action française
Revue des deux mondes
Revue de synthèse historique
Revue du siècle
Revue hebdomadaire
Revue historique
Revue politique et littéraire
Revue universelle
Le Soleil
Le Temps
Vient de Paraître
La Volonté

WORKS BY JACQUES BAINVILLE

L'Allemagne. 2 vols. Paris: Plon, 1939.
L'Allemagne romantique et réaliste. Paris: Fayard, 1927.
L'Angleterre et l'Empire britannique. Paris: Plon, 1938.
"Anti-démocrates d'extrême gauche." *Revue de l'Action française,* VII
    (July 15, 1902), 121–28.
Après la Guerre: Comment placer sa fortune. Paris: Nouvelle Librairie Na-
    tionale, 1919.
Bismarck. Paris: Editions du Siècle, 1932.
Bismarck et la France. Paris: Nouvelle Librairie Nationale, 1918.
Bonaparte en Egypte. Paris: Flammarion, 1936.
Chroniques. Paris: Plon, 1938.
Comment est née la Révolution russe. Paris: Nouvelle Librairie Nationale,
    1917.
"Comment est née la Révolution russe." *Revue des deux mondes* (April 15,
    1917), 869–93.
Comment s'est faite la restauration de 1814. Paris: Editions Self, 1948.
Les Conséquences politiques de la paix. Paris: Nouvelle Librairie Nationale,
    1920.

Couleurs du temps. Versailles: Bibliothèque des Oeuvres Politiques, 1928.

Le Coup d'Agadir et la Guerre d'Orient. Paris: Nouvelle Librairie Nationale, 1913.

Le Critique mort jeune. Paris: Editions du Monde Moderne, 1927.

Dictators. Trans. J. Lewis May. London: Jonathan Cape, 1937.

Le Dix-Huit Brumaire. Paris: Hachette, 1925.

Doit-on le Dire?. Paris: Fayard, 1939.

L'Empereur. Paris: Flammarion, 1939.

Esquisses et portraits. Paris: J. and R. Wittmann, 1946.

Les Etonnements de Michou. Paris: Calmann-Lévy, 1934.

Filiations. Paris: A la Cité des Livres, 1923.

La Fortune de la France. Paris: Plon, 1937.

La France. 2 vols. Paris: Editions Self, 1947.

"Franco-allemand." *Revue universelle* (December 1, 1929), 611–12.

Heur et Malheur des Français. Paris: Nouvelle Librairie Nationale, 1924.

Histoire de deux peuples. Paris: Nouvelle Librairie Nationale, 1919.

Histoire de deux peuples continuée jusqu'à Hitler. Paris: Fayard, 1933.

Histoire de trois générations, 1815–1918. Paris: Fayard, 1918.

Histoire de trois générations avec un épilogue pour la quatrième. Paris: Fayard, 1934.

History of France. Trans. A. G. and C. G. Gauss. New York: Appleton & Co., 1926.

Italy and the War. London: Hodder & Stoughton, 1916.

Jaco et Lori. Paris: Grasset, 1927.

Le Jardin des lettres. 2 vols. Paris: Editions du Capitole, 1929.

Journal, I, 1901–1918. Paris: Plon, 1949.

Journal, II, 1919–1926. Paris: Plon, 1949.

Journal, III, 1927–1935. Paris: Plon, 1949.

Journal inédit, 1914. Paris: Plon, 1953.

Lectures. Paris: Fayard, 1937.

Louis II de Bavière. Paris: Fayard, 1964.

Maximes et réflexions. Paris: A la Cité des Livres, 1931.

"Le Mois historique de l'Italie: mai 1915." *Revue des deux mondes* (October 1, 1915), 559–87.

Les Moments décisifs de l'histoire de France. ed. Pierre Gaxotte. Paris: Robert Cayla, 1949.

Napoléon. Paris: Fayard, 1931.

Napoléon. Preface by André Maurois. Paris: Fayard, 1958.

"Nos Calvinistes en Allemagne." *Revue de l'Action française* (April 1, 1900), 553–64.

Nouveau Dialogue dans le salon d'Aliénor. Paris: Chez Marcelle Lesage, 1926.

Paraboles hyperboliques. Paris: Editions du Capitole, 1931.

Petit Musée germanique, suivi de la Russie en 1916. Paris: Société Littéraire de France, 1917.

Polioute. Paris: A la Lampe d'Aladdin, 1926.

La Presse et la guerre: choix d'articles. Paris: Bloud et Gay, 1915.

"Quatre Mois en Russie pendant la guerre." *Revue des deux mondes*, XXXIV (August 15, 1916), 778–814.

Réflexions sur la politique. Paris: Plon, 1941.

Ed. *La République de Bismarck, ou origines allemandes de la Troisième République*. Paris: Nouvelle Librairie Nationale, 1905.

Richelieu. Paris: Beytout, n.d.

La Russie et la barrière de l'est. Paris: Plon, 1947.

Une Saison chez Thespis. Paris: Editions Prométhée, 1929.

Les Sept Portes de Thebes. Paris: Les Editions du Cadran, 1931.

Au Seuil du siècle. Paris: Editions du Capitole, 1927.

La Tasse de Saxe. Paris: Grasset, 1928.

La Troisième République. Paris: Fayard, 1935.

Tyrrhenus. Saint-Félicien-en-Vivarais: Le Pigeonnier, 1925.

Vertu de l'amitié. Paris: Private Printing, 1935.

Vie de Napoléon. Paris: Flammarion, 1935.

Le Vieil Utopiste. Paris: Les Cahiers d'Occident, 1st year, no. 3, 1927.

Vitalité du capitalisme. Liège: Editions Dynamo, 1960.

OTHER BOOKS, ARTICLES, AND MEMOIRS

Andrew, Christopher. *Théophile Delcassé and the Entente Cordiale*. New York: St. Martin's, 1968.

Ardagh, John. *The New French Revolution*. New York: Harper & Row, 1968.

Ariès, Philippe. *Le Temps de l'histoire*. Monaco: Editions du Rocher, 1954.

Aulard, Alphonse, *Taine: historien de la Révolution française*. Paris: Colin, 1901.

Barnes, Harry Elmer. *A History of Historical Writing*. 2nd. rev. ed. New York: Dover Publications, 1962.

Barrès, Maurice. *Mes Cahiers*. Vol. II. Paris: Plon, 1930.

———. *Scènes et doctrines du nationalisme*. Vol. I. Paris: Plon-Nourrit et Cie, 1925.

Beau de Loménie, Emmanuel. *Maurras et son système*. Paris: Centre d'Etudes Nationales, 1965.

———. *Les Responsabilités des dynasties bourgeoises*. 5 vols. Paris: Denoël, 1943–1973.

Beaunier, André. *Les Idées et les hommes*. Paris: Plon, 1916.

Bedel, Maurice. "Réception de M. Jacques Bainville à l'Académie Française." *Revue des deux mondes* (December 1, 1935), 708–710.

Bellesort, André. *Les Intellectuels et l'avènement de la Troisième République.* Paris: Grasset, 1931.

Benda, Julien. *The Treason of the Intellectuals.* Trans. Richard Aldington. New York: Norton, 1969.

Bidou, Henri: "M. Bainville à l'Académie." *Revue de Paris*, VI (November 15, 1935), 451–55.

Binion, Rudolph. *Defeated Leaders.* New York: Columbia University Press, 1960.

Bordeaux, Henry. *De Baudelaire à Soeur Marguerite.* Paris: Flammarion, 1936.

———. "Charles Maurras et l'Académie Française." *Les Oeuvres libres* (January, 1953), 3–58.

———. "Un Grand Journaliste doublé d'un grand historien: Jacques Bainville." *Ecrits de Paris* (April, 1958), 65–75.

———. *Histoire d'une vie.* Vol. V. Paris: Plon, 1964.

———. "La Mort de Jacques Bainville." *Revue universelle*, LXIV (March 15, 1936), 703–13.

———. *Quarante Ans chez les quarante.* Paris: Fayard, 1959.

Brasillach, Robert. *Notre Avant-Guerre.* Paris: Les Sept Couleurs, 1951.

Britsch, Amadée. "Une Nouvelle Histoire de France." *Le Correspondant* (October 10, 1924), 88–97.

Brogan, D. W. *French Personalities and Problems.* New York: Knopf, 1947.

Brower, Daniel R. *The New Jacobins: The French Communist Party and the Popular Front.* Ithaca: Cornell University Press, 1968.

Buthman, William C. *The Rise of Integral Nationalism in France.* New York: Columbia University Press, 1939.

Cahuet, A. "La Réception de M. Jacques Bainville à l'Académie Française." *L'Illustration* (November 16, 1935), 343.

Cameron, Rondo. *France and the Economic Development of Europe: 1800–1914.* Princeton: Princeton University Press, 1961.

Carr, E. H. *The Bolshevik Revolution.* Vol. III. New York: Macmillan, 1953.

Carré, Jean-Marie. *Les Ecrivains français et le mirage allemand.* Paris: Bouvin, 1947.

Caute, David. *Communism and the French Intellectuals: 1914–1960.* New York: Macmillan, 1964.

Chaigne, Louis. *Histoire de la littérature française: les lettres contemporaines.* Paris: Editions Mondiales, 1964.

Chaumeix, André. *Le Lycée Henri Quatre.* Paris: Gallimard, 1936.

Clouard, Henri. "Jacques Bainville." *Mercure de France* (February 15, 1936), 225–36.

Colton, Joel. *Léon Blum, Humanist in Politics.* New York: Knopf, 1966.

Curtis, Michael. *Three Against the Republic: Sorel, Barrès, and Maurras.* Princeton: Princeton University Press, 1959.

Curtius, Ernst Robert. *Französischer Geist im neuen Europa.* Stuttgart: Deutsche Verlags-Anstalt, 1925.

Daudet, Léon. *L'Avant-Guerre: études et documents sur l'espionnage juif-allemand en France depuis l'affaire Dreyfus.* Paris: Nouvelle Librairie Nationale, 1913.

———. *Ecrivains et artistes.* Paris: Editions du Capitole, 1927.

———. *Souvenirs des milieux littéraires, politiques, artistiques, et médicaux.* Paris: Nouvelle Librairie Nationale, 1926.

———. *Le stupide dix-neuvième siècle.* Paris: Nouvelle Librairie Nationale, 1922.

———. *Vers le Roi.* Paris: Grasset, 1934.

Davies, Norman. *White Eagle, Red Star: The Polish-Soviet War, 1919–1920.* New York: St. Martin's, 1972.

Delandsheere, Paul, and Alphonse Ooms. *La Belgique sous les Nazis.* 2 vols. Brussels: n.p., n.d.

Demartial, Georges. *La Guerre de 1914: comment on mobilisa les consciences.* Paris: Editions des Cahiers Internationaux, 1922.

Dictionnaire de biographie française. Paris: Librairie Letouzey et Ane, 1941.

Dictionnaire national des contemporains. Paris: Lajeunesse, 1936.

Digeon, Claude. *La Crise allemande de la pensée française, 1870–1914.* Paris: Presses Universitaires de France, 1959.

Dimier, Louis. *Les Maîtres de la contre-révolution.* Paris: Librairie des Saints-Pères et Nouvelle Librairie Nationale, 1907.

———. *Les Préjugés Ennemis de l'histoire de France.* Paris: Nouvelle Librairie Nationale, 1917.

———. *Souvenirs d'action publique et d'université.* Paris: Nouvelle Librairie Nationale, 1920.

———. *Vingt Ans d'Action française.* Paris: Nouvelle Librairie Nationale, 1926.

Dubech, Lucien. *Les Chefs de file de la jeune génération.* Paris: Plon, 1925.

Ebray, Alcide. *La France qui meurt.* Paris: Société Française d'Imprimerie et de Librairie, 1910.

Elwitt, Sanford. *The Making of the Third Republic: Class and Politics in France, 1868–1884.* Baton Rouge: Louisiana State University Press, 1975.

Fabrègues, Jean de. *Charles Maurras et son Action française.* Paris: Librairie Académique Perrin, 1966.

Fagniez, Gustave. "A Propos d'une nouvelle histoire de France." *Séances et Travaux de l'Académie des Sciences Morales et Politiques: Compte Rendu* (November–December, 1924), 315–38.

Farmer, Paul. *France Reviews its Revolutionary Origins: Social Politics and*

Historical Opinion in the Third Republic. New York: Octagon Books, 1963.

Le Fauteuil de Jacques Bainville: Discours de réception de M. Joseph Pesquidoux à l'Academie française et réponse de M. André Bellesort. Paris: Plon, 1937.

Le Fauteuil de Raymond Poincaré: Discours de réception de M. Jacques Bainville à l'Académie française et réponse de M. Maurice Donnay. Paris: Plon, 1935.

Febvre, Lucien. "Politique royale ou civilisation française." *Revue de synthèse historique,* XXXVIII (December, 1924).

Feyel, Paul. "Les Livres nouveaux." *Revue bleue* (November 15, 1924), 289–90.

Fraenkel, Ernst. *Military Occupation and the Rule of Law: Occupational Government in the Rhineland, 1918–1923.* London: Oxford University Press, 1944.

Garraty, John A. "The New Deal, National Socialism, and the Great Depression." *American Historical Review,* LXXVI (October, 1973), 907–44.

Gatzke, Hans. *Stresemann and the Rearmament of Germany.* Baltimore: The Johns Hopkins University Press, 1954.

Gaxotte, Pierre, ed. *Charles Maurras, 1868–1952.* Paris: Plon, 1953.

Géraud, André [Pertinax]. *The Gravediggers of France: Gamelin, Daladier, Reynaud, Pétain, and Laval.* Garden City, N.Y.: Doubleday, 1944.

Gérin-Ricard, Lazare de. *L'Histoire de France de Jacques Bainville.* Paris: Editions Edgar Malfère, 1939.

Gérin-Ricard, Lazare de, and Louis Truc. *Histoire de l'Action française.* Paris: Edition Fournier-Valdès, 1949.

Geyl, Pieter. *Napoleon, For and Against.* Trans. Olive Renier. New Haven: Yale University Press, 1967.

Gilbert, Pierre. *La Forêt des Cippes.* Vol. I. Paris: Champion, 1918.

Girardet, Raoul. "Notes sur l'esprit d'un fascisme français, 1934–1939." *Revue française de science politique,* V (1955), 529–46.

Goguel, François. *La Politique des partis sous la Troisième République.* Paris: Seuil, 1946.

Gorgolini, Pietro. *Le Fascisme.* Trans. Eugène Marsan. Preface by Jacques Bainville. Paris: Nouvelle Librairie Nationale, 1923.

Grimm, Friedrich. *Du Testament de Richelieu à Jacques Bainville.* Geneva: *Le Mois Suisse,* 1941.

Guiraud, Jean. *Cours d'histoire de France pour les écoles primaires.* Paris: Girard, 1914.

———. *Histoire partiale, histoire vraie.* 4 vols. Paris: Beauchesne, 1911–1917.

Halpen, Louis, "Jacques Bainville: Histoire de France." *Revue historique,* CXLVII (September–October, 1924), 99–100.

Hauser, Henri. *Le Principe des nationalités.* Paris: Alcan, 1916.

Havard de la Montagne, Robert. *Histoire de l'Action Française.* Paris: Amiot-Dumont, 1950.

Herrick, Jane. *The Historical Thought of Fustel de Coulanges*. Washington, D.C.: The Catholic University of America Press, 1954.

Histoire de la Librairie Arthème Fayard. Paris: Fayard, n.d.

"Hommages à Jacques Bainville." *Revue universelle*, LXIV (March 1, 1936), 513–676.

Hughes, H. Stuart. *The Obstructed Path: French Social Thought in the Years of Desperation*. New York: Harper & Row, 1968.

Johannet, René. *Eloge du bourgeois français*. Paris: Grasset, 1924.

———. *Le Principe des nationalités*. Paris: Nouvelle Librairie Nationale, 1923.

Joll, James. *Three Intellectuals in Politics*. New York: Harper & Row, 1960.

Joseph, Roger, "Le Poète Jacques Bainville." *Revue moderne des arts et de la vie* (March 1, 1961), 23–25.

———. *Qui est Jacques Bainville?* Orleans: Lhermitte, 1967.

Keylor, William R. *Academy and Community: The Foundation of the French Historical Profession*. Cambridge, Mass.: Harvard University Press, 1975.

———. "Clio on Trial: Charles Péguy as Historical Critic." William R. Keylor and Dora B. Weiner, eds. *From Parnassus: Essays in Honor of Jacques Barzun*. New York: Harper & Row, 1976.

Keynes, John Maynard. *The Economic Consequences of the Peace*. London: Macmillan, 1920.

Kindleberger, Charles. *Economic Growth in France and Britain: 1851–1950*. Cambridge, Mass.: Harvard University Press, 1964.

———. "The Postwar Resurgence of the French Economy." Stanley Hoffmann, *et al.*, eds., *In Search of France*. New York: Harper & Row, 1965.

King, Jere C. *Foch versus Clemenceau*. Cambridge, Mass.: Harvard University Press, 1960.

Lacouture, Jean. *De Gaulle*. Trans. Francis K. Price. London: Hutchinson & Co., 1965.

Langlois, Charles-Victor, and Charles Seignobos. *Introduction aux études historiques*. Paris: Hachette, 1898.

Langlois, Charles-Victor. *Questions d'histoire et d'enseignement*. Paris: Hachette, 1902.

Lasserre, Pierre. *La Doctrine officielle de l'université*. Paris: Mercure de France, 1912.

Latzarus, Louis. *La France veut-elle un roi?*. Paris: Editions du Siècle, 1924.

Lavisse, Ernest, ed. *Histoire de France depuis les origines jusqu'à la Révolution*, 9 vols. Paris: Colin, 1900–1911.

——— and Alfred Rambaud, eds. *Histoire générale du IVe siècle à nos jours*. 12 vols. Paris: Colin, 1892–1901.

Lazareff, Pierre. *Deadline*. Trans. David Partridge. New York: Random House, 1942.

Lecler, Joseph. "L'Oeuvre historique de Jacques Bainville." *Etudes* (June 5, 1935), 633–47.

Leeds, Stanton. *These Ruled France*. Indianapolis: Bobbs-Merrill, 1940.

Leger, François. "Le Dessein de Jacques Bainville." *L'Ordre français* (November, 1964), 45–58.

Linville, Lyle E. "Jacques Bainville: His Political Life and Thought in the Era of the Great War." Ph.D. dissertation, Kent State University, 1971.

Malraux, André. *Felled Oaks*. Trans. Irene Clephane. New York: Holt, Rinehart, and Winston, 1971.

Marcel, Jean. *L'heure classique de la France et le conseil de Bainville*. Paris: Private Printing, 1935.

Marcus, John T. *Neutralism and Nationalism in France*. New York: Bookman Associates, 1958.

Maritain, Jacques. *Carnet de Notes*. Paris: Desclée de Brouwer, 1965.

———. *Journal de Raïssa*. Paris: Desclée de Brouwer, 1963.

Maritain, Raïssa. *Les Grandes Amitiés*. Paris: Desclée de Brouwer, 1949.

Marty, Albert. *L'Action Française racontée par elle-même*. Paris: Nouvelles Editions Latines, 1968.

Massis, Henri. *Défense de l'Occident*. Paris: Plon, 1927.

———. *Maurras et notre temps*. 2 vols. Paris: La Palatine, 1951.

———, ed. *Le Souvenir de Jacques Bainville*. Paris: Les Amis des Beaux Livres, 1936.

———, and Alfred de Tarde [Agathon]. *L'Esprit de la Nouvelle Sorbonne*. Paris: Mercure de France, 1911.

Mathiez, Albert. *La Monarchie et la politique nationale*. Paris: Alcan, 1917.

Maurras, Charles. *L'Allée des philosophes*. Paris: Editions Crès, 1924.

———. *Devant l'Allemagne éternelle: gaulois, germains, latins*. Paris: Editions 'à l'Etoile,' 1937.

———. *Dilemme de Marc Sangnier*. Paris: Nouvelle Librairie Nationale, 1921.

———. *Enquête sur la monarchie*. Paris: Nouvelle Librairie Nationale, 1909.

———. *Ironie et poésie*. Saint-Félicien-en-Vivarais: Au Pigeonnier, 1923.

———. *Jacques Bainville et Paul Bourget*. Paris: Editions du Cadran, n.d.

———. *Kiel et Tanger*. Paris: Nouvelle Librairie Nationale, 1916.

———. *Mademoiselle Monk*. Paris: Stock, 1923.

——— [Octave Martin]. *Le Parapluie de Marianne*. Paris: Editions de 'La Seule France,' 1948.

———. *Póesie et Vérité*. Lyons: Lardanchet, 1944.

———. *Pour un Jeune Français*. Paris: Amiot-Dumont, 1949.

———. *Quand les Français ne s'aimaient pas*. 2nd ed. Paris: Nouvelle Librairie Nationale, 1926.

———. *Romantisme et révolution*. Paris: Nouvelle Librairie Nationale, 1925.

———. *Au Signe de Flore*. Paris: Les Oeuvres Représentatives, 1931.

———. *Tombeaux*. Paris: Nouvelle Librairie Nationale, 1921.

———. *Trois Idées politiques*. Paris: Champion, 1898.

Maurras, Hélène et Nicole, eds. *La République ou le roi: correspondance in-édite de Maurice Barrès et Charles Maurras, 1888–1923*. Paris: Plon, 1970.

Mayer, Arno J. *Dynamics of Counterrevolution in Europe, 1870–1956*. New York: Harper Torchbooks, 1971).

———. *Politics and Diplomacy of Peacemaking: Containment and Counterrevo-lution at Versailles, 1918–1919*. New York: Vintage Books, 1969.

Meynier, Albert. "A Propos du 'Napoléon' de M. Jacques Bainville." *La Révolution française: Revue de la Société de l'Histoire de la Révolution*, LXXXV (October–December, 1932), 315–20.

Micaud, Charles. *The French Right and Nazi Germany, 1933–1939*. New York: Octagon Books, 1964.

Mirabel, André. *La Comédie du nationalisme intégral*. Paris: Grasset, 1947.

Mitchell, Allan. *Bismarck and the French Nation*. New York: Bobbs-Merrill, 1971.

Monod, Gabriel. "Historiens contemporains." *La Revue politique et littéraire* (May 15, 1875), 1077–83.

Morland, Jacques. "Enquête sur l'influence allemande." *Mercure de France* (November–December, 1902), 289–382, 647–95.

Morse, Edward. *Foreign Policy and Independence in Gaullist France*. Prince-ton: Princeton University Press, 1973.

Murat, Comtesse. *Souvenirs sur Jacques Bainville*. Paris: Editions d'Histoire et d'Art, 1938.

Nolte, Ernst. *Three Faces of Fascism*. Trans. Leila Vennewitz. New York: Holt, Rinehart, and Winston, 1966.

Osgood, Samuel. *French Royalism under the Third and Fourth Republics*. The Hague: Nijhoff, 1960.

———. *French Royalism since 1870*. The Hague: Nijhoff, 1970.

Paxton, Robert. *Parades and Politics at Vichy*. Princeton: Princeton Univer-sity Press, 1966.

Péguy, Charles. "De la Situation faite à l'histoire et à la sociologie dans les temps modernes." *Cahiers de la quinzaine*, 8th series (1906).

Picard, Gaston. *Nos Ecrivains definis par eux-mêmes*. Paris: Goulet, 1925.

Plumyène, J. and R. Lasierra. *Les Fascismes français*. Paris: Editions du Seuil, 1963.

Poincaré, Raymond. *How France is Governed*. Trans. Bernard Miall. Lon-don: Unwin, 1913.

Porter, Charles W. *The Career of Théophile Delcassé*. Philadelphia: University of Pennsylvania Press, 1936.

Prévost, Jean. "Histoire de France." *Nouvelle Revue française* (October 1, 1924), 478–79.

Pujo, Maurice. *Les Camelots du roi.* Paris: Flammarion, 1933.

Rambert, Louis. *L'Action Française pendant la guerre.* Paris: L'Action Française, 1919.

Reboul, Jacques. *M. Bainville contre l'histoire de France.* Paris: Editions du Siècle, 1925.

Remond, René. *The Right Wing in France from 1815 to de Gaulle.* Trans. James M. Laux. Philadelphia: University of Pennsylvania Press, 1966.

Renauld, Ernest. *L'Action Française contre l'Eglise Catholique et contre la monarchie.* Paris: Tolra, 1936.

Roubaud, A. "Une Synthèse de l'histoire de France." *Revue de synthèse historique,* XXXVIII (December, 1924), 163–70.

Roudiez, Léon. *Maurras jusqu'à l'Action Française.* Paris: Bonne, 1957.

Rousseaux, André. "Jacques Bainville." *Vient de Paraître* (April, 1924), 197–99.

Roussel, Ernest. *Les Nuées maurrassiennes.* Paris: Flory, 1936.

Schuker, Stephen A. *The End of French Predominance in Europe: The Financial Crisis of 1924 and the Adoption of the Dawes Plan.* Chapel Hill: University of North Carolina Press, 1976.

Scott, William E. *Alliance against Hitler: The Origins of the Franco-Soviet Pact.* Durham: Duke University Press, 1962.

Séances et travaux de l'Académie des sciences morales et politiques: compte rendu (November–December, 1924).

Sembat, Marcel. *Faites un roi, sinon, faites la paix.* Paris: Figuière, 1913.

Soucy, Robert. *Fascism in France: The Case of Maurice Barrès.* Berkeley: University of California Press, 1972.

———. "The Nature of Fascism in France." Walter Laqueur and George Mosse, eds. *International Fascism: 1920–1945.* New York: Harper & Row, 1966, 27–55.

Stock, Phyllis H. "New Quarrel of Ancients and Moderns: The French University and its Opponents, 1899–1914." Ph.D. dissertation, Yale University, 1965.

Szekeley de Doba, André, *et al. Jacques Bainville.* Paris: Editions du Capitole, 1927.

Talbott, John E. *The Politics of Educational Reform in France, 1918–1940.* Princeton: Princeton University Press, 1969.

Tannenbaum, Edward R. *The Action Française.* New York: Wiley, 1962.

Taylor, A. J. P. *The Course of German History.* New York: Capricorn Books, 1962.

Thibaudet, Albert. *Histoire de la littérature française.* Paris: Stock, 1936.

Thomas, Hilah. "The Thought of Jacques Bainville on Germany: A Study in the Loyalties of Integral Nationalism." Honors thesis, Smith College, 1962.

Tint, Herbert. *The Decline of French Patriotism: 1870–1914*. London: Weidenfeld & Nicolson, 1964.

Treich, Léon, ed. *Almanach des lettres françaises et étrangères*. Paris: Crès, 1924.

"Trois Nouveaux Académiciens." *Annales politiques et littéraires* (April 10, 1935), 347–48.

Vallette, Alfred. "Une Enquête franco-allemande." *Mercure de France* (April–June, 1895), 1–65.

Valois, Georges and Francois Renié. *Les Manuels scolaires*. Paris: Nouvelle Librairie Nationale, 1911.

Vanderem, Fernand. *Le Miroir des lettres*. Paris: Flammarion, 1929.

Vidal, Henri. *La Pensée de Jacques Bainville en matière économique et sociale*. Paris: Université de Paris, Faculté de Droit, Thèse pour le doctorat, Etablissements Busson, 1944.

Viereck, Peter. *Metapolitics: From the Romantics to Hitler*. New York: Knopf, 1941.

Villermont, F. de. "Absence de Jacques Bainville pour l'anniversaire de sa mort." *Revue hebdomadaire*, XLVI (February 13, 1937).

Virtanen, Reino. "Nietzsche and the Action Française." *Journal of the History of Ideas*, XI (April, 1950), 194–214.

Weber, Eugen. *Action Française*. Stanford, Calif.: Stanford University Press, 1962.

―――. *The Nationalist Revival in France, 1905–1914*. Berkeley: University of California Press, 1959.

Werth, Alexander. *De Gaulle*. Middlesex, Eng.: Penguin, 1965.

Whibley, Charles. "A History of France." *English Review* (November, 1924), 626–29.

Wieder, Joachim. *Jacques Bainville: Nationalismus und Klassizismus in Frankreich*. Breslau: Priebatsch, 1939.

Willis, F. Roy. *France, Germany, and the New Europe, 1945–1967*. London: Oxford University Press, 1968.

Wilson, Stephen. "Fustel de Coulanges and the Action Française." *Journal of the History of Ideas*, XXXIV (1973), 123–34.

―――. "A View of the Past: Action Française Historiography and its Socio-Political Function." *Historical Journal*, XIX (1976), 135–61.

Wolfe, Martin. "French Interwar Stagnation Revisited." Charles K. Warner, ed. *From the Ancien Régime to the Popular Front*. New York: Columbia University Press, 1969.

Wolfers, Arnold. *Britain and France Between Two World Wars* (New York: Norton, 1966), 201–11.

Wright, Gordon. *France in Modern Times*. Chicago: Rand, McNally & Co., 1960.

———. *Raymond Poincaré and the French Presidency*. Stanford, Calif.: Stanford University Press, 1942.

Index